International Marketing

International Marketing
Consuming Globally, Thinking Locally

ANDREW McAULEY
Department of Marketing, University of Stirling

JOHN WILEY & SONS, LTD
Chichester • New York • Weinheim • Brisbane • Singapore • Toronto

Other Wiley Editorial Offices

John Wiley & Sons, Inc., 605 Third Avenue,
New York, NY 10158-0012, USA

WILEY-VCH Verlag GmbH
Pappelallee 3, D-69469 Weinheim, Germany

John Wiley & Sons Australia, Ltd, 33 Park Road, Milton,
Queensland 4064, Australia

John Wiley & Sons (Canada) Ltd, 22 Worcester Road
Rexdale, Ontario, M9W 1L1, Canada

John Wiley & Sons (Asia) Pte Ltd, 2 Clementi Loop #02-01,
Jin Xing Distripark, Singapore 129809

Library of Congress Cataloging-in-Publication Data

McAuley, Andrew.
International marketing : consuming globally, thinking locally / Andrew McAuley.
     p. cm.
     Includes bibliographical references and index.
     ISBN 0-471-89744-2
     11. Export marketing. 2. International economic relations. 3. Globalization. I. Title.
HF1416 .M345 2001
658.8'48–dc21   00-54571

British Library Cataloguing in Publication Data

A catalogue record for this book is available from the British Library
ISBN 0 471 89744 2

Typeset in Palatino by Deerpark Publishing Services Ltd, Shannon.
Printed and bound in Great Britain by Biddles Ltd, Guildford and King's Lynn.

This book is printed on acid-free paper responsibly manufactured from sustainable forestry in which at least two trees are planted for each one used for paper production.

Dedication

For Andy and Rachel

'the time was not enough'

Contents

Acknowledgements

This will probably not be an exhaustive list (I'll save that for the Booker Prize) as there are always many people who assist one's thinking over the years whose input in many subtle ways often goes unnoticed but runs deep; an 'inarticulate speech'. To those friends and family who have taken an interest in this project along the way and periodically asked about its progress; thanks for the guilt trip!

More specifically I would like to thank my publisher, Steve Hardman at John Wiley, for his unending patience, support and good humour. A better publisher to work with would be hard to find, I think. A large drink is due. A big thank you also to the rest of the Wiley team for taking this book from manuscript and turning it into a finished product.

My thanks also to those people, listed elsewhere, who have contributed case studies to this book. Their contributions have much enhanced the final product.

Thanks are also due to the reviewers who have offered advice and commented on the original proposal and in particular to Professor Hugh Munro, Wilfrid Laurier University; Professor Tony Millman, University of Buckingham and Dr Stuart Rooks, Oxford Brookes University who provided many useful suggestions on the draft manuscript.

On a more personal note I should like to acknowledge Professor John Cole, formerly of the Department of Geography, University of Nottingham. To him my sincere thanks for helping to create in me that special spark which made me think. To the many students who over the years mainly at Stirling but also in Canada, Jamaica and Hong Kong have often added the poignant questions which have kept that thinking alive.

Special thanks to Susan for her tireless love and support not to mention the initial proof reading!

When you finish a painting there is a time when it feels like the best you have ever done. This feeling passes. Then it gradually dawns on you that the painting in your head has not appeared on the canvas. Somewhere in the process it has become muted and you are left staring at a blank canvas which once again challenges you. You know there is more to come. I fear that finishing this book will be the same. However, I can still see the potential in my head. So when you're ready Steve!

Andrew McAuley
October 2000

List of contributors

Stephen J. Arnold, School of Business, Queen's University, Kingston, Ontario, Canada

Bradley R. Barnes, Leeds University Business School, Leeds, UK

Angela Carroll, Huddersfield University Business School, Huddersfield, UK

John Fernie, School of Management, Heriot-Watt University, Edinburgh, UK

Amjad Hadjikhani, Department of Business Studies, Uppsala University, Uppsala, Sweden

Suzanne Horne, Department of Marketing, University of Stirling, Stirling, UK

Ulf Johansson, Department of Business Administration, Lund University, Lund, Sweden

Jeryl Whitelock, Department of Business Studies, University of Salford, Salford, UK

CHAPTER 1

Introduction

Chapter objectives

After studying this chapter you should be able to:

- Appreciate the importance of international marketing
- Understand its relevance to the policy maker, business owner and marketing manager
- Distinguish between exporting, international marketing and global marketing
- Understand the structure of this book; its chapter flow and learning features

Introduction

Think about what you have been doing recently – how many of the products or services you have recently consumed originated solely in your own country? Whether we talk about the music you have just been listening to, the last soft drink you had, the film you recently went to see at the cinema, or the clothes you wear, there is a good chance some of these will have been supplied by a company located elsewhere in the world, albeit they may have a partnership with a local producer. These are just the obvious ones. If you think about the component parts for your hi-fi or personal computer, they may well have been designed, manufactured and assembled in different locations around the globe. It is true that consumer tastes in many areas are converging. People around the globe welcome quality, service and value in the goods and services which they purchase. At the same time there is a movement against the globalisation of world markets by various pressure groups who view multinationals as 'evil' players, who obstruct the development of economies in developing countries, or are responsible for exploitative employment practices.

There is only one thing certain in international marketing, and that is that the environment, be it economic, social, political or technological, will consistently evolve and develop. During the course of writing this book, international marketers have been hit by the Asian financial crisis and its world-wide domino effect as other economies slowed down. Currently, there is concern among International Monetary Fund members about the weakness of the euro and the high price of oil on the world markets. The Organisation of Petroleum Exporting Countries is being brought under pressure to increase production and so reduce oil prices. The USA is to release 30 million barrels from its national reserve in an attempt to achieve the same objective. These environmental influences may seem distant from the small exporter, but they can have very significant effects on the cost of producing goods for the manufacturer, and ultimately on the competitiveness of their product in winning international orders.

In recent weeks there have been significant protests across Europe by consumers frustrated by the high price of fuel. In all likelihood these problems will pass, but other influences will emerge to challenge the international company. However, a whole host of influences have to be managed effectively in order to achieve international success. Table 1.1 shows the recent rankings for global competitiveness as calculated by the World Economic Forum. Aside from the USA gaining top position, the list is dominated by European countries, with Asian representation led by Singapore, Hong Kong and Taiwan. How many of the goods you have recently purchased were manufactured in one of these three territories?

Why do you purchase goods and services from international suppliers? Probably because you are attracted by their design, quality, reputation, pricing or availability. Your views will have been influenced by, for example, friends, family, the Internet, advertising on television or in the press, or the sales person in the retail store where you shopped. The role of personal selling is also very important in the business to business market.

All of these influences on your purchasing activity are part of the concern of marketing, and the aim of this book is to explore and understand how companies

Table 1.1 Global competitive rankings (source: World Economic Fourm, 2000)

Rank	Country
1	USA
2	Singapore
3	Luxembourg
4	Netherlands
5	Ireland
6	Finland
7	Canada
8	Hong Kong SAR
9	UK
10	Switzerland
11	Taiwan
12	Australia
13	Sweden
14	Denmark
15	Germany

can use marketing to help them succeed in the international marketplace. A business needs many components to help it succeed, including for example, employees, financial strength, research and development and, naturally, a product or service. A holistic view of business is important but the focus of this book is those businesses who wish to adopt the marketing philosophy in running their business. This philosophy is focused on understanding, creating, communicating and delivering customer related values, that is, those needs and wants which customers wish to see in the products and services they consume, whether in the business to business market or in the consumer market. Satisfied customers are essential if a business is to thrive. It may sound trite, but without customers a business will not continue to exist. Marketing's task is to find and retain customers for the business, whilst working with other functions within the business to achieve this efficiently and effectively.

Some familiar terms

Needs, wants and values

Needs relate to the basic requirements which we, as human beings, need to survive. Thus, food, water, shelter constitute our basic needs. Our wants, in terms of marketing, are the wide range of products and services which we desire for whatever reason. Customers buy products and services for all sorts of reasons which reflect their own values. It may be because the item is functional (buying things for what they do), symbolic (buying things for what they mean) or experiential (obtaining value from the transaction experience itself). Thus, by understanding customer related values the marketer can begin to design products and services which match these values, before going on to communicate and deliver these values to the customer.

Marketing

There are many different definitions of marketing. One of the most familiar ways of thinking about marketing is referred to as the marketing mix or 4Ps (Product, Price, Promotion and Place). This book assumes that the reader has a basic understanding of the principles of marketing. What this book concentrates on is the application of marketing to international markets. The framework used here may be slightly different to that which you are used to. Namely, as Figure 1.1 shows, the terminology used refers to understanding the customer's values, creating the product or service to satisfy those values, communicating to the customer that your product or service embodying the values they seek is available, and finally delivering the product or service to the customer to their satisfaction. Four key words sum this up: Understand, Create, Communicate and Deliver. This way of thinking about marketing will be further expanded upon in Chapter 6, and used as a means to explore relevant issues within the international context which relate to the marketing activities associated with the marketing cycle.

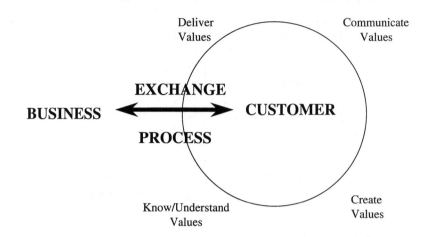

Figure 1.1   The basic marketing cycle (source: adapted from Figure 6.1; Bathie, 1998).

What then is international marketing all about?

International marketing is really all about the application of marketing skills and techniques to markets beyond the domestic market. These marketing skills and techniques are universal – it is in their application to different markets that variations occur, because of the environmental differences which will be encountered. These may be as a result of the interaction of the domestic and target markets' culture, the variation likely to occur because of human managerial abilities, or the influence of the broader political, social, economic and technological, competitive environments (Figure 1.2).

International marketing can be defined quite simply as 'the performance of business activities that direct the flow of a company's goods and services to consumers or users in more than one nation for a profit' (Cateora et al., 2000). Alternatively, Albaum et al. (1998) spell it out in a little more detail as 'that segment of business concerned with the planning, promoting, distribution, pricing, and servicing of the goods and services desired by intermediate and ultimate consumers'.

Many of the topics discussed in this book would equally be at home in a international business text. Box 1.1 provides an outline of the subject matter of international business. However, an international marketing approach to this material is different and unique because it looks at the material from the point of view of the customer. In contrast to the definitions of marketing previously outlined, there is no reference to the customer in Box 1.1. Under a marketing perspective, the customer – be they in the consumer or business to business market – is the starting point. The business is built around the customer. Everything that is done in the business should use the customer as the point of reference. In a marketing orientated firm the customer is the fulcrum around which the business revolves. It is this approach which distinguishes the discussion of international activities from a marketing, as opposed to an international business, perspective.

BOX 1.1 DEFINITION OF INTERNATIONAL BUSINESS

International business involves commercial activities that cross national frontiers. It concerns the international movement of goods, capital, services, employees and technology, importing and exporting, cross-border transactions in intellectual property (patents, trademarks, know-how, copyright materials) via licensing and franchising, investments in physical and financial assets in foreign countries, contract manufacture or assembly of goods abroad for local sale or for export to other nations, buying and selling in foreign countries, the establishment of foreign warehousing and distribution systems, and the import to one foreign country of goods from a second foreign country for subsequent local sale.

(source: Bennett, 1996)

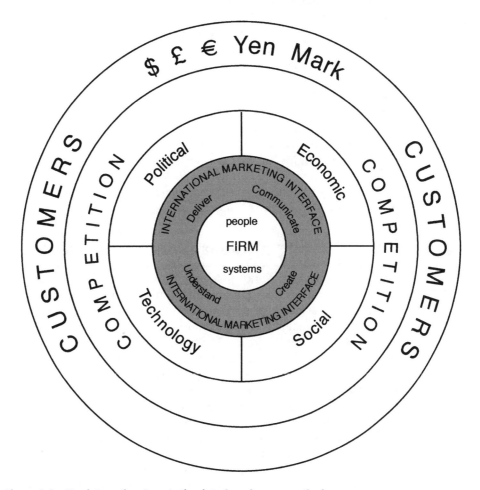

Figure 1.2   The international marketing interface (source: author).

Exporting, international marketing and global marketing

The terms exporting, international marketing and global marketing are sometimes used interchangeably. However, they relate to different and quite distinct strategies in terms of the commitment to marketing and the activities it involves. Exporting a consignment of goods to an international customer involves transportation, packaging, labelling, documentation, adherence to relevant technical standards, insurance and payment. Exporting in itself falls short of international marketing, primarily because it does not involve the company in marketing activities directed at the end customer. Instead the focus of the business relationship is on the intermediary who is purchasing the goods. Exporting may be referred to as active or passive depending on the degree of proactive involvement the business exhibits in dealing with its international customers.

Whether a company moves beyond exporting depends on its ambitions for its international operations. More will be said about the process of internationalisation and market entry in Chapter 4. It is possible that a company will primarily be a domestic operator with only occasional sales going to other countries. However, if sales to international markets significantly increase, the company may adopt different marketing strategies for each international market, facilitated through international subsidiaries. Each market is seen as distinct, and while the headquarters of the company has some input into the process, the products or services are tailored for each market, along with communication, pricing and distribution strategies. This is international marketing.

Global marketing, strictly speaking, is where a company has recognised that customers belonging to similar segments exist in a number of different national markets. As a result, marketing activities are directed at standardising as much as possible of the product or service and reaching the customers with similar communication, pricing and distribution strategies.

International marketing involves products and services

The global economy is not just about manufactured products. Services make a significant contribution to international investment activity. For example a breakdown of cross-border merger and acquisition activity in 1997 (UNCTAD, 1998) reveals that primary industry accounted for 7% in terms of value, secondary or manufacturing accounted for 34.5% and the tertiary sector accounted for 58.6%. From 1990 to 1997 reorganisation was particularly active in the financial, telecommunications, electrical power, gas and chemical industries. This was partly due to the world-wide trend towards greater liberalisation, deregulation and privatisation, and subsequent expansion by firms seeking to make themselves more competitive. The financial sector was particularly active in 1997, where the value of deals involving banks and insurers totalled 17.1% of all deals in that year. Table 1.2 list some of the larger deals.

The significance of service sector companies can also be seen in the activities of Tesco, the UK based supermarket, which by 2002 could have 45% of its shopping

Table 1.2   Mega deals in the financial sector, 1997 (source UNCTAD, 1998)

Value in US$ billion	Buyer	Acquired firm
18.4	Zurich Versicherungs GmbH (Switzerland)	BAT Industries PLC (UK)
10.0	Allianz AG Holding Berlin (Germany)	AGF (France)
6.2	Assicurazioni Generali SpA (Italy)	Aachener und Muenchener (Germany)
5.3	Merrill Lynch & Co. Inc. (US)	Mercury Asset Management Group (UK)
4.5	ING Groep NV (Netherlands)	Banque bruxelles Lambert SA (Belgium)
4.3	Nordbanken (Sweden)	Merita Oy (Finland)

space outside the UK. Stores in Ireland and Central Europe employ some 27 000 people. The company first moved into Hungary in 1994 and then to Poland in 1995, before entering the Czech Republic and Slovakia in 1996. The company plans to have 69 hypermarkets across Hungary, Poland, the Czech Republic and Slovakia by 2002. These hypermarkets will be 100 000 square feet or more, and will allow the inclusion of food and non-food ranges emphasising choice, quality, and value. Recent developments are detailed in Table 1.3.

Asia is the second international region in which Tesco operates. The Tesco Lotus business in Thailand has 17 hypermarkets, and a partnership with Samsung in South Korea manages two hypermarkets. The first Tesco store for Taiwan is planned for 2001. Further ambitious expansion plans involve developing to 34 hypermarkets in Thailand by 2002 and to over 50 hypermarkets in South Korea by 2005.

The company is also moving towards global sourcing, and has established three sourcing centres in Hong Kong, India and Thailand. These currently source 30% of Tesco non-food products, excluding health and beauty products. By 2003 it is anticipated that this will be 50%, when a fourth sourcing centre is opened in Central Europe.

The company appears to be following a classic 'think globally, act locally' strat-

Table 1.3   Tesco's growing interest in Central European markets (source: Tesco Annual Report, 2000)

	Hungary	Poland	Czech Republic	Slovakia
Number of stores	39	34	10	8
Sales area (square feet (× 1000))	980	690	980	620
Stores opened in 1999	4	3	2	2
Planned to open by 2000	6	6	2	3

egy, by having a format which is internationally transferable, but which at the same time can be adapted locally. Thus, the stores in Central Europe and Asia tend to have more products on sale, with a higher proportion of non-food ranges. The whole operation is geared towards one-stop shopping. Tesco combines its retailing skills and high service standards to serve these markets, and at the same time acquires local knowledge which it uses to good effect.

The approach apparently adapted by Tesco to its international development is reflected in the title of this book, namely, 'International Marketing: Consuming Globally, Thinking Locally'. Tesco's chief executive, Terry Leahy, has stated that successful retailers will be those which can manage changes in domestic and foreign markets to emerge as global forces.

Relevance of international marketing

Global trade is encouraged by supra-national organisations and national governments as we shall see in Chapter 2. There is much to be gained in terms of economic development by encouraging companies to trade internationally. This can be basic exporting or may end up as a joint venture with a partner company or a direct investment in a new plant in another country. As the figures for foreign direct investment in Tables 1.4 and 1.5 show there are significant sums of capital involved in such investment. Thus, foreign direct investment outflows according to UNCTAD (2000) estimates in 1999 amounted to US$800 billion while inflows were estimated at US$865 billion (these figures do not match due to data inconsistencies). The tables detail the top five sources and recipients of such flows.

FDI is the largest source of external finance for many developing countries. Governments recognise its importance and are opening their economies to encou-

Table 1.4 Top five sources of FDI outflows to developed countries (source: UNCTAD, 2000)

1999	$ million
UK	199289
USA	150901
France	107952
Germany	50596
Netherlands	45858

Table 1.5 Top five recipients of FDI inflows to developed countries (source: UNCTAD, 2000)

1999	$ million
USA	275533
UK	82182
Sweden	59968
France	39101
Netherlands	33785

rage the flow of trade, technology, information, investment and financial flows. FDI into Latin America and the Caribbean exceeded US$90 billion, while inflows to all the developing countries in Asia grew to US$ 106 billion. Flows to Central and Eastern Europe and to Africa remained modest at US$ 21 billion and US$ 9 billion, respectively.

Attracting such flows of capital is important to national economies and, in turn, many of the plants created feed products back into the global economy thus further stimulating importing and exporting. Much of this activity is dominated by large companies or what UNCTAD refer to as transnational corporations (TNCs). Table 1.6 shows the top ten largest non-financial TNCs ranked by international assets for 1998. This list is drawn from the top 100 list which shows remarkable stability in that 57 of the top 100 TNCs have been on the list since 1990. Almost 90 are head-quartered in the EU, Japan or the US. The list is dominated by motor vehicles; petroleum exploration and distribution; and electronic and electrical equipment. However, utility and telecommunications companies are increasing their presence while pharmaceutical and chemical firms reduced their entries in 1998 due to merger and acquisition activity.

With this kind of investment in international activity it should be apparent that international marketing is a relevant component of the global economy. Thus, whether as a government policy maker, a business owner or a marketing manager for a company an understanding of the complexities of international marketing can add substance to business activities. However, it should be noted that such activity is not only relevant for the large companies in Table 1.6 but small and medium sized companies (SMEs) and indeed micro companies can make a contribution to the global economy through their activities as we shall see in Chapter 5.

Structure of this book

Essentially this book falls into five sections. The first part (Chapters 2 and 3) deals with the broader international environment within which companies operate. The second (Chapters 4 and 5) focuses on the firm and the processes associated with going international. In particular Chapter 5 concentrates on the activities of SMEs. This is explored both from a theoretical and practical perspective. In the third section (Chapters 6–8) the marketing activities associated with international marketing are dealt with. The fourth section (Chapter 9) deals with the technical side of international marketing by discussing documentation, payments, insurance and financing issues. The final part (Chapters 10 and 11) is devoted to issues which are of interest because of their topicality. In this case globalisation, the Internet and franchising are discussed.

Chapter outline in more detail

Following this introductory chapter, attention will be given, in Chapter 2, to the macro influences on the world's economy. Contrasts will be drawn between the advanced, transitional and developing economies. The role of trading blocs,

Table 1.6   The worlds top ten TNCs ranked by international assets, 1998 (source: UNCTAD, 2000)

Rank	Corporation	Country	Industry	International Assets	International Sales	International Employees
1	General Electric	USA	Electronics	128.6	28.7	130000
2	General Motors	USA	Motor Vehicles	73.1	49.9	NA
3	Shell, Royal Dutch	Netherlands/UK	Petroleum	67.0	50.0	61000
4	Ford Motor Company	USA	Motor Vehicles	NA	43.8	171276
5	Exxon corporation	USA	Petroleum	50.1	92.7	NA
6	Toyota	Japan	Motor Vehicles	44.9	55.2	113216
7	IBM	USA	Computers	43.6	46.4	149934
8	BP Amoco	UK	Petroleum	40.5	48.6	78950
9	Daimler-Benz	Germany	Motor Vehicles	36.7	125.4	208502
10	Nestlé SA	Switzerland	Food/beverages	35.6	51.2	225665

national governments and supra-national bodies, such as the World Trade Organisation, will be discussed.

In Chapter 3 the cultural dimensions of international marketing will be considered, and readers will be encouraged to explore their own cultural influences and how this perception affects their view of the world. How culture influences the activities of marketing within the marketing cycle will be explored.

The process of internationalisation will be discussed in Chapter 4, including an examination of the key theories of internationalisation, what motivates companies to internationalise, and what market entry options are available to them.

Since SMEs often play such a vibrant role in international activities, Chapter 5 is devoted to them. What advantages do they face? How are they hindered because of their size or access to fewer resources, be they human or financial? The key influence of the driven entrepreneur will be apparent in the success of these smaller firms.

The next three chapters are really the marketing heart of the book, focusing as they do on the key marketing activities associated with the marketing cycle. Chapter 6 will begin with an explanation of the framework being used to structure this discussion, namely, understanding the customer, creating the product or service, and communicating with the customer, before delivering the customer related values enshrined in the product or service. Thus, Chapter 6 deals with market selection, market research, and market segmentation in relation to understanding the customer. Chapter 7 goes on to deal with creating and communicating customer related values. In the first half of the chapter this will involve a discussion of global brands, country of origin effects, pricing and packaging; whilst in the second half the discussion will focus on the basic elements of communication, the role of advertising, standardisation versus adaptation, and how to develop a communication plan. Chapter 8 completes the discussion of the key marketing activities, by analysing how companies can efficiently and effectively deliver customer value. Topics considered include customer value management and customer satisfaction.

This then leads into a related discussion in Chapter 9 of the documents required to successfully move goods around the globe, how to organise payments for exports, the role and purpose of insurance, and the options available for financing international activities.

The final two chapters provide an opportunity to broaden the discussion into topical issues. Thus, in Chapter 10 the impact of globalisation and the Internet on the international marketer will be discussed, along with the growing anti-corporate movement. Finally franchising, which is currently an increasingly popular mode of internationalising business activities, will be dealt with in Chapter 11.

To the student: some learning features

This book is not intended to be an encyclopaedic guide to international marketing. It assumes a pre-existing knowledge of marketing. It will provide a useful overview of the subject, and does concentrate on some of the more interesting topics within the subject, for example, the impact of culture, how companies internationalise their activities, the role of SMEs, globalisation, franchising and the Internet. However, no text book should be read cover to cover. Instead you should use the contents list at the front and the index at the back of the book to guide you to the topic you seek. In case you should decide to read a complete chapter, it is hoped that you will find the style of this book to be very readable. Inevitably some topics are drier than others, but overall the intention has been to enliven this subject and make it as accessible as possible. It is intended that the chapter objectives outlined at the beginning of each chapter will assist you to gauge your progress, by telling you what you should understand by the time you reach the end of the chapter. Each chapter has a list of references, websites, where used, and suggestions for further reading. This should give you a starting point for further study. You should endeavour to find your own examples from current literature (academic journals, newspapers, business magazines, etc.) or websites as appropriate. New examples will help to freshen and enliven the topics discussed in this book. At the end of each chapter there are questions for discussion which can be used for private study or in a tutorial/seminar situation.

Conclusion

There is an African saying which states that a person is not a person until they are involved with other people. Perhaps a company does not really begin to understand the complexities of marketing across cultures until that first step towards an international presence is taken. For many this can be a long and interesting journey. It is hoped that this book will stimulate at least some of you to journey further.

References

Albaum, G., Strandskov, J. and Duerr, E. (1998), *International Marketing and Export Management*, Addison Welsey, Harlow.

Bathie, D. (1998), *Principles of Marketing, Retail Marketing MBA Module 1*, Institute for Retail Studies, University of Stirling.

Bennett, R. (1996), *International Business*, M&E Pitman Publishing, London. Tesco Annual Report (2000).

Cateora, P.R., Graham, J.L. and Ghauri, P.N. (2000), *International Marketing*, European Edition, McGraw-Hill, London.

UNCTAD (1998), *World Investment Report 1998*, United Nations Conference on Trade and Development, Geneva.

UNCTAD (2000), *World Investment Report 2000*, United Nations Conference on Trade and Development, Geneva.

World Economic Fourm (2000), *The Global Competitiveness Report 2000*, World Economic Forum, Geneva.

Further reading

Jensen, R. (1999), *The Dream Society: How the Coming Shift from Information to Imagination will Transform your Business*, McGraw-Hill, London.

Paliwoda, S.J. (1999), Viewpoint: international marketing: an assessment, *International Marketing Review*, 16 (1), pp. 8–17.

Yip, G.S. (1997), Patterns and determinants of global marketing, *Journal of Marketing Management*, 13 (1–3), pp. 153–164.

The following web sites may also be of interest.
Michigan State University Center for International Business Education and Research. http://ciber.bus.msu.edu/
World Economic Forum. http://www.weforum.org/
United Nations Conference on Trade and Development (UNCTAD) http://www.unctad.org

CHAPTER 2

Trading places: an overview of the world economy

Chapter objectives

After studying this chapter you should be able to:

- Explain the current macro influences on the world's economy
- Highlight the contrasting experiences of the advanced, transitional and developing economies
- Understand the role of the key global organizations in policing world trade
- Understand the function of trading blocs and national governments in shaping world trade
- Relate to the human impact of these global economic influences
- Appreciate the influence of these environmental factors on marketing

Introduction

It is important to have an overview of the characteristics of world trade in order to properly understand a nation's place within the global economy. It is then possible to view the activities of an individual firm within this framework, and assess its contribution to international trade.

World trade is a dynamic system and the economies within it are like corks bobbing on the ocean, constantly adjusting to sea changes, and attempting to chart a safe course for the economic welfare of the nation. In simple terms global trade is increasing. One estimate (Steingraber, 1996) puts it 225% up in the last 25 years. The reason for this can be attributed to the following factors:

- Excess production capacity
- Trade and investment liberalization (lower tariffs, fewer regulations)
- Elimination of subsidies
- Opening up of public procurements
- Shift from planned to market economies

There is much discussion of globalization in the media and we frequently hear discussion of the 'global village' and that we live in an ever-shrinking world. These, of course, are subjective views and very much depend on the location of the viewer. As we shall see in Chapter 3 our view of the world very much depends on where we start from. Thus a westernized European or North American view is very different to that of a Chinese person living in the relatively remote and under-developed western parts of China which, in turn, will be different from a person living in Afghanistan. For better or worse there is an aspiration towards a western free market lifestyle by many people around the globe, with its inherent assumption that 'west is best'. Travel around this globe and certainly in many parts there is an erosion of individual identity. One of the key motives for travelling is being lost, as shopping centre after shopping centre the world over begins to look just like the ones we have at home. According to Carr et al. (1998) the top 100 global retailers already represent one-fifth of the world's retail market and continue to take market share from their smaller competitors. Table 2.1 lists the 35 most global retailers. Many names will be familiar to you.

So there is a 'sameness' creeping gradually into the world which, in marketing terms, raises interesting questions as people ask 'why do I pay a different price for the same product in different parts of the world?' Partly this is because when the first international operations were established, the local operations were given considerable leeway to develop channel strategies and tactics, thus allowing a responsiveness to local market conditions. However, this independent decision making has resulted in inconsistencies in pricing structures, brand positioning and logistics capabilities across markets. In this new century it is likely that retailers will make the necessary strategic, organizational, operational and system changes to act globally.

Thus, the globalization process is hard to ignore but what exactly does it involve? De Wilde (1991) characterizes globalization as describing three world-wide economic and technological trends. These are:

1. The cumulative effect of information technology, computers, world-wide media and the rise of integrated telecommunications-cable-infometrics systems.
2. The development of global capital markets with the ability to move resources

Table 2.1   Thirty-five most global retailers (Carr et al., 1998)

Nine US	23 European			Three Asian
Costco	Ahold	GIB Group	Promodes	Dairy Farm
Home Depot	Aldi	Ikea	Rewe	Ito Yokado
JC Penney	Auchan	Intermarche	Tengelmann	Jusco
Office Depot	Boots	J Sainsbury	Tesco	
Office Max	Carrefour	Leclerc	WH Smith	
Staples	Casino	Lidl&Schwarz	Delhaize	
TJX	Comptoirs	Marks&Spencer	Le Lion	
Toys 'R' Us	Modernes	Metro		
Wal-Mart	Edeka	Makro		

rapidly in response to new opportunities. This creates a premium for firms at the forefront of technology, and limits the impact of conventional national economic policy instruments.

3. The generation of export-orientated business strategies as the global market becomes accessible to entrepreneurs everywhere.

This gradual shift to globalization is arguably the most important trend underpinning an understanding of the world's economy and the 'Trading Places' within it. In this chapter we will discuss the structure of the world economy by looking at the advanced, transitional and developing economies (Section 'The nuts and bolts of the world economy'); outline the role and contribution of a number of global organizations whose job it is to shape the framework of the global economy, including the World Bank, the World Trade Organization, and the International Monetary Fund (Section 'The institutional framework: global players and referees'). In the section 'Supra-national trading blocs' a number of key trading blocs will be discussed, including the Association of Southeast Asian Nations, the European Union and Caribbean Community and Common Market. This section will end with a brief discussion of the relevance of national governments. The section 'The human context' will attempt to convey the influence of the changing global economy on the lives of humans in their role as worker, manager and employer. The relevance of this global 'bigger picture' to marketing will be discussed in the conclusions to this chapter.

The nuts and bolts of the world economy

The world economy

The post World War II period was characterized by relatively steady and smooth growth from 1950 to 1975 (Figure 2.1). The World Bank (1997) has characterized the last quarter of the 20th Century as the age of shocks and adjustment. These shocks were created by the oil crisis in the 1970s, the third world debt crisis in 1982 and the domino effect of the collapse of communism in 1989. As a result the world's economies have been occupied in responding and adjusting to these events. Although stylized, this framework provides a basic appreciation of the global economy.

Of course the fate of the world's economies is not just the result of these macro events, but the outcome of the interaction of politics, economic and investment policies, institutions (e.g. World Bank, International Monetary Fund (IMF)) and factors such as technology. Political changes had an enormous impact in the 1980s and early 1990s, as liberalization of the world economy continued and state controlled economies reoriented themselves to a free, or freer, market. These economies are said to be in transition (see Box 2.1). This coupled with the work of the World Trade Organization (the organization formerly known as GATT) in reducing tariff and non-tariff barriers has allowed freer movement of goods around the world. This in turn gave rise to new patterns in the flows of trade around the globe.

BOX 2.1: TRANSITION ECONOMIES EXPLAINED

The end goal of the transition economy is to build a market economy which will create long-term growth in living standards. This change is different from reform in other countries because it is systemic change. Reforms are designed to restructure the institutional basis of the social system. This is not an easy task and has, for many countries taken longer than was first thought in the early days of new found freedom.
Three sets of reform characterize transition:

- Freeing prices, trade and entry to markets from state control, whilst stabilizing the economy. Thus budget deficits have to be controlled and inflation held in check as much as possible, whilst decentralizing production decisions to enterprises, households and giving agents the ability to trade freely by responding to demand and supply.
- Ownership of property has to be clarified, and state control turned over to private ownership where necessary. Institutions which support market exchange, for example, the legal system, have to be created or re-created as required.
- A social service network has to be put in place to ease the pain of transition, since the change may lead to an initial increase in unemployment. Since economic growth is partly dependent on increased productivity, the population has to be carried along with the reform process and not left behind in its wake.

(source: The World Bank, 1996)

According to the IMF (1997) this vibrant situation was set to continue, with world output expected to expand by 4–4.5% in 1997 and 1998. Whilst the figure for 1997 was correct at 4.2% the 1998 figure was 2.5%, due to the slowing down of the world economy following the Asian financial crisis in 1997–1998.

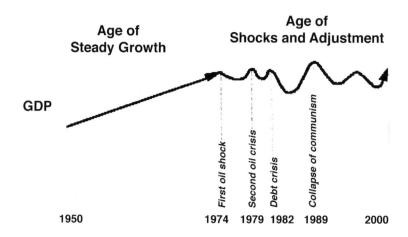

Figure 2.1 Stylized history of economic growth and development. Source: World Bank http://www.worldbank.org/.

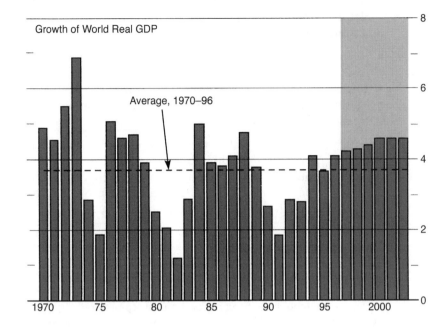

Figure 2.2   Growth of world real GDP. Source: IMF (1997).

However, the underlying pattern of progress has been supported by low inflation in the USA and UK, improved economic performance in Canada and western Europe, and better prospects in most of the world's developing countries, especially China and Southeast Asia. The latter will experience a setback due to the financial difficulties dating from late 1997, but longer term stability is expected to return. In the former communist-run economies of eastern Europe and the former Soviet Union, signs of growth have also been identified by the IMF. However, despite this optimism, a glance at Figure 2.2 will show that each growth phase is followed by a downturn.

Despite this, the IMF appear hopeful for the following reasons:

- Few of the signs that normally signal a downturn are present – for example, rising inflation, price instability, increasing fiscal imbalances or exchange rate fluctuations.
- There is still plenty of economic slack to be taken up in Japan and continental Europe as demand slows in countries in the more mature phase of their growth cycles including the USA and the UK.
- Finally, there is growing demand in the transition economies and in some of the more successful developing world economies which will continue to stimulate growth and trade.

The IMF believe that average world GDP growth could average 4.5% per annum between 1996 and 2002, compared with 3.75% from 1970 to 1995.

Not everything in macroeconomics runs smoothly, and problems to upset the best projections could be:

- Risks of overheating if inflationary pressures are allowed to rise without a quick response.
- Uncertainties about economic and monetary union in Europe.
- The sustainability of capital flows to emerging market countries, as highlighted by the problems in Thailand and other Southeast Asian countries in 1997–1998.

Current projections suggest that world output will rise by 3.5% in 2000 while world trade will grow by 6.2%. Within this general picture there is some variation, and whilst it is not the intention to provide an encyclopaedic guide to each country's situation, some contrasts will be drawn below to provide a flavour of the environment within which the international marketer operates.

Prospects in the advanced economies

Developed economies were not immune to the Asian financial crisis and so Japan, Korea, Hong Kong and Singapore felt its direct impact on their economies. However, Japan seems to be recovering faster than was expected (2% growth in the first quarter of 1999), but with the US expected to face a cyclical downturn, the immediate question for the world economy is how far domestic growth in Japan and Europe can be maintained to support world trade. Should the downturn in the US be sharper than currently expected by the IMF, then there may be a wider negative impact on the recoveries in the Asian economies, and eventually in Latin America.

Australia weathered the Asian crisis better than its neighbour New Zealand. Growth in 1998 in Australia reached 5% while New Zealand slipped into recession. Part of the answer to this was that Australia had outperformed its neighbour in export growth in 1995–1997; 9% a year compared to 3.5% in New Zealand. This stronger position, combined with the renegotiation of commodity contracts at favourable prices before the crisis, provided a cushion to soften the impact of the Asian crisis.

Prospects in the transition economies

During the 1990s the transition economies have experienced both significant financial volatility and macroeconomic stability. Relative stability and growth gave way to crisis in Russia in August 1998 in banking and financial sectors, which affected their relationship with international creditors. Some progress has been made, but the crisis has also slowed down the speed of reform in Russia and the political situation remains unsteady. The war in Chechnya represents another significant drain on Russian resources. It seems that those economies in Eastern Europe which have undergone the most reform have proved the most resilient to macroeconomic discord. Progress in 1994–1998 is highlighted in Table 2.2 but comparison with western economies shows that significant gaps remain in economic activity.

There is no doubt that the way forward for the transitional economies is to

Table 2.2   Selected countries in transition: average annual growth rates 1994–1998; 1998 GDP per capita in dollars and indicators of export performance 1994–1998. Source: adapted from IMF (1999)

Country/unit	Average growth	Per capita GDP	Average export growth
Croatia	5.5	6839	6.8
Czech Republic	2.2	12479	12.8
Estonia	4.2	7607	29.7
Hungary	3.1	10202	21.9
Latvia	3.2	5557	15.3
Lithuania	2.1	6437	26.9
Poland	6.0	7658	18.6
Slovak Republic	5.9	9817	12.2
Slovenia	4.3	14305	8.6
Russia	−4.2	6474	5.3
EU 15	2.5	20031	–
Japan	1.1	23979	–
USA	3.4	30057	–

continue trade liberalization, and the development of the institutional framework to support a market economy. However, broader reforms are necessary if growth is to be maintained and enhanced in the longer term, and if the benefits are to be more widely shared. These 'second generation' reforms, as the IMF (1997) has called them, include the need to accelerate social progress and invest in human capital by increasing the quality of public expenditure; strengthen the efficiency and robustness of the financial sector; reform and eventual privatization of state-owned enterprises; address corruption and improve governance; improve the quality and timeliness of statistical data collection.

Prospects in the developing countries

The developing economies of Asia, many of whom were noted for rapid economic growth in the 1990s – the so-called 'tiger economies', faced a financial crisis in 1997–1998. Thus countries like Indonesia, Philippines and Thailand saw their economic progress halted. Elsewhere other developing countries had financial crises of their own in Mexico in 1994–1995, and in Brazil and other Latin American countries in 1998-1999. Whilst the worst of the emerging market crisis seems to be over and, for example, Brazil is showing strong signs of recovery, it may take some time for the situation to fully stabilize. However, commodity prices seemed to have bottomed out and exports are increasing, supported by competitive exchange rates.

The role of the developing countries in the world is increasing, as evidenced by their share of world GDP. It is possible that China could equal the shares of the US or the EU within a decade. (Figure 2.3). However, their integration into the world economy requires careful planning, as increasing inward flows of capital to such

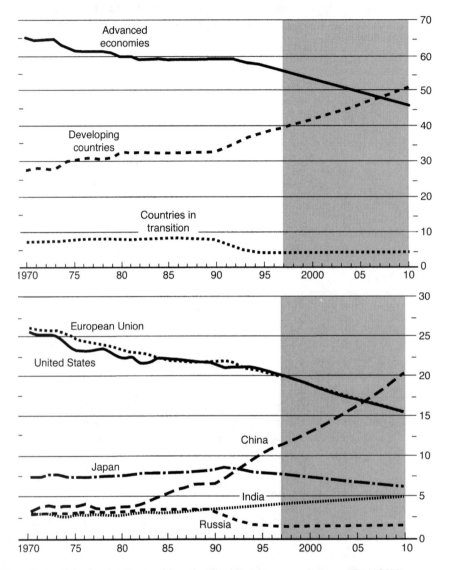

Figure 2.3 Changing relative positions in the global economy. Source: IMF (1997).

countries can result in overheating if foreign direct investment (FDI) is used to replace domestic saving.

Currently, many developing countries in Africa have been affected by changes in commodity prices. This has suited any countries which are oil exporters, for example Nigeria, as the price has been rising. However, other non-oil commodity prices are weak, which constrains growth in many developing countries. Previous economic difficulties have resulted in major structural reforms being undertaken

Table 2.3   Percentage share of GDP exports and population by economic groupings for 1999. Source: IMF (2000)

	Gross domestic product (GDP)	Exports of goods and services	Population
Advanced economies	57.4	77.6	15.5
Developing countries	36.8	18.0	77.7
Countries in transition	5.8	4.4	6.8

in the developing countries. These include the privatization of utilities and transportation companies, public sector reforms, the introduction of fiscal control measures, and the general improvement of the climate for inward investment.

Another noticeable development among African nations is the growth of co-operation in trade and politics. This includes such initiatives as the common external tariff being implemented by the West African Economic and Monetary Union; trade agreement with the EU concluded by Tunisia, Morocco and South Africa; plans to establish a free trade area in 2000 for the Common Market for Eastern and Southern Africa. Growth for Africa as a whole is projected to be 5% in 2000. However, political problems persist and further hamper development. As the last century closed it was estimated (IMF, 1999) that one-third of sub-Saharan Africa was involved directly or indirectly in military conflicts. Natural disasters can also introduce an unpredictable influence as the cyclone which affected Mozambique early in 2000 illustrated. This natural event put back economic development by between 5 and 10 years.

Overall, then, the global economy continues to be dominated by the advanced economies, especially when share of population is taken into account (Table 2.3).

The purpose of this review has been to illustrate the interconnectivity of the global economy. The Asian financial crisis is a useful example of how eventually the global economy can be affected by a regional problem. Add to the macroeconomic events a mixture of political failure ending in war, together with the impact of natural disasters, human perceptions of business confidence and the resultant capital flows and the difficulties faced by international players become clear. This review demonstrates that situations beyond the control of an individual firm can very rapidly affect the trading conditions of that firm. However, the global economy is not all bad news for the individual firm, as we shall see in this next section, where we will review some of the organizations who attempt to manage and police the global economy to ensure that everyone can benefit from trade.

The institutional framework: global players and referees

The World Bank

The World Bank was founded in 1944 and consists of a number of organizations as detailed in Box 2.2. It is based in Washington DC and provides approximately $30 billion each year to client countries. By working with other organizations, including the EU, other development banks, national aid programmes and export credit agencies, the Bank can leverage an additional $8 billion annually in cofinance deals to assist its work.

The Bank's key mission is to fight poverty. In order to achieve this the Bank emphasizes:

- Investing in people via health and education
- Protecting the environment
- Supporting and encouraging private business development
- Strengthening the ability of governments to deliver quality services, efficiently and transparently
- Promoting reforms to create a macroeconomic environment which will attract investment and allow long-term planning
- Social development, inclusion, governance and institution-building as key elements of poverty reduction.

BOX 2.2: MEMBERS OF THE WORLD BANK GROUP

The World Bank Group consists of:

The International Bank for Reconstruction and Development (IBRD)

The IBRD provides loans and development assistance to middle-income countries and creditworthy poorer countries. Funds are raised through the sale of bonds in international capital markets.

The International Development Association (IDA)

The IDA assists the world's poorest countries through the provision of interest-free loans. Its aim is to reduce poverty. Funds are dependent on contributions from member countries.

The International Finance Corporation (IFC)

The IFC promotes growth and development in developing countries by financing private sector investments and by providing technical assistance to governments and businesses.

The Multilateral Investment Guarantee Agency (MIGA)

This organization protects foreign investors against loss caused by non-commercial (political) risk and thus encourages investment in developing countries. It also helps the developing countries to disseminate information on investment opportunities.

The International Centre for Settlement of Investment Disputes (ICSID)

When problems arise in the relationships between host countries and their investors the ICSID is available to arbitrate.

In terms of regional spending in 1998 the World Bank lent $28,593.90 billion. Of this 34% went to East Asia and the Pacific; 21% to Latin America and the Caribbean; 18% to Eastern Europe and Central Asia; 14% to South Asia; 10% to Central and Southern Africa and 3% to the Middle East and North Africa.

Many of the activities and policy aims of the Bank have implications for the broader economic environment within which international marketers find themselves operating. If more of the world's countries can be brought out of poverty then the potential for an increase in trade and prosperity is there. Likewise, by supporting exporters through the insurance offered by the MIGA, and by acting against corruption, the Bank helps to build an environment of trust and confidence for exporters.

The World Trade Organization

This organization began its existence as the General Agreement on Tariffs and Trade (GATT). It was formed in 1947 just after World War II, when it was felt that future conflicts could be partly avoided if the world's nations were more integrated and prosperous via trading links. Not surprisingly, the US led the initial grouping, which included 22 other countries. The basic principles of GATT were:

- Non-discrimination in trade
- Domestic industry should be protected only through customs tariffs
- Measures such as dumping and subsidies should not interfere with fair competition
- Tariffs should be reduced through multilateral negotiations.

Membership has grown over the intervening years and in 1992 GATT had 103 members which accounted for approximately 80% of the world's trade. By 1994 the organization had 118 members and countries applying for membership included Saudi Arabia, many of the former centrally planned economies of Eastern Europe and, crucially, China. In 1995 GATT became the World Trade Organization (WTO) and currently (September 2000) membership stands at 138 countries. Its headquarters are in Geneva, Switzerland and it has a staff of 500 working for it. World trade in 1997 was 14 times the level in 1950 which helps to put into perspective the growth and importance of the WTO.

The functions of the WTO are to:

- Administer WTO trade agreements
- Provide a forum for trade negotiations
- Handle trade disputes
- Monitor national trade policies
- Provide technical assistance and training for developing countries
- Co-operate with other international organizations.

The WTO operates by securing agreement from its member countries. Decisions in the WTO are typically taken by consensus and they are ratified by members' parliaments. These agreements form what is known as the multilateral trading system, and they form the legal basis for international commerce. Essentially, they are contracts, guaranteeing member countries' trade rights, and binding governments to keep their trade policies within agreed limits for the benefit of all. Agreements exist to cover goods, services and intellectual property. Problems between member countries over trading rights are handled by a dispute settlement process, where the focus is on interpreting agreements and commitments, and ensuring that countries' trade policies conform with them. The complexity of the world trading system is highlighted by the fact that between 1947 and 1994, GATT dealt with 300 disputes. During the life of the WTO so far (1995 to March 1999) 167 cases have been brought forward for arbitration (see Box 2.3 for examples of recent disputes).

BOX 2.3: TRADE DISPUTES BROUGHT TO THE WTO

Inevitably, the world trading partners sometimes fall out over trade related issues. One option in order to find a resolution is to go to the WTO, who act as referee. The first stage of this process is for any member to request a meeting with any other which, it believes to be breaking WTO rules to protect its economy. If the dispute is not settled in 60 days, the plaintiff can ask for a panel, drawn from international-law experts, to adjudicate. This body should report within 6 months.

Examples of complaints include a plea by the EU, the US and Canada that Japan's alcohol taxes are biased against imports.

A plea by the US against South Korea that its inspections of fruit and vegetables are so detailed that the produce rots on the quayside.

A case brought by Venezuela and Brazil against the US on its rules on pollutants in petrol.

In September 1997 the EU was found by the WTO to discriminate in favour of former colonies in banana imports. This ruling had a negative impact upon the Caribbean.

The current round of talks, begun in Seattle in November 1999, is the eighth in the history of GATT/WTO. They tend to last for a long time; 9 years on average. Gaining agreement from such a diverse group is very difficult, and views on free trade tend to fluctuate depending on where an individual country is in the economic cycle. Thus, depression and protectionism tend to go hand-in-hand. One of the key difficulties of the WTO is that it is impossible to please everyone. The latest round of talks illustrate this from the different objectives (Business Week, 1999) which the three key groupings (US, Europe and the Developing Nations) bring to the negotiating table. For example the US would wish to concentrate on:

- Ending European farm subsidies
- Reducing tariffs on goods and services
- Protecting e-commerce from taxes and regulation
- Adding environmental protections to trade agreements
- Ensuring labour rights, through co-operation between the WTO and the International Labour Organization
- Protecting biotech products from labelling requirements.

Whereas Europe sought to:

- Maintain current farm subsidies
- Restrict labelling requirements for bioengineered foods

- Create a committee to foster labour rights
- Strengthen antitrust enforcement
- Retain current investment rules.

Meanwhile the Developing Nations' agenda was focused on:

- Relaxing antidumping enforcement
- Creating special rules for developing nations
- Opening more markets for farm, clothing and textile goods
- Limiting intellectual property safeguards.

The Seattle round became infamous for the coalition of protesters which it attracted and the street disturbances which followed. Images were transmitted around the world of the WTO meeting against a background of a vandalized McDonalds and street riots. Somehow it seemed the protesters blamed global ills: deforestation, child labour, overfishing, pollution and the loss of jobs to low-wage competition all on the 'faceless bureaucrats' of the WTO rather than linking it to the spending power of the global consumer.

The International Monetary Fund (IMF)

This organization was founded in 1945 at a conference held in Bretton Woods, New Hampshire in the US. From an initial membership of 39 it has grown to 182 member countries and a staff of approximately 2,700. The former centrally planned economies of Eastern Europe and the Soviet Union have joined, and are at various stages of completing their transition to a market economy. In essence the IMF exists because the member countries see the value of maintaining a stable system of buying and selling their currencies, so that payments in foreign money can take place between countries smoothly and without delay. In a more expanded form its statutory purpose is to:

- Promote international monetary co-operation
- Facilitate the expansion and balanced growth of international trade
- Promote exchange stability
- Assist in the establishment of a multilateral system of payments
- Make its general resources temporarily available to members experiencing balance of payments difficulties
- Shorten the duration, and lessen the degree of imbalances of payments of members.

To achieve these aims, the IMF provides a surveillance service in which it appraises members' economic situations, and produces the World Economic Outlook twice per annum. Technical assistance, for example, developing a central bank, collection and use of statistical data, and the training of officials, represents another strand of the IMF's work. The IMF has a range of financial measures, credits and loans, which it uses to support policies of adjustment and reform in countries with problems. Table 2.4 provides an overview of its financial provision in 1999.

In the past decade the IMF has been active in assisting the countries of Central

Table 2.4   Total fund credit and loans outstanding (April 1999) one special drawing unit (SDR) approximately equalled $1.34467 in February 1999. Source: IMF: http://www.imf.org/

Zone	Billions SDRs
World	63.6
Africa	6.7
Asia	20.3
Europe	18.3
Middle East	0.7
Western Hemisphere	17.6

Europe, the Baltic countries and Russia in their transition. It has also supported the economies of Mexico in 1995, and those countries affected by the Asian financial crisis in 1997–1998. As part of this latter activity, loans were arranged for Korea, Indonesia and Thailand. Again in the summer of 1998 when the Russian rouble collapsed, the IMF was on hand to assist.

Organization for Economic Co-operation and Development (OECD)

The OECD consists of 29 countries who support the principles of a market economy, pluralist democracy and respect for human rights. This is a rich but, they would claim, not an exclusive club, although the members do produce two-thirds of the world's goods and services. The original 20 members, from Western Europe and North America, came together in 1961, taking over the work of the Organization for European Economic Co-operation which had been formed to administer the Marshall Plan scheme for the reconstruction of Europe. Japan, Australia, New Zealand and Finland subsequently joined, and more recently Mexico, the Czech Republic, Hungary, Poland and Korea. The secretariat is based in Paris with a staff of some 1,850.

The key aims of the OECD and its members are to:

- Promote policies designed to achieve the highest sustainable economic growth and employment, and a rising standard of living for the population. This must be done under conditions of financial stability, and member countries must contribute to the expansion of world trade on a multilateral and non-discriminatory basis
- Undertake to co-operate with each other to ensure economic growth, reduction of the obstacles to trade in goods and services, and liberalization of capital movements, and to contribute to the economic development of all the world's countries.

The OECD participates in the collection of economic statistics and has interests in the environment, the developing countries, public service management, social policy, agriculture, energy, science and technology. It also participates in dialogue with non-members including Russia and Asian and Latin American countries.

In keeping in touch with new developments in the world's economy, the OECD Trade Directorate produces reports on special topics. For example, recent work has looked at e-commerce, since this is rapidly increasing as a means of conducting commercial transactions and facilitating international trade. In investigating a range of e-commerce issues such as taxation, protection of privacy, consumer protection, and the social and economic impact of e-commerce, the OECD is at the forefront of international discussions. Clearly, as well as being innovative, the OECD and its member countries are concerned about the growth of e-commerce and its impact on taxation, tariff issues, and general jurisdiction issues in international trade.

Supra-national trading blocs

There are a number of regional trade agreements in place around the globe, and in recent years there has been a significant extension in their scope. The North American Free Trade Area (NAFTA) involving the US, Canada and Mexico came into existence in 1993. In South America there is an organization called Mercosur (Argentina, Peru, Paraguay, Uruguay). Perhaps the two will one day join, and certainly Chile has expressed an interest in joining NAFTA. Within Europe the EU is expanding its reach by forming the European Economic Area with the remaining members of the European Free Trade Association. The EU also has agreements with a number of former communists states in Central Europe, as well as deals with North African countries and Mercosur. In Asia the Asia-Pacific Economic Co-operation forum (APEC) exists with a goal of free trade in the Pacific by 2020, as well as ASEAN, and ANZCERTA, a pact between Australia and New Zealand. The Economist (1998) estimated that in the previous 50 years, 153 regional trade agreements had been notified to GATT or the WTO, with most still currently in force.

In this section more details will be provided on selected regional economic associations. Examples of other associations intended to foster economic co-operation are listed in Table 2.5.

Association of Southeast Asian Nations (ASEAN)

ASEAN was formed in 1967 in Bangkok with Indonesia, Malaysia, Philippines, Singapore and Thailand being the founder members. Since then Brunei Darussalam joined in 1984, Vietnam in 1995, Laos and Myanmar in 1997 and Cambodia in 1999. The combined ASEAN nations have a population of 500 million and a GDP of $737 billion, and a total trade of $720 billion. The secretariat is based in Jakarta.

The purpose of the Association is:

- To accelerate the economic growth, social progress and cultural development in the region, through joint endeavours in the spirit of equality and partnership, in order to strengthen the foundation for a prosperous and peaceful community of Southeast Asian nations.
- To promote regional peace and stability through abiding respect for justice and

Table 2.5 Examples of other regional economic groupings

Grouping	Member states
Andean Common Market (ANCOM)	Bolivia, Colombia, Ecuador, Peru, Venezuela
Arab Common Market (ACM)	Egypt, Iraq, Jordan, Kuwait, Libya, Syria
Arab Magreb Union (AMU)	Algeria, Libya, Mauritania, Morocco, Tunisia
Asia-Pacific Economic Co-operation Forum (APEC)	Australia, Brunei, Canada, Chile, China, Hong Kong, Indonesia, Japan, South Korea, Malaysia, Mexico, New Zealand, Papua New Guinea, Peru, Philippines, Russia, Singapore, Taiwan, Thailand, US, Vietnam
CAIRNS Group (named after Cairns, Northern Queensland in Australia where the inaugural meeting took place in 1986)	Australia, Argentina, Bolivia, Brazil, Canada, Chile, Colombia, Costa Rica, Fiji, Guatemala, Indonesia, Malaysia, New Zealand, Paraguay, Philippines, South Africa, Thailand, Uruguay
Central American Common Market (CACM)	Costa Rica, El Salvador, Guatemala, Honduras, Nicaragua
Economic Community of West African States (ECOWAS)	Benin, Burkina Faso, Cape Verde, Ivory Coast, Gambia, Ghana, Guinea, Liberia, Mali, Mauritania, Niger, Nigeria, Senegal, Sierra Leone, Togo
Latin American Integration Association (LAIA)	Argentina, Bolivia, Brazil, Chile, Colombia, Ecuador, Paraguay, Peru, Uruguay, Venezuela
North American Free Trade Agreement (NAFTA)	Canada, Mexico, US

the rule of law in the relationship among countries in the region, and adherence to the principles of the United Nations Charter.

■ To promote active collaboration and mutual assistance on matters of common interest in the economic, social, cultural, technical, scientific and administrative fields.

In terms of the economic aspect of the ASEAN's activities, when it was first formed intra member trade was very low, only about 12–15% of their total trade. By focusing on tariff reduction between members, it was possible to increase this through the Preferential Trading Arrangement of 1977 and a number of similar subsequent measures. By 1992 the members were discussing an ASEAN Free Trade Area (AFTA) with the aim of eliminating tariff and non-tariff barriers in order to promote greater economic efficiency, productivity and competitiveness. The target date to achieve this was by 2005.

In addition to trade and investment activities, the members of ASEAN are committed to developing the Trans-ASEAN transportation network. This consists of initiatives to improve and develop air, sea, road, rail and inland waterway networks. ASEAN is also promoting the interoperability and interconnectivity of national telecommunications equipment and services. However, despite good intentions, strong rhetoric, and announcements, ASEAN is still a long way from being a operational free trade area.

Caribbean Community and Common Market (CARICOM)

CARICOM consists of Antigua and Barbuda, The Bahamas, Barbados, Belize, Dominica, Grenada, Guyana, Haiti, Jamaica, Montserrat, Suriname, St. Kitts, Nevis, St. Lucia, St. Vincent and the Grenadines and Trinidad and Tobago.

CARICOM was established by the Treaty of Chaguaramas, which was signed by Barbados, Jamaica, Guyana and Trinidad and Tobago and came into effect on August 1, 1973. This was the outcome of earlier co-operation under the British West Indies Federation which was founded in 1958.

The mission statement of the grouping is 'To provide dynamic leadership and service, in partnership with community institutions and groups, toward the attainment of a viable, internationally competitive and sustainable community, with improved quality of life for all'.

The Caribbean Community has three objectives:

- Economic co-operation through the Caribbean Single Market and Economy (CSM&E)
- Co-ordination of foreign policy among the independent member states
- Common services and co-operation in functional matters such as health, education and culture, communications and industrial relations.

The principal organizations of the Community are the Conference of the Heads of Government and the Community Council of Ministers. Other bodies include the Council for Trade and Economic Development (COTED), which promotes trade and economic development of the Community and oversees the operations of the CSM&E. The Council for Foreign and Community Relations (COFCOR) determines relations with international organizations and third states. The Council for Human and Social Development (COHSOD) promotes human and social development. Finally The Council for Finance and Planning (COFAP) co-ordinates economic policy and financial and monetary integration of member states.

In general the members of CARICOM have suffered from an over reliance on primary products and tourism. By co-operating intraregionally it was hoped that the drawbacks of small market size, economic fragmentation, and external dependence would be overcome. CARICOM's goal of regional integration was intended to act as a catalyst for growth, by allowing for market expansion, harmonization of production strategies, and the development of economies of scale. Integration would also eliminate excess capacity in the manufacturing sector and stimulate investment in new sectors of the market. While the path to integration has not always been smooth, the institutional framework created by CARICOM, the intraregional dialogue and trade, and functional co-operation, have proved resilient.

European Union (EU)

The EU is perhaps the best known of all the trading blocs representing 350 million consumers in Western Europe, and generating exports worth $813 billion and purchasing $801 billion of imports in 1999. Its headquarters is in Brussels, Belgium and it has a number of important institutions including the European Commission, the Council of Ministers, the European Court of Justice, the European Parliament, the European Council and the Economic and Social Committee.

The EU had its roots in the Treaty of Paris, 1951, which created the European Coal and Steel Community. This marked the beginning of co-operation which led to the establishment of the European Economic Community (EEC) under the Treaty of Rome in 1957. The founding members were Belgium, France, West Germany, Italy, Luxembourg and the Netherlands. The EEC expanded with the accession of Denmark, Ireland and the UK in 1973; Greece in 1981, Portugal and Spain in 1986 and most recently, Austria, Finland and Sweden in 1995.

The aim of the EU to achieve one set of trade rules, a single tariff and a single set of administrative procedures, took a huge step forward in 1992 with the creation of the Single Market. This allowed for a number of important measures including the free movement of people, capital, and open access to public sector contracts for all EU firms.

In 1998 the EU began the process which could increase its geographical area by 34% and the population within its boundaries by 105 million. It accepted applications for membership from Bulgaria, Cyprus, the Czech Republic, Estonia, Hungary, Latvia, Lithuania, Malta, Poland, Romania, the Slovak Republic, Slovenia and Turkey.

The requirements for membership state that each country must have achieved:

- Stability through democratic institutions, the rule of law and human rights and the protection of minorities
- The existence of a market economy and the ability to cope with competitive pressures within the EU
- The ability to take on the obligations of membership including adherence to political, economic and monetary union

and has created:

- The conditions for the integration of its administrative structures, so that EU legislation can be transposed into its national legislation, and implemented effectively via administrative and judicial structures.

Another key development within the EU was the introduction of the euro in 1999. This is part of a process called Economic Monetary Union (EMU) which aims to create a single currency whilst providing an alternative to the US dollar in international trade. So far the euro has been weak and it has not yet emerged as a serious alternative to the US dollar. Eleven of the EU countries have joined the EMU: Austria, Belgium, Finland, France, Germany, Italy, Ireland, Luxembourg, the Netherlands, Portugal and Spain. There will be no notes or coins issued until 2002, but purchases can be made in euros using debit or credit cards or travellers' cheques.

Many shops have introduced dual pricing in euros as well as the local currency. By the end of 2002, it is anticipated that those countries which have joined the EMU will begin to withdraw their own coins and notes, leaving the Euro as the sole currency. For some member countries monetary union is a precursor to political union, while for others, notably the UK regardless of whether or not monetary union is achieved, a federal structure is preferred.

European Free Trade Area (EFTA)

EFTA was established in 1960 by Austria, Denmark, Norway, Portugal, Sweden, Switzerland and the UK. Its goal was to remove import duties, quotas and other obstacles to trade in Western Europe while supporting liberal, non-discriminatory trading practices in the rest of the world. Iceland joined in 1960, Finland in 1986 and Liechtenstein in 1991.

With the development of the European Community six members have left EFTA leaving Iceland, Liechtenstein, Norway and Switzerland as the current members. In 1992 all EFTA members except Switzerland entered into an Agreement on the European Economic Area (EEA) with the 15 members of the EU. This extends the EU single market concept to the three EFTA states and allows for close co-operation on project not related to trade, for example, the environment, education and training. The headquarters of EFTA are in Geneva while the Secretariat in Brussels deals with the EU to administer the EEA.

In addition to the EEA, EFTA has a range of formal trade relations with other partners including for example, Turkey, Israel, Morocco, the Palestine Liberation Organization, Egypt, Tunisia and most former communist countries in Eastern Europe. Negotiations are underway (since 1998) with Canada to conclude a transatlantic agreement.

National governments

National governments, as we have seen already, appear to play a dual role in international trade. Sometimes they work for trade liberalization measures in co-operation with other countries, and at other times, as in trade disputes, show secular interests are the key driving force behind policy decisions. This duality is seen again in this section when we review the range of possible measures open to national governments to specifically dissuade or encourage trade with their country.

Restricting trade

Free trade is widely believed to be beneficial to all trading nations and allows international specialization. When firms are able to serve international markets, economies of scale are achieved leading to lower prices in the importing market. However, not all nations wish to see a totally free trade system and some nations implement more trade laws than others. Some of these trade laws are the product of culture, for example, whisky may not be imported into Saudi Arabia, but generally, these laws favour the local producer and hinder the activities of international firms. These trade distortion practices are either referred to as tariff barriers or non-tariff barriers.

Tariff barriers are explicit taxes and charges imposed on imports. They can and should be taken into account by companies when devising their marketing strategies, especially in terms of price. Poorer nations can use them to protect local industry and to raise revenue and politicians can claim to be standing up for their citizens. The most common forms of tariff are as follows:

- Ad valorem. This Latin phrase represents a duty which is based on a percentage of the value of the goods landed at the port of entry.
- Specific duty. This duty is based on the weight, volume, length, number of units in the shipment.
- Alternative duty. Applicable rate is that which provides the higher amount of duty.
- Component or mixed duties.
- Temporary import surcharge.
- Compensatory import taxes.
- Anti-dumping duties.
- Customs union or common market which maintains an external tariff.
- Countervailing duty. This is designed to raise the price of imported goods to the current price of the nearest domestic competitor.
- Drawback duty. This is paid if the imported goods are re-exported.
- Tariff schedule. These can be single column i.e. same tariff regardless of origin or multi-column i.e. different depending on origin of goods.
- Much Favoured Nation Status. This allows for bilateral trade or preferential rates of duty.

Non-tariff barriers are often more difficult to deal with as they can be more surreptitious than tariff barriers. They can be imposed at relatively short notice making it difficult for marketers to plan for them. Non-tariff barriers include:

- Specific limitations including quotas and import restraints
- Discriminatory governmental and private procurement policies including 'buy national' and state subsidies to companies
- Restrictive custom practices on validation, classification, documentation, health, safety and hygiene
- Selective monetary controls and discriminatory exchange rate controls
- Restrictive administrative and technical regulation standards for products, packaging, labelling and marketing.

Encouraging trade

Most national governments will support trade development because, in a narrow political sense, it means jobs, a successful economy and other things being equal, more votes at the next election for the party in power. Clearly governments support trade through membership of the WTO and involvement with the other 'international referees', as well as by participating in regional economic groupings as discussed earlier in this chapter. However, the WTO has some concern that the growth of free trade zones and trade blocs may lead to increased protectionism rather than promoting trade liberalization.

Governments vary in their degree of involvement in encouraging companies to export, but examples of the kinds of activities which may be undertaken are given below. Governments can encourage companies to export by providing information sources on the mechanics of exporting, as well as acting as a clearing house for specific opportunities; they may provide grants to enable market research; provide assistance for companies to attend international trade fairs or exhibitions; encourage trade to 'difficult' markets through providing insurance (see Box 2.4). Trade missions may also be led by the government trade development body to specific markets which are regarded as good potential markets. Governments also concern themselves with inward investment for footloose companies, which helps to diversify the economy, create jobs and perhaps bring new technology to the domestic market (this is discussed again in Chapter 4).

BOX 2.4: INTO AFRICA – GOVERNMENT SUPPORT FOR EXPORTERS

US based exporters and SMEs based in Africa seeking to purchase US products and services will benefit (after 1999) from an experimental finance program launched by the Export–Import Bank of the US. The program will make short-term insurance available in 11 sub-Saharan countries where routine financing is currently unavailable, namely in Chad, Equatorial Guinea, Madagascar, Malawi, Mauritania, Mozambique, Nigeria, Sao Tome and Principle, Tanzania and Togo.

(adapted from Industry Week, 1999)

The human context

Every generation probably feels that it has faced more change than any preceding one. This may well be true, but what is different today is that the pace of change, when allied to technological changes, is probably more rapid and far reaching in its consequences. In 1978 approximately one-third of the world's workforce lived in centrally planned economies. Another third lived in economies only partially linked to the international trading system because of protective measures. By the turn of the century fewer than 10% of the workforce were living in markets semi-detached from the world economy.

Such change is never easy and insecurity, technological change, and the decline of traditional social structures affects both the rich and poor countries. Poverty remains a serious problem, and could increase as the world's workforce grows from 2.5 billion in 1995 to 3.7 billion in 2025. Currently almost one billion workers live on a dollar or less a day while many work in very poor conditions. World-wide approximately 120 million people are unemployed and many have lost hope of finding work.

Compare the following examples of workers experience of the global economy (The World Bank, 1995).

The worker

'Duong is a Vietnamese peasant farmer who struggles to feed his family. He earns the equivalent of $10 a week for 38 h of work in the rice fields, but he works only 6 months of the year – during the off-season he can earn very little. His wife and four children work with him in the fields, but the family can afford to send only the two youngest to school. Duong's 11-year-old daughter stays at home to help with housework, while his 13-year-old son works as a street trader in town. By any standard Duong's family is living in poverty. Workers like Duong labouring on family farms in low- and middle-income countries, account for about 40% of the world's labour force.

Hoa is a young Vietnamese city dweller experiencing relative affluence for the first time. In Ho Chi Minh City she earns the equivalent of $30 a week working 48 h in a garment factory – a joint venture with a French firm. She works hard for her living and spends many hours looking after her three children as well; her husband works as a janitor. But Hoa's family has several times the standard of living of Duong's and, by Vietnamese standards, is relatively well-off. There is every expectation that both she and her children will continue to have a vastly better standard of living than her parents had. Wage employees like Hoa, working in the formal sector in low- and middle-income countries, make up about 20% of the global labour force.

Francoise is an immigrant in France of Vietnamese origin who works long hours as a waitress to make ends meet. She takes home the equivalent of $220, a week after taxes and including tips, for 50 h work. By French standards she is poor. Legally, Francoise is a casual worker and so has no job security, but she is much better off in France than she would have been in Vietnam. Her wage is almost eight times that earned by Hoa in Ho Chi Minh City. Francoise and other services sector workers in high-income countries account for about 9% of the global labour force.

Jean-Paul is a 50-year-old Frenchman whose employment prospects look bleak. For 10 years he has worked in a garment factory in Toulouse, taking home the equivalent of US $400 a week – 12 times the average wage in Vietnam's garment industry. By next month he will lose his job when the factory closes. Unemployment benefits will partly shield him from the shock, but his chances of matching his old salary in a new job are slim. Frenchmen of Jean-Paul's age who lose their jobs are likely to stay unemployed for more than a year, and Jean-Paul is encouraging his son to work hard in school so he can go to college and study computer programming. Workers in industry in high-income countries, like Jean-Paul, make up just 4% of the world's labour force.

These four families – two living in Vietnam, two living in France – have vastly different standards of living and expectations for the future. Employment and wage prospects in Toulouse and Ho Chi Minh City are worlds apart, even when incomes are adjusted, as here, for differences in the cost of living. Francoise's poverty wage would clearly buy Hoa a vastly more affluent life-style. And much more of the world's work force, like Duong, works outside the wage sector on family farms and in the informal sector, generally earning even lower labour incomes. But the lives of urban workers in different parts of the world are increasingly intertwined. French consumers buy the products of Hoa's labour, and Jean-Paul believes it is Hoa's low wages that are taking his job, while migrant workers, like Francoise feel the brunt of Jean-Paul's anger. Meanwhile, Duong struggles to save so that his children can be educated and leave the countryside for the city, where foreign companies advertise new jobs at better wages.

If low incomes, poor working conditions and insecurity are to be effectively tackled then a combination of sound domestic policy and a supportive international environment are needed. To achieve this the World Bank recommends that governments should:

- Follow market-based growth plans which create a demand for labour, expand workforce skills and raise productivity
- Continue to open up trade and attract inward investment
- Construct a framework for labour policy that complements informal and rural labour markets, supports collective bargaining in the formal sector, protects the vulnerable and does not act in favour of the better-off workers
- Encourage as rapid as possible progress in the transition economies without excessive or permanent costs for labour

The manager

The international marketing manager must have the skill to look at people and situations from different perspectives, be willing to adjust to new and different conditions, have an analytical ability to interpret the findings. Korey (1995) suggests that managers should be able to look at problems from multiple perspectives. Creative thinking needs to be part of the decision-making process and can be enhanced if the following perspectives are used subject to the normal economic, political and market perspectives:

- Technical perspective – from the point of view of technology and rationality
- Organizational perspective i.e. corporate organization, company structure and general social infrastructure
- Personal perspective – from the point of view of the individual(s) affected
- International perspective – regarding the social responsibility of the transnational business, ethical basis, values and morality
- Cultural perspective – including religion, language, education and intercultural dimensions.

By using multiple perspectives and obtaining a larger range of views, the suggestion is that ultimately risk is reduced. Allied to this the manager requires an orderly approach to problem solving. This requires good organization and efficiency on the part of the manager, taking responsibility for one's action and being skilled at problem solving.

Markets should not be seen as domestic and international. The distance from the headquarters should not affect how marketing is conducted. Marketing management requires the integration of all marketing activities (understanding, creating, communicating and delivering) within the organization.

This view is echoed by de Wilde (1991) who states that innovative approaches are needed for managing in a global economy. Two processes are required in order to become a global-thinking manager. The first is conceptual/strategic and requires the communication of knowledge. Thus it is important to appreciate the interrelatedness of the global environment. A shift in investment from a high-wage economy to a low-wage economy will allow cost savings and increase competitiveness in the global market. Or, for example, in attempting to break into the Latin American market a strategic alliance with Spanish or Hispanic firms can accelerate cultural understanding and increase the likelihood of success.

The second is skills-based and can draw on case-based management education. The suggestion is that the global manager requires:

- Intercultural negotiating skills. How does one deal with the Japanese or what is an appropriate way to behave in Saudi Arabia. Do the Slovaks differ from the Czechs?
- Ability to read different markets in different cultural contexts. Do different trends drive different markets across the world and therefore does our marketing have to be adapted?
- Ability to understand comparative politics. National governments have different approaches to, for example, intellectual property law.
- Ability to understand that cultural frameworks define markets, pricing and competition.

The employer

Transnational businesses have a certain social responsibility thrust upon them when they operate internationally. This is in addition to the expectation of the host country that they will create wealth.

External manifestations of the social responsibility include:

- Community service
- Environmental protection (air, land and water pollution)
- Packaging used and its impact on pollution
- Transmission of new values (through advertising of new products) and new technology.

Social responsibility can also be pursued through internal measures including:

- Physical working conditions
- Women's, multicultural and minority rights
- Education and training of employees
- Industrial relations.

Attempting to create a partnership with employees as co-producers and having the 'right' attitude has much to do with achieving international success. The organization in terms of its senior executives has the responsibly for forming this attitude and conveying it to the lower levels of managers and the workers. Perlmutter (1969) defined an organization's approach to international markets as ethnocentric, polycentric or geocentric. Although an article written over 30 years ago the conceptualization offered still has a resonance today.

An ethnocentric approach believes that the employees and practices of foreign cultures are inferior to those of the domestic market. All policies whether human resource management, finance, marketing or production related reflect the home-country policies.

Such an approach may be appropriate if markets served were virtually identical to the home country. However, it is in greater danger of being out of line with local conditions, and more importantly the emerging global trends which could be different from the home-country situation on which policy is based.

Polycentrism takes the view that all cultures are different and that all foreign based activities should be left to get on with their work as long as they contribute profitably to the organization. A variation on this theme is regiocentrism. Regiocentrism recognizes that certain similarities exist between different countries within a geographic region and adopt policies which treat these markets in a similar way. Thus, an American manager might perceive France, Italy, the UK and Denmark to be the same since they are all European, whereas from a European perspective significant variations exist between consumers in these countries.

The problem with either the polycentric approach, or regiocentrism to a lesser degree, is that economies of scale are not realized, lessons learned by the organization are not translated into other operating theatres, facilities may be duplicated and divergent policies on recruitment, training and sales policies followed.

The final category of Perlmutter's typology is geocentrism. This approach holds that there are global similarities in both cultures and markets. Unlike the ethnocentric approach in which domestic personnel and ways of managing are thought to be superior and polycentric approaches where cultural superiority rests with the host country; geocentric approaches do not assume either local or domestic practices to be best. Under this approach to management, polices are devised to balance local practices and global practices. In this the ideal is to achieve the best of both worlds, so that economies of scale are realized, and responsiveness to local conditions can be maintained. Executives with a global outlook can drive such polices and contribute towards a geocentric organization.

In a study of Canadian firms Calof and Beamish (1994) found that there were significant differences in the performance among companies who followed one of Perlmutter's typologies. The most dramatic difference was with overall international performance. Export intensity (international/total sales) was 27% for ethnocentric firms, 45% for polycentric firms and 68% for geoocentric firms. On average geocentric firms had an average of $66 million in export sales compared to $47 million for polycentric and $32 million for ethnocentric firms. Calof and Beamish state that the firms were all of similar size with no significant differences in total sales or number of employees, thus concluding that the differences in sales and intensity did not arise because of the size of the firm. Rather, attitudes, centricity, emerged as the dominant factor differentiating performance. Other evidence from the study indicated that firms who moved to a geocentric approach experienced an improved international performance.

For an organization to increase its successful involvement with international trade it can follow a policy of looking for executives with geocentric attitudes. This can be facilitated by employing people who have worked or attend an educational institution outside their country of birth. They may also speak more than one language or have participated in an international exchange programme. For existing staff, geocentric attitudes can be encouraged with suitable training programmes, placement on international assignments and the facilitation of reading newspapers and magazines from other countries. Clearly, companies can also benefit from the increasing importance of the Internet with its information search and delivery potential. The development of an international outlook or experience is a crucial building block to understanding internationalization. This will be discussed further in Chapter 4. Its importance is echoed in a quotation from an executive in the Calof and Beamish study who states 'The best investment a firm can make is in having an international board. It is more important to have international board experience than product experience'.

Conclusions: the marketing context

The preceding discussion in this chapter has described the background against which marketers must act their part in the global economy. This background, as we have seen, is complex, full of uncertainty and subject to change which is often rapid and unpredictable. The marketer must be alive to the opportunities which come along and be prepared to take advantage of windows of opportunity as they open. This, as we shall see later in this book, is open to both the small and medium sized enterprise as well as the multinational ,without discrimination. The particular factors influencing the small firm will be dealt with in Chapter 5, but to conclude the final comments in this chapter will deal with the macro issues which will drive the global economy in the future in which marketers will have to operate.

Steingraber (1996) believes that the globalization issue itself is the crucial factor. It is viewed as having unstoppable momentum. Changes in the technology we use, methods of transportation and communication, coupled with the growth in global trade, are creating a trading environment in which anything can be made and sold anywhere.

A second driver of globalization is technology which contributes to the globalization process by helping to create new products and services which stimulate demand and growth in the world's economy.

A third driver of globalization, and one of particular interest to marketers, is the convergence of customer needs. It is argued that the availability of information, and the increase in travel and education levels, leads to a greater awareness of and likely acceptance of standard products across countries. This standardization/adaptation debate is one we will return to later in Chapter 7. However, for now it is worth remembering that people throughout the world share similar needs and desires, but that these needs and desires can be satisfied in quite different ways due to the variable influence of culture, tradition or way of managing a business.

One of the most profound shifts to take place is the expected shift in economic power to the developing countries in the next 25 years. It is forecast that the developing world will account for 65%, up from 40%, of the worlds GDP in 2020. It is also forecast that the GDP of East Asia will outstrip that of North America or Europe by $1 trillion within 10 years and China's GDP will be larger than the US's by 2020. Thus, companies with a marketing presence in Asia will be in a position to jump to positions of greater global dominance by virtue of being in these growing markets.

The second macro-trend which marketers will face is shorter supply chains. Steingraber (1996) quotes one company which found 39 handlings between the production line and retail shelf while Digital calculated that some computer parts travel 250 000 miles before reaching the customer! The argument is that such lengthy supply chains will not stand up to the competitive demands of the 21st Century which will include:

- Shorter product life cycles
- Diminishing brand value
- Smarter and more demanding customers
- New-technology enabled distribution channels
- Increased pressure on prices and financial results.

The third trend identified is technology convergence which is transforming the workplace, sourcing of materials, creation of products and services, and their delivery to the market place. The Internet, for example, represents a distribution channel as well as a market. New linkages are made and markets created which were unthought of only a few years ago. This creates enormous possibilities for marketers and offers the opportunity to unleash the very core of a marketer's response, namely, a creativity in linking a business to its customers. In time developments in technology will allow marketers to interact on a one to one basis with customers in their own homes, as the computer or next generation of televisions become much more than just a delivery of programmes.

Finally, no matter how certain the future of the global economy may seem, the only real certainty is that nothing is certain and change is inevitable. As the first draft of this chapter was being written the impact of the financial crisis in Southeast Asia was being felt in Japan and South Korea with smaller, but discernible ripples being felt in Europe, for example, loss of export orders and a decrease in investment, including postponement of foreign direct investment by companies.

In September 1997 Japan's GDP growth rate was forecast as 2.9%; in 1998 by November it was forecast at 0.9%; while South Korea and Thailand saw projected growth of 6–7% turn into a projected fall in output (The Economist, 1997). The impact on New Zealand and Australia which only export around 12% of GDP to Asia will be less than Japan and the US which export 44% and 30% respectively to Asia. Ironically, in some EU countries this slowdown will allow a cooling off period and reduce pressure for interest rate increases.

Prior to the Asian crisis the growing economic dominance seemed unstoppable but now there is talk of the 'New Atlantic Economy' driven by the US and Europe. The tired economic image of these regions has been shed by deregulation, for example, in the telecom, finance and airline sectors; the development of new technologies, the creation of the euro and a shared system of business values underpinned by a common business school education experience. The 'Old' economy of steel, cars and energy has given way to the so-called 'New' economy of pharmaceuticals, technology and telecommunications.

The lesson from all of this, if we still needed it, is the integrated nature of the global economy. It offers vast opportunities but the impact of shocks must also be absorbed from time to time. Such is the nature of the trading world in which most of the world's population live. For countries, the managers and the workers, total control is impossible and the metaphor of the bobbing cork is a powerful one.

Questions for discussion

1. Discuss what aspects of globalization are apparent in your local economy. For instance, how does it affect employment opportunities and your personal purchasing habits?
2. Prepare for a discussion on the current state of the global economy which updates the situation outlined in this chapter. What are the current opportunities, difficulties and general trends?
3. Using the WTO, World Bank or IMF, search their websites to discover what their current concerns are for the global economy.
4. Select a trading bloc and research what issues are currently dominating the member nations' thoughts.
5. Using web based sources select a country and assess its attractiveness as a market.
6. Research what assistance is offered to exporters by your national government. How does the assistance offered compare to your nearest economic competitors?
7. Discuss the human impact of globalization. What are its advantages and disadvantages? Has it made the world a fairer place?
8. How does an understanding of the global economy affect the international marketer?
9. What management skills are important in the global economy of the 21st Century?
10. Is globalization creating a global consumer?

References

Business Week (1999), *Bracing for a Battle in Seattle*, Nov. 8 (3654), p. 38.

Calof, J.L. and Beamish, P.W. (1994), The right attitude for international success, *Business Quarterly*, 59 (1), pp. 105–110.

Carr, M., Hostrop, A. and O'Connor, D. (1998), The new era of global retailing, *Journal of Business Strategy*, 19 (3), p. 11; (5) InfoTrac http://www.galegroup.com/

Korey, G. (1995), Multilateral perspectives in international marketing dynamics, *Journal of Business and Industrial Marketing*, 10 (3), pp. 74–82.

De Wilde, J. (1991), How to train managers for going global, *Business Quarterly*, 55 (3), p. 41 (4) InfoTrac http://www.galegroup.com/.

Industry Week (1999), Into Africa, *Industry Week*, 248 (10), p. 10.

International Monetary Fund (1997), *World Economic Outlook*, IMF World Economic and Financial Surveys, Washington, DC.

International Monetary Fund (1999), *World Economic Outlook*, IMF World Economic and Financial Surveys, Washington, DC.

International Monetary Fund (2000), *World Economic Outlook*, IMF World Economic and Financial Surveys, Washington, DC.

Perlmutter, H.V. (1969), The tortuous evolution of the multinational corporation, *Columbia Journal of World Business*, 4 (Jan/Feb), pp. 9–18.

Steingraber, F.G. (1996), The new business realities of the twenty-first century, *Business Horizons*, 39 (6), p. 2; (4) InfoTrac http://www.galegroup.com/.

The Economist (US) (1997), Variable fallout: Asia and the world economy, *The Economist (US)*, Nov. 29, 345 (8045), pp. 79–81.

The Economist (US) (1998), Alphabetti spaghetti: are regional trade agreements a good idea? *The Economist (US)*, Oct. 3, 348 (8088), pp. 19–20.

The World Bank (1995), *World Development Report*, World Bank, Washington, DC.

The World Bank (1996), *World Development Report*, World Bank, Washington, DC.

The World Bank (1997), *World Development Report*, World Bank, Washington, DC.

Further reading

Bales, K. (1999), *Disposable People: New Slavery in the Global Economy*, University of California Press, Berkeley, CA.

Hunter, J.L. (1999), The World Trade Organisation ministerial: setting priorities for the twenty-first century, *European Business Journal*, 11 (3), pp. 146–149.

Hejazi, W. and Safarian, A.E. (1999), Trade, foreign direct investment, and R & D spillovers, *Journal of International Business Studies*, 30 (3), pp. 491–511.

Kostecki, M. and Fehervary, A. (eds.) (1996), *Services in the Transition Economies: Business Options for Trade and Investment*, Pergamon, Oxford.

Kozul-Wright, R. and Rowthorn, R. (eds.) (1999), *Transnational Corporations in the Global Economy*, Macmillan, Basingstoke.

Malhotra, N.K., Agarwal, J. and Baalbaki, I. (1998), Heterogeneity of regional trading blocs and global marketing strategies: a multicultural perspective, *International Marketing Review*, 15 (6), pp. 476–506.

Rodilk, D. (1999), *The New Global Economy and Developing Countries: Making Openness Work*, Frank Cass & Company Ltd., New York.

Scase, R. (1997), The role of small businesses in the economic transformation of Eastern Europe: real but relatively unimportant? *International Small Business Journal*, 16 (1), pp. 13–21.

Simon, H. and Otte, M. (2000), The new atlantic economy, *Harvard Business Review*, 78 (1), pp. 17–20.

Smallbone, D., Piasecki, B., Venesaar, U., Todorov, K. and Labrianidis, L. (1998), Internationalisation and SME development in transition economies: an international comparison, *Journal of Small Business and Enterprise Development*, 5 (4), pp. 363–375.

The following web sites were also consulted and provide a useful starting point for further study:

APEC	http://www.apecsec.org.sg/
ASEAN	http://www.asean.or
CAIRNS	http://www.dfat.gov.au/trade/negotiations/cairns_group/
CARICOM	http://www. caricom.org/expframes3.htm
EFTA	http://www.efta.org
EU	http://www.europa.eu.int/
IMF	http://www.imf.org
MERCOSUR	http://www.mercosur.org/english/default.htm
NAFTA	http://www.nafta-sec-alena.org/
OECD	http://www.oecd.org
WTO	http://www.wto.org
The World Bank	http://www.worldbank.org

CHAPTER 3

Get a good guide-book: the influence of culture on international marketing

Chapter objectives

After studying this chapter you should be able to:

- Describe the elements of culture and their influence on international marketing
- Appreciate the limitations of your own 'world view'
- Understand how all stages of the marketing cycle have a cultural dimension
- Consider how best to manage cultural interactions

Introduction

It is people that often make involvement with international marketing exciting but frustrating. A concern for the cultural dimension can evoke extreme reactions, for example, Hanns Johst is quoted to have remarked on one occasion 'Whenever I hear the word culture, I release the safety catch on my revolver'. In essence this view captures the complexity of the challenging but often frustrating cultural landscape in which companies now find themselves operating. It is hoped that the reaction of the international marketing manager is less extreme than that of Johst!

With many of the recent changes to the political map of the world, old boundaries are being re-established as many older cultures stake a claim to their place in the 21st Century. Consequently the political map of the world, particularly in Europe, more closely resembles pre-World War I atlases than those of the late 20th Century. While these changes may seem remote from the day-to-day concerns of the international marketing manager, they can have very significant reverberations. Newly emerging states, for example, are often keen to stamp their own identity on all activities, and demand the use of local language where before the language of the colonial power would have been the standard business language. In Belarus, for example, the Government has reverted to the Belorussian

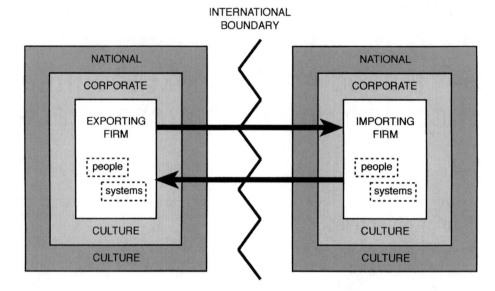

Figure 3.1   The influence of culture on the buyer-seller relationship. Source: author.

language for all official documents. This creates problems in completing appropriate documentation and clearly has cost and time implications for the exporting company.

It is important to realize that the link (Figure 3.1) between the selling firm and its international customer is not simply a linear relationship. The influence of culture can be identified at a number of levels. Thus, the relationship between buyer and seller is played out against the backcloth of both nations' culture. In addition, the corporate culture of both organizations, itself a mixture of each organization's way of doing things, and its relationship with the individuals within each organization, interacts to create the environment within which the exchange will take place. These cultural identities act as a prism refracting or distorting the one's view of the other. How well this is first, recognized and secondly, managed within each organization will strongly influence the success of the venture.

Viewed in this way culture cannot be ignored in any study of international marketing management. It provides a useful starting point to understanding the stage on which international business takes place. It is both a privilege and a luxury, as a student, to take a step back from one's own cultural perspective and attempt to appreciate its influence. In day-to-day business the time is often not there to fully appreciate its influence, and yet countless decisions are made automatically because of it. Fundamentally, cultural influences are a defining feature of our own humanity and provide a framework for our actions.

The purpose of this chapter is to begin by considering the definitions of culture which have been put forward before going on in the Section 'The foundations of our cultural understanding' to discuss the role of geography and our inner view of the world as the basis for cultural understanding. Following these introductory and scene setting sections, the relationship between culture and marketing will be dealt with using the typology introduced in Chapter 1, namely, understanding the customer, creating the product, communicating with the customer and delivering what was promised to the customer. Each of these aspects of the marketing cycle will be considered from a cultural perspective. The more practical aspects of culture and marketing will be raised in the Section 'Doing business with culture' where issues such as how culture affects management styles, training needs and cross-border alliances will be discussed.

Culture: no one definition

Unsurprisingly there is no one universally accepted definition of culture. It remains a construct which is difficult to define. Kroeber and Kluckhohn (1952) identified over 160 definitions of culture! Namenwirth and Weber (1987) from a sociologist's perspective, defined culture as a 'system of ideas' that provided a 'design for living'. Anthropologists Hall and Hall (1990) view culture as a system for creating, sending, storing and processing information. Hofstede (1994) defines culture as 'the collective programming of the mind which distinguishes the members of one group or category of people from another'. Culture is learned, not inherited. We absorb it from our social environment. It has to be distinguished from human personality and human nature, although the boundaries between them are open to debate (Figure 3.2).

Human nature is what all humans have in common. It allows us to feel fear, anger, love, happiness and sadness, share with others through talking about our experience of the environment. What we do with these feelings is modified by culture. An individual's personality is their unique set of mental programming, partly inherited and partly learned. By learned, we mean it is modified by the personal experiences one has in life and by the influence of culture.

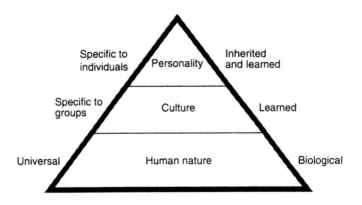

Figure 3.2   Three levels of human mental programming. Source: adapted from Hofstede (1991).

Despite the diversity of approaches, there are many common threads which the various definitions share, and so it is generalized as a shared pattern of being, thinking and behaving; something (further examples are given in Box 3.1) learned from childhood through socialization; something deeply rooted in tradition that permeates all aspects of any society. Perhaps Hill (1997) puts it most succinctly and defines it as 'a system of values and norms that are shared among a group of people and that when taken together constitute a design for living'.

Almost everyone belongs to a number of different groups and categories of people at the same time therefore, inevitably, carrying several layers of mental programming with them, corresponding to different layers of culture. For example:

- A national level according to one's country (or countries for people who migrated during their lifetime)
- A regional and/or ethnic and/or religious and/or linguistic affiliation level, as most nations are composed of culturally different regions and/or ethnic and/or religious and/or language groups
- A gender level, whether a person was born a girl or a boy
- A generation level, which separates grandparents from parents from children
- A social class level, associated with educational opportunities and with a person's occupation or profession
- For those who are employed, an organizational or corporate level according to the way employees have been socialized by their work organization.

BOX 3.1: VIEWS OF CULTURE

Culture…is that complex whole which includes knowledge, belief, art, law, morals, custom, and any other capabilities and habits acquired by man as a member of society (Tylor, 1891)

…culture is the socially inherited assemblage of practices and beliefs that determines the texture of our lives (Sapir, 1949)

Culture is the term used to refer to the way that members of a group act in relation to one another and to other groups (Lasswell, 1966)

Culture is a learned, shared, compelling, interrelated set of symbols whose meanings provide a set of orientations for members of a society. These orientations, taken together, provide solutions to problems that all societies must solve if they are to remain viable (Terpstra and David, 1985)

Culture is an integrated system of learned behaviour patterns that are distinguishing characteristics of the members of any given society (Czinkota and Ronkainen, 1995)

Not all these layers will be in harmony necessarily, for example, across generation, gender or religious values.

It is worth noting that the focus of attention here is national culture, and not corporate culture, which in itself can be a major influence on approaches to international marketing. In some ways cultural boundaries between nations are becoming increasingly blurred, as global alliances and media level help to emphasize sameness and ignore differences (Fukuyama, 1995). Indeed there can be as much variation within nations as between them (Fukuyama, 1995; Locke, 1995).

One of the key contributions to our understanding of culture and its influence comes from Hofstede (1991) who states that differences, and specifically cultural differences, reveal themselves in various ways through values, rituals, heroes and symbols. Ultimately Hofstede developed five dimensions to describe the culture of the 58 countries in his study. These were:

- Masculinity (values associated with earnings, advancement, assertiveness) versus femininity (values associated with friendly atmosphere, getting along with people, nurturance)
- Individualism (a concern for yourself) versus collectivism (a concern for the priorities of the group to which you belong)
- Uncertainty avoidance – a love of formal rules and an intolerance of ambiguity
- Power distance – the extent to which a hierarchy is a part of life
- Long term orientation versus short term orientation.

In terms of masculinity it was found that within Europe Austria, Italy, Switzerland, the UK, Ireland and West Germany (as was) had the highest scores while feminine cultures where found in Scandinavia, Holland and the former Yugoslavia. Better off nations were found to be more individualistic and the poorer ones more collective orientated. Uncertainty avoidance is higher in the Latin European and Mediterranean countries than in the English speaking countries. Latin countries also score highly on the power distance dimension while most of the countries score highly on the short time dimension.

In an attempt to apply Hofstede's work to the internationalization strategies of retailers Kasper and Bloemer (1996) examined the four dimensions in relation to 17 European national cultures. The following cultural clusters were identified:

- The English speaking countries Ireland and the UK
- The German speaking Countries (Austria, Switzerland, Germany) and Italy
- The Scandinavian countries and the Netherlands
- Belgium, Spain and France
- Greece, Portugal and the former Yugoslavia.

Within the internationalization literature the suggestion is that retailers will go for expansion into culturally close countries. This proposition was examined by studying the strategies adopted by eight retailers namely, Ikea, The Body Shop, Douglas, Otto, Carrefour, Spar, Ahold and Superconfex.

It was concluded that the European retailers prefer to enter geographically close countries first and often, but not always, these were culturally close. It was also found that standardized retail formats are exported to culturally close countries (Ikea, Douglas, Superconfex and to some extent Spar). In addition those countries (France, Germany and Belgium) with a high degree of uncertainty avoidance apply entry modes giving them a high degree of control. The same was true for power distance in the case of the examples from France and Germany. The relationship

Table 3.1 The results of eight case studies with respect to the propositions; are they supported or not by the case description? (source: Kasper and Bloemer, 1996)

	Proposition	IKEA	Body Shop	Douglas	OTTO	Carrefour	SPAR	AHOLD	Super-confex
1	Starting in culturally close countries	Yes	Not fully	Yes	No	Partly	No	No	Yes
2	Standardized retail formats to culturally close countries	Yes	No	Yes	No	Not avail.	Partly	No	Yes
3	High on UAI[b] in home country, high control	No	NR[a]	Yes	Yes	Yes	NR	NR	Yes
4	High on PDI[c] in home country, high control	No	NR	No	No	Yes	NR	NR	Yes
5	High on IDV[d] in home country, low control	No	Yes	No	No	No	Yes	No	No

[b] UAI, uncertainty avoidance.
[a] NR, not relevant in this case.
[c] PDI, power distance.
[d] IDV, individualism.

between a low degree of control and a highly individualistic home culture held only for the Body Shop and for Spar (Table 3.1).

While the cultural map as developed in this study does not fully explain the internationalization process of the retailers concerned, it does add a further possible dimension to the material which will be discussed in Chapter 4 and highlights why it is more difficult to maintain a presence in one country than another.

Hofstede is not alone in making a significant contribution to our understanding of the role of cultural differences in business activities. Other authors, for example, Laurent and Trompenaars have also offered relevant insights. A study by Laurent (1983) of French, German and British managers working for an American multinational found that their values and behaviours are more French, more German and more British than their compatriots working for local, domestic companies. Apparently the more the managers were exposed to another culture's way of doing things the more they identified with their own cultural beliefs.

Trompenaars (1993) over a 10-year period interviewed some 15 000 managers from 28 countries. From this five dimensions were identified which are as follows:

- Universalism versus particularism: societal versus personal obligation
- Individualism versus collectivism: personal versus group goals
- Neutral versus affective relationships: emotional orientation in relationships
- Specific versus diffuse relationship: degree of involvement in relationships
- Achievement versus ascription; legitimation of power and status.

These dimensions are not so dissimilar from Hoecklin's (1995) attempt to combine them by focusing on the dimensions which distinguish nations trying to work more closely together without abandoning their differences while attempting to create global competitiveness from diversity. These are:

- Power distance: how convinced are people that differences in power are given and accepted?
- Uncertainty avoidance: how much are people prepared to deal with the unexpected?
- Collectivism/individualism: which carries most weight?
- Universalism/particularism: which has the greatest impact?

If managers can use the frameworks developed by researchers in this area then they have a means of understanding some of the differences they will encounter in doing business and managing across cultures.

The foundations of our cultural understanding

Our basic perceptions of the world are built up by any number of influences. Geography was one such influence on me and I find it useful as a starting point to engage students in a discussion about culture. Geographic concepts of space and time are a useful tool with which to explore our knowledge of the world. Think about your appreciation of distance and area. Look at Figure 3.3 which depicts the comparative size of countries and some smaller units. Did you have any apprecia-

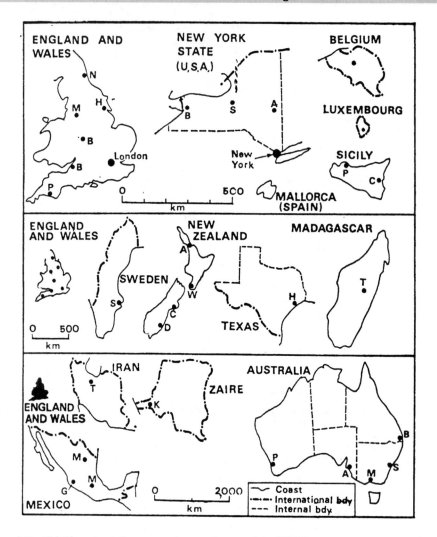

Figure 3.3   Thinking about distance and area. Source: Cole (1979).

tion that one state in the US was almost as big a England and Wales or that England and Wales could fit quite comfortably into the northern tip of Australia? Look at Figure 3.4 which shows some of the largest countries in the world along with France, the UK and Japan on the same scale. Consider Figure 3.5 with its examples of elongated and fragmented countries. Now think what the relevance of all of this is to marketing? In the case of the UK some 56 million consumers are crowded into a relatively small space whereas in Canada only 25 million people are concentrated into the major cities along the St. Lawrence and in places like Vancouver, Calgary, Edmonton in the west. This distribution has implications for distribution policy, advertising strategies and basic issues to do with cultural identity, particularly in

Figure 3.4   Larger or smaller than you thought? Source: Cole (1979).

the case of the French speakers in Quebec. In some countries such as the UK, the population is used to national newspapers being available across the country by the end of the morning. Other countries are so large and fragmented that they are dominated by stronger regional newspapers.

An appreciation of the sense of scale is important for all marketers. Cultural distance is very different from physical distance and both have to be dealt with for a successful relationship with a customer to be developed. Our knowledge of the world around us can be very extensive at the local scale but can be much more limited when considered at the continental or world scale. The extent of our knowledge can tell us something about our view of the world and how it will be curtailed in certain ways. Now try Exercise 3.1 before reading any further.

The view of the world which we carry around in our heads can be explored in other ways as well. The country of origin has been shown by researchers to have a significant effect on the perceptions of consumers with regard to, for example, the

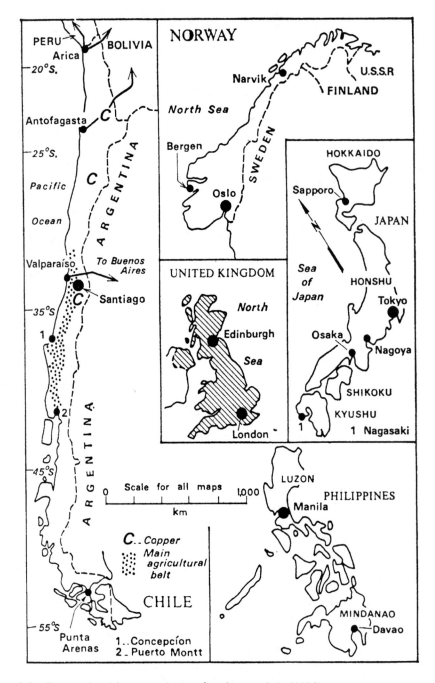

Figure 3.5   Elongated and fragmented countries. Source: Cole (1979).

quality of products. It is possible to have a composite view of such matters. Each year in my international marketing classes I ask the following questions, try them for yourself.

EXERCISE 3.1: YOUR MENTAL MAPS

For the following exercise you will need three sheets of plain A4 paper.
   On the first sheet draw a map of your university/college campus. Mark as many key buildings and landmarks as possible.
   Now draw a map of your local town/city centre. Identify as many streets, shops, landmarks, etc. as you can.
   Finally, draw a map of the world. Name as many countries as you can.

Now ask yourself the following questions:

What country did you place at the centre of the map and why?
Is this country out of proportion to the rest of the map? Why is this?
Is your drawing more accurate for places you have visited?
Are there any gaps in your map? What does this mean?
Do you think your level of cultural awareness of the world is represented by this map?
Does you mental map indicate anything about how effective you would be as an
   international marketing manager?
What will you do now to improve your mental map as a result of this exercise?

EXERCISE 3.2: SHARED PERCEPTIONS?

Which country:

Makes the highest-quality products?
Makes the best-looking products?
Has the most advanced technology?
Does the best job of selling its products to other countries?

In terms of quality, Germany and Japan are often the first choices especially in terms of electronic products and cars. For style and design, particularly in fashion, Italy and France are the key players. The US, Germany and Japan feature with regard to technology, while the US is always out in front as the world's best seller. From year to year there is remarkable consistency in the countries being mentioned, which helps to illustrate the potency of shared perceptions based on our evaluations of various indicators. There is also consistency across culture too. Teaching a course in Jamaica recently I was questioned by a sceptical student about how marketing could be applied equally to different cultural groups. The exercise outlined above illustrated the point that consumers share common perceptions half a world away. Again the same exercise repeated in Hong Kong gives identical results. Of course there is always the course outlier, like the one student who answered Switzerland to every question one year. She was, of course, Swiss!

These perceptions are important and can strongly influence the success of a company's international activity. In the UK Marks and Spencer has a good reputation for customer service, quality and value in the high street. However, the company has always struggled to replicate its success abroad, especially in Canada and the US where the expectation of customer service is at a higher level, and it is more difficult to differentiate your offering from the competition than it is in the UK. Interestingly in 1999 Marks and Spencer closed their Toronto store and had announced their intention to withdraw from the Canadian market.

Culture and marketing

Traditionally anthropologists have defined culture as revolving around material culture (technology, economics); social institutions (social organization, political structures); education (literacy rates, level available); belief systems (religion, superstitions, power structure); aesthetics (music, drama, dance, graphic and plastic arts) and last but not least language (spoken and written). These expressions of culture can have a very direct influence on the marketing activities of a company, and the following section will highlight how they impact on our framework of understanding the customer, creating the product, communicating with the customer and finally delivering value to the customer.

Understanding the customer

At the very basic level confusion can occur from the first point of contact and the role of personal space. Western business people are often made to feel uncomfortable by the Africans or Arabs standing too close to them during discussions. On the other hand Africans and Arabs feel rejected by the distance maintained by westerners. Getting to grips with such social mores is part of business success and is set to become increasingly important.

Research by A.T. Kearney (Zubrod, 1996) points to a world in which the marketer will face even greater cultural diversity in the 21st century. It is possible that China will supplant the US as the largest economy in the world in just a few years. By 2020, nine of today's developing economies will be among the world's 15 largest economies. The list could look like, China, US, Japan, then India, Indonesia, Germany, South Korea, Thailand, France, Taiwan, followed by Brazil, Italy, Russia, UK and Mexico. The drivers behind the growth of these developing economies are attributed to population growth, together with increasing living standards and per capita GDP, the increase in trade and financial flows since World War II, and the increase in the number of economies adopting a liberalized economic model.

British Airways has met cultural problems in the air with some of its recent business activities. Customers from Singapore said that the alliance with Quantas in Australia looked like the whites of the old world uniting. This may be further exacerbated with the two airlines agreeing in 1999 to merge their Hong Kong operations as well. Reservation agents placed Indian wives in rows next to strangers, which made their husbands uncomfortable. The cabin crew would close gallery cart drawers with their feet, which is unacceptable for Thais and others who believe feet should be far away from food.

As an attempt to clearly create a global image artists were commissioned to produce African murals, Japanese calligraphy and Scottish plaid amongst other designs. These were then transposed onto the ticket jackets, cabin crew scarves, business cards and perhaps most strikingly onto the tails of the planes. This was viewed as a strategy to increase the global credibility and to be seen less as a British based airline. The £60 million rebrand begun in 1997 was abandoned in June 1999 after market research which showed that the change had been a public relations disaster. Passengers from outside the UK tended to like it but UK passengers who make up 40% of BA's business disliked it. Within 18 months the airline planned to have the Union Jack back on the tail of over half the fleet as the repainting programme rolled out.

To effectively manage international operations, sensitivity to cultural needs of the markets, sources and organizations in foreign countries will be essential. The starting point for this is to understand the customer. However, as the British Airways story illustrates, not losing sight of your key customer groups is crucial.

Belief systems

Whilst religious observance may be on the decline in westernized societies, it is a key influence on the behaviour patterns of large sections of the world's population. In some countries, for example Iran and Afghanistan, religion may be the very foundation of the government, and a dominating factor in many business decisions. There are over 840 million followers of Islam in the world and in those countries where fundamentalists have a major influence on society, patterns of consumption and gender roles can be tightly defined. Major religious festivals, such as Ramadan, can significantly alter working and consumption patterns. Thus enough food will be consumed before sunrise to sustain the individual until after sunset. Strength and stamina during the working day can be affected and therefore employers have to be sensitive to this. Certain food types are also restricted, for example pork by Judaism and Islam. The role of women is often strictly controlled by Islam, as was the case in Afghanistan when the Taliban took over the government and almost immediately passed laws forbidding females to work or have access to education. This is an approach which other culturally distant societies will find strange. Islamic religion also rejects excessive profit, which is seen as exploitation, and thus impacts on the pricing of products and services. Another consideration is the fact that the day of rest for followers of Islam is Friday, for Jews it is Saturday and for Christians it is Sunday. Often these can provide an insight into why people behave as they do. For the marketer it can be a difficult cultural influence to spot as it is an 'unseen' factor to a large extent, although in some societies it can be reflected in a dress code.

The influence on marketing comes in the form of influencing patterns of consumption, for example, of certain food types and the observance of set days as holidays. New product development can be stimulated by belief systems as Box 3.2 illustrates. Belief systems can also give rise to single-issue pressure groups including those opposed to the legalization of Sunday shopping in the UK or those against the service provided by abortion clinics in the US. For marketers there is often a fine line to be followed in dealing with such issues, as inevitably extreme opinions will be present within their customer base.

BOX 3.2: CULTURE INFLUENCES NEW PRODUCT DEVELOPMENT

As Egypt becomes more of a consumer society manufacturers are trying to find the balance between religious observance and how individuals wish to live their lives. One of the latest products to emerge is the 'Sharia swimsuit'. Until now observant Muslim women either had to sit on one side or go into the water in their clothes. This new swimsuit is a high-necked swimming costume with sleeves and a small skirt to be worn over long trousers. It first appeared a few years ago but was expensive and hard to find in the shops. This year (2000) it is widely available and comes in new cuts and colours.

In the increasingly secular westernized world, it could be argued that belief systems now encompass such trends as represented by environmental pressure groups, animal welfare groups, vegetarians and various strands of thought under the New Age Movement. These 'belief systems' also have had a significant impact on marketers in their attempt to understand customers. This has its expression in more basic packaging, a concern to include recycled material in new products, the production of food in which the animals are treated humanely or allowed to roam free during their productive lives as in the case of hens and pigs.

The variation across the globe in the influence of belief systems, whether the more traditional religious, or those stemming from secular concerns, creates interesting ethical dilemmas for Multi National Enterprises (MNEs), for example, in environmental policy do you operate within the limits of the domestic market, which will often be stricter, or under the more lax laws of the (developing) host market?

It can be a mistake to think that 'we are all more or less the same'. Belief in such things as female genital mutilation, polygamy and witchcraft can quickly create a heated debate between Africans and western critics, who particularly denounce female mutilation as a barbaric and primitive act, while many Africans see it as a cultural tradition. Avoiding cultural judgements and redefining the problem as a health issue is a possible way forward. Such creative thinking can be a useful tool in the marketer's kit bag, to avoid a culture clash and direct confrontation. Belief systems, including the belief in nothing at all, are strong throughout the world, and do influence how people act.

Aesthetics

Ideas of beauty and of good taste are strongly related to culture. This affects the type of music, art, folklore, dance and drama which society produces. Often these are reflected in strong regional difference within an apparently uniform national culture to the outsider.

The implications of this for the marketer affect product or packaging design, colours used in the product, or in advertising. In addition music used in the background in advertising will also be influenced. The symbols associated with a product can also be problematic, for example, the owl which is normally associated with wisdom in the western world means bad luck in India. One company involved in exporting shoes to Arab countries overlooked the fact that the design on the sole resembled a Star of David, and thus the product failed to sell.

Time

In westernized societies the clock is the boss. Efficiency is judged by making deadlines, making meetings on time, getting down to business quickly without spending any time on social introductions. However, in other parts of the world a rush to do business implies arrogance and a potentially untrustworthy person. Being kept waiting is not a measure of lack of importance almost the reverse. For the Japanese an essential element of doing business is to get to know the person socially. This can take time but it is time well spent if the transaction is to be a success.

In some cultures the perception of lateness varies. In westernized markets, someone turning up 5 min late for a meeting would be acceptable. Ten minutes late and the host will expect a good reason for the delay. If the delay reaches 15 min it may be deemed that the person is not coming. However, in Arab markets such delays would be considered trivial as they view 15 min as a westerner would view 3 min, and therefore the person is still likely to turn up. It is likely that as the world becomes more globalized such behaviour within the business world is less likely to occur.

Creating the product

For an international company engaged in international production strategies, the quality of the education system in the host country can have significant impact on its employment policy. The degree to which remedial education and training will have to be undertaken can add to the costs of the operation. Many companies source supplies from around the world. This exposes the company to challenges including an extended supply chain, multiple languages, different players, and distinct regulations.

Country of origin effect

The role of national images has been a part of marketing research since the 1960s. Most studies indicate that national origin is an important attribute in both consumer and organizational markets. Stereotypes can be positive or negative and so it is an important part of international strategy to manage a product or service's national image. Generally speaking it is a good strategy to be perceived as a local company, perhaps by having a local name, if the target market is nationalistic. Alternatively the appeal of imported products can add value to the purchase, create something of the exotic in the brand, and therefore offer differential advantage. Some companies are perceived as global players and are 'owned' by everyone, for example Coke, Pepsi, Whirlpool, Kodak, Shell. Even a smaller player like McCain, the largest manufacturer of frozen chips, has been mistaken for a Scottish company when in fact it is Canadian owned.

Usinier (2000) identifies five other elements in addition to the 'made in' label which affect consumers' perception of product personality.

- The image of imported products in opposition to national products or the image of national versus international products
- National images of generic products: yoghurt calls to mind the Balkans, perfume evokes France, and the US by a pair of jeans
- The national image of the manufacturing company
- The image diffused by the brand name
- The image of the 'made in' label in the sense of the manufacturing origin legally appended to the product.

There are many influences acting on a consumer when they evaluate a product or service. In general, past research has shown that in developed countries, local products are perceived to be of a higher quality than imported products. However, resistance to imported products tends to be lowered as income level, education, and travel experience increase. It is also reduced by better guarantees and after sales service.

As Niss (1996) points out the image of the country of origin is made up of cognitive and affective components. The former being the country's perceived socio-economic, cultural and political attributes while the latter are the buyer's feelings and attitudes towards the country in question, through past experience, association or contact with its people and products. Any attempts to disassociate the image from the reality are likely to fail (Usinier, 2000) thus there would be no advantage in selling poor quality products under a good 'made in' label.

Images are not static; think how trends and fashions change for the tourism 'product' and also how vulnerable they are to short term problems, for example, American tourists very quickly avoid many parts of the world when the perceived threat from terrorists increases. Consequently such perceptions can seriously impact on vulnerable developing economies or those over dependent on tourism.

Pricing

On first sight it may be thought that pricing is not a cultural issue. Prices are fixed and that is that. However, even in westernized economies the price of larger ticketed items can be flexible. There are usually discounts to be had in the purchase of houses, cars, and more specialized/expensive electronic and electrical equipment. We do not think it proper to negotiate a price for items purchased in the supermarket. Yet in some cultures the bartering process is an integral part of the purchasing activity, for example, in purchasing a carpet in a souk in Tunisia.

Consider the entrepreneur starting a business in the UK who went to source product from craftspeople in Indonesia. He was struck by the use of the phrase 'morning price' during his discussions. This was exactly what it sounds like, i.e. the price at this moment in time. By the afternoon or another day the price may have changed! I have heard a similar approach used by beach hawkers in Barbados where one seller used the phrase 'As the sun goes down the price goes down'. Price then is not always fixed and is subject to cultural norms.

Legal aspects

In an attempt to deal with the potential conflict between different jurisdictions, some 34 countries abide by an international treaty which sets the rules and jurisdiction of contractual disputes involving the international sale of goods. (Giermanski, 1994). The treaty is known as the Convention of Contracts for the International Sales of Goods.

INCOTERMS also help to make clear what exactly is covered in the terms of sale (more details in Chapter 9).

Communicating with the customer

Language

Perhaps, this is the most obvious cultural barrier in that it prevents effective communication. It also can be seen as a basic requirement in our attempts to understand the customer. Language in itself is an expression of culture and it could be argued that in any one market, the number of different languages reflects the potential number of cultures. The language of business is often held to be English, and indeed in many cases English will be used to establish the initial deal, but the actual language of the market may be very different.

Most of you will all have experienced problems of language when travelling. Often errors are made in signage due to the use of the wrong tense. However, most problems with language result from a very literal translation from the original. In doing this the nuances, critical to understanding, are often lost. When Gerard Depardieu was filming Cyrano de Bergerac he told an interviewer that when he was 9 he had witnessed a rape. The verb he used was 'assister' which is French for 'to be present at'. Unfortunately the interviewer interpreted it as 'to assist' and when the article appeared it caused some controversy. In business bad translation can be equally disastrous, and even more costly in goodwill and undermined authority. Some problems of an over literal translation are seen in the examples in Box 3.3.

BOX 3.3: HAVING FUN WITH LANGUAGE!

The literature is littered with examples of mistranslation including the following:

'Please leave your values at the front desk' Notice in a Paris hotel lift (elevator to some!)

'Drop your trousers here for best results' Notice in a Bangkok Dry Cleaners

'We take your bags and send them in all directions' Notice in a Copenhagen Ticket Office

A US airline advertised 'rendezvous' lounges at airports in Brazil to lure business customers, not realizing that in Portuguese, the word 'rendezvous' implies a room for making love.

The American chicken magnate, Frank Perdue's slogan 'It takes a tough man to make a tender chicken' was translated into Spanish as 'It takes a virile man to make a chicken affectionate'. While the later is probably literately true it is not quite what the company was trying to communicate!

Ferraro (1996) reports that American companies have advertised cigarettes with low 'asphalt' instead of tar and computer 'underwear' instead of software. Trunick (1996) illustrates the kinds of practical problem which an misinterpretation can lead to. You do not want to sell 100 of your products at $19 rather than $91. Conversely, you do not want to buy 100 items thinking you are paying $19 each and end-up being billed $91 each. Mistakes can easily be made since Germans say their numbers backwards to US convention. For example, 91 would be 'one and ninety'. Without use of an interpreter, it would be easy to hear the numbers and think 19 instead of 91.

Companies can make use of specialist translation services, who provide not only the necessary level of language skills, but are alive to the nuances of the languages and are able to cope with specialized technical terms in electronics, design and engineering. There is a general trend towards a better appreciation of languages in business. Companies are increasingly realizing that language cannot be treated as an afterthought if they are to compete internationally, and that their international image will depend on a professional and sophisticated approach to communication. If in any doubt it is good practice to translate the material from language A to language B then have a different person translate the material from language B to A. If the sense remains the same as in the original piece then you can be confident with your translation.

The use of a brand name can give a marketer a very powerful icon on which to develop a relationship between a product and the customer. The choice of a brand name for the international market can be very difficult particularly if it is to be sold across a number of international boundaries. Some manufacturers overcome the problems of translation by producing brand names which have no literal meaning in any language and therefore can be free from any misinterpretation, for example, Kodak and Hoover.

An important issue connected to language, which has all sorts of implications for doing business, is the level of literacy around the world. The influence of education comes both from the formal education provided by state or privately run institutions, and from the informal social education provided by family members. There are variations created by the level to which education is continued (primary, secondary or tertiary), the status accorded to education in a society, and the degree of access to it which people have. In particular societies, females have a lower level of access than their male counterparts.

Miller (1995) quotes the example of Bertlesmann, the multinational bookclub giant, and their attempted entry into the Indian market. When the company looked at India they saw a potential market of almost 1 billion people. Many were well educated, middle class and spoke English, which are the characteristics of Bertlesmann's target market. However, they have to have viable addresses, and 70% of Indians live in rural areas with unreliable addresses. In addition only one-third of those are literate. This still left millions of urban dwellers who spoke English, but after several test campaigns the company concluded that out of a population of 900 million it would probably net 200 000 subscribers, with little room for growth.

Learning the local language assists greatly with adjusting to the new environment, because efficient communication can reduce the frustrations, misunderstandings and aggravations which can result from misuse of words. In addition it can provide a feeling of confidence and self-assurance, and allow deeper insight to the values of the host culture than would otherwise be possible.

Business people are often reported as having difficulty when negotiating with Asian business people as they are unlikely to say 'no' directly to a proposal but will reply in ways synonymous with 'no'. This is illustrated in Box 3.4.

BOX 3.4: SAYING 'NO' (ADAPTED FROM ENGHOLM, 1991)

To the question; 'Has my proposal been accepted?' An Asian response could take the form of:

The conditional 'yes': 'If everything proceeds as planned, the proposal will be approved'.
The counter-question: 'have you submitted a copy of your proposal to the Ministry?'
A critical comment: 'Your question is difficult to answer'.
A refusal: 'We cannot answer your question at this time'.
The tangential reply: 'Will you be staying longer than you originally planned?'
The 'Yes, but...' reply: 'Yes, approval looks likely, but...' The meaning of 'but' could mean 'it might be approved'.
The answer is delayed: 'You will know shortly'.

Part of the difficulties of the above example is that the Japanese are part of a high-context culture, as are people from the Middle East and Latin America. A high-context communication or message is one in which most of the information is either in the physical context or internalized in the person, while very little is in the coded, explicit, transmitted part of the message. In contrast a low-context message is the very opposite since the mass of the information is vested in the explicit code (Hall, 1976).

The issue with primarily verbal exchanges is to know to what extent the non-verbal gestures, gesticulations and attitudes mix with the verbal, explicit messages. This is less important in a language such as English which is very precise but will be crucial where the language used is French which can be alternately vague and precise (Usinier, 2000).

Deliver to the customer

As more and more firms operate in world markets, such activities are adding to the complexity of business, through trying to deal with cultural differences, currencies, new business practices and logistical challenges. The role of logistics becomes crucial to global competitiveness and this creates a tension between the need to standardize as much as possible, while taking account of national and regional cultural diversity. At the same time there is a significant loss of control and familiarity, as executives attempt to manage, or co-ordinate via alliances, the company's logistics.

There are conflicting views on the degree of adaptation to local circumstances which a company should undertake. Zubrod (1996) reports that alignment to geographic forces affecting an industry is responsible for only 40% of relative globalization success. However, overcoming cultural barriers is a long-term task requiring 3–5 years' effort. It is suggested that companies can go too far in 'thinking local'. As the transportation sector becomes more global, a restructuring focused on local options or standards would be detrimental. It is more likely that over time world class benchmarks and standards will be applied and accepted. The research suggested that the global nature of customer service requirement would increase by 82% over a 10 year time-span, while the local and regional aspects of that driver would only change 26% and 52%, respectively. In addition it was found that global competitive threats will increase 52%, while on a local basis they will change only 11% and regionally 28%. The message here is clear for the level of cultural adaptation which a company should aspire to.

Zubrod (1996) concludes that globalization is increasing the complexity of doing business and logistics are crucial to global competitiveness. However, often companies go 'too local' and tailor their strategies to reflect too much cultural diversity. This can often lead to a relatively large drop in global performance. He argues that it makes little sense to focus on the traditional triad approach of North America, Europe and Asia-Pacific, since market characteristics allow a company to leverage its strengths more effectively than geographic proximity. Therefore it makes little sense to treat emerging markets like Indonesia in the same way as sophisticated markets such as Australia and Japan.

The prescription is to identify clusters of counties and regions that have common market, strategic or business challenges, in order to allow learning and transference of knowledge between markets within the groupings.

Doing business with culture

For Levitt with his 'Orwellian 1984' view of the global corporation, whereby the global corporation operates '...as if the entire world (or major regions of it) were a single entity; it sells the same things in the same way everywhere'. He goes even further 'Different cultural preferences, national tastes and standards...are vestiges of the past...with persistence and appropriate means, barriers against superior technologies and economics have always fallen away. ' This is scary stuff – economic imperialism full of subjective value judgements of the worst kind. Levitt has gone down in the textbooks as *the* main proponent of this view. However, inevitably the world has moved on, and the once popular trend towards global marketing has been fine-tuned in the 1990s by more market-responsive approaches which recognize the importance of identifying local differences within a global strategy. Political changes within, for example, the former USSR, the Eastern Bloc and Yugoslavia have accentuated the importance of local cultures.

It is therefore becoming increasingly important that groups of countries are not lumped together. From, for example, the Japanese perspective, it may be that most of Europe seems like a similar market. However, those companies in Europe could quite easily distinguish between consumers in Germany, Spain and Holland. Likewise all Americans may look the same but there can be distinct regional markets with the country, for example, Miami with its high Latin population is a very non-American American city. When the Berlin wall came down in the dramatic political upheaval of 1989 there was a tendency for companies to regard the 'former Eastern European' countries as a distant cohesive entity. This too is a mistake as Box 3.5 illustrates in advice given by Lufthansa.

BOX 3.5: BUSINESS ETIQUETTE IN EASTERN EUROPE AS SEEN BY LUFTHANSA

General rules:

- Do not band the countries of Eastern Europe together. It is important to recognize that just as each has its own language, culture and traditions, its approach to business is also very different.
- Avoid using the term 'Eastern Europe'. Most countries are proud of their independence and do not take kindly to being grouped as one.
- The question 'How are you?' is often taken quite literally, so if you do ask, be prepared for a lengthy answer.
- Have plenty of business cards and trade literature with you. An exchange of business cards follows introductions at any meeting or negotiation.
- Translate as much as possible into the relevant language. This eases initial introductions and makes for good business etiquette.
- Prepare your visit well in advance. Find out about local conditions, facilities, personnel and government.
- Ensure presentations to new companies are brief, to the point and well documented.

Source: Lufthansa Information Services Bulletin, July 1996

The management of cultural diversity is an important part of international activities, whether the firm is operating alone or in a partnership of some sort. In this section management styles, cross-cultural management alliances and training needs will be considered.

Management styles

A number of studies have looked at how culture can influence the decisions made by managers. It appears, from the evidence gathered, that culture can influence:

- How a problem is defined/identified
- The objectives motivating choice
- The communication of problems and recommendations
- The decisiveness of recommendations.

In any summary of management styles one should guard against falling back on stereotypes as a means of defining differences. However, a number of well researched studies point to common styles held by managers from a common cultural background. From a European perspective Myers et al. (1995) found that the Irish, Spanish and British tended to emphasize charismatic leadership while consensus management was valued by Finnish and Swedish managers. A more systematic and routinised style was apparent in the Austrian and German managers, with all individuals working towards a common set of goals. In contrast the French tended to hold meetings but then followed their own individual goals afterwards. The four types of management styles and their key traits identified from these characteristics are listed in Box 3.6.

BOX 3.6: LEADING FROM THE FRONT

Charisma
- Reliance on individual's leadership ability. Rules and procedures hinder performance. Self-motivation. Dominance.

Managing from a distance
- Lack of discipline. Pursuit of personal agendas. Strategic/conceptual thinkers. Ineffective communication. Ambiguity.

Consensus
- Team spirit. Effective communication. Attention to organization detail. Open dialogue. Consensual decision-making.

Towards a common goal
- Valuing functional expertise. Authority based leadership style. Clear roles of responsibility. Discipline oriented. Identify with systems and controls.

Source: Myers et al. (1995).

The authors could not identify a common European style of management, but could see a more homogeneous style emerging if managers gained more experience in cross-national management teams. This, of course, would be a long term trend, but could be facilitated by the merger and acquisition activity of MNEs, and the greater openness of the job market in Europe following the creation of the Single Market. As the Single Market standardizes the technical and regulatory environment, then there is a far greater likelihood of a social convergence in management styles.

A number of studies have investigated the influence of management. In a comparison of British, American and Japanese managers it was found that American managers tend to be more assertive, the British less likely to take risks, and the Japanese to pay more attention to detail. Lewis (1996) found French managers to be more autocratic than German counterparts while Swedish companies are much more democratic.

Americans doing business in Australia should not assume that they do not have to make adjustments to their business practices just because they share a common language, a British heritage, a Christian tradition and belief in democracy (Sunoo, 1998). American business people have a tendency to impose change and to give orders; to base their trust on people's performance, behaviour and reputation; and to define the quality of their lives in terms of their private lives. In contrast the Australians tend to resent being given orders and favour a collaborative approach to decision making; to base their trust on people's sense of loyalty and commitment, and to assess the quality of their lives not just in terms of their free time but all aspects of their lives. Consider the example given in Box 3.7.

BOX 3.7: THE US AND OZ

What do you do when…
1. Before completing your report, you need some additional information from another department. As you tell this to your boss, you recommend he call the head of the other department in order to move things more quickly. Your manager does not seem impressed with your idea and asks you to go back to your office. Why?
2. You are tired of the discussion, and want to move on to a new topic. You ask your Australian business associate, 'Can we table this for awhile?' But to your dismay, the colleague keeps right on discussing just what you want to put aside. Are Australians that inconsiderate?

Culturally sensitive behaviour would be:
1. 'Jack's as good as his master,' according to an old saying in Australia. It means nobody acts as if they are better than anybody else. Australians are sensitive to anyone attempting to pull rank. Americans can often speak with self-assurance and a bravado that in a more relaxed Australian business environment can appear superior. An Australian sensing this will make fun of you or push you off your pedestal.
2. To 'table something' in Australia is to bring it forward for discussion. The English spoken in Australia is often closer to British than American, e.g. brolly (umbrella), cozzie (bathing suit) and lollie (candy (also money in UK)). Words will be shortened whenever possible so 'G'day' is the standard greeting down under.

Cross-cultural management and alliances

For cross-cultural management strategies to succeed they should be based on cultural implications that derive from basic values, beliefs, world views and social relationships. In the case of US businesses doing business in China, Xing (1995) illustrates how these firms should be concerned with the underlying forces that influence Chinese business practices. Thus, for example, the common approach by Americans to solve a problem is to follow the following steps:

- Identify, define the problem
- Analyze and understand the problem
- Set a goal/objective
- Identify, evaluate and select the options available
- Plan and schedule
- Implement and control
- Follow-up and assess the outcome.

This 'classic' pattern will be familiar to most westernized readers. It is analytical, logical, linear, orderly and explicit. However, it can have its limitations:

- Flexibility and economy of thinking may suffer from a rigidly fixed pattern
- The process of thinking is much more integrated and not necessarily segmented and linear
- An analytical approach is not always applicable to managerial issues.

In contrast to this the Chinese mind is influenced by Confucianism, family-ism, a group orientation and a spiritual ideal of life. Thus, because of this tradition the Chinese think in terms of concrete analogy which places the situation in a form more easily grasped in its entirety. Synthesis, intuition, concrete image and use of proverbs are often the first Chinese priorities. Xing likens the different approach by the Chinese as being akin to the difference between masculinity and femininity.

Thus, effective cross-cultural management strategies must be based on the implications of actual cultural mechanisms and not on any temporary fashions which only run skin-deep and are likely to generate disorientation. Three key pointers for American (westernized) businesses going to China are:

- Build up a primary understanding of the major forces that have framed the Chinese culture
- Maintain an open and adaptable mind for different management and negotiation styles and practices
- Minimize value judgements exclusively based on American cultural terms about Chinese business deviations.

The prospect of coping with an entirely new culture can seem daunting, and has resource implications depending on the size and experience of the firm. One option for attempting to deal with market entry and local culture is to link with a domestic firm in the target country. This exposes the company to two cultural fronts, namely, the country and the local organization. This double-layered acculturation process encourages learning and can be useful in future expansion plans. This was illustrated in research reported by Zacharakis (1996) who cites a study of 13 Dutch firms and their 225 foreign ventures between 1966 and 1988. As would be expected, entry was more successful where the new country's culture was similar to the domestic culture. Having to cope with country and company cultural adjustments slowed down the initial success of the venture, but due to the intensity of the learning experience the success of future ventures was increased. In other words the organization was applying its experience and gaining from it.

In another study (Dunham, 1996) the CEO of Conoco relates how the company became involved in the Russian oil business in the Timan Pechora Region. Through the company's commitment to relationship building at all levels, it survived the political evolution from Gorbachev to Yeltsin. The pragmatic approach adopted by the company involved talking to all parties involved, whether in or out of government, about their prospects. Underlying Conoco's efforts was a philosophy based on a desire to be a true partner of local interests, both in the business community and in the societal sense. A great deal of time was spent talking to local people explaining why Conoco believed its presence would benefit all. This also involved listening to local concerns. Eventually a joint venture company was established to develop the old field at Ardalin. The first oil was produced in 1994 and Conoco believe that the experience and the respect gained from this project will help them in the future to develop bigger projects.

The advice offered by the CEO is pertinent and transferable in general to market entry decisions across cultural boundaries.

- Be true to your core beliefs and practices
- Take time to let people know who you are
- Honour the local history and culture
- Act like the guest you are
- Persevere.

While the former communist dominated economies of Eastern Europe have experienced many changes since the fall of the Berlin wall in 1989, economic and cultural change do not always proceed at the same pace. Randall and Coakley (1998) have studied the impact of culture on the strategies of joint ventures between Western companies and organizations located in Russia and Belarus. They observed Russian managers as they attempted to fuse their cultural norms, past training and work experiences with the demands of the market-in-transition. Managerial behaviour very often remained steeped in the achievement of production goals in lieu of marketplace edicts, and the maintenance of labour in spite of cost and profit implications for the company. Many managers still held the view that technological superiority was paramount in the attainment of social welfare and national security.

Randall and Coakley observe that cultural change lags behind structural change and this will inevitably impact on any joint venture partnership. However, the crucial factor here, as with many of the issues raised in this chapter, is that through an awareness of cultural differences and the beliefs of others, productive, creative and profitable collaborations can be achieved.

Any search for an international partner is not solely based on a good cultural fit.

The companies will be concerned with the strategic issues of partner characteristics, product-market synergy and the financial strength of the potential partner. However, the underlying importance and potential impact of the cultural dimension cannot be understated, and should be viewed as an essential foundation of any international joint venture. As Box 3.8 illustrates even the exchange of a business card in Japan can be a culturally significant experience.

BOX 3.8: BUSINESS CARD ETIQUETTE.

Business cards serve an important function in doing business in Japan, and the exchange of business cards is an integral part of Japanese business etiquette. Japanese business people exchange cards when meeting someone for the first time who may have significance in the future. As Japanese business becomes increasingly internationalized, those Japanese business people most likely to interface with non-Japanese are often supplied with business cards printed in Japanese on one side and a foreign language, usually English, on the reverse side. This is aimed at enhancing recognition and pronunciation of Japanese names, which are often unfamiliar to foreign business people. Conversely, it is advisable for foreign business people to carry and exchange with their Japanese counterparts a similar type of card printed in Japanese and their native language. These cards can often be obtained through business centres in major hotels.

When receiving a card, it is considered common courtesy to offer one in return. Not returning a card might convey the impression that you are not committed to a meaningful business relationship in the future. In consideration of the numerous opportunities for exchanging cards in Japan, it is advisable to use a business card holder – a case that resembles a compact wallet that prevents cards from becoming creased and tattered and allows for easy access.

When presenting and receiving business cards, several basic points should be kept in mind to avoid committing a faux pas. Business cards should be presented and received with both hands. When presenting your card, make sure your name is not upside down from the recipient's point of view and that the card is presented with the appropriate side up, again from the recipient's point of view, if printed in more than one language. When receiving a business card, it should be handled with care. If you are sitting at a conference or other type of table, the card is usually placed on the table in front of you for the duration of the meeting. It would be considered rude to put a prospective business partner's card in your pocket before sitting down to discuss business matters.

Source: JETRO http://www.jetro.go.jp/top/index.html

Training needs

With a planned program of awareness raising, it is possible for companies to prepare for many of the potential problems which executives may face when, for example, dealing with international customers, negotiating joint ventures, entering new markets or if they go to work abroad. The crucial emphasis behind any such training program should be to encourage a mutual respect: cultures are not better or worse than each other, they are just different. Cultural interpretation and adaptation are critical to the comparative understanding of the practice of national and international management.

In order to manage the cultural gap between US managers and their Chinese hosts, Gross and Dyson (1997) suggest that managers must be attuned to the subtle attitudinal and motivational variations of the two business cultures. The gap is not so large that it cannot be negotiated with forethought. Over time, as the experience on both sides increases, the culture gap will decrease as long as both sides are committed to learning from each other. For example in attempting to employ local managers, the US managers should not expect the Chinese applicants to discuss their achievements in great detail, given China's cultural bias against boasting.

Problems associated with cross-cultural alliance can be reduced through training and efforts to increase communication and to promote social networks. Following a study of Anglo-French alliances, Schoenberg et al. (1995) identified three management practices, parity, heightened communication, and individual training as being the best way of overcoming the downside of cultural diversity, whilst building mutual trust in order to exploit the opportunity offered. The key components of parity are: parity in terms of language, parity in terms of management numbers and hierarchical distribution, and parity in terms of terms and conditions of employment.

In terms of communication, a key activity was to reinforce formal communication procedures to ensure constant clarification and better circulation of information by putting all communications in writing. This helped to overcome different cultural approaches and language difficulties and allowed for continuous checking of understanding. By formalizing the communications process, it overcame the difficulties of relying on informal discussion and transmission 'at the coffee table' since this is less likely to occur between employees of different nationalities, especially if language skills are not developed.

Training for the individual was the third essential managerial issue. Since national cultures are enacted at the individual level, it is important that employees are given assistance in adapting to their new multicultural environment. For many alliances language training was a first step. One company, which had adopted English as the official company language, was conscious of the negative symbolic effects it had raised in terms of national parity. Its solution was to spend heavily on language training for the French managers, until it absorbed 20% of the training budget. However, it did not solve the problem, as many executives found it difficult to attend all the sessions and so, despite extensive training, many felt disadvantaged at meetings since English was not their natural language. The company, having assessed the cost-benefit of the training, concluded that language training is no substitute for hiring bilingual staff.

Cross-cultural training programs had greater success, especially those that both mixed participation from different nationalities and formed a component of some wider training. However, in the final analysis training is no substitute for experience abroad, which creates mental openness and sensitivity to understanding foreign practices more effectively. Schoenberg quotes one British personnel director who states 'It is very useful to run cultural awareness programmes but posting managers abroad is still the best way for them to understand foreign practices. Our company has realized that it would have been much better to have more cross-cultural exchanges and cross-national teams before starting our cross-border partnerships. We would have avoided some costly mistakes!'

Conclusions

Culture is one of those concepts we all like to be involved in; whether this is to praise or criticize some peculiar expression of it. Culture is a living active process. It can be developed only from within, it cannot be imposed from without or above, although some political systems have tried and largely ultimately failed in their attempt.

We should be grateful for variety and the fact that a homogeneous, externally produced culture cannot be sold ready made to the masses. Culture does not work like that. However, this did not stop the large global corporations from attempting to turn us into a Coca-Cola drinking, McDonalds eating, Marlboro smoking, Levis wearing mass of hedonistic consumers. While the consumer culture is a powerful influence around the world, and one which we all buy into to a greater or lesser extent, we are fortunate that culture, however commercialized, can never be adequately described solely in terms of the buying and selling of commodities (Fiske, 1989).

Thankfully it goes much deeper involving both nature and nurture. We are shaped by our material culture in the shape of technology and economic systems, while the structure of social organizations including education, belief systems and political structures all make a contribution. Naturally, for most people, language provides the most obvious cultural barrier, although for some colour causes a greater emotional response.

As far as business is concerned, economic behaviour does not take space in a cultural vacuum. Factors such as character, world outlook, values and attitudes all play a role in the economic transformation of societies. It has been acknowledged by numerous authors that the post World War II Japanese economic miracle cannot be fully understood without grasping the principles of Japanese culture.

In the late 1980s there was a flurry of text books produced in international marketing and in international business where the word 'Global' seemed obligatory in the title. The connotations of serving a global market in the same way everywhere was strangely out of keeping with the grim reality of what was actually happening in the world.

To the most casual observer the time lag between text and reality must have been obvious. In 1989 the Berlin wall came tumbling down and gradually a new freedom swept the former Eastern Bloc. Likewise commentators found themselves speaking of the 'former Soviet Union'. Later in the 1990s the Republic of Yugoslavia, no longer held in check by a strong Tito, gradually imploded into the worst war seen in Europe since 1939–1945, that is until Kosovo in 1999. It is apparent that the world often seems held in balance between centrifugal and centripetal forces. While the above examples are tearing themselves apart, other areas of the world are coming together in closer economic union. The debate in EU is all about the development of a single currency and how far political union may be both desirable and possible. In North America the Canadians, US and Mexico entered into the NAFTA, while in Southeast Asia The Association of Southeast Asian Nations (ASEAN) continues to develop and grow since its foundation in 1967. On April 30, 1999 ASEAN admitted Cambodia as its tenth member, fulfilling its vision to establish an organization for all Southeast Asian countries. ASEAN now comprises Brunei Darussalam, Cambodia, Indonesia, Laos, Myanmar, Malaysia, the Philippines, Singapore, Thailand and Vietnam. With Cambodia's entry, the ASEAN region now has a total population of about 500 million, a total area of 4.5 million square kilometres, a combined gross national product of $685 billion, and a total trade of $720 billion.

Many of the destructive changes brought about by these events can be traced to the latent cultural expressions of peoples who had an external and alien culture imposed upon then. It worked for a while but, in time, these older more potent cultures have re-emerged to shape the destinies of many national groups. The down side of this has been a polarization into nationalism as expressed in the free elections of 1996 in Bosnia. For the international marketer the potency of culture is obvious.

The life of nations is largely lived in the imagination; a phrase once used by Enoch Powell, a UK politician, himself not renowned for cultural openness, but this phrase neatly encapsulates the link between reality and the perceived world where (marketing) decisions are made. Only by understanding the importance of culture in the market place can the international marketer venture forth with some confidence.

Finally as Fagiano (1990) suggested: 'By developing your own cultural sensitivity and choosing a local presence who is willing and able to help you appear as native as possible, you can do more than just avoid disastrous advertising gaffes. You can succeed in international marketing'.

There is an element of luxury in being able, from an academic viewpoint, to sit back and contemplate the role of culture in international marketing. In the fast moving day to day world of business, executives will have little time to actively address it. In a sense, the ways of dealing with cultural diversity should be so embedded in the thinking process that managers can make a seamless transition from one culture to another. However, this will only happen if, at some point in developing new business relationships, due care is paid to the role of mental software in the process.

Questions for discussion

1. Why study culture?

2. Describe a 'culture shock' you have experienced, perhaps when travelling. What did you learn from it?
3. Make a list of stereotypical views of three of the following countries (or add some of your own) Australia, Brazil, China, Germany, Japan, Libya, Scotland and the US. How far do you think these 'views' differ from reality?
4. Can human beings be culturally free?
5. How does your culture affect your behaviour? Does it influence your purchasing habits?
6. Find an example of a product or service which failed to understand the culture of the market it entered. What should the company concerned have done to make a successful market entry?
7. Why does language seem to cause many of the problems in international marketing?
8. Find an example of where the management style of different nations has given rise to conflict in a business?
9. 'Culture cannot be imposed'. Discuss, in relation to so-called global products, for example, Coca-Cola, Mastercard and McDonalds.
10. Is the world-wide web a culture free international marketing tool? Discuss.

References

Cole, J.P. (1979), *Geography of World Affairs*, Penguin Books, Harmondsworth.

Czinkota, M.R. and Ronkainen, I.A. (1995), *International Marketing*, Dryden Press, New York.

Dunham, A.W. (1996), Conoco's excellent Russian adventure, *Journal of Business Strategy*, 17 (5), pp. 12–15.

Engholm, C. (1991), *When Business East Meets Business West: the Guide to Practice and Protocol in the Pacific Rim*, John Wiley and Sons, New York.

Fagiano, D. (1990), Learning to market as the Romans do, *Management Review*, 79 (5), p. 4 (2).

Ferraro, G.P. (1996), The need for linguistic proficiency in global business, *Business Horizons*, 39 (3), pp. 39–46.

Fiske, J. (1989), *Understanding Popular Culture*, Unwin Hyman, London.

Fukuyama, F. (1995), *Trust: the Social Virtues and the Creation of Prosperity*, Free Press, New York.

Giermanski, J. (1994), Can you talk international trade? *Transportation and Distribution*, 35 (7), pp. 34–36.

Gross, A. and Dyson, P. (1997), China: managing the culture gap, *HR Focus*, 74 (2), p. 15.

Hall, E.T. (1976), *Beyond Culture*, Doubleday, New York.

Hall, E.T. and Hall, M.R. (1990), *Understanding Cultural Differences*, Intercultural Press, Yarmouth.

Hill, C.W. (1997), *International Business: Competing in the Global Market Place*, Irwin, Chicago, IL.

Hoecklin, L., (1995), *Managing Cultural Differences: Strategies for Competitive Advantage*, Addison-Wesley, Wokingham.

Hofstede, G. (1991), *Cultures and Organisations: Software of the Mind*, McGraw-Hill, London.

Hofstede, G. (1994), *Uncommon Sense about Organisations: Cases, Studies and Field Observations*, Sage, Thousands Oaks, CA.

Kasper, H. and Bloemer, J. (1996), Cultural closeness and its impact on internationalisation strategies: some examples from the European retail industry, *EMAC Annual Conference 1996*.

Kroeber, A.L. and Kluckhohn, C. (1952), Culture - a critical review of concepts and definitions, *Papers of the Peabody Museum of American Archaeology and Ethnology*, XLV11 (1), Harvard University.

Lasswell, H.D. (1966),*The Analysis of Political Behaviour*, Archon, Hamden, CN.

Laurent, A. (1983), The cultural diversity of Western conceptions of management, *International Studies of Management and Organisation*, XIII (1/2), Spring/Summer, pp. 75–96.

Lewis, R.D. (1996), How to lead in another language, *Management Today*, pp. 82–84.

Locke, R.M. (1995), *Remaking the Italian Economy*, Cornell University Press, Ithaca, NY.

Miller, R. (1995), To use or not to use: the role of English in cross-border marketing, *Direct Marketing*, 58 (8), pp. 20–21.

Myers, A., Kakabadse, A. and Gordon, C. (1995), Effectiveness of French management: analysis of the behaviour, attitudes and business impact of top managers, *Journal of Management Development*, 14 (6), pp. 56–72.

Namenwirth, J.Z. and Weber, R.B. (1987), *Dynamics of Culture*, Allen and Unwin, Boston, MA.

Niss, H. (1996), Country of origin marketing over the product life cycle: a Danish case study, *European Journal of Marketing*, 30 (3), pp. 6–22.

Randall, L.M. and Coakley, L.A. (1998), Building successful partnerships in Russia and Belarus: the impact of culture on strategy, *Business Horizons*, 41 (2), pp. 15–22.

Sapir, E. (1949), *Selected Writings of E. Sapir in Language, Culture and Personality*, Mandelbaum, D.G. (ed.), University of California Press, Berkeley CA.

Schoenberg, R., Denuelle, N. and Norburn, D. (1995), National conflict within European alliances, *European Business Journal*, 7 (1), pp. 8–16.

Sunoo, B.P. (1998), Adapting to the land down under, *Global Workforce*, 77 (1), pp. 24–25.

Terpstra, V. and David, K. (1985), *The Cultural Environment of International Business*, South-Western Publishing Co., Cincinatti, OH.

Trompenaars, F. (1993), *Riding the Waves of Culture*, The Economist Books, London.

Trunick, P.A. (1996), Trade shows: where culture meets commerce, *Transportation and Distribution*, 37 (12), pp. 66–67.

Tylor, E.B. (1891), *Primitive Culture: Researches into the Development of Mythology, Philosophy, Religion, Language, Art and Customs*, Murray, Boston, MA.

Usinier, J.-C. (2000), *Marketing Across Cultures*, FT-Prentice-Hall, London.

Xing, F. (1995), The Chinese cultural system: implications for cross-cultural management, *SAM Advanced Management Journal*, 60 (1), p. 14 (6).

Zacharakis, A. (1996), The double whammy of globalisation: differing country and foreign partner cultures, *The Academy of Management Executive*, 10 (4), p. 109 (2).

Zubrod, J. (1996), How important is local culture to global logistics? *Transportation and Distribution*, 37 (12), pp. 61–63.

Further reading

Doney, P.M., Cannon, J.P. and Mullen, M.R. (1998), Understanding the influence of national culture on the development of trust, *Academy of Management Review*, 23 (3), p. 601 (17).

Elenkov, D.S. (1998), Can American management concepts work in Russia? A cross-cultural comparative study, *California Management Review*, 40 (4), pp. 133–156.

Gesteland, R.R. (1999), *Cross-Cultural Business Behaviour: Marketing, Negotiating and Managing Across Cultures*, Copenhagen Business School Press, Copenhagen.

Harris, S. and Dibben, M. (1999), Trust and co-operation in business relationship development: exploring the influence of national values, *Journal of Marketing Management*, 15 (6), pp. 463–483.

Hennart, J-F., and Larimo, J. (1998), The impact of culture on the strategy of the multinational enterprise: does national origin affect ownership decisions?, *Journal of International Business Studies*, 29 (2), pp. 515–538.

Hofstede, G. (1998), Attitudes, values and organizational culture: disentangling the concepts, *Organisation Studies*, 19 (3), pp. 477–491.

Holden, N. (1998), Viewpoint: international marketing studies - time to break the English-language strangle-hold, *International Marketing Review*, 15 (2–3), pp. 86–100.

Husted, B.W. (1999),Wealth, culture, and corruption, *Journal of International Business Studies*, 30 (2), pp. 339–360.

Money, B. R. (1998), International multilateral negotiations and social networks, *Journal of International Business Studies*, 29 (4), pp. 695–710.

Morosini, P., Shane, S. and Singh, H. (1998), National cultural distance and cross-border acquisition performance, *Journal of International Business Studies*, 29 (1), pp. 137–158.

Morris, M.W., Williams, K.Y., Leung, K., Larrick, R., Mendoza, M.T., Bhatnagar, D., Li, J., Kondo, M., Luo, J.-L. and Hu, J.-C. (1998), Conflict management style: accounting for cross-national difference, *Journal of International Business Studies*, 29 (4), pp. 729–748.

Parnell, J.A. and Hatem, T. (1999), Cultural antecedents of behavioural differences between American and Egyptian managers, *Journal of Management Studies*, 36 (3), pp. 399–418.

Peñaloza, L. and Gilly, M.C. (1999), Marketer acculturation: the changer and the changed, *Journal of Marketing*, 63 (3), pp. 84–104.

Pornpitakpan, C. (1999), The effects of cultural adaptation on business relationships: Americans selling to Japanese and Thais, *Journal of International Business Studies*, 30 (2), pp. 317–338.

Stöttinger, B. and Schlegelmilch, B.B. (1998), Explaining export development through psychic distance: enlightening or elusive? *International Marketing Review*, 15 (5), pp. 357–372.

In addition the following journals have published relevant special issues:

International Business Review (1998), Special Issue: Culture and International Business, 7 (4).

Journal of International Business Studies (1999), Special Issue: New Trends in International and Multicultural Management, 30 (4).

CHAPTER 4

The process of internationalization

Chapter objectives

After studying this chapter you should be able to:

- Discuss how our understanding of SME internationalization has been shaped by the published definitions
- Explain three key theories of internationalization
- Identify the main motives driving international involvement
- Describe the main market entry options
- Outline the key influences on successful export marketing

Introduction

Hardly a week goes by without some reference to the cliché that we live in a 'shrinking world' or the 'Global Village'. Certainly, for many, the so-called shrinking can be experienced in the journey times for long distance travel or in the rapid technological improvements in communication which facilitate the ever faster exchange of more detailed information. This, of course, can result in curious situations where, for example, from the comfort of our own home we can watch the latest disaster, natural or man-made, unfold in real-time as we watch, emotionally involved yet at a safe physical distance.

There is an inevitability about the development of an ever-integrated world in terms of communications as the technology advances. What we as humans chose to do with it remains very much in the balance, and few of us fully appreciate the impact it will have on our lives in the future. Likewise business is affected by an increasing internationalization, and for some sectors and individual companies there is also an inevitability about their international development. The high technology sector is seen by many as needing to be international from day one, as a rapidly changing technological base reduces the window of opportunity before new products are introduced. Companies in relatively small domestic markets are often forced to seek growth through the development of new markets around the world. Even a traditionally insular economy like the US has begun to realize that, by increasing exporting activity, economic performance can be sustained and improved. Elsewhere in the world the rapid advances made, until 1997, by the progressive so called 'tiger economies' were largely based on an aggressive export-orientated economic development. Of course, rather like the value of stocks and shares, successful international involvement has no magic formula and success can be short lived.

Internationalization can be viewed on a number of levels. On a popular cultural level, many people around the world would like to think of themselves as more international as education levels rise, as more leisure travel is undertaken, and as their lives become more influenced by international media conveying cosmopolitan tastes in food and fashion. At the level of the nation-state it is possible to see an increased internationalization in the suppression of trade barriers and the coming together of individual countries in economic blocs. As part and parcel of this process we see simpler documentation and customs procedures, as markets become more and more integrated. Finally, at the level of the individual firm a whole host of activities can contribute towards an increased international orientation namely: location of production facilities; technology transfer; sourcing of inputs; acquisition activities; tapping into international sources of finance as well as recruiting people from around the world.

Thus, the phenomenon of internationalization is the central concern of this chapter. The structure of the discussion will be as follows. The next section will look at the definitions of internationalization which have been put forward by various authors. Following this the three dominant theories of the internationalization process will be reviewed, namely, foreign direct investment (FDI), the stages model and the network approach. The motives, constraints and opportunities affecting companies will then be discussed, before going on to outline the key modes of market entry open to companies. Finally, the factors influencing success and failure in the internationalization process will be outlined before some concluding thoughts on the chapter are offered.

Definitions

One problem with attempting a definition of internationalization is trying to find one on which everyone can agree. A brief review of the literature will reveal that such a definition does not exist. Instead there are almost as many definitions as there are contributions to the body of research knowledge on this topic. The present author has to admit to contributing to the profusion of definitions when, following a study in 1988, the following definition was produced: 'Internationalization may be viewed as an approach to management which allows an organization to integrate domestic and international opportunities with internal resources'. Each new study has a different perspective and it is difficult to point to a simple coherence in the literature on the subject of internationalization. But then again why should there be any simple solution to such a complex process? This is an issue we shall return to later in the chapter, but first let us consider some of the key themes within the definitions offered.

The origin of much of the work on internationalization stems from studies in the 1960s on the nature of export behaviour. Simmonds and Smith identified the promotion of an 'international outlook' or 'internationalization' among managers as a more successful route to increasing exports than any appeal to nationalistic motives. This work became formalized into models of export behaviour, mainly by a number of Swedish researchers including Johanson and Wiedersheim-Paul (1975) who stated that 'internationalization usually refers to either an attitude of the firm towards foreign activities or to the actual carrying out of activities abroad'. For them it was the interaction of these attitudes and actual behaviour which describe the internationalization process.

These attitudinal and behavioural themes continued to be echoed in the literature by Joynt and Welch (1985) who talked of business internationalization as the need 'to stimulate greater international orientation amongst its [Norway's] smaller companies'. More importantly they also state that a crucial component of the whole internationalization process is the 'internationalization of people and their attitudes'.

Another theme apparent in some of the definitions of internationalization is that it is a gradual process during which firms acquire, integrate and utilize their knowledge about foreign markets and operations. As this happens over time, the firms gradually increase their commitment to international markets. Some research work on this topic has suggested that internationalization evolves as firms gradually increase their commitment and exposure to risk. This is reflected in their market entry mode which may progress through (i) exporting, (ii) agency representation, (iii) overseas licensing, (iv) overseas sales subsidiary, and finally (v) the establishment of an overseas production subsidiary.

Apart from these recurrent themes there remains no one agreed definition. Part of the problem is that few studies use identical methodologies, and therefore cross-cultural or longitudinal studies are rare. Other criticisms of the work into internationalization have included its over-association with the exporting mode, lack of empirical evidence for the stages model, discrepancies based on the unit of observation, and a neglect of service-based companies and of purchasing behaviour.

Aaby and Slater (1989) call for improvement in the research design, and for more research to be based on previous findings. They criticize much of the previous research for being simplistic, partly because of the approaches used which fail to recognize the complexity of the relationships between firm characteristics, competencies, strategy and performance. In terms of design, they suggest that improvements need to be made in the area of performance measures and longitudinal studies.

Johanson and Vahlne (1990) see part of the problem of developing the concept of internationalization as the result of the fact that the basic ideas are drawn from a number of disciplines including economic theory, organization theory and marketing theory. For the future they think that researchers should investigate how firm

internationalization processes are related to market or network internationalization, industry internationalization, technical development, concentration and
deconcentration processes.

If a broadly acceptable definition is to be found, then it must be reasonably
holistic to allow for the range of views in the literature. One definition which fits
into this category is provided by Beamish (1990) who sees internationalization as
'...the process by which firms increase their awareness of the direct and indirect
influence of international transactions on their future, and establish and conduct
transactions with other countries'. Perhaps this is as good a starting point as any for
a working definition on the subject of internationalization.

Theories of internationalization

In the literature, the process of internationalization has been encapsulated in
various ways by three contrasting schools of research thought; FDI theory, the
'Stage' models and by the network perspective on internationalization. Of these,
FDI and the stage models have received the most attention in the literature, while
the network perspective is the most recent, and increasingly the most popular,
approach.

In all the schools of thought the explanation, both conceptual and empirical, is
mainly in the context of larger multinational, manufacturing companies. Since
small firms, for all sorts of reasons, experience different management practices
compared with larger firms, then it is likely that their experience of internationalization will also be different. This issue will be explored further in the next chapter
but, for now, this chapter will concentrate on the theories themselves.

Foreign direct investment

Many governments around the world have established special bodies to attract
foreign investment (see Boxes 4.1 and 4.2). In today's world this is a highly competitive field, with much wooing of potential investors by offering attractive incentives, including tax breaks and rent-free periods. The key benefit to the host country
is the influx of jobs and the hoped-for impact on suppliers to a new plant. The
economy is diversified, imports often reduced, and new technologies are introduced to the economy.

There is, however, a down-side to this activity in that many promises are not fully
realized in terms of the number or types of jobs created, i.e. assembly rather than
R&D or higher level management jobs. Traditionally, these so-called branch plants
are also vulnerable in times of economic downturn. Many vulnerable communities
around the world have welcomed much needed jobs, only to see them evaporate as
quickly as they came. Despite this, efforts to attract investment continue unabated.

The theory of FDI has developed from neo-classical and industrial trade theory,
and supports 'internalization' of a firm's activities in the process of internationalization. This view explains international expansion behaviour with the argument
that firms choose their optimal structure for each stage of production by evaluating

the costs of economic transactions. From this, firms choose the organizational form and location for which overall transaction costs are minimized. Thus, transactions which are perceived to be high risk and requiring significant management time or other resource commitments are more likely to be 'internalized,' as part of a hierarchically structured organization. Conversely, transactions with limited investment requirements and less risk are more likely to take place *between* firms, and across market boundaries, and are therefore 'externalized.'

BOX 4.1: FDI AND PAPUA NEW GUINEA

Since 1992 the Investment Promotion Authority has worked to attract foreign investment projects with high foreign exchange earnings prospects, while creating jobs and contribution towards import substitution. Priority activities include:

- Minerals and petroleum exploration
- Agriculture, forestry and fishing
- Shipbuilding and repair
- Tourism.

The secondary processing of agricultural products and assembly of consumer durables is also encouraged. The incentives offered for such investments include:

- Loans for industry
- Wage subsidies
- Feasibility study grants
- Investment guarantees, e.g. right to remit earnings and to repatriate capital.

An additional range of incentives include tax incentives:

- Tax free zones lasting up to 10 years
- Export incentives, e.g. tax free earnings on exports for a 3 year period.

Critics of FDI argue that research in the area is used primarily to explain a pattern of investment, and not a long-term process of internationalization (Melin, 1992). Aharoni (1966) views FDI, in the context of small firms, as a managerial decision-making process. This study of US investors in Israel identified five stages of activity which characterize the FDI decision process:

1. An 'initiating force' which triggers a non-investor
2. Investigation
3. The decision to invest (involving increased commitment within the firm)
4. Review and negotiation within the firm
5. Organizational change 'through repetition' over time.

The interviews of Buckley et al. (1990) with managers of UK manufacturing firms also suggest an evolutionary approach to internationalization, reflecting incremental investment resulting from a process of managerial learning over time. Thus, FDI, as we shall see in the next section, exhibits characteristics similar to those associated with the stages approach.

> ### BOX 4.2: FDI AND NEW ZEALAND
>
> The New Zealand government assesses the attractiveness of foreign investment on the following criteria:
>
> - The creation of new job opportunities or the retention of existing jobs that might otherwise be lost
> - The introduction into New Zealand of new technology or business skills
> - The development of new export markets or increased export market access for New Zealand exporters
> - Added market competition, greater efficiency or productivity, or enhanced domestic services in New Zealand.

Stage models

The stage models are based on the premise that internationalization is a process. It is viewed as an evolutionary development over time and consists of a number of phases. Typically the models follow the following generic phases:

1. No interest in exporting
2. Exporting begins via intermediaries
3. The firm begins to export more directly and enthusiastically
4. The firm may establish a presence in the export market in the form of a marketing or sales outlet
5. Finally, at the most advanced point, a manufacturing plant is established.

Two concepts strongly associated with the models are psychic distance and geographic proximity. Psychic distance refers to the tendency for those people involved in first time exporting to trade with countries with which they feel comfortable culturally. So, for example, English speaking nations will be more likely to trade with each other initially, even if the geographic distance is greater than their nearest neighbour. The issue of geographic distance is straightforward in that the initial exporting will take place to countries in close proximity. Both concepts work together to influence the destination of the first export order.

A number of models have been proposed along these lines and, rather like the definition issue, they are variations on a theme rather than radically different, as Table 4.1 illustrates.

The models draw on organizational behaviour and learning theory to capture both firm behaviour and managerial learning over time (see Box 4.3). Much of the conceptual and empirical foundation in this school of research was initiated by Johanson and Wiedersheim-Paul (1975), and then Johanson and Vahlne (1977), whose establishment chain model suggests that internationalization activities occur incrementally, and are influenced by increased market knowledge and commitment.

The basic theory is that the perceptions and beliefs of managers both influence,

Table 4.1   Content review of export development models. Source: Leonidou and Katsikeas (1996)

Johanson and Wiedersheim-Paul (1975)	Bilkey and Tesar (1977)	Wiedersheim-Paul et al. (1978)	Wortzel and Wortzel (1981)	Cavusgil (1982)	Czinkota (1982)	Barrett and Wilkinson (1986)	Moon and Lee (1990)	Lim et al. (1991)	Rao and Naidu (1992)	Crick (1995)
	Stage I No interest in exporting/not even filling an unsolicited order	Stage I Domestic oriented firm/no willingness to start exporting/ limited information collection and transmission		Stage I Pre-involvement/ selling only in the home market/no interest in export related information	Stage I Completely uninterested firm/no exploration of feasibility to export	Stage I Non-exporters who never considered exporting		Stage I Awareness/ recognition of exporting as an opportunity	Stage I Non-exporters indicating no current level of export nor any future interest in exporting	Stage I Completely uninterested firm
	Stage II Passive exploration of exporting/ possible filling of an unsolicited order	Stage II Passive non-exporter/ moderate willingness to start exporting/ moderate information collection and transmission		Stage II Reactive involvement/ evaluation of feasibility to export/ deliberate search for export related information	Stage II Partially interested firm/ exporting is a desirable but uncertain activity	Stage II–III Non-exporters who investigated exporting and precious exporters		Stage II Interest in selecting exporting as a viable strategy		Stage II Partially interested firm
	Stage III Management actively explores the feasibility to export	Stage III Active non-exporter/ High willingness to start exporting/ Relatively high information collection and transmission			Stage III Exploring firm/ Planning for export and actively exploring export possibilities			Stage III Intention to initiate exports		Stage III Exporting firm

Table 4.1 (continued)

Johanson and Wiedersheim-Paul (1975)	Bilkey and Tesar (1977)	Wiedersheim-Paul et al. (1978)	Wortzel and Wortzel (1981)	Cavusgil (1982)	Czinkota (1982)	Barrett and Wilkinson (1986)	Moon and Lee (1990)	Lim et al. (1991)	Rao and Naidu (1992)	Crick (1995)
Stage I No regular export activity/no resource commitment abroad	Stage IV Experimental exporting to some psychologically close country		Stage I Importer pull/foreign customer orders	Stage III Limited experimental involvement/limited exporting to psychologically close countries	Stage IV Experimenting exporter/favorable export attitude but little exploration of export possibilities	Stage IV Current exporters with no direct investment abroad	Stage I Lower stage of export involvement	Stage IV Trial and adoption of exporting	Stage III Sporadic involvement in exporting activities	Stage IV Experimental exporter
			Stage II Basic production capacity marketing							
Stage II Exporting to psychologically close countries via independent reps/agents	Stage V Experienced exporter/optimal export adjustment to environmental factors		Stage III Advanced production capacity marketing	Stage IV Active involvement/systematic exporting to new countries using direct distribution methods	Stage V Semi experienced small exporter/favorable attitude and active involvement in exporting		Stage II Middle stage of export involvement		Stage IV Regular involvement in exporting activities	Stage V Experienced small exporter
			Stage IV Product marketing channel push							
Stage III Exporting to more psychologically distant countries/establishment of sales subsidiaries	Stage IV Exporting to additional countries psychologically more distant		Stage V Product marketing channel pull	Stage V Committed involvement/allocating resources between domestic and foreign markets	Stage VI Experienced large exporter/very favorable export attitudes and future export plans		Stage III Higher stage of export involvement			Stage VI Experienced larger exporter

and are shaped by, incremental involvement in foreign markets. This results in a pattern of evolution, from the managers having little or no interest in international markets, to trial initiatives in, and evaluation of, psychically close markets. Managers then pursue active expansion into more challenging and unknown markets, becoming increasingly committed to international growth.

BOX 4.3: STAGES MODEL: LET'S SURF AGAIN

This company was founded in 1981 in Newcastle, England, UK. Its set-up was in itself an interesting process, in that it was started by a Swedish entrepreneur in the UK and, because of patent protection in the UK, was immediately forced to export – a truly international firm from the outset. Whilst not directly reflecting the classic stages model, its history helps to illustrate 'stages' of gradual market expansion and product development. The first main products which the company marketed were surf boards and surf skis. These were sold into identified markets in France, Australia and the US. Five years after it was founded, the company acquired a clothing manufacturer in order to develop a range of leisure wear, which it again sold to the same markets where it had successfully marketed its surf boards. This time, of course, it had bene- fited from the market knowledge and experience gained from the first round of inter- national involvement. Further new product development produced a kayak which again was to be sold into the company's already established key markets.

The stage models of internationalization have triggered significant empirical work, in an attempt to verify the models across different industrial contexts. The model has been criticized for being over systematic and categorical in the definition of the phases, in that it implies a sequential or incremental progression from one stage to another, which not all firms will necessarily go through. It is difficult to justify viewing internationalization as a single pre-determined path, and not to allow for the individuality of organizations and the actions of the decision-makers within them.

Since the late 1980s research has shown that many companies are engaging in rapid and more direct forms of internationalization. The stages model is ill- equipped to deal with this dynamic process. Many of the early models were based on very small samples of large firms, whose wider relevance must be ques- tioned. Further, the implied sequential process is not inevitable and there is evidence of companies moving backward and forwards or even jumping stages within the model. Evidence also of rapid internationalization by high-technology products, whose window of opportunity on the world market can be quite limited, has further added to the criticism.

Why then has this theory survived so long? One reason is that nothing better has come along. The model remains intuitively appealing to our search for order and neat explanations in the chaos of the international environment. However, while elements of the model may provide useful insights into our understanding, it is long past the time when the stages approach should be accepted as the best explanation of the internationalization process. As stated by Johanson and Vahlne (1992), the foreign market entry process is '…unclear, complex, continuously changing… strategy emerges out of interplay between actors in the foreign market and the focal firm'. This *interplay between actors* has received increasing attention in the literature, in the context of network research. Thus, the third school of internationalization research will now be discussed: the network perspective.

A network perspective

Businesses cannot exist in 'splendid isolation'. They must interact with suppliers, intermediaries of various sorts, and customers, meet the competition and find ways of organizing their international environment to create the most efficient structure. In short, links will be created between the departments/individuals of the firm and all those organizations/individuals with whom it interacts. Clearly, some of these links will be more important than others to the firm, and will require a higher degree of commitment on behalf of the two parties. Some will be relatively new, others long-established. Some will be merely based on a business relationship while others will extend into friendship. Depending on the size of the firm these links or networks will cover a great range of complexity.

The idea of business networks is not a new one, although its prominence has been on the increase recently. Much work has been conducted across a variety of disciplines on the structure of networks and in defining what they are. Often networks are characterized as sets of exchange relationships between individuals or organizations. Within the relationship the exchange components can be the product or service, information, financial or social elements. Yanagida (1992) states that networks can be more than social groups 'they can be active and energetic organizations that challenge individual members and provide a forum for the exchange of information'. Perhaps more importantly 'they offer business people a powerful tool in their own personal development as well as in the development of their business'.

The dual role of networks, as interaction at a formal organizational level between businesses, and as a social interaction or exchange between individuals, is a common theme in many definitions. However, it is inevitable that the two dimensions will overlap and any analysis needs to be able to take this into account. It is possible to think of three types of networks, for example, those based on production networks, personal networks and symbolic networks. Production networks occur within and between organizations; personal networks involve friendship and are based on trust; symbolic networks are related to collective community values.

As a result, the network perspective offers a complementary view to FDI theory, given that the latter does not account for the role and influence of social relationships in business transactions (Granovetter, 1985). Also, internationalization decisions and activities in the network perspective emerge as patterns of behaviour influenced by various network members, while FDI theory assumes rational strategic decision-making (Sharma, 1992). Compared with the unilateral process suggested by the stage models, the network perspective introduces a 'more multilateral element' to internationalization (Johanson and Vahlne, 1990, 1992) creating a spider's web of influences on the process covering both formal and informal networks.

Motives, constraints and opportunities

Firms enter into the international arena for a variety of reasons. No classification can be regarded as inclusive of all possible reasons; instead they act as a shorthand guide to be adapted to all sorts of situations. Likewise all firms operate within a framework of constraints; not all opportunities can be responded to positively, and they need to be evaluated within the overall context of the businesses aims. Motives are also directly related to the mode of market entry adopted by a company, as we shall see in the Section 'Modes of entry'.

Motives

Ask any group of international marketing students to come up with a list of the key reasons as to why companies should want to get involved with global trade, and it is likely that the list will include most of the classic reasons, but what is more difficult is to find agreement on is how the motives should be classified. The traditional way in the literature is to regard export motives as push and pull factors.
   Push factors include:

- Excess capacity
- Having a unique product
- Having a company specific advantage
- Having a marketing advantage
- Being driven by the owner/key decision-maker
- A desire to spread cost and risk.

These are also termed internal factors.
   The pull or external factors are:

- Receiving an unsolicited or chance order
- Operating in a saturated or highly competitive domestic market
- Being receptive to peer competitive pressures
- Being stimulated by export stimulation programs.

Some students find this a difficult classification to endorse, since the difference between a pull and a push can be difficult to judge; for example, a saturated home market could be seen as both a pull and a push factor. Perhaps greater clarity is offered by the use of the terms reactive and proactive, which can be cross-tabulated against internal and external as seen in Table 4.2.

Constraints and opportunities

It is worth bearing in mind that not all companies are in a position to take advan-

Table 4.2 A classification of international involvement motives

	Internal	External
Proactive	Driven by owner-manager/key decision makers Desire to increase profits Having a unique product/service Having a company specific advantage, e.g. in marketing, technology	Perceived international market opportunities Export development activity by governments, trade associations, banks
Reactive	Excess production capacity Spreading costs and risk	Unsolicited order Small domestic market Saturated domestic market Peer competitive pressure

tage of all opportunities which may present themselves. Indeed, it is possible that not all opportunities will be recognized by the decision-makers in the company. It is this perceptual variation and ability to process information which helps to create the variability on the map of international activities.

Little, quoted in Yanacek (1998) has identified the top ten constraints faced by companies marketing products or services internationally. These are:

- Building distribution networks
- Designing market entry strategies
- Identifying market opportunities
- Dealing with political and commercial risks
- Obtaining information on alternatives to direct exporting
- Securing working capital and export financing
- Collecting foreign receivables
- Providing after sales customer service
- Dealing with tariff barriers and quotas
- Dealing with export laws, regulations and procedures.

Of course on the other side of the coin, it is worth remembering that not all companies wish to become internationally active (see Box 4.4). This can occur for a variety of reasons, some of which, particularly in smaller companies, can be associated with the personal characteristics of the entrepreneur. Some find it difficult to delegate responsibility and, therefore, it is difficult for the company to grow. Others have reached what some authors have called the 'comfort level', and do not wish to see an expansion of the business. While outsiders may wish to see growth and while it may be frustrating to watch a company, in a sense, under achieve, it is also dangerous to force change upon such a company.

BOX 4.4: NO TEDDY BEAR'S PICNIC

In a remote part of Scotland there is a small company producing soft toys. Meanwhile on a visit to Scotland were executives from Disney who had seen the company's products and liked them. The executives were keen to cut a deal but had been warned that the company was sceptical. In attempting to contact the company the ensuing telephone conversation went something like this:...

    Disney: 'Hello, is that the Teddy Bear Company?'
    Teddy: 'Aye.'
    Disney: 'Hi, I represent Disney and we're mighty impressed by your cute teddy
              bears...'
    Teddy: 'Who?'
    Disney: 'Disney. You know Donald Duck, Mickey Mouse, Florida.'
    Teddy: 'Disney?'
    Disney: 'That's right.'
    Teddy: 'Never heard of you. Good-bye.'

The moral of this story is, global brands beware!.

Work with Scottish arts and crafts businesses (McAuley, 1999) has shown that, despite being exposed to similar opportunities at trade fairs, some companies are quicker than others to take advantage of the possibility to trade internationally. The key feature which appears to separate the 'instant' exporter from the others is the personality of the entrepreneur.

As well as what might be termed these 'softer' constraints, there are the more traditional ones related to worries about:

- Available resources whether human or financial
- Having the time to devote to international activities
- State of the market
- Getting paid
- Exchange rate volatility
- Need for and cost of insurance
- Getting the right (cheap) information
- Cost of marketing activities
- Political risk
- Suitability of the product/service
- Cultural differences.

The firm faces many decisions in its attempt to internationalize its activities: what volume of trade is desirable? how many countries to market in? which countries to select? The degree of market attractiveness will be influenced by a number of factors related to:

- Geographic characteristics
- Demographic characteristics
- Economic characteristics

- Technological characteristics
- Socio-cultural characteristics.

Having evaluated the relative attractiveness of the potential markets in relation to the company's product/service it is better placed to select those markets where the 'fit' is apparently best. This then prepares the way for one of the dominant decisions of the internationalization process, namely, the mode of market entry decision.

Modes of entry

The firm has a number of choices when it is attempting to evaluate a mode of market entry. It should be remembered that there is no one method which is suitable for all firms under a particular set of circumstances. Instead there are a number of options which companies and the individuals within them have to weigh up under the pertaining market situation. Box 4.5 highlights those favoured by exporters in Canada and Latin America.

BOX 4.5: MARKET ENTRY: A CANADA–LATIN AMERICA STUDY

Based on 15–18 business people from each of the following areas – Nova Scotia, Venezuela, Peru, Chile and Costa Rica – the following views were noted.

- Few were involved in FDI decisions.
- Nova Scotian companies stated that the decisions made were often hasty and short sighted and lacked strategic vision.
- Chilean exporters stressed the importance of using local agents as an information source. Most used foreign buyers and distributors.
- Venezuelan exporters used a more direct approach, after some trial and error, which involved more channels, including the establishment of commercial subsidiaries in the US.
- Overall it was observed that exporters tended to take greater control of market channels as they mature and increase their market commitment.

The company will have a number of broad strategic choices which it will have to address including: is a domestic export-based strategy, or a production-based strategy in the host country, more appropriate? It may be that the host country will only welcome the exporter if it involves a presence in the host market. Such a presence will require a commitment, at the very least, to international marketing or a production plant, unlike a pure domestic export-based strategy. Under such a strategy the responsibility could be devolved to the intermediary being used.

A number of specific factors will shape their choice. These will include the:

- Speed of entry required
- Financial resources available
- Flexibility required
- Degree of risk aversion

- Period over which the investment is expected to provide a return
- Long-term objectives of the organization
- Degree of marketing control.

Firms can also make use of outside advice on market entry concerns as Box 4.6 illustrates.

BOX 4.6: MARKET ENTRY: TARGET WESTERN EUROPE – ADVICE GIVEN TO CANADIAN EXPORTERS

Try to obtain language and cultural expertise, and use this in all aspects of negotiation, marketing and promotion. You will not only be seen as respectful, but will be able to differentiate your company from many competitors.

Clients in the European market are well-versed in international affairs. If you wish to gain their respect, be prepared to discuss these issues intelligently.

Approach distribution strategy very carefully. This area is crucial and complex. Do not hesitate to seek advice from other exporters and/or trade consultants.

Trade shows are plentiful and useful in this market. Participation through federal and provincial government programs is a good first step.

Despite a more homogeneous Europe (since 1992) the region will not be one uniform market in the near future. Consequently, be sensitive to distinctive national and even sub-national requirements.

There are a number of ways to classify the options open to companies, and no one method is correct. The approach used in this book is to look at indirect and direct market entry together with strategies which do or do not involve foreign investment. This is outlined in Table 4.3 and discussed below.

Indirect market entry

This is often referred to as passive exporting or as being the result of an 'export pull' effect, since people outside the company stimulate the activity. The main strategies which come under this category are:

(i) Responding to unsolicited or chance orders. For some companies, this is the first introduction to international markets, which may stimulate them to explore the feasibility of exporting more seriously as the stage models would suggest. It does have that advantage of being new, unexpected business. It illustrates the fact that there are potential, as yet unreached, customers in the world, and it involves no product adaptation costs or promotion costs.

However, on the downside, the company is not geared up for exporting, and therefore there are relatively high costs involved because of the learning curve which has to be gone through. For example, a one-off distribution channel will be relatively expensive as no economies of scale are available. The potential benefits of this initial involvement depend on the company's medium-term response to the unsolicited order.

Table 4.3   Classification of modes of market entry

Indirect market entry	Strategies without foreign investment

Unsolicited orders
Domestic based intermediaries
  Courier/express services
  Export management companies
  Export houses
  Trading companies
  Piggybacking
  Brokers
  Jobbers
	Licensing
	Franchising
	Management contracts

Direct market entry	**Strategies with foreign investment**

Domestic based intermediaries
  Freight forwarders
  Consortium exporting
  Export department
Foreign based intermediaries
  Agents
  Distributors
	Marketing subsidiary
	Manufacturing subsidiary
	Joint ventures
	  Joint equity venture
	  Contractual joint venture

(ii) Use of a range of home-based intermediaries. This can include making use of courier/express delivery services, export management companies, export houses, trading companies, piggybacking, brokers and jobbers. Effectively by using the services of these intermediaries, the experience is little different than undertaking a domestic sale, as there is no direct export marketing experience being gained.

Courier and express delivery services will be of little use for bulk items, as they will have weight restrictions, but for low-weight high-value items they are an option. It is a cost efficient way for a micro-business to reach international clients, for example, in the jewellery or hand-made ceramic businesses.

Export management companies are estimated to handle approximately 10% of all manufactured goods. They offer a personal service to clients who come to view them as an extension of their own business. It may even be that the buyer does not realize they are dealing indirectly with the exporter. For the exporter without the personnel or funds to run an export operation, this route offers market entry at low investment.

An export house will buy directly from the domestic manufacturer on behalf of an international client. This is a straightforward sale for the domestic company with the export house taking responsibility for organizing the export of the goods.

Trading companies gather together, transport and distribute goods from many companies. Names from the past include the East India Company and the Hudson Bay Company, and today the United Africa Company is a major player on that continent. They handle a huge range of items across the consumer and business to business markets. In Japan the 'sogo shosha' have a long history of trading as both importers and exporters, and offer integrated financial and insurance services as part of the package.

Piggybacking, or complementary marketing as it is sometimes known, allows one firm to use the distribution channels of another firm to reach an international customer. It may be that the existing exporter has excess capacity in the channel, or they may be keen to expand the range of products carried by seeking out complementary, non-competing products to those already carried. The request can also come from an existing customer for another product to be sourced. The domestic firm may then seek a third party offering a complete export package, based on its existing channels, to meet this request.

Successful piggybacking can work well for both the piggybacker and the carrier. The former gains a ready market and the experience of an existing exporter, while the latter increases the product range and makes more efficient use of channels which would have been served anyway.

Brokers and jobbers tend to deal mostly in commodities. Brokers bring buyer and seller together and do not necessarily have an ongoing relationship with their clients, but maintain a network of producers and buyers throughout the world. Jobbers take title to the goods but do not take physical possession; instead they organize the transportation of the goods.

All of these indirect approaches to market entry have the common advantage of being low cost, as no international sales force is required, but they do not allow the company to develop its own skills and knowledge of the exporting process. By using the expertise of others it is likely that most deals will run smoothly for the company, but crucially direct contact with the end customer is non-existent. Under these circumstances the firm must accept that its involvement in international markets is very shallow.

Direct market entry

This is an active form of exporting and can involve the use of domestic and international based intermediaries. The commitment and investment required are greater than in indirect exporting, but the rewards can also be greater. Within the domestic market the main types are:

(i) Use of freight forwarders. These companies provide advice and guidance and offer a documentation and delivery service. They act on behalf of the producer, and are indispensable to an exporter who does not possess the skills in-house to handle the paperwork associated with exporting. A full-service freight forwarder will provide information on shipping, routing, schedules, charges, labelling, certification and consular requirements. By consolidating orders into larger shipments, the freight forwarder can offer a more cost effective service to the smaller exporter than they could obtain independently.

(ii) Consortium exporting. Under this a number of companies, normally non-competing, come together in order to combine their skills and resources, especially managerial and financial. They bid for contracts and projects as a group while remaining independent. Often these are linked to large construction projects where a consortium is formed, with one lead organization driving the group forward.

(iii) Export department. Larger companies will be able to form an in-house export department to run all exporting activities. Home-based salespeople travel abroad, perhaps in defined geographical areas, in search of orders.

Those methods involving the use of international-based intermediaries include:

(i) Use of agents. Agents represent the exporter abroad and are normally paid on a commission basis. They will have territorial sales rights, but may work for more than one company and carry more than one product line. The exporter may remain responsible for the inventory. This is the most common means of market entry for exporters, and is a relatively inexpensive method. However, it is important that a 'who does what' agreement is drawn up and understood by both sides before entering into any relationship, as bad agents do exist and can be difficult to get rid off. On a positive note, they offer market knowledge and access to networks.

(ii) Use of distributors. Distributors operate in a very similar way to agents, but the distributor takes title (ownership) of the goods. This means that they purchase the goods from the exporter before going on to re-sell them. The advantage of this method to the exporter is that cash flow is more assured, but there is a loss of control over the price to the end-user, and no direct knowledge about who the end user is.

Strategies without international investment

The next group of strategies involve international production strategies without direct investment. Those without direct investment include:

(i) Licensing. This involves providing permission for another operator (the licensee) to make use of a production process, trademark or patent in return for a lump sum payment and an annual royalty. The royalty would be based on a percentage of sales or profit. It is a popular method for companies, especially SMEs, who desire market entry without a large capital outlay.

One advantage of such an arrangement is that income can be obtained for older processes which are technically obsolete in the domestic market, e.g. the UK car company Rover has licensed older models of engines to the Chinese market. The original manufacturer gains an entry to international markets with relatively low risk and low cost. It may also be the only route to market entry if import restrictions exist which deny other means.

There are some potential disadvantages which have to be considered. These include a certain loss of control of the technology, which could be developed by the new operator and inadvertently create a new competitor for the original company. There can also be problems with the payment process, and in making sure that the original deal is honoured in that the technology is not passed on to any third party. Thus the supervision costs of the agreement can escalate.

(ii) Franchising. This involves the selling of a marketing concept as part of a business package which will include such things as the corporate image, trademarks and a training program for the new franchisee. The franchisee owns and manages the operation on a day-to-day basis within the regulations laid down by the franchise owner.

Currently this is a fast growing form of market entry. The types of sectors involved include business services, food, home care services, property care, car services and retailing. Many of the initial entries into the emerging markets of Eastern Europe were franchises. Usually a master franchise for a particular territory will be agreed with one partner who will have the right to issue subfranchises.

The advantage of this system is a rapid and relatively low cost market entry, which helps to create a global image. The original business idea is maximized with the minimum of investment. There can be control problems in relation to variable quality provided by the individual franchisee, which may reflect badly on the brand as a whole, e.g. when McDonald's had to close down its Paris operation. It is also possible the concept may be closely copied and a competitor may enter the market quickly.

(iii) Management contracts. These involve putting in a management system plus the personnel to operate the venture. The international company supplies the capital. This again provides rapid entry and help to fill obvious management gaps. For example, in Eastern Europe after the fall of the Berlin Wall in 1989, a number of joint ventures were created in the hotel sector to meet the rapid increase in demand for tourist facilities, as the number of visitors grew. Management contracts are also popular in the management of private hospitals.

The turnkey operation is a particular version of this method of market entry. This is often associated with large-scale construction contracts, whereby a company builds and commissions a facility, for example a power station or dam, for a government customer. Over an agreed period of time the running of the facility is passed from the original builder to the government or its appointed body.

Strategies with international investment

(i) Establish a marketing subsidiary. This mode is favoured where the company feels that its own marketing skills are better than any agent it could engage. Having the 'local' presence is deemed to be important to the image of the company in the country. By creating this feeling of presence, the company enhances its own credibility, and perhaps acceptability, in some politically sensitive markets.

(ii) Establish a manufacturing or assembly subsidiary. Wholly owned production facilities are a popular strategy for many larger companies. The organization can be attracted to this option in order to seek new markets, obtain access to resources, or improve the efficiency of their operation, partly through increased productivity.

This option allows full control with no dilution of profits to other operators or agents, and can reduce transports costs. It also allows the company to take advantage of financial incentives from the host government, lower labour costs, access to raw materials and perhaps avoid punitive import taxes. However, the capital cost involved can be prohibitive, and in certain politically risky countries the future can be uncertain. However, as we saw earlier in Chapter 2, there are many incentives offered to footloose international investment.

A variation on this approach is to establish a local presence by acquiring or merging with a local firm. This is a faster route to entering the market than building a brand new facility. It gives immediate market intelligence, market share and established channels of distribution. There can be disadvantages in amalgamating two distinct company cultures, a product line and/or a management team that was underperforming. However, this mode, which was much in fashion in the 1960s and 1970s, seems to be making a comeback in the early years of the new century.

(iii) Joint ventures. This option provides an important local feel to the investment without carrying all the risk. The partner can also provide the all important knowledge and access to networks, as well as reducing political and cultural barriers which might have been present in acquisition or in developing a wholly owned subsidiary. Some governments specifically encourage this form of investment rather than experience too many international operators moving in. On the down side there is a certain loss of control and a risk that the partner organization may not be all that it appeared. Within the corporate structure there can also be tensions between the corporate culture and ambitions versus the local identity. There are two distinct types of joint ventures: joint equity venture and contractual, as in strategic business alliances.

A joint-equity venture consists of domestic and international companies coming together to share ownership and control in a venture. This may involve buying in to a company or forming a new local business. As the name implies, such an arrangement involves investment over a period of time, which does not have to be fixed. Often such a business set-up is required by the government as the only means of market entry allowed. Alternatively the firm's own economic reasons may force such co-operation. The astute choice of partners is essential to the venture's success, as disputes can be time consuming and expensive. It is important that the partners work to establish and develop a relationship which will evolve over time.

A contractual joint venture is of fixed duration, with the specific duties of each partner well defined. Under such a scheme, a company contracts a manufacturer abroad to produce its product and provide all supporting services in the market. There is, of course, a loss of control in this arrangement, but if it works it can lead to closer co-operation between the companies, and certainly involves less capital than direct investment in production facilities.

The relationship between internationalization theories and market entry modes

While the Johanson and Vahlne model emphasizes managerial learning, the internationalization process is also reflected in the mechanisms used for mode of entry. For example, firms improve their foreign market knowledge through initial expansion with low risk, indirect exporting approaches to similar, 'psychically close' markets. Over time and through experience, firms then increase their foreign market commitment. This in turn enhances market knowledge, leading to further commitment, including equity investment in off-shore manufacturing and sales operations. Interestingly, in the same way recent FDI literature captures the concept of organizational learning, the Johanson and Vahlne model encapsulates the essence of FDI whereby the firm is ultimately expected to internalize its activities, by moving over time from purely domestic operations to finally establishing host country production.

Interestingly, Johanson and Vahlne's more recent perspective has evolved somewhat from their early work, and reflects their ongoing research exploring the management of foreign market entry. For example, their 1992 study of internationalization in the context of exchange networks found that although foreign market entry is a gradual process (reflecting their original stage model), it results from interaction, and the development and maintenance of relationships over time. These findings support Sharma and Johanson (1987), who found that technical consultancy firms operate in networks of connected relationships between organizations, where relationships become 'bridges to foreign markets,' and provide firms with the opportunity and motivation to internationalize. This view is supported by other authors who argue that network relationships provide a firm with access to external resources (Jarillo, 1989), new market contacts, and enhanced flexibility and market reputation (Bridgewater, 1992). Related to this, Johanson and Mattsson (1988) suggest that a firm's success in entering new international markets is more dependent on its relationships within current markets than on market and cultural characteristics.

Whatever method of entry is chosen, it is important to minimize the risk of failure. Careful planning and good preparation for market entry can help to offset unforeseen setbacks in the market entry process. Success can never be taken for granted and failure can never be eliminated entirely, but the research literature does point to some key characteristics of successes and failures which will be discussed in the next section.

Success and failure in the internationalization process

There is often almost an obsession with trying to know in advance if a venture is going to be successful. Partly the attitude of an individual relates to their own perception of risk. Some decision makers are prepared to jump with only 50% certainty or less, while others are highly risk averse and will only jump when they think they have 95% certainty or more! Nothing ventured, nothing gained is not a bad maxim for business. If taking risks is not for you, try a different career. On the other hand, there is some literature in entrepreneurship which suggests that entrepreneurs never take risks, because they have so carefully assimilated the information needed that they know they are onto a winner.

Of course nothing can guarantee success; not even a monopoly situation in the long-term, as many state owned businesses have found to their cost throughout the world. The environment does not stand still. Market awareness and knowledge is important, as Box 4.7 illustrates. However, the very best information gathering exercise is only as good as the interpretation or spin put upon it by the individuals concerned. There is perhaps a rather understated view, which says that marketing cannot guarantee success, but that an enterprise will fail less badly because of it. Marketers should be a little bolder than this at least!

BOX 4.7: MARKET ENTRY – GETTING IT WRONG

Not everything goes smoothly all the time for market entry and the literature is full of famous errors. Failure can occur for all sorts of reasons, e.g. poor intermediaries, poor communication, not getting paid.

For one company attempting to exploit the Dutch market from a base in the UK, failure was based on poor market research. A showroom was opened in Holland to sell female clothing. The company attempted to simply transfer the product to the new market, and in so doing made the mistake in marketing of giving the market the wrong product. Colours and styles which had gone down well in England were found to be unacceptable in the Dutch market. The company also encountered problems with regard to the size of its garments. It did not take into account the difference in stature between customers in the two markets. The company found, too late, that the Dutch customer was taller and larger than its UK market. Formal market research would have revealed the special characteristics of the new market, and allowed the company to adapt its products to the fashion tastes of the Dutch buyers.

In hindsight the company had learnt a lot as the interviewee stated: 'I think that if the company is going to go into the Dutch market then you have to sort of cater for their way of thinking. You maybe have to hire Dutch designers if you go into things like that because it is so specialized. They are different people – its like the French, they have a different attitude towards fashion'.

So what are the factors which influence success in the internationalization process and what should be done to guard against failure? Various studies have attempted to identify the elements which are crucial to the success of the export venture. These include:

- Having a long-term view
- Being committed to 'exporting'
- Finding good representation
- Paying attention to detail
- Being focused on customer service
- Being flexible and patient.

Much of the literature focuses on exporting success because, as we have seen before, this is the dominant internationalization activity for most businesses. Attention has been given to the degree of export experience, i.e. experienced exporters versus new exporters; or to how the export intensity (exports as a percentage of total turnover) relates to the level of internationalization, size of the firm or product type.

While smaller firms can be active exporters as we shall see in Chapter 5, the larger company does have the advantages of greater human resources and financial strength. There is an assumption then that they have more spare capacity to devote to internationalization activities while benefiting from economies of scale. At the same time they perceive less risk in international markets, which gives them added confidence. On the other hand Aaby and Slater (1989) in their review of the literature find contrary evidence, which suggests that small firms are not inhibited by their size and can in fact benefit from it.

Often a broad distinction is made between products devoted to the consumer market and those serving the business to business or organizational market. Partly because of the cultural differences between international markets, goods for the consumer market are subject to greater scrutiny than those destined for the business market. This is especially true where the exported products are component parts to be incorporated or consumed in the production of another product. Thus the route to export success in the business market can be more straightforward. So then what are the key success factors?

Export success factors

Not surprisingly the marketing activities of a business have some influence on the success of a venture. Within the literature a number of factors have been identified; these include:

- Market selection
- Product strategy
- Packaging characteristics
- Pricing strategy
- Credit strategy
- Communication strategy
- Distribution strategy
- After sales support
- Experience of staff.

Other authors have identified firm-specific characteristics including:

- Technology intensity
- Planning process
- International networks
- Quality control
- Financial strength.

Of course success is dependent on the context within which the business finds itself. Thus, the third group of success factors relate to the external environment, namely:

- Friendly diplomatic relations
- Trade pacts and agreements
- Export subsidies and support (including information provision, tax breaks)
- Low trade barriers (tariffs and other trading restrictions)
- Stable political and trading environment
- Good infrastructure.

Inevitably a number of models exist in the literature which attempt to pull together the determinants of export marketing performance. Cavusgil and Nason (1991) selected the following variables: organization characteristics, management characteristics, top management commitment, product and marketing strengths, suitability of product to the market. Aaby and Slater (1989) included technology, market knowledge, planning, marketing strategy, organizational size, commitment and expected profit. More succinct models of export determinants were proposed by Louter et al. (1991) and Holzmuller and Kasper (1991). The former included company, attitude, and strategy characteristics and the latter grouped the determinants into culture, business and manager characteristics.

Based on an extensive literature review, Valos and Baker (1996) attempted to identify tangible and intangible export performance determinants. While the study was based within the Australian context it clearly has a wider resonance.

Thus the tangible determinants were:

- Distribution – inadequate channel relationships prevent successful export marketing
- Product – having a unique product, product packaging, willingness to adapt products, good quality, and good pre/after sales service
- Customer contact – frequent customer contact assists export success
- Control – having good management control systems
- Research and development – provides new and innovative products
- Technology – those able to apply technology are more successful
- Supplier – having suppliers who perform reliably
- Finance – under capitalization of activities hinders performance.

While the intangible factors were identified as:
  (i) Attitudinal

- Management commitment – persistence and involvement are crucial
- Perceived importance – exporting is seen as attractive, with the possibility of higher returns than in the domestic market
- Export orientation – having an international outlook or vision
- Confidence – being confident and having a positive attitude to risk.

(ii) Skill related factors included:

- Management – education levels of the managers and the close interaction between managers and workers
- Marketing – lack of, or poor, marketing planning and analysis can cause export failure
- Export specific skills – foreign language skills, knowledge of export procedures and financing expertise, experience of living and working internationally.

(iii) Knowledge:

- Knowledge – lack of foreign market knowledge affects export success.

Success rarely comes automatically and in export marketing, as with many other activities, it requires careful planning, commitment and perhaps most importantly having a product or service that customers actually want. For the smaller firm making use of networks and knowing when and how to obtain advice and information can also be an important contributor to success. The people involved in any business must believe that the world is the market. For the entrepreneurs and the entrepreneurs within organizations, opportunities are there if you look for them and you should nurture an 'attack mentality'. Flexibility, especially in mode of market entry is important, so that a business is prepared to work with agents, distributors or enter into joint ventures to exploit opportunities. You may not succeed first time, but there will be plenty of advice on offer to assist you (Box 4.8) if you know where to find it.

BOX 4.8: HOW TO SUCCEED IN INTERNATIONAL BUSINESS (BY REALLY TRYING).

1. Focus on key markets. Each market generally requires its own unique adaptations; successfully establishing a position in each takes considerable commitment.
2. Control the important elements. Let local managers control the downstream activities with the corporate management concentrating on technology, product and investment decisions.
3. Reduce the investment burden. Worry about control rather than ownership. Use agents, distributors and joint ventures, which reduce the investment required.
4. Pursue a phased development. Develop a multinational approach with units serving specific areas, rather than units everywhere serving the whole world.
5. Implement the strategy well. Use well qualified managers with local knowledge, including foreign nationals.
6. Follow exports with investment. To gain insider status, invest in marketing and sales networks, production facilities, perhaps even R&D capacity.
7. Think internationally.

Adapted from McClenahen (1988)

Conclusions

Internationalization, therefore, is not a process which can be easily simplified. The heterogeneous nature of firms makes the emergence of a generally applicable theory or model of the process extremely difficult to achieve. There are many questions left to answer. Do we need to start with an agreed definition and, perhaps, some sub-definitions or is a common definition to be built up from the different research strands which have emerged? Can more cross-fertilization between different disciplines and research ideas be encouraged? Can better methodologies be designed on an international basis and involving longitudinal studies? Can the work be made more relevant to the exporter and the policy maker providing them with best practice recommendations? Can more reflective articles be produced, leading to an acceptable paradigm of internationalization and perhaps above all, while acknowledging the difficulties in researching SME internationalization, can enough debate and discussion be stimulated to make future research efforts more focused?

While interest in internationalization will continue to attract much attention from academics and policy makers, who will address many of the questions above, it must be remembered that firms will carry on developing new international strategies as the business world evolves in the 21st Century. This almost inevitable drive towards 'globalization' has been illustrated in previous research which incorporates the key themes of this chapter, namely, the stage approach, motives and market entry.

Experience has shown that while the stimulus for involvement, together with the chosen mode of entry, does vary by firm and market, there does appear to be a growing enthusiasm exhibited by the firm once international activity is underway (Figure 4.1). What emerges is that, while passive firms displayed little active involvement in the early phases they, like their more active counterparts, display more enthusiasm for international activities as internationalization moves into the middle stages of development. At this stage all the firms were actively seeking growth. These firms were too young to discover what will happen in the later stages of internationalization, but an extension of the trend would suggest that the general forward thrust of their involvement will continue.

These findings are encouraging in that casual or accidental exporting does seem to encourage firms to upgrade their international activities, even when they have not been at the forefront of developing these markets. A great deal of progress has been made over the last 25 years in attempting to understand SME internationalization, and there is currently much research interest in understanding networks better, and greater use of qualitative and longitudinal methodologies which will do much to enhance our understanding of the internationalization process. Success in all of this cannot be guaranteed for the smaller firm, but we are better able now to understand what influences the global performance of the SME.

```
                    The Internationalisation Process

                                        INTERNATIONALISATION PHASE

  STIMULUS          MODE           EARLY              MIDDLE          LATE
  _____

                    E*           ACTIVE           A
  PUSH --------- X ----- INVOLVEMENT ----- C  S        -----> ?
                    P                              T  E  G
                    O            LITTLE            I  E  R
  PASSIVE------- R ----- INVOLVEMENT ----- V  K  O -----> ?
                    T                              E  I  W
                    I            ACTIVE            L  N  T
  PULL---------- N ----- INVOLVEMENT ----- Y  G  W -----> ?
                    G
  _____
```

Figure 4.1　The internationalization process. Source: author.
* for example exporting.

Questions for discussion

1. What would your suggestion be for a definition of internationalization? Is it any different for firms from different sectors or industries? Does size, however measured, make any difference?

2. What do you understand by the terms: psychically close or psychically distant markets?

3. Discuss the contribution of the stages model in understanding the internationalization process. Do you agree it is intuitively appealing as an explanation? Why?

4. Can you find any examples of firms in your country (nationally or locally) who are internationalized? How have they achieved internationalization? Can you apply any of the theories of internationalization reviewed in this chapter to their behaviour? Can you provide a better way of explaining how they have internationalized?

5. Select an international company and using secondary sources (company websites may be useful) see if you can piece together the pattern of their international expansion. What does this pattern reveal?

6. Discuss why some firms might not wish to become involved in exporting or international marketing?

7. Is it possible to classify the modes of market entry by degree of commitment required, available resources, and motivation? Are any other dimensions required? What, in your view, is the central determinant of choice of mode?

8. Why are joint ventures a popular mode of market entry?

9. Success in international marketing is difficult, if not impossible, to guarantee. What do you think are the most vital elements of success? Can you classify the elements into distinctive groupings?

10. Can a firm succeed in exporting or international marketing without being good at marketing? Discuss and justify your response.

References

Aaby, N.E. and Slater, S.F. (1989), Management influences on export performance: a review of the empirical literature 1978–88, *International Marketing Review*, 6 (4), pp. 7–20.

Aharoni, Y. (1966), *The Foreign Investment Decision Process*, Graduate School of Business Administration, Harvard University, Boston, MA.

Barrett, N.I. and Wilkinson, I.F. (1986), Internationalization behaviour: management characteristics of Australian manufacturing firms by level of international development, in: Turnbull, P.W. and Paliwoda, S.J. (eds.) *Research in International Marketing*, Croom Helm, London, pp. 213–233.

Beamish, P.W. (1990), The internationalization process for smaller Ontario firms: a research agenda, in: Rugman, A.M. (ed.), *Research in Global Strategic Management - International Business Research for the Twenty-First Century: Canada's New Research Agenda*, JAI Press Inc, Greenwich, pp. 77–92.

Bilkey, W.J. and Tesar, G. (1977), The export behaviour of smaller Wisconsin manufacturing firms, *Journal of International Business Studies*, 8 (1), pp. 93–98.

Bridgewater, S. (1992), *Informal Networks as a Vehicle of International Market Entry: Future*

Research Directions, Warwick Business School Research Paper No. 54, University of Warwick.

Buckley, P.J., Pass, C.L. and Prescott, K. (1990), Measures of international competitiveness: empirical findings from British manufacturing companies, *Journal of Marketing Management*, 4 (2), pp. 175–200.

Cavusgil, S.T. (1982), Some observations on the relevance of critical variables for internationalization stages, in: Czinkota, M.R. and Tesar, G (eds.) *Export Management: An International Context*, Praeger, New York.

Cavusgil, S.T. and Nason, J. (1991), Assessment of company readiness to export, in: Cavusgil, S.T. and Thorelli, H. (eds.), *International Marketing Strategy*, Pergamon Press, Oxford.

Crick, D. (1995), An investigation into the targeting of UK export assistance, *European Journal of Marketing*, 29 (8), pp. 76–94.

Czinkota, M.R. (1982), *Export Development Strategies: US Promotion Policy*, Praeger, New York.

Granovetter, M.S. (1985), Economic action and social structure: the problem of embeddedness, *American Journal of Sociology*, 91 (3), pp. 481–510.

Holzmuller, H.H. and Kasper, H. (1991), On a theory of export performance: personal and organizational determinants of export trade activities observed in small and medium-sized firms, *Management International Review*, Special Issue, pp. 45–70.

Jarillo, J.C. (1989), Entrepreneurship and growth: the strategic use of external resources, *Journal of Business Venturing*, 4 (2), pp. 133–147.

Johanson, J. and Mattsson, L.G. (1988), Internationalization in industrial systems - a network approach, in: Hood, N. and Vahlne, J.-E. (eds.), *Strategies in Global Competition*. Croom Helm, London, pp. 287–314.

Johanson, J. and Vahlne, J.-E. (1977), The internationalization process of the firm - a model of knowledge development and increasing foreign market commitments, *Journal of International Business Studies*, Spring/Summer, pp. 23–32.

Johanson, J. and Vahlne, J.-E. (1990), The mechanism of internationalization, *International Marketing Review*, 7 (4), pp. 11–24.

Johanson, J. and Vahlne, J.-E. (1992), Management of foreign market entry, *Scandinavian International Business Review*, 1 (3), pp. 9–27.

Johanson, J. and Wiedersheim-Paul, F. (1975), The internationalization of the firm - four Swedish cases, *Journal of Management Studies*, 12 (3), pp. 305–322.

Joynt, P. and Welch, L. (1985),A strategy for small business internationalisation, *International Marketing Review*, 2 (3), pp. 64–73.

Lim, J-S., Sharkey, T.W. and Kim, K.I. (1991), An empirical test of an export adoption model, *Management International Review*, 31 (1), pp. 51–62.

Louter, P.J., Ouwerkirk, C. and Bakkar, B.A. (1991), An inquiry into successful exporting, *European Journal of Marketing*, 25 (6), pp. 7–23.

McAuley, A. (1999), Entrepreneurial instant exporters in the Scottish arts and crafts sector, *Journal of International Marketing*, 7 (4), pp. 67–82.

McClenahen, J.S. (1988), How U.S. entrepreneurs succeed in world markets: they think positively - and globally, *Industry Week*, 236 (9), p. 47; (3) InfoTrac http://www.galegroup.com/

Melin, L. (1992), Internationalization as a strategy process, *Strategic Management Journal*, 13, pp. 99–118.

Moon, J. and Lee, H. (1990), On the internal correlates of export stage development: an empirical investigation in the Korean electronics industry, *International Marketing Review*, 7 (5), pp. 16–26.

Rao, T.R. and Naidu, G.M. (1992), Are the stages of internationalization empirically supportable? *Journal of Global Marketing*, 6 (1/2), pp. 147–170.

Sharma, D. (1992), International business research: issues and trends, *Scandinavian International Business Review*, 1 (3), pp. 3–8.

Sharma, D.D. and Johanson, J. (1987), Technical consultancy in internationalisation. *International Marketing Review*, 4 (4), pp. 20–29.

Valos, M. and Baker, M. (1996), Developing an Australian model of export marketing performance determinants, *Marketing Intelligence and Planning*, 14 (3), pp. 11–20.

Wiedersheim-Paul, F., Olson, H.C. and Welch, L.S. (1978), Pre-export activity: the first step in internationalization, *Journal of International Business Studies*, 9 (1), pp. 47–58.

Wortzel, L.H. and Wortzel, H.V. (1981), Export marketing strategies for NIC and LDC-based firms, *Columbia Journal of World Business*, Spring, pp. 51–60.

Yanacek, F. (1988), The road to exports, *Transportation and Distribution*, 29 (2),pp. 32–36.

Yanagida, I. (1992), The business network: a powerful and challenging business tool, *Journal of Business Venturing*, 7 (5), pp. 341–346.

Further reading

Bartlett, C.A. and Ghoshal, S. (2000), Going global: lessons from late movers, *Harvard Business Review*, 78 (2), pp. 132–142.

Bridgewater, S. (1999), Networks and internationalisation: the case of multinational corporations entering Ukraine, *International Business Review* 8 (1), pp. 99–118.

Chetty, S.K. (1999), Dimensions of internationalistion of manufacturing firms in the apparel industry, *European Journal of Marketing*, 33 (1/2), pp. 121–142.

Chetty, S. and Holm, D.B. (2000), Internationalisation of small to medium-sized manufacturing firms: a network approach, *International Business Review*, 9 (1), pp. 77–93.

Coviello, N. and McAuley, A. (1999), Internationalisation processes and the smaller firm: a review of contemporary empirical research, *Management International Review*, 39 (3), pp. 223–256.

Holmlund, M. and Kock, S. (1998), Relationships and the internationalisation of Finnish small and medium-sized companies, *International Small Business Journal*, 16 (4), pp. 46–63.

Keogh, W., Jack, S.L., Bower, D.J. and Crabtree, E. (1998), Small technology-based firms in the UK oil and gas industry: innovation and internationalisation strategies, *International Small Business Journal*, 17 (1), pp. 57–72.

Leonidas, C.L. and Adams-Florou, A.S. (1999), Types and sources of export information: insights from small business, *International Small Business Journal, 17 (3), pp. 30–48.*

Leonidou, L. and Katsikeas, C. (1996), The export development process: an integrative review of empirical models, *Journal of International Business Studies*, 27 (3), pp. 517–551.

Morgan, R.E. and Katsikeas, C.S. (1997), Theories of international trade, foreign direct investment and firm internationalisation: a critique, *Management Decision*, 35 (1/2), pp. 68–79.

Muniz-Martinez, N. (1998), The internationalisation of European retailers in America: the US experience, *International Journal of Retail and Distribution Management*, 26 (10), p. 29; (9) InfoTrac http://www.galegroup.com/

O'Farrell, P.N., Wood, P.A. and Zheng, J. (1998), Internationalisation by business service SMEs: an inter-industry analysis, *International Small Business Journal*, 16 (2), pp. 13–33.

Sluyterman, K.A. (1998), The internationalisation of Dutch accounting firms, *Business History*, 40 (2), p. 1; (21) InfoTrac http://www.galegroup.com/

Stewart, D.B. and McAuley, A. (1999), The effects of export stimulation: implications for export performance, *Journal of Marketing Management*, 15 (6), pp. 505–518.

Tesar, G. and Moini, A.H. (1998), Longitudinal study of exporters and nonexporters: a focus on smaller manufacturing enterprises, *International Business Review*, 7 (3), pp. 291–313.

CHAPTER 5

SMEs: key players in a global economy

Chapter objectives

- What is meant by the term small and medium sized enterprise (SME) and how it is defined
- Their key characteristics
- Their contribution to the global economy
- The constraints and opportunities which they face
- The skills and competencies they require to be successful

Introduction

A popular myth is that it is more difficult for small firms to become involved in exporting or international marketing. This is usually based on three interrelated issues:

- Smaller firms have less awareness and knowledge of foreign markets and so their confidence, competence and ambitions are limited
- They cannot achieve the same economies of scale as larger firms in relation to production, international marketing or administration
- They lack the necessary financial and managerial resources.

The empirical evidence to support this view has been mixed. In fact some studies have suggested that the smaller firm can be more flexible in international trade, and can therefore be a formidable competitive force. Many countries have recognized the potential importance of the SME to their future growth. Consequently governments have been supportive of the development of indigenous small and medium sized firms as a way of increasing their participation in the global economy.

This is a reversal of the trend experienced in many countries since the 1950s. At that time the drive was to expand business and to achieve economies of scale, and until the mid-1970s employment in small businesses throughout the world was declining. This has now been reversed and in countries as diverse as Australia and South Korea, SMEs are responsible for a significant and growing share of export activity. This is true in many European countries as well as in the US and Japan (see Box 5.1 for a US example).

BOX 5.1: JOIN THE GLOBETROTTERS (ADAPTED FROM BUSINESS WEEK, 1999)

During the first 7 months of 1999 exports in the US reached $545.7 billion, which is up $2.2 billion on the same period in 1998. Evidence that smaller firms are contributing to this is derived from the value of loans guaranteed by the Small Business Administration. These have risen by 600% since its inception in 1994. The 1998 figure of $159.1 million in loans was up 12% from 1997. The sector benefiting from this are small technology consulting firms, software companies and suppliers to large retailers. The hottest market for these smaller exporters is in Europe.

This resurgence can be identified as being the result of:

- Changing consumer preferences increasing demand for specialized, not standardized, products, and the ability of smaller firms to adapt their product offerings to meet emerging market needs
- Changing manufacturing techniques. Until the 1960s, process innovation favoured large scale operations seeking economies of scale. Now new production technology based on electronic processes allow smaller firms to complete on cost and quality with larger firms
- Developments in IT. New technologies allow information to travel quickly and cheaply, thus the competitive advantage of being a large vertically integrated company – when information flows were expensive and slow – has been removed
- Changing competitive conditions. As product life cycles shorten and consumer taste change more rapidly, the smaller firm is often more adaptable and cost effective.

A recent study (Voss et al., 1998) of 297 SMEs in Europe (Italy, UK, Belgium, Denmark, Germany, Ireland and Sweden) found that only three (1%) of the companies reached world class standards. However, over half the SMEs had the potential to compete internationally given growth, improvement and perseverance. SMEs were judged to be customer orientated, response focused, and concerned with new products. Their competitive edge comes from speed, responsiveness and a closeness to customers. It would appear that the time is ripe for the smaller firm to play a significant role in the global marketplace. The aim of this chapter is to highlight some of the issues which SMEs face in the global economy. Thus the next section ('What are SMEs?') will explore how SMEs are defined internationally, before going on to the following section to look at the characteristics of the smaller firm. The constraints and opportunities faced by SMEs will then be discussed. This is followed by an examination of the skills and competencies needed by SME exporters. This section will make reference to culture, information needs, strategic alliance, training and support for SMEs.

What are SMEs?

One of the difficulties of talking about small or medium sized firms in a global context is the fact that the terms 'small' and 'medium' mean different things to different people. It is difficult to see how one definition based solely on size would be applicable throughout the world. Further, definitions which are suitable for the organization of national statistics often make little or no sense at the regional or local scale. Thus, a country may regard a company of 200 or fewer employees as small yet at the local level it may be the most important employer in the locale. The impact of economic cycles can also be dramatic, for example, many westernized economies have experienced a shaking out of employment from older heavy industries, which were relatively labour intensive compared to the newer 'sunrise' industries in electronics and biotechnology. Therefore in considering classifications based on size, it should be noted that this is only one dimension and does not place the company in its full context.

As there is no standard agreement on what constitutes a small or medium sized firm, research conducted into such firms also displays a variety of standards. This, of course, makes the direct comparison of results more problematic. Researchers have used a mixture of employment size or turnover figures to define small. For example, Culpan (1989); Ali and Swiercz (1991) used sales of $5 million or less; Rabino (1980) called firms with less than $10 million in sales as small. While Beamish et al. (1993) had a cut-off point of $25 million or less to separate small from medium. Using numbers of employees Samimee and Walters (1990) used 1–99 employees to define small; Reid (1984) defined small Canadian enterprises as between 100 and 500 employees; Roy and Simpson (1981) selected 500 or less to classify small from medium; Voss et al. (1998) defined micro as 5–20 employees, small 21–50 and medium as 51–200.

Perhaps one of the most pragmatic definitions derives from the first major report into small firms in the UK. This was the Bolton Report (1971) which argued that a small firm was:

- An independent business
- Managed by its owner or part owners; and
- Had a small market share.

The UK Companies Act of 1985 defines small and medium as laid out in Table 5.1.

In order to collect and organize statistics the Department of Trade and Industry uses the following scale, which is probably one of the most useful definitions, based on size, namely:

Table 5.1   Definitions of size

Criterion	Small firm	Medium firm
Turnover	Not more than £2.8 million	Not more than £11.2 million
Balance sheet	Not more than £1.4 million	Not more than £5.6 million
Employees	Not more than 50	Not more than 250

- Micro 0–9 employees
- Small 0–99 employees (includes micro)
- Medium 50–249 employees
- Large over 250 employees.

As we have seen, there is variation even within national boundaries, so how much more difficult is it to obtain a consensus internationally? The EU has attempted to adhere to a standard definition to allow for a cross-EU comparison. Before such a scheme was introduced the standards were very variable, for example, the UK used to regard small as 200 employees or less from the time of the Bolton Report in 1971. In Holland by comparison the measure was 100 employees or less. The current EU definition is detailed in Table 5.2.

While the EU now provides a common standard, the problems of international definition are still enormous. In the US, for example, many of the statistics are based on small firms being those with 500 or fewer employees. New Zealand uses the following classification: micro (0–5), small (1–19), medium (20–99) and large (100+).

The discussion suggests that a size based definition of the small firm is perhaps too crude a measure on which to focus. Alternatively, Paliwoda and Thomas (1998) suggested that the criteria which are important are those which place the company in the context of its absolute and relative size in the national market place in which it operates. Interestingly their approach is not that different from the 1971 suggestion by The Bolton Committee. Thus a small firm is characterized by:

- Having only a small share of the market
- Being managed in a personalized way by its owners or part owners, and does not have an elaborate management structure

Table 5.2   EU SME definitions [a]

Criterion	Micro	Small	Medium
Maximum number of employees	10	50	250
Maximum annual turnover	–	7 mecu	40 mecu
Maximum annual balance sheet total	–	5 mecu	27 mecu
Maximum % owned by one, or jointly by several enterprises(s) not satisfying the same criteria	–	25%	25%

[a] To qualify as an SME, both the employee and the independence criteria must be satisfied and either the turnover or the balance sheet total criteria.

- Not being large enough to have access to the capital market for the public issue or placing of securities.

Once a company breaches any of these criteria it has ceased to be a small firm.

Regardless of how size is measured, a number of authors have pointed to the important contribution which SMEs make to national economies. Storey (1994) asserts that irrespective of how size is measured, the majority of enterprises in Europe (85–99.5% according to definition) are small and medium sized. Again, depending on the size criteria used, they account for one-third to one-half of private sector employment in Europe. In Taiwan SMEs make up 98.5% of the total number of companies, 75–80% of all employment and 47% of the total economy (The Economist, 1998). Some countries, for example, South Africa, are still to experience the growth of SMEs. Kaplinsky and Manning (1998) report that SMEs (defined as 1–99 employees) are responsible for less than 20% of manufacturing employment.

It is important to bear their contribution, real or potential, in mind, and not to become swamped by measures of size. While, as we have seen, there is a lack of universal agreement on how SMEs are defined, there is probably more consensus on their key characteristics as we shall explore in the next section.

Characteristics of SMEs

From inception the one issue which dominates the mind of the small business owner is how to survive. Many small businesses fail within the first 3 years of being in business, so it is not surprising that survival is uppermost in the mind of the owner. If the 3 year barrier is crossed, then the small firm is perhaps in a position to begin to grow and develop. There is much literature related to this issue and, of course, not all firms wish to grow beyond a certain comfort level.

Small firms are not just little versions of big firms. Larger firms are inherently more complex in their organization and structure. They will be divided into more functional or specialized departments, with many layers of management. This leads to an increasingly complex decision making process as the layers of management increase. Although small firms are simpler than this, they too can exhibit complex attitudes, behaviour and decision making, depending on the personality of the owner manager, where the responsibility for decision making resides. This is unlike the case in a larger firm, where the complexities of different management levels will, in theory at least, produce a more rational form of decision making.

It sometimes seems that the smaller firm is perhaps over criticized for being too reactive in its environment rather than forging ahead in a buoyant fashion. Thus smaller firms are often characterized as having:

- Too regional a focus
- Undertaking only limited market research
- Being reactive; responding to unsolicited orders
- Making little or no use of public or private support agencies

- Concentrating on personal visits, agents and trade fairs to sell products/services.

The traditional pattern of these firms is to establish a domestic presence first and then to export. This approach links to the theories of internationalization discussed in Chapter 4. Thus, these firms have:

- Their core business well established
- Good business skills
- Solid financial capability
- Sound product portfolio.

They then turn their attention to the potential for growth offered by the international market. Even when this becomes a feature of their activities, the main focus of the business remains the domestic market, and any competitive threat there often results in the neglect of international markets. In a study in Australia, Rennie (1993) identified these firms as being on average 27 years old before exporting began, and as having approximately 20% of their sales derived from exports.

However, this picture of rather sluggish entry into the international arena is at best unfair, and a highly inaccurate representation of the experience of many small firms, and not just those in the high-technology sector. It is important to realize that, far from being constrained by these traditional views of 'smallness', some small firms can take on the world market and win from day one. While evidence (Young, 1987; Hedlund and Kverneland, 1984) has been around for some time of rapid and more direct internationalization, it has normally been associated with high-technology based sectors. Indeed some authors, for example, Burrill and Almassy (1993), view internationalization as a 'requirement' for newly formed ventures in the electronics sector.

Case study evidence of the 'born international' syndrome has been highlighted by a number of authors, who have produced some interesting material although the emphasis is, once again, on advanced technology firms (Box 5.2).

BOX 5.2: BORN GLOBAL DOWN UNDER

Exports account for 95% of Cochlear's $440 million sales. This Australian company produces implants for the profoundly deaf. Its international strategy is based on a technological lead which is maintained by strong links with hospitals and research units around the world. In addition it undertakes collaborative research with a network of institutions in its own domestic market and in Switzerland, Germany and in the US. It is a prime example of a company that was 'born global' (Rennie, 1993).

International new ventures are defined by Oviatt and McDougall (1994) as 'a business organization that, from inception, seeks to derive significant competitive advantage from the use of resources and the sale of outputs in multiple countries'. For them, some of the international new ventures are able to link resources from multiple countries to meet the demand of markets that are inherently international.

Others have an international vision from the outset, an innovative product or service marketed through a strong network and a tightly managed organization focused on international sales growth. Success for these companies requires more than simply applying successful domestic strategies abroad, as McDougall and Oviatt (1996) found; it appears to demand changes in the overall strategy of the organization.

Evidence from a study of 300 Australian companies also reveals the rapid internationalization of SMEs (Rennie, 1993). These companies, operating within the high value-added manufacturing sector, managed to attain as much as 76% of their sales from exports after only 2 years of operation. On average these firms were only 14 years old and were responsible for 20 of Australia's high value-added manufacturing exports.

For 40% of these companies the key competitive lever was technology. This allows them to offer superior quality and value based on innovative technology and product design. Being close to their customer was seen as being vital to success. Thus, by seeking out a particular group of customers, and by understanding and satisfying their needs better than anyone else in the world, they created a market with virtually no competitors. With this philosophy many of the companies ran the business efficiently with the help of the humble fax. A simple fax machine allowed them to run cheap and responsive sales and service operations with customers in different time zones and languages. After an initial sales trip to meet the customer this is how the business was conducted.

Rapid internationalization is not just confined to high-value added sectors or high-technology products. The author has found evidence of 'instant internationals', defined as firms achieving international business within one year of start-up, within what might be regarded as the relatively sleepy sector of arts and crafts companies. Profiles of three of these companies are presented in Box 5.3.

BOX 5.3: PROFILES OF THREE INSTANT INTERNATIONALS

Company 1
  This company was founded in 1993 and is located in the central belt of Scotland. The founder is a textile designer who produces fashion and furnishing accessories. Her entry into the export markets occurred after a contact, one of the judges at her final degree show who liked her work, showed it to knitwear designers she knew in Germany, Holland and Ireland. These designers also liked her work and the first export orders followed. Since then she has also exported to Japan. This clearly illustrates the value of network, and the fact that the move was unplanned by the entrepreneur herself.

Company 2
  This weaving company was founded in the far North of Scotland in 1991 and is involved in the production of fashion accessories. The key influence here on their exporting activity was that a previous company had existed from 1986 to 1990. Crucially, the international networks developed by the designer associated with the original company were maintained by the new company as a part of their business

strategy. This planned use of networks paved the way for the international success and the company now has agents in France, Italy, Japan and the US. Indeed the company's entire turnover has traditionally come from export markets. It is only since 1995 that the domestic market has been given serious marketing consideration.

Company 3

This young company, founded in 1995, is located North of Inverness and is involved with jewellery design and making. The entry to the export market occurred when at a trade fair in London. The entrepreneur was approached by a Japanese buyer for a small gallery in Yokohama City. The buyer 'liked the design, then the price'. The gallery has since reordered and the company is seeking to extend its business in Japan. Clearly in this case the trade fair was a crucial catalyst in the beginning of exporting, but from the entrepreneur's point of view it was an unplanned development.

With this kind of evidence, perhaps we should be less critical of the smaller firm and see it in a more positive framework. Firms large or small all have the possibility to get involved in the global market. What often makes the difference is the drive and determination of the individual involved. It is this more than anything which defines the direction a business will go in. The smaller firm will have a very different experience to the larger firm, but a different set of constraints simply leads to a different set of opportunities as we shall see in the next section.

Constraints and opportunities for SMEs

In entering the international market the smaller firm will experience a number of challenges. Its response to these challenges helps to determine the framework of constraints and opportunities within which it will operate. Often the most significant challenge for the small firm is the increased cost of doing business internationally. Indeed this is often perceived as being higher than it actually is, and can result in companies deciding not to enter the international market. A substantial investment of time and resources is required in order to succeed. Patience is required as planning is time consuming as new legal, financial, production and marketing issues have to be investigated. Add to this the need for long distance travel and an appreciation of cultural issues and it is possible to appreciate the impact that exploiting international opportunities can have on a small firm. Box 5.4 provides one version of a practical guide to knowing if a business is ready to face the world markets.

BOX 5.4: ARE YOU READY FOR INTERNATIONAL BUSINESS?

Q. How will I know if my company is ready for international business?

A. A company that succeeds in international ventures often exhibits many of the following characteristics:

1. Exceptional domestic demand for a product and a demonstrated international market.
2. Decline in domestic sales of a product after more technically advanced competitors have been introduced. This product could be exported to economies at earlier stages of the technology life cycle.
3. A unique product that is difficult to duplicate abroad.
4. Secure capitalization, operations and management to sustain an international venture.
5. Strong relationship with creditors.
6. The ability to expand staff and facilities if necessary.
7. An understanding of global markets and the willingness to devote the necessary time and resources to a new venture.
8. Senior management's commitment to provide resources and direction.
9. Personnel experienced or trained in international business.

(adapted from Murray, 1993)

There can be many factors which contribute to constraining export growth and development, for example, the company may experience delays because of language differences, laws and regulations, accounting and legal systems, business practices, and currency problems. The smaller firm is held back by the very obvious lack of resources which it will often have. This covers issues from straightforward lack of capital, to a multitude of human resource constraints related to its skill base, to practical operating problems of managing a number of international markets.

A study by Prince (1995) into the export performance of Dutch companies found that although size was a discriminating factor between exporting and non-exporting firms, the larger firms did not export a larger share of their sales than the smaller companies. Other discriminating factors between exporters and non-exporters included: emphasis on competitive strategies, and ability to speak a foreign language.

Firms who derived more of their sales from exports had the following management characteristics: higher number of foreign languages spoken; greater active search for export orders; greater number of weeks spent abroad; and ownership of subsidiaries abroad. As can been seen some of these factors are tautological but within the literature the following problems have often been highlighted:

Constraints on export growth

Exchange rates

Exporting companies always find it harder to sell their goods and services abroad when the value of their domestic currency is high. Thus, for the international customer it takes a lot more of their currency to buy a particular good. If the value of the exporter's domestic currency falls, then the good becomes cheaper for the international customer to acquire. In situations where the domestic currency is highly valued, businesses will find goods harder to sell and experience reduced profits. Most smaller businesses will try and maintain their market position during such periods rather than lose market share to competitors.

Getting paid

Problems can occur in getting paid for the smaller business. Internationally there are countries with good and bad reputations for paying on time. Surprisingly it is not always the more 'obscure' who are bad payers, for example, within Europe France, Germany, Italy and Spain all have a reputation for a poor payment record. More will be said about payment methods in Chapter 9 but generally speaking many companies will trade on open account with local and other long standing and well known customers. Once outside the local region business is more likely to be cash with order, letter of credit, cash on delivery, or cash on shipment.

Payment problems can make companies more cautious about their expansion into exporting, especially if they have had a bad experience. However, they can use export credit insurance to cover their trade, and this will include the checking of the financial standing of their trading partners by the insurance provider (see Chapter 9 for details).

Finance

Related to payment problems are issues to do with financing. Problems can arise with customers if they do not have sufficient financing arrangements in place, particularly for the purchase of expensive capital equipment. This can be especially a problem in developing or under-developed countries, where there is a shortage of capital in the market.

Political instability

Depending on the severity of the situation, this can lead to a temporary or permanent withdrawal from the market. Most companies wish to show that their commitment to the market is long-term, and will be keen to re-establish trade with their customers as soon as possible. The wars in the Balkans, the Gulf War and fighting in East Timor have all seriously disrupted trade with these areas. Businesses can also leave themselves exposed to financial loss by not having their trade with international customers insured. There are from time to time international embargoes on certain countries who have been deemed to fall outside international conventions, for example, in the treatment of their own people or minorities within their borders; or who have sponsored international terrorism. Thus, South Africa, Iran, Iraq, and Libya have all experienced such pressure. Indeed, Iraq is currently forbidden to sell its oil on the international market beyond a certain quota.

Production capacity

Clearly if there is a lack of production capacity then developing international customers can cause pressures and problems. Investment in additional capacity may be required, coupled with keeping up to date with the latest technological improvements. This potential constraint can be avoided with proper planning for export market entry.

Management attitudes

The attitude of management can be crucial, especially in terms of the time and resources which they are prepared to devote to export activity. If a relatively large domestic market exists, this may dissuade involvement, as will problems in finding good agents, and their supervision and motivation. Lack of language skills will also be prohibitive, or at least will favour a concentration strategy on markets with similar language rather than market spreading. The cost of maintaining an overseas office may also be off-putting to a management team lacking a long term perspective.

Human resource issues

Related to some of the problems outlined above can be issues to do with looking after employees who may have to live and work internationally. Depending on the scale and size of the operation, there are additional expenses associated with having expatriates: setting up compensation and benefits plans, calculating taxes for domestically paid salaries, finding suitable housing and schooling and conducting cross-cultural training. Staff can benefit from training in language skills, communication skills, listening skills and awareness of norms (Box 5.5).

Clearly the SME faces similar challenges to those faced by the larger companies, but has to meet them with fewer resources. These challenges can range from the practical – for example, compensation, selection and relocation of employees – to the laws and regulations of the foreign market. The experience base of managers is often more limited, with fewer having international expertise. Some studies have shown that firms with access to managers with international experience have yielded faster international revenue growth than companies led by CEOs with only domestic experience.

BOX 5.5: INTERNATIONAL HUMAN RESOURCES AT IAMS

If staff are placed abroad then they must be communicated with frequently given that the corporate investment in them is enormous. In the case of IAMS Co., maker of premium pet foods, they first moved out of the US market in 1991 by establishing a base in the Netherlands. The employees were given a great deal of support from the human resources department before and after the move. Being small makes communication easier and more frequent. Expatriates can be sent home-country magazines, newsletters and other relevant information. The company also maintains links with spouses to make sure everything is going well and if the company can do anything to improve the experience. This commitment to open communication is seen as the key to international success, and helps to illustrate how a 'holistic' approach to international marketing is regarded as crucial. Following the initial move to the Netherlands the company entered Singapore and Latin America in 1993 and currently (2000) employs 2000 people with sales of over $800 million.

Reuber and Fischer (1997) in a study of Canadian software SMEs found that internationally experienced management teams are viewed as a resource which influences SMEs in behaviours leading to a greater degree of internationalization. These firms tend to use more international strategic partners and delay less in obtaining international sales after start-up.

Opportunities for SMEs

Opportunities exist for the smaller firm in international markets for those that are willing to take this risk. There can be many reasons for a smaller firm's success, for example, having a exceptional unique product or being in a strong financial position with good credit relations. Even an apparent disadvantage, for example, declining domestic sales, can act as an impetus for a successful export development.

McClenahen (1988) suggests that much success for SMEs is based on attitude:

- Believing that the world is your market
- The market is out there if you go to find/create it
- Having an attack mentality
- How to understand and crack the foreign market, aim to become a 'business insider' in foreign markets, ensure that bureaucracy is kept to a minimum
- Being led by an entrepreneurial attitude
- Desire to create something new 'and international is new'
- Being flexible in their approaches
- Being prepared to use multiple methods of market entry
- Buy-in advice/expertise when needed – export houses or freight forwarders can supply the knowledge to shift products.

The best SMEs have an entrepreneurial management style, characterized by informal approaches to planning, and heavy reliance on networks rather than bureaucratic planning procedures associated with larger organizations. Other factors which assist the SME to make best advantage of available opportunities include:

Export market development

The best companies keep on the look out for new opportunities. Their information gathering may use national providers of information, consular representatives, and trade magazines to source new contacts. This should be an on-going activity designed to fit in with the strategic objectives of the business.

Agents and distributors

The best advantage of having an agent or distributor working for you in the market is that there is someone in the market who can keep in constant contact with customers and potential customers. Clearly the selection of the right agent or distributor is an important factor. Generally the qualities in an agent or distributor which assist companies to take best advantage of available opportunities are (Watson et al., 1998):

- Access to appropriate potential customers
- Understanding of the company's specialties
- Ability to represent the company in the best possible way
- Enthusiasm for selling the products
- Having good technical knowledge
- Having complementary product lines
- Regularly communicating with the company

International visits

Visiting potential international markets is a crucial component for the SME. Despite advances in telecommunication opportunities, there is still much to be said in favour of the face to face contact with new or existing customers. Visits allow the most accurate information and impressions of the market to be gathered. It also indicates a degree of commitment to the market and local intermediaries and customers.

Trade exhibition and missions

Trade exhibitions can be costly, but the smaller firm can target and benefit from a presence at relevant events. A major event will attract many potential customers and intermediaries, which allows the opportunity for vital face to face contact. For the experience to be fully exploited an efficient system of follow-up must be in place to pursue contacts made at the exhibition. This may involve a simple phone call, or sending additional information or samples to agents or potential customers. They also provide an opportunity to see what competitors are doing, as well as establishing a market presence, and can be used to create a high profile launch of a new product or range.

Export skills and competencies

Exporters are not all equal. They have different levels of knowledge, different approaches to management, face different barriers and are motivated by a range of factors. Previous studies have assessed the impact of top managers' exposure to international markets, and its effect on internationalization behaviour. Success has been correlated with the extent to which the manager has engaged in international travel; the number of languages spoken; whether an individual was born abroad, lived and/or worked abroad. In this section we will look at the skills and competencies required by the SME exporter generally, and also as specifically influenced by culture, information needs, the use of alliances and training provision.

Skills: a varied and evolving need

Douglas and Craig (1995) suggest that different skills are needed at each 'stage' of exporting. For initial market entry competence in selection and capitalizing on opportunities are important, whereas for expansion in the local market, skills in product management, adaptation of product and promotional programmes become more important.

If a smaller firm is able to learn from its experiences, and is capable of being flexible and efficient, then these export marketing skills will become part of their core competencies. A crucial element of this is the strategic intent of the firm's management. The literature often points to a shared vision and the desire to become a strong international player as an important component of success.

Albaum et al. (1998) identified key skills as:

- Planning and market intelligence
- Product management
- Customer analysis
- Selection and development of markets
- Promotion and communication
- International pricing.

In a study of SME exporting skills Broderick (1998) used the above categories and added to them dimensions to do with finance, distribution, and further marketing and management competencies. The development of export competency was observed at different stages of exporting, and firms were classified as passive, experimental or proactive. It was found that competence development varied significantly between the less active (passive) and the more active (proactive) firms as outlined in Table 5.3. This categorization could prove useful for those agencies involved in assisting exporters with their international activities, as undoubtedly there is a strong link between skills and the experience and learning required for decision making in international markets.

Foreign language skills are often seen as important for companies to be successful as exporters. However, few small companies have the resources to train people or recruit specialists solely for their language skills. The idea that English has been replaced by the customer's own language as the international language of business is more an aspiration than reality for the SME. Instead of trying to speak all the languages of potential customers, more realistic targets have to be set. Visser (1995) found that SMEs were experimenting with a variety of approaches to deal with the requirements of international communication. The use of freelance translators or language consultants was a cost-effective way of obtaining specialist support, while the employment of a local agent solves language problems and provides market intelligence.

Work by Eyre and Smallman (1998) has combined the outcomes from previous studies and produced a composite table listing the skills required by European SME managers (Table 5.4). It is difficult to see why such attributes as interpersonal skills,

Table 5.3   Skills/competencies at different stages of internationalization. Source: Broderick, 1998

Stage of internationalization	Export marketing competencies
Passive exporters: no intention to expand export activity	Unless these are experiences exporters, now re-focusing on the domestic market, these firms are likely to have only sufficient basic export administrative skills for order fulfilment, if a passive exporter; otherwise little export skills. No desire to invest in developing skills in either export administration or marketing, possibly due to a lack of awareness of the potential benefits
Experimental exporters: export intention increasing. Firms have desire to make it happen backed by research, market testing and some adaptation	More active experimental firms progress from basic export administration skills to developing skills in general market intelligence, enabling selection and testing of markets. Still lack more advanced skills for specific market intelligence, as a basis for a structured export plan. Responsiveness to local market conditions needs improvement through product management and communication skills, to enable adaptation. Conscious of specific skills gaps
Proactive exporters: strong intention to expand international activities, backed by strategically oriented rather than exploratory actions	Strong export marketing skills in most areas equal to those developed for the domestic market enabling systematic market research, selection and development. Key area for development is long term planning skills to maximize efficiency and enable alternative strategic directions to be evaluated

Table 5.4 A unified model of European management skills. Source: Eyre and Smallman, 1998

Ability to involve people (interpersonal skills)	Communication skills (listening, consulting, explaining, dialogue, communicating supportively). Skills in psychology (understanding people, gaining power and influence). Capacity to work in multi-level teams. Capacity to co-ordinate, to create enthusiasm and to motivate. Managing conflict
International skills	International experience. Competence in several languages (three minimum). Geographical mobility. Global thinking. Understanding cultural differences. Capacity to work in multi-national and multi-cultural teams
Flexibility	Aptitude to manage change. Aptitude to manage diversity. Tolerance of ambiguity and uncertainty. Managing stress. Developing self-awareness. Capacity to learn (self-evaluation and openness)
Intuition	Intuition. Creativity, ability to innovate, problem solving
Broad vision	Aptitude to have a general view of a situation (combining several disciplines, considering the historical context, and taking a systematic approach). Deep understanding (sociological, philosophical, ethical)

international skills, flexibility, intuition and broad vision should not be regarded as vital to SME mangers in other westernized developed countries.

In testing this model with a sample of 32 UK companies, the skills required by an export manager were evaluated (Table 5.5). Only 20 of the companies had a need for an export manager and the top rated skills were technical and language ability. International skills were mentioned but a long way down the list.

Table 5.5 Required knowledge, experience and skills in an export manager

Knowledge, experience and skills	Number of times mentioned
Technical	15
Languages	8
Commercial	4
Exporting	3
International	2
Interpersonal	2
Adaptable	1
Exporting knowledge	1
Intelligence	1
Professional qualification	1

Eyre and Smallman also investigated the skills of a sample of 50 French companies. They found that 54% of the SMEs had an export department with between one and ten staff. In the remaining 46% the managing director took responsibility. Only 15 reported that the export staff had qualifications in international trade. Most, 54%, had degrees but these were in technical disciplines. Language skills were strong with 59% having two foreign languages, normally including English.

It appears that SME managers can find themselves doing jobs which they are not necessarily qualified for, thus emphasizing the vital skills of flexibility and adaptability within such businesses. It also contrasts them with large firms and their more structured management layers.

The structure of business also allows the SMEs to expand and contract with the market, allowing change to be absorbed. Thus, for example, Leadwell, a company making milling machines at Taichung on the West coast of Taiwan, has many subcontractors as employees, about 400. When business is good it subcontracts work but when trade is poor only it own factories are used. While this system may not be as efficient in terms of logistics as if everything were done by a large company, it has allowed the company to weather the bad times of the Asian financial crisis in 1997. Having a business structure which can be prepared for good and bad economic cycles is a useful foundation.

Cultural influences

Cultural differences too can play their role in defining the behaviour of SMEs based on 'inherent' skills. In an article in praise of Taiwan's success, The Economist (1998) suggests that the Chinese ability to network, and guanxi (connections, which does not always mean corruption) provides them with an advantage. They also value profit and prudence in a way similar to the ideals of shareholder capitalism, mostly because Confucian ideals require them to hand on as big an inheritance as possible to their children. They achieve a balance between financial conservatism and being natural gamblers with a keen eye for opportunity.

As discussed earlier in this book, it is important for empirical research on export performance to be aware of the cultural dimension. Thus, the cultural distance to the export market is a crucial factor in the overall performance of the firm. The important feature in economic terms is the impact of the gap between actual and expected behaviour of the people representing the seller and the buyer. Such gaps can result in transaction costs and/or transaction breakdown. Madsen (1994) graphically illustrates the cultural gaps which can exist (Figure 5.1).

The buyer and seller will be strongly influenced by their respective cultural backgrounds (Gap 1). This gap will however, by moderated by the sales person's perception of the buyer's cultural background. Depending on the sales person's perception he/she will adapt his/her behaviour to what he/she thinks will be acceptable to the buyer. The sales person will also have a perception of what behaviour he/she expects from the buyer. The sales person will only rarely obtain a full understanding of the buyer's culture so a gap (Gap 2) will persist. Likewise

SELLER

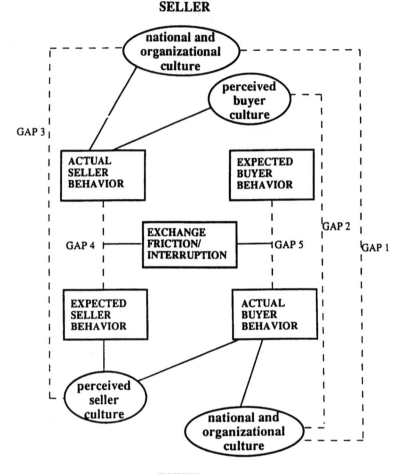

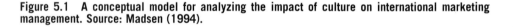

Figure 5.1 A conceptual model for analyzing the impact of culture on international marketing management. Source: Madsen (1994).

the buyer will operate under similar constraints (Gap 3) with regard to the sales person.

The end result of this will be a gap between the actual and perceived seller behaviour (Gap 4) and between actual and perceived buyer behaviour (Gap 5). From a marketing perspective Gaps 4 and 5 are crucial as they create the discontinuities in the exchange process which can increase transaction costs.

Training, of course, can alleviate the impact of the gaps. Thus, Gap 2 can be reduced through marketing research and education of the sales staff. Gap 3 can be reduced through market communication.

Here we have a useful framework for conceptualization of the impact of culture on export performance. The examples in Boxes 5.6 and 5.7 illustrate how culture can both be a hindrance and a helping hand to exporting.

BOX 5.6: CULTURE PUTS THE BRAKES ON EXPORTING

In common with other exporters the SME cannot escape the influence of culture. When two entrepreneurs formed a company to import British folding bicycles to the US in 1994 they thought they were onto a winner. The Bickerton Portable Bicycle is a very compact folding bicycle which enjoyed enormous market success in the UK. A large scale mail order campaign was launched including an announcement that the bikes were arriving by Concorde. However, what they had overlooked was at that time the idea of unfolding a bicycle and riding down through the neighbourhood was as far removed from the American culture as English scones and clotted cream. The entrepreneurs had failed to take into account how Americans think.

(adapted from Miller, 1996)

BOX 5.7: A HELPING HAND FROM CULTURE

For the SME linking a product to a wider emotional context can provide a valuable edge in the marketplace. Many Canadians and Americans can claim at least one Scottish ancestor. It is often evident that these people in pursuing their 'Scottishness' are more Scottish than the Scots! Specialist Scottish SME food companies are well established as niche suppliers to this potential customer base. Scottish heritage is effective in North America and in fragmented retail structures such as Holland and Germany.

(adapted from The Grocer, 1996)

Export development and the role of information

Despite the significance of information in developing export activities, much of the literature suggests that this is relatively ad hoc especially for SMEs (Leonidas and Adams-Florou, 1999). As a firm proceeds through export stages, information assists with strategic problems including what market expansion strategy to adopt, where to introduce new products and how to evaluate the overall export performance. However, many SMEs do not fully appreciate the need for marketing research. Often the research is not rigorous, formal or systematic. This can be the result of:

- A lack of sensitivity to differences in customer tastes, habits and preferences
- A limited appreciation of different marketing environments

- A lack of knowledge about information sources and an inability to use them properly
- A tendency to use experience in place of market research.

While much of the above may be true in relation to developing new export markets, many firms make a perfectly successful entry into international markets without spending much time and effort on information gathering. The business environment is often too dynamic for the luxury of formal market research. An opportunity arises and the firm will decide to take advantage of it based on an informal mixture of intuition and experience. Many of the national agencies for the provision of export information (as we saw in Chapter 2) charge for their services which acts as a deterrent for the smaller firm. Often this information is too general and not market specific enough to meet their perceived needs. To be fair, many of the providers are in a difficult situation of having to meet so many different needs and expectations that it is almost impossible. Once firms have some experience of international activities, they tend to develop their own networks for information gathering, and may only use national providers for specific opportunities. In turn, the national providers perhaps have more to offer the new exporter with limited experience, to whom the general information is of more interest. Targeting of such services is important but can be difficult.

In a study of export award winners in the UK, this changing pattern of use was found. Respondents were asked to distinguish between providers of information which they had perhaps used once or twice, a category referred to as 'have used', and those which they found themselves returning to time after time. This category was referred to as 'frequently used'.

In terms of 'have used' the top five are chambers of commerce, British Overseas Trade Board/Department of Trade and Industry, overseas embassies, banks and trade fairs. However, those 'frequently used' are almost entirely different with only trade fairs moving from the 'have used' category to 'frequently used' status. The top five 'frequently used' were:

- Overseas agents
- Personal contacts overseas
- Trade fairs
- Overseas subsidiary company
- Personal contacts in the UK.

The implication of the contrast between the 'have used' and 'frequently used' categories is that a number of organizations, although used by exporters, do not receive repeat business. The conclusion is the assistance given was not helpful, or inappropriate to the changing needs of the exporter.

For those sources which the exporters had used at any time, they were asked to indicate how useful the assistance was which they received. From the analysis three groupings emerged. These were given the descriptive labels of positive, neutral and negative (Table 5.6).

The interpretation given to this pattern was that the sources included in the positive group were those which the exporters had found to be the most useful.

Table 5.6   Utility of information sources

	Rank
Positive	
Personal contact overseas	1
Overseas agent	2
Trade fairs	3
Personal contact UK	4
Overseas subsidiary company	5
Overseas company office	6
Neutral	
BOTB/DTI	7
Chambers of commerce	8
Bank(s)	9
Overseas embassies	10
Trade associations	11
UK embassies	12
Negative	
Public libraries	13
Commercial libraries	14=
Professional institutions	14=
CBI	16=
University/polytechnic	16=

In contrast those in the negative category had been least useful. Between the two extremes there were a set of providers who did not evoke feelings of great satisfaction or dissatisfaction from the users. Thus, from the viewpoint of the users you have the emergence of in and out-suppliers of information relating to their needs.

The findings suggest that there is great variation in the pattern of sources of export information used, and that some sources are not regarded by the companies as being of great use to them. It appears that personal contacts, and those sources where there is a high chance of interaction (overseas agents, personal contacts overseas and trade fairs) between the inquirer and the provider, tend to be most popular. It is possible that firms are missing out on useful sources of export information from, for example, commercial and public libraries, simply because they are non-traditional points of contact for the firm. These are sources of information which have been scored poorly by the exporters but often public libraries contain, or have access to, a range of business information which the cost-conscious company could access at a relatively low price. Clearly, if these organizations wish to convey this to their potential users, there is an important awareness-raising task to be performed in order to achieve a higher profile in this area.

Watson et al. (1998) in a study of 20 SME firms found that informal networks were the most valued source of information. People located in the international markets were particularly found to be useful, as were the commercial sections of embassies and trade associations. In terms of the information they sought, most needed help to find agents and distributors and to identify lists of potential customers.

While information is an important issue it should be remembered that, from a marketing point of view, success in overseas markets is still largely based on delivering what you promised to the customer and, as Archer (1991) cautioned, a firm must avoid spending 'so much time keeping itself informed that it will have no time for exporting'.

Strategic alliances

Hansen et al. (1994) in a study of Danish exporters explored the role of market responsiveness, technology and export co-operation in contributing to the success of SME exporters. The study used as its database the export behaviour of almost 200 companies in Jutland, a peripheral area within Denmark. Due to the small size of the Danish economy, the SMEs are under pressure to export if they wish their businesses to develop.

Market responsiveness occurs because the companies undertake a high level of process and product adaptation for the export markets, thus they specialize in providing new or specialty products for particular groups of customers. A second strength of the group is the use of technology to innovate in the production process, including use of just-in-time systems. Thus, while the companies themselves are not engaged in high-tech production, they integrate new technologies into their internal organization in ways that diffuse innovation. The third key feature was their use of alliances. This enabled them to finance higher levels of investment, to absorb greater risk, to access knowledge and know-how more rapidly, and allowed increased specialization, and therefore increased efficiency. Alliances were helped by the geographical proximity and cultural similarity among the firms, thus the social network helped to create an environment of mutual trust.

This use of an alliance of some sort is not unusual in SME exporting. Joynt and Welch (1985) reported the encouragement by the Swedish government of alliances between geographical distant companies. Likewise Kaufmann (1995) observed that SMEs would often use distribution agreements, and sometimes production co-operation, to expand into foreign markets and therefore improve their international competitiveness. By co-operating, the companies realize synergies that otherwise would call for a merger. Co-operation is an efficient alternative, as long as the sum costs are less than the cost of going it alone.

Berra et al. (1995) have observed 'learning by co-operating' in companies involved in the Italian clothing industry. From the study of a large database, recording some 1051 contractual ventures and direct investments from 1987 to 1991, they identified some 709 deals at the international level. Of these 362 were co-operative deals and 347 were non-co-operative. It was found that in this particular industry the international growth of the SMEs took place through co-operative contractual deals (68%) than by non-co-operative deals (32%). This contrasted with the larger companies were non-co-operative strategies prevail (54%). The kinds of co-operative operations included are:

- Commercial and distribution agreements
- Manufacturing licensing
- Long term subcontracts
- Commercial licensing
- Transfer of trade-marks and of granting patents
- Management contracts
- Transfer of know-how and turnkeys (the later being a management contract for the construction of a plant, training of personnel and the initial operation of a plant for a local investor)
- Portfolio investments.

It appears that the companies in the study attempt to reproduce the same pattern of linkages at the international level as they operate on the domestic level. In Italy the SMEs decentralize their production within the country through networks of companies and industrial districts, whose horizontal connections (among the SMEs themselves) and vertical connections (with large companies) provide flexibility and low costs.

Training and support for SMEs

Many OECD countries are changing their industrial policies to support SMEs (OECD Observer, 1995). These policy changes will enable many of them to enhance or develop for the first time their export capability. Assistance is being developed in countries such as Canada, France, Germany, Italy and the UK to train and support SME managers. This includes free or subsidized consultancy services. Another form is the use of 'business angels', senior retired executives who have significant managerial experience and who know about the difficulties of business start-up or growth or who have knowledge of a particular technology.

In the US, Australia, Canada and the UK, attempts are being made to reduce the burden of administrative procedures on the SME by developing one stop shopping, either physical or virtual, to reduce the time spent on such activity.

Many OECD countries are providing better access to finance than is available through the private banking sector. Thus seed money, venture capital and loans, and credit guarantees are being provided. Often SMEs pay a premium rate for loans of up to 4%, and this raises criticism that banks are not providing the services needed by SMEs. It may be, of course, that the banks have correctly assessed the risk for their loans to SMEs, but it is likely there will be increasing competition amongst financial providers to meet the needs of the SMEs in the future.

Of particular interest are measures to increase the research and development rate in SMEs, which may lead to increased export competitiveness. Whilst many have innovative products on offer, the challenge often is to maintain that lead with future products. As well as direct financial assistance, there are measures to encourage networking and partnerships with other businesses, universities or other research institutions, plus advice on licensing arrangements.

Conclusions

Large firms will go on existing but many observers expect that much of the growth in business activity in the global economy will be the result of small, innovative, flexible enterprises which are formed and reformed by a workforce of highly skilled people, especially those with an understanding of IT. Small firms do have their constraints, as we have seen in this chapter, but they can be flexible and develop customer intimacy which leads to a competitive advantage. The SME born globals, discussed in this chapter, are part of Ken Ohmae's 'borderless world' where ideas, goods and people flow freely around the world creating a genuine global economic village, at least for those in the first world.

SMEs are traditionally characterized as being more agile and responsive to the marketplace and as a result can experience rapid growth (which in itself can lead to other problems). The small firms also benefit from having less internal politics to cope with, which allows them to focus more directly on the objectives of the business. Solomon et al. (1997) suggest that firms must build internal structures correctly from the beginning, get personally involved and use outside experts where necessary. Entrepreneurial leadership can create new enterprises which can thrive in the global economy, such as the growth and development of Lonely Planet (see Box 5.8).

BOX 5.8: THE LONELY PLANET STORY

In 1973 Tony and Maureen Wheeler printed 1500 copies of a 96-page travel guide, Across Asia on the Cheap, at their own expense. Thus, the 'Lonely Planet' travel imprint was born. Initial distribution was door-to-door to Sydney bookstores. Having recovered their costs, they made enough money to begin travelling again, which in turn led to shoestring guides to Hong Kong, Australia, Papua New Guinea, Nepal and Africa. By the early 1980s they were headquartered in Melbourne and in 1984 opened a sales office in San Francisco, followed by London in 1990. Today the organization employs some 300 people working in Australia, London and Paris, and a team of writers travelling and writing around the globe. They publish 270 titles covering just about every corner of the globe. The market is global with 43% of sales (1997–1998) in Europe, 35% in the US and Canada, 13% in Australia and 9% in Asia-Pacific region. Product development for the future includes in flight videos for corporate clients, street maps, restaurant guides and a specialist image library.

An SMEs global venture can be less dramatic than its larger cousins', but just as effective in business terms. For example, one firm based near Nottingham, which produced filter rings, was based in premises little bigger than 200 m^2. The workshop was filthy and totally unpretentious. However, during the course of a 1 h interview it was obvious that the business was international. During the visit orders came in by fax and telephone calls from Sweden, France, Germany and Italy. By being a specialist player in a niche market, this small company had effectively cornered the European market in its particular product category.

Internationally, the development of SMEs has been recognized as a crucial stage in the transformation of the former communist economies of Eastern Europe to capitalism. For example in Hungary, Poland, the Czech and Slovak Republics, numbers of SMEs are growing with government support for restructuring in economic, education, training and competition policies. Some 20% (Frost, 1996) of the new SMEs are in manufacturing and, in time, some of these will be the exporters of the future.

Developed economies also recognize the potential contribution from SMEs and have identified target markets and sectors as in the case of Scotland (Box 5.9). The Small Business Administration in the US has identified the following barriers to the growth of SMEs in this century as being: access to credit, capital, education, training, and to information. The growth in the role of SMEs will partly come about because of: increased globalization, increased connectivity, a preference for heterogeneity, diversity and complexity, and the customization of products and services. Many governments promote export development and have a variety of schemes in place to support such activity. Appendix II illustrates the kind of support available in the UK, US and Australia. Such support is available to all companies but SMEs can find it particularly valuable given their resource constraints.

BOX 5.9: SCOTTISH SMES FACE AN INTERNATIONAL CHALLENGE

In attempting to identify future prospects for Scottish companies, including SMEs, Scottish Trade International, a government organization, have identified the following priority markets for Scottish exporters.

Developed markets, i.e. those which already take a substantial proportion of Scottish exports, e.g. France, Germany, US.

Developing markets where Scottish exporters have made some progress over the last few years, e.g. Hong Kong, China, Taiwan, South Korea, Singapore, Malaysia, United Arab Emirates.

Emerging markets where Scottish exporters are beginning to show some interest, e.g. South Africa, India, Russian Federation.

Within these geographical areas the following sector have been identified as offering potential future growth:
- Food and drink
- Textiles
- Value-added engineering
- Oil and gas
- Electronics
- Software and multimedia
- Financial services
- Education, training and research services.

The SME, especially those at the 'S' end of SME, will always face particular constraints to do with time, cost and skill. There is also a tendency to view marketing negatively, or with suspicion, and the time factor can be used as an excuse for not paying much attention to it. However, there is much evidence in the literature to suggest that even successful SMEs who make it past the 3 year barrier begin to think about grafting marketing onto their business in some way. In the next three chapters we will explore what marketing is all about within the framework of the Marketing Cycle, namely, understanding the customer, creating the product or service, communicating with the customer and finally delivering the product or service to the customer. This process is relevant to all firms who have international activities, regardless of their size.

Questions for discussion

1. What is the definition of small and medium sized enterprises used in your country? How well does it fit the profile of businesses in your local area?
2. Compile a list of advantages and disadvantages which you think the smaller firm faces in attempting to participate in the global economy.
3. How important is the entrepreneur or owner-manager to the success of a small exporting firm? Discuss.
4. Small firms are just little big firms. Discuss and justify your view.
5. You are about to undertake a survey of exporting businesses in your local economy. Devise a series of questions which you might include in your questionnaire related to: background details of the business, their information gathering processes; their export strategy, and their plans for further developing export markets. You should be able to devise at least six questions in each category.
6. Select a market and a product or service, and then by only using information obtained from the Internet, see how many sources of appropriate and useful information you can find for your selected market and product/ service. Evaluate the Internet as a source of information for the smaller company.
7. Select an SME which has experienced rapid development and perhaps is now an internationally recognized brand. Research its growth and development and attempt to identify the crucial influences upon its development.
8. How can strategic alliances help the smaller firm in its international activities?
9. What support in terms of export assistance is available for the smaller firm in your local area, state or nation? How useful is this assistance?
10. Interpersonal skills, especially communication skills, are the most important resource for the small firm because this allows the 'firm' to network. Discuss.

References

Albaum, G., Strandskov, J. and Duerr, E. (1998), *International Marketing and Export Management*, Addison-Wesley, Harlow.

Ali, A. and Swiercz, P.M. (1991), Firm size and export behaviour: lessons from the midwest, *Journal of Small Business Management*, 29 (2), pp. 71–78.

Archer, M. (1991), *Canadian Export Management*, Maurice Archer Books, Oakville, Ontario.

Beamish, P.W., Craig, R. and McLellan, K. (1993), The performance characteristics of Canadian versus UK exporters in small and medium sized firms, *Management International Review*, 33 (2), pp. 121–137.

Berra, L., Piattti, L. and Vitali, G. (1995),The internationalisation process in the small and medium-sized firm: a case study of the Italian Clothing industry, *Small Business Economics*, 7 (1), pp. 67–75.

Bolton Report (1971), *Small firms: Report of the Committee of Inquiry on Small Firms*, chaired by J.E. Bolton, Cmnd. 4811, HMSO, London.

Broderick, A. (1998), Behavioural and entrepreneurial perspectives on skills dvelopment and learning in SMEs as they internationalise, in: Hulbert, B., Day, J. and Shaw, E. (eds.), *Proceedings 1996–1998, Academy of Marketing UIC/AMA Symposium on the Marketing and Entrepreneurship Interface*, pp. 331–345.

Burrill, G.S. and Almassy, S.E. (1993), *Electronics '93 the New Global Reality: Ernst and Young's Fourth Annual Report on the Electronics Industry*, Ernst and Young, San Francisco, CA.

Business Week (1999), Join the globetrotters, *Business Week*, Nov. 8 (3654), p. 10.

Culpan, R. (1989), Export behaviour of firms: relevance of firm size, *Journal of Business Research*, 18 (3), pp. 207–218.

Douglas, S. and Craig, C.S. (1995), *Global Marketing Strategies*, McGraw-Hill, New York.

Eyre, P. and Smallman, C. (1998), Euromanagement competences in small and medium-sized entreprises: a development path for the new millennium? *Management Decision*, 36 (1), pp. 34–42.

Frost, M. (1996), Helping small business in Eastern Europe, *OECD Observer*, Feb/Mar (198), pp. 51–55.

Hansen, N., Gillespie, K. and Gencturck, E. (1994), SMEs and export involvement: market responsiveness, technology, and alliances, *Journal of Global Marketing*, 7 (4), pp. 7–27.

Hedlund, G. and Kverneland, A. (1984), *Are Established and Growth Patterns for Foreign Markets Changing? The Case of Swedish Involvement in Japan*, Institute of International Business, Stockholm School of Economics.

Joynt, P. and Welch, L. (1985), A strategy for small business internationalisation, *International Marketing Review*, 2 (3), pp. 64–73.

Kaplinsky, R. and Manning, C. (1998), Concentration, competition policy and the role of small and medium-sized enterprises in South Africa's industrial development, *Journal of Development Studies*, 35 (1), p. 139; (14) InfoTrac http://www.galegroup.com/

Kaufmann, F. (1995), Internationalisation via co-operation - strategies of SMEs, *International Small Business Journal*, 13 (2), pp. 27–33.

Leonidas, C.L. and Adams-Florou, A.S. (1999), Types and sources of export information: insights from small business, *International Small Business Journal*, 17 (3), pp. 30–48.

Madsen, T.K. (1994), A contingency approach to export performance research, *Advances in International Marketing*, 6, pp. 25–42.

McClenahen, J.S. (1988), How U.S. entrepreneurs succeed in world markets: they think positively - and globally, *Industry Week*, 236 (9), p. 47; (3) InfoTrac http://www.galegroup.com/

McDougall, P.P. and Oviatt, B.M. (1996), New venture internationalisation, strategic change, and performance, *Journal of Business Venturing*, 11 (1), pp. 23–40.

Miller, R.N. (1996), Cultural barriers in cross-border marketing, *Direct Marketing*, 58 (11), pp. 66–69.

Murray, M.F. (1993), Answers to small business questions on international opportunities, *Journal of Accountancy*, 176 (2), pp. 52; (2) InfoTrac http://www.galegroup.com/

OECD Observer (1995), Globalisation and industrial competitiveness, *OECD Observer*, Dec/Jan (197),p. 38; (5) InfoTrac http://www.galegroup.com/

Oviatt, B.M. and McDougall, P.P. (1994), Toward a theory of international new ventures, *Journal of International Business Studies*, 25 (1), pp. 45–64.

Paliwoda, S.J. and Thomas, M.J. (1998), *International Marketing*, Butterworth-Heinemann, Oxford.

Prince, Y.M. (1995), *Export Performance of SMEs*, Research Report 9503/E, EIM Small Business Research and Consultancy, Zoetermeer.

Rabino, S. (1980), An examination of barriers to exporting encountered by small manufacturing companies, *Management International Review*, 20 (1), pp. 67–74.

Reid, S. D. (1984), Market expansion and firm internationalisation, in: Kaynak, E. (ed.), *International Marketing Management*, Praeger, New York.

Rennie, M.W. (1993), Born global, *The McKinsey Quarterly*, Autumn, pp. 45–52.

Reuber, A.R. and Fischer, E. (1997), The influence of the management team's international experience on the internationalisation behaviors of SMEs, *Journal of International Business Studies*, 28 (4), pp. 807–826.

Roy, D. A. and Simpson, C.L. (1981), Export attitudes of business executives in the smaller manufacturing firm, *Journal of Small Business Management*, 19 (2), pp. 16–22.

Samiee, S. and Walters, P.G.P. (1990), Influence of firm size on export planning and performance, *Journal of Business Research*, 10 (3), pp. 235–248.

Solomon, C.M., Marsh, M. and Burke, R. (1997), Growing companies hit global home runs, *Workforce*, 76 (6), pp. 72–80.

Storey, D.J. (1994), *Understanding the Small Business Sector*, Routledge, London.

The Economist (1998), Taiwan's economic success shows what the Chinese can do if you let them, *The Economist*, Nov. 7.

The Grocer (1996), Authenticity is all-important, *The Grocer*, Sep. 7, 218 (7270), p. 79.

Visser, C. (1995), Theory and practice: a defence of small business language strategies, *European Business Journal*, 7 (2), pp. 49–55.

Voss, C., Blackmon, K.L., Cagliano, R., Hanson, P. and Wilson, F. (1998), Made in Europe: small companies, *Business Strategy Review*, 9 (4), pp. 1–21.

Watson, K., Hogarth-Scott, S. and Wilson, N. (1998), Key issues in export market development for small and medium sized UK businesses, in: Hulbert, B., Day, J. and Shaw, E. (Eds.) *Proceedings 1996–1998*, Academy of Marketing UIC/AMA Symposium on the Marketing and Entrepreneurship Interface, pp. 355–365.

Young, S. (1987), Business strategy and the internationalisation of business: recent approaches, *Managerial and Decision Economics*, 8, pp. 31–40.

Further reading

Bell, J. (1997), A comparative study of the export problems of small computer software exporters in Finland, Ireland and Norway, *International Business Review*, 6 (6), pp. 585–604.

Gibb, A.A. (1997), Small firms' training and copetitiveness. Building upon the small firm as a learning organisation, *International Small Business Journal*, 15 (3), pp. 13–29.

Graham, P.G. (1999), Small business participation in the global economy, *European Journal of Marketing*, 33 (1/2), pp. 88–102.

Levinson, J.C. (1998), *Guerrilla Marketing: Secrets for Making Big Profits from your Small Business*, Houghton Mifflin, New York.

Madsen, T.K. and Servais, P. (1997), The internationalisation of born globals: an evolutionary process? *International Business Review,*, 6 (6), pp. 561–583.

Philp, N.E. (1998), The export propensity of the very small enterprise, *International Small Business Journal*, 16 (4), pp. 79–93.

Wei, Ho-C. and Christodoulou, C. (1997), An examination of strategic foreign direct investment decision processes: the case of Taiwanese manufacturing SMEs, *Management Decision*, 35 (7/8), pp. 619–630.

CHAPTER 6

Understanding customer values

Chapter objectives

After studying this chapter you should be able to:

- Describe the marketing cycle as it relates to the international customer
- Appreciate what is meant by understanding customer values
- Explain market research, market selection and segmentation.

Introduction

There is nothing particularly difficult about the basic principles of marketing. After all, what could be more straightforward than trying to meet the customer's needs and satisfy them? Essentially this involves doing some market research, producing a product or providing a service, telling potential customers that the product or service is available, and finally making the product or service available to them either directly or, for example, via shops, mail order or over the Internet. The difficulties begin when you begin to deal with customers in the real world, because even within a domestic market they can be very varied in their needs, wants and expectations. This becomes even more acute when you start to trade across international boundaries. Of course, the issue of culture once again underpins this debate, but then is it fair to say that we are all so different? If we are, then how come companies like Coca-Cola, Pepsi, Levis and Marlboro are so well known around the world?

The aim of this chapter is to present a conceptualization of the marketing cycle whereby we can understand the relationship between marketing and the buyers and sellers engaged in the exchange process. This conceptualization will then be used as the framework to explain the marketing activities associated with each stage of the marketing cycle in an international context. Thus, in this chapter the processes of understanding the customer, involving market research, the market selection process, and segmentation will be discussed.

The marketing cycle

In order to appreciate the approach used in this chapter and in Chapter 7 this section will review the underpinning philosophy of marketing as used in this book. This will provide the reader with the foundation on which to construct ideas about the application of the marketing concept within the international context.

Marketing is all about a particular view of how the business process operates. It argues that by focusing on a set of activities, the objectives of a business can be achieved. At the centre of these activities must be the customer; the business achieves its objectives by satisfying the customer's objectives.

Businesses only succeed by generating sales through the exchange of products or services with individual consumers or other organizations. People and organizations will exchange with the seller because they are motivated by the use they will put the product or service to after they have obtained it. In some instances the buying process will be rational and the decision made on least cost including, for example, such factors as price, distance to travel to obtain the product/service, and time involved. However, people buy products and services for all sorts of reasons, some of which are tangible and some of which are intangible (psychological and social factors). Often there is a greater perceived prestige in owning products which are sourced internationally, and may be perceived as being more exclusive and more prestigious to own.

This adds a new dimension to our attempt to understand the customer's objectives. We must recognize that these can be a varied bundle of tangible and intangible factors, and that the customer will measure the value of the products or services offered in the exchange in terms of how far their objectives are met. Thus customers will pay for products and services that satisfy them and assist them to achieve an objective. The perception of the value of the product/service in their terms will determine how much they buy and how much they will be willing to pay. This focus on the customer is the distinguishing feature of marketing as an approach to business.

One of the more populist writers in business, Tom Peters, has referred to this need to know the customer as recognizing 'the smell of the customer', not literally of course! However, he is trying to convey a closeness to the customer and their complexities. Marketing management should aim to understand these complexities, and implement business activities which will deliver customer related values and thus achieve the objectives of the business.

In this brief discussion of marketing we have used the terms exchange and value. These terms can be confusing, especially value, which is not to be equated with money or price. It is worth saying a little more about these terms. Exchange occurs in all aspect of life, both professionally and socially. At the core of the business–customer relationship is the exchange of values and it is this process which the marketer attempts to manage. These exchanges can be one-off or isolated transactions or they can be long-term relationships between the business and the customer. If the one-off transaction comes about as a result of the customer's expectations or values not being satisfied, then this is not good for the business as it does not lead to repeat business. Essentially this is an 'I win, you lose' situation from the business' point of view. To turn this exchange into a mutually satisfying one for both sides, the values of each have to be met, creating an 'I win, you win' situation. The customer gains value from the product or service and the business gains revenue with a good chance of future business from a satisfied customer.

The best business–customer relationships depend on an understanding of the customer's values and the ability of the business to achieve those values. Thus the customer may need, for example, precision accuracy in calibration, fast delivery, personal attention, customized products. Whatever is important to the customer should be the focus of the businesses attention as well. By sharing the customers values we get closer to the 'smell of the customer'.

None of this is easy. Whilst the concept of marketing is not difficult to grasp, its ongoing application can be difficult to implement in domestic and international markets.

The first stage in applying marketing is to understand the customer, including their characteristics, needs, wants, values and perceptions. This should be the key focus of the market research activities within a business. The second stage is to design a product or service which will embody the customer's values. There is no point to the first two stages if the business does not communicate with potential customers to tell them what it has to offer, thus communicating values is the third stage. Finally, delivery of the values must take place at the point of exchange. This process is shown in Figure 6.1 (Bathie, 1998) and is the marketing cycle, where the middle loop represents the marketing activities within the exchange process. The inner loop of the cycle describes the customer's view of the world and the foundations of their behaviour. This loop determines the behaviour of the outer loop, the business's activities.

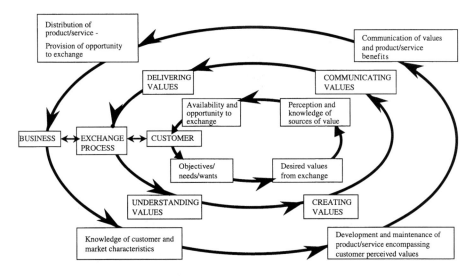

Figure 6.1   The marketing cycle. Source: Bathie (1998).

This section has outlined the marketing cycle within the context of understanding, creating, communicating and delivering customer related values. In the remainder of this chapter processes related to understanding the customer in the international arena will be discussed. The topics of creating products and services will be dealt with in Chapter 7, while delivering customer values will be discussed in Chapter 8, thus completing the discussion of the marketing cycle.

Understanding the customer

Introduction

The environment in which companies operate is becoming increasingly competitive. It is likely that this is a trend which will continue in the future as customers become more discerning and less loyal. Thus, as new competitors emerge, as laws and regulations change, and as technology opens up new opportunities and threats, so the relative importance of understanding the customer increases.

It is not enough to produce a good product and to sell it aggressively on the international market. The better companies are more interested in developing longer term relationships with their international customers, be they other companies or consumers. This is important because customers are often bombarded with an ever increasing number of products and services from which to choose. Therefore the final choice is based on a complex decision-making process which assesses price, service, quality and value.

As we saw in Chapter 3, the cultural background of customers can have a significant effect on customers' opinions. It is likely that across a number of markets customers will be selecting the same product but for different reasons. If this is the case, then it becomes crucial for the company to conduct suitable market research, in order to understand the needs of the target market, so that it can communicate appropriate values to a particular group of customers. The famous marketing maxim of 'staying close to your customers' is crucial to international success. These customers can in turn be segmented and marketed to in ways which the company believes to be appropriate for their characteristics.

In this section we will consider appropriate steps which can be taken to facilitate market selection, before focusing on market research and how it can contribute to understanding the customer. A discussion of market segmentation will then follow.

Market research

Within this context, market research becomes the crucial tool with which to understand the customer. Thus market research has the following goals:

- It helps create accurate judgements
- It reduces risk
- It provides an understanding of customers' needs

- It allows marketers to identify and analyze potential markets
- It provides an assessment of global demand.

The key aims of international market research are to provide reliable information, insight and consistency. These will change little – however, in the future it is likely that through the introduction of new technology the means by which the information is gathered, organized, analyzed and presented will change radically. For example, companies who supply electronic point of sale data to companies have an enormous wealth of information at hand. They know what consumers buy – not what they say they buy. In the future the research organization may be bypassed as the brand owner talks directly with their customers, for example, Toyota car owners can visit a website, register their car, and talk to designers and tell them what they like and dislike about their car and what they would like to see in their next car. While purists will argue about the importance of sampling in such information gathering, it may well be that such conversations will take the place of traditional market research, which tends to be a snapshot at one point in time rather than an ongoing dialogue between a company and its customers.

How this will develop in the household market will depend on the penetration of PCs into the home, and how they form part of a communications package, integrated, perhaps, with the next generation of televisions and the activities of cable/satellite operators.

Most companies will acknowledge the need to undertake market research before they rush off into foreign markets. However, sometimes for reasons of arrogance or cost, less research is undertaken than is necessary, or the wrong questions are asked. This can have disastrous results in the end (see Box 6.1 for an example) which can put an end, even if only temporarily, to international activity.

BOX 6.1: SIZE DOES MATTER

This company, based in Bradford, UK began as a market trader selling ladies' sweaters, which it bought from wholesalers. Gradually as the business grew and developed, the owners decided to design and manufacture their own range of products. This development was a success and the business continued to grow. In time it was felt that there was an opportunity to export their products to another country, and Holland was chosen as the initial export market. The owners were confident of success, and after the first delivery to the Dutch market they sat back and waited for the sales to take off. Unfortunately they never did, and it was only in hindsight that they began to seriously look at the market which they had entered. It emerged that the colours popular in Holland were different to those popular in the UK at the time and in addition the average Dutch women was larger than the average UK women. Thus, in terms of sizing, only part of the company's range was of interest to the Dutch consumer, and then the offering was further disadvantaged by not being available in the preferred colours. Rather than try to put things right the company took the exit route from the international market and once again became a solely domestic operator.

Methods and what to ask

Traditional approaches to market research have concentrated on qualitative and quantitative methodologies. There has been for many years a heated debate between proponents of qualitative and quantitative research methodologies. Unfortunately they are often seen as being diametrically opposed to each other, and that research can only follow one particular methodological path. This is very much an error, and rather like looking at the world with one eye closed, making judgements of depth very difficult. Both approaches do different things but they can complement each other. Quantitative is good for the what and where questions related to purchasing habits, while qualitative deals with the why and how people buy. Pawle (1999) argues that we need to assimilate both approaches and that one without the other is unbalanced. To illustrate his point he draws on a gender metaphor (Table 6.1).

There can be a tendency, particularly in smaller companies, to rush into research without proper planning. This is almost worse than not doing any market research at all! Prior planning can help avoid poor performance. Laflin (1999) suggests that two key questions should be asked during the planning phase: 'How will I tell if the project has been a success?'; and 'Why am I conducting this research?'. In answer to the first question, measures such as whether the project was completed on time and within budget will be relevant, as will an assessment of whether the right information was collected from the right people. The real answer to the second question comes in the future and varies with the objectives of the research; was a damaging decision avoided or a good decision made, did revenues increase?

Certainly before embarking on any research, you should have a clear idea of what you are trying to achieve, how you will go about collecting data, how it will be analyzed, and how the outcomes will be addressed. In more detail, as part of the planning process you will need to address:

- What method will be used?
- What questions will be asked?
- Who will be interviewed?
- How will you get contact information for potential respondents?
- When and where will data be collected?
- Which parts of the work will be done internally and which will be done externally?

Table 6.1   Contrasting contributions of qualitative and quantitative approaches

Qualitative	Quantitative
Feminine in nature	More masculine
Intuitive and understanding	Aggressive (more shallow but concrete)
Taps the rich veins of experience	Shallower interpretation
Extends quantitative and drives quantitative analyses	Agencies revert back to 'results' not 'findings'
More conclusions	

- What statistical analysis will be performed?
- How will the results be communicated in the organization?

While the above can be generally applied to market research activities, it is worth developing these ideas a little further within the context of international market research. Recommended steps are to:

1. Profile your target segments and clients, not just from secondary statistical data but from first hand observation and discussion. How do the customers in the target market(s) behave in the sector you wish to enter? How do their buying tastes and preferences differ to those in your domestic market where you have experience?
2. Interview members of the target segments to see how well they fit your pre-conceived ideas about them. It may be that little refinement is necessary, and you can sell existing products or services without adaptation. On the other hand such interviews can reveal the need for a modification which will enhance your chances of success. Stewart-Allen (1999) notes the case of Hansen Soft Drinks, a California-based carbonated drinks maker, who found that European consumers found their white plastic screw-on top conveyed cheapness.
3. Use local researchers who appreciate the methods which work best in respective markets.
4. Use a variety of methods to get a well-rounded understanding of the market. A mixture of quantitative and qualitative can provide information on preferences and strength of beliefs, but also the anecdotes which can be used in communication campaigns.
5. When looking at the data produced by research, focus on outcomes, the actions to follow from the data. Ask yourself, 'What do I do as a result of this data? What will I do that will be different to the pattern in existing domestic markets?'

In-house or bought in?

It is suggested, by many observers, that much of market research can be undertaken by the company itself rather than buying in assistance. However, this will require a time and resource commitment, as rarely is there a short cut to everything the company needs to know. It is easy to see how a company would be motivated to the DIY approach on grounds of cost. It is generally more expensive to conduct research in foreign markets because of the additional travel, co-ordination and translation costs which are often involved. A typical usage and attitude survey can cost between 75 and 120% more in terms of the price paid to a research organization. Crucially, the relative impact of this cost on the smaller company is much greater if the strategy subsequently developed is the wrong one. Failure in one international market can easily lead to the whole exporting adventure being abandoned.

MacFarlane (1991) outlines the types of activities undertaken by a consultancy before any primary research is undertaken. This process involved seven steps and these are outlined below. They provide an insight into the services offered by such organizations to exporters.

1. Check reference information on countries, products, markets and competitors.
2. Conduct secondary research online and in the library.
3. Select any studies which appear to be of interest. Contact the publishers and request an abstract/contents page in order to see if it is worth purchasing.
4. Select a foreign firm or firms to assist in the study or perform most of the work
5. Ask for proposals for foreign fieldwork and analysis, particularly where language skills are required.
6. Finalize the client proposal, including business reference information, secondary research, multi-client studies, subcontracted fieldwork and analysis.
7. Begin the primary research study, working closely with the client and arranging for frequent interim meetings to ensure that work is progressing at a good rate and in line with the proposal.

New directions: using the Internet

The evolving nature of the global economy (discussed in Chapter 2) in itself creates new challenges for market research. Markets emerge where little formal statistical information exists, and so for companies interested in doing business in these new markets, the challenge to market researchers can be quite great.

Already we are experiencing the boom in accessibility of information as, for example, the Internet makes downloading a bizarre range of details possible. This can only be expected to continue in the 21st Century. McKie (1996) states that 'The average weekday edition of the New York Times contains more information than most people in 17th century England would have seen in an entire lifetime'. The distinction which will become increasingly important, if marketers and researchers are to avoid information gridlock, will be the capability to unbundle data and knowledge, i.e. to be able to see the story behind the reams of tables which the computer database will make available. Anyone who has used the Internet to search for information will understand how easy it is to become side-tracked by link after link, whilst losing sight of what the search was about!

As more companies become involved in selling across international boundaries, particularly as more SMEs enter the arena, so too will the demand for international market research increase. McKie states that some companies are rejecting the traditional route of test marketing or piloting products in new markets. Examples are quoted of companies in the youth or fashion markets who claim not to use research because they have their finger on the pulse. However, in reality these companies have informants on the ground observing and talking to people, and feeding the information gained back to the centre. Thus, this is not a total rejection of research, but an change in emphasis from the conventional methods to less formal and controlled methods (see Box 6.2 for an example).

BOX 6.2: DOT COM RESEARCH

Being short of a budget to conduct conventional research, one company came up with an innovative solution – use the Internet. Therefore, in order to approach snowboarders to find out what was 'cool' or not, the company visited various sites on snowboarding, e-mailed people and use the talk sites to set up informal group discussions. Some valuable insights were gained as well as some flaming for the commercial aspects of the project.

Undoubtedly in the future there will be even greater potential to set up virtual focus groups on the net, while e-mail could allow for vast distribution of self-completion questionnaires. This is already happening within organizations and could be a way of conducting cheap international market research.

James (1999) reports that Avon Products, who previously dispatched interviewers to 17 US cities to survey Avon representatives at local shopping malls, attempted a parallel survey in 1997 with representatives online. The data correlation was so high, and the online approach so much more cost effective, that mall based meetings were dropped.

The Internet is cheaper, faster, easier than traditional telephone, personal interviews or postal surveys, and the revenues generated are increasing (Table 6.2). The companies can conduct wide open polls, opt-in polls, invitation only polls, password protected sites and Internet based panels. There are some concerns in the industry that proper social science methods are followed where required, for example, random sampling, respondent privacy. Some companies are using quota sampling to allow for differences between the online population and the general population – here addressing concern of social exclusion and the creation of an offline underclass. Others bar access, once an individual has participated in a survey, for 3 months. Clearly these methods are an additional tool in markets where online access is high and growing, but many markets exist around the world were such techniques would not be possible.

The market selection process

Issues surrounding mode of entry have been discussed in Chapter 4, however, it is worth saying a few words about market selection here in relation to understanding the customer at the macro level. In reality firms, large or small, will be guided and

Table 6.2 Growth in online research in the US (adapted from James, 1999)

Year	Revenue ($ million)
1996	3.3
1998	28.3
1999	74.4
2000	170 (estimated)

attracted to markets for all sorts of reasons, but essentially they go there because they see an opportunity. How that opportunity comes about can be because of careful planning, but it can also be because of the chance outcome of a whole series of occurrences. It should, however, be noted that not all firms in all situations will ask, or need to ask, the detailed questions often associated with market selection; in some instances the opportunity will present itself to the firm, unsolicited. Experience and intuition play their role in opportunity taking, so it is important to view the systematic approaches to market selection outlined below as the luxury model based on ample time and no previous experience.

In first attempting to select international markets for entry, a firm's choice will broadly be determined by its own characteristics and by those of the environment. Thus, firm characteristics such as the:

- Level of international experience
- Degree of integration into networks
- Human and financial resources available
- The nature of the business sector
- Long-term business objectives
- Attitude of the key-decision makers

and environmental factors; such as:

- How internationalized the industry sector is
- How internationalized the host market is
- What the host market's potential is
- How far the market is geographically or physically distant including
- How similar the potential market is to the one already served in the domestic market.

will all influence the choice of which international markets to consider for entry.

Preliminary screening of the markets can then take place. This will involve a macro approach which may include data grouped under such headings as:

- Economic size and structure (economic potential for growth)
- Social and cultural data (distinctive features of the society)
- Environmental data (legal and political data)
- Marketing environment (consumer behaviour, level of competition, support services, e.g. warehousing, distribution, advertising agencies).

A number of different measures have been suggested as a means to evaluate the risks involved in entering a new country. The Business Environment Risk Index (BERI) takes into account a range of factors as listed in Table 6.3 along with their respective weighting in the index.

Each criterion is scored as being: unacceptable; poor; average; above average; or superior, in terms of the country concerned and a score calculated based on the weightings associated with each criterion. Thus, scores higher than 80 represent advanced economies with a favourable environment for investment; scores of 70–79 are not so favourable, but still an advanced economy; the 55–69 category represent

Table 6.3 Criteria included in the BERI index

Criteria	Weighting
Political stability	3
Economic growth	2.5
Currency convertibility	2.5
Labour cost/productivity	2
Short-term credit	2
Long-term loans/venture capital	2
Attitude toward the international investor	1.5
Nationalization	1.5
Monetary inflation	1.5
Balance of payments	1.5
Enforceability of contracts	1.5
Bureaucratic delays	1
Communications	1
Local management and partners	1
Professional services and contractors	0.5

immature economies; while those falling into the 40–54 category are high risk countries. A score of less than 40 suggests that no serious consideration should be given to such a market.

A second macro screening technique is the shift-share approach (Green and Allaway, 1985; Papadopoulos and Denis, 1988). Using this technique, the average growth in the rate of imports for a particular product in a group of countries can be calculated. Each country's actual growth is compared to the average growth rate, and the difference is termed the 'net-shift', thus identifying growing and declining markets.

While both the approaches outlined here have some merit, they are limited in that the BERI index focuses on political stability and the shift-share method on imports and their relative growth. It can be argued that they do not take enough account of other macro criteria or, especially in the case of micro or smaller enterprises, the crucial influence of the entrepreneur or owner-manager.

A third approach which does try to include the competencies of the individual firm is an adaptation of the Boston Consulting Group's growth-share matrix. The two single dimensions are replaced with composite dimensions based on market/country attractiveness and competitive strength. These composite dimensions are based on the variables detailed in Table 6.4.

These criteria can be scaled and weighted as appropriate to the individual company, and the end result would be the plotting of the markets/countries within the matrix (Figure 6.2). Thus, markets/countries can be seen as primary markets (A countries) which offer the best opportunities; secondary markets (the B countries) which have some economic or political risk suggesting some caution; and the tertiary or C countries, which are high risk and any involvement would be short-term and opportunistic.

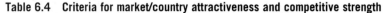

Table 6.4   Criteria for market/country attractiveness and competitive strength

Market/country attractiveness	Competitive strength
Market size	Market share
Market growth	Marketing skills
Buying power of customers	Product fit to market demands
Market season and fluctuations	Price
Average industry margin	Contribution margin
Competitive conditions (concentration, intensity, entry barriers)	Image
Market prohibitive conditions (tariff and non-tariff barriers)	Technology position
Government regulations (price controls, local content, compensatory exports)	Product quality
Infrastructure	Market support
Economic and political stability	Quality of distributors and service
Psychic distance	Financial resources
	Access to distribution channels

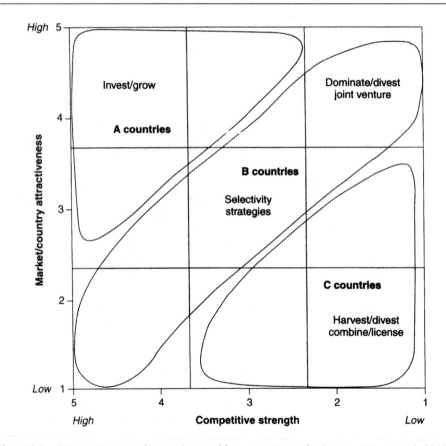

Figure 6.2   The market attractiveness/competitive strength matrix. Source: Hollensen (1998).

Overall, market screening can be expensive in money and time if data is gathered directly from international markets. The reliability of secondary data can also be dubious, or it may be based on groupings and categories which are not standardized internationally. Often with such a vast range of information available, it can be difficult to reduce the number of potentially relevant variables to those which are really critical. Perhaps not enough attention is given to the pragmatic or entrepreneurial drive within the systematic approaches to market selection. A decision process solely based on these techniques would be difficult to justify. Moseley (1996) has suggested a more practical approach to market selection which is detailed in Box 6.3.

BOX 6.3: PRACTICAL MARKET SELECTION (MOSELEY, 1996)

Mosely suggested a number of key questions which should be addressed:

- How big is the market?
- How big is the sector?
- Is there an imported sector? (Can we create one?)
- What are prices/tariffs? (Can we price profitably?)
- What are legal restraints? (Pack/product changes?)
- What distribution? (License vs. direct?)
- Promotional opportunities? (What can we offer?)
- Competition? (How will they respond?)
- Ease of payment?

In order to obtain information to provide answers to these questions Mosely suggests three stages:

Stage 1: Check published statistical information; contact commercial attachés in local embassies of the countries in question.

This provides a screen of the countries in question, and depending on the range of countries and on the depth of data available, could be completed in a couple of weeks. It will become apparent that there is an enormous difference in the data available, which varies more by category than by geographical market, apart from the less-developed countries of the world. The second aspect is the cost of secondary reports, which will often be prohibitive for the smaller exporter. Efficient screening will allow anomalies to be resolved, for example, in one report Hong Kong was listed as a potential attractive market for a particular product because of the large market penetration. However, what was overlooked was the fact that all of the product was being re-exported from Hong Kong, which was acting as an entrepot. At the end of Stage 1 a shortlist of countries can be produced.

Stage 2 involves qualitative research to determine which country will offer the most attractive opportunities. Smaller firms will look for the easier opportunities and, while they may not be the best in the long-term, they will be the easiest to penetrate with limited resources. The degree of attractiveness will vary by category but common factors include:

- Look at what the competition is doing. If they are present in the market and successful, then it improves the chances of success, as they will have already prepared the market.

- Examine the real point of difference, and therefore the key benefit of the brand or product/service, and find out whether there is a niche in the market where your brand could realistically attain top 5 status. There is no point entering a crowded market and becoming brand 49!
- Analyze how easy it is to do business in these markets and how comfortable you would feel at operating in them. This involves considering legal constraints, cultural aspects, and particularly, the language spoken.
- Are there any special reasons why you would find resistance to your product/service in a particular country? This could be related to political or religious issues, for example, American companies doing business in Iran, Iraq, or Libya.

At the end of this stage the exporter has a reasonable view of the key markets, the conditions for entry, and some idea of strategy.

Stage 3: Visit the market. This is vital not just to meet potential intermediaries, such as agents and distributors, but to get a real feel for the market. Talk to consumers in formal qualitative groups, but also in bars and cafes, see where your brand will fit in, what uniqueness will it offer to the market? Such material cannot only be used to reach consumers, but also it will help sell the brand to the intermediaries. Observe, breathe and think the market, and you will be ready for developing the market entry strategy.

Segmentation as an aid to understanding

The purpose of segmenting markets is to take a relatively complex world and break it down into manageable bite-size chunks. These chunks or segments share common consumption characteristics, and can therefore be targeted by companies. Once the prime target markets have been identified, then standard segmentation techniques can be applied. Competitive advantage is achieved by using segmentation strategies to thoroughly understand and appropriately respond to the core values and needs of the consumers within the segment. Traditionally for a market segment to be viable it is said to require four features:

- It must be identifiable so that the size and purchasing power of the segment can be measured
- It must be reachable in order that the segment can be communicated with effectively
- It must be large enough to be sustainable and profitable
- And it must be more homogeneous than the market as a whole.

Companies can either treat each country as an individual entity and target all consumers within its borders, or attempt to serve consumers with the same needs and wants across many countries in global market segments. Arguably with increasing globalization there is an increasing trend towards global market segments, as national boundaries cease to be as important, with the growth of regional trading blocs; the establishment of global investment and production strategies; the expansion of world travel; an increase in the education and literacy levels; the growth of global media and the influence of the Internet allowing a greater freedom of access to information. Firms cannot escape these influences, and even if they do not compete at the global or supra-national level, they may well find international competitors seeking a foothold in their domestic market. Partly as a result of these influences, consumers in different countries often have more in common than consumers within the same country. This process is vastly reinforced by the growth of a common 'language' which consumers share world-wide, namely the brand. The dominance of the branded product in the car market, fashion, electronics, cosmetics, fast food, soft and alcoholic drinks is well known.

The basis for international segmentation has often begun with grouping countries together using macro-level variables, as discussed earlier in this chapter, including geographic, political, economic and cultural data. However, culture is a difficult measure to use, due to the difficulties associated with defining and measuring cultural characteristics. Proxies tend to be used, including social structures, education systems and living standards. Economic measures include degree of urbanization, demographic transition, changes in income distribution and in the occupations of the labour force. While this macro approach may provide groups of countries to target, this approach does not reveal any details about the consumers within those countries. Micro-segmentation gets closer to the customer, and this has been based on product related factors, for example, perceived product characteristics, and on consumer related factors, for example, lifestyle and values. While the latter consumer-focused approach gets closer to the customer, it is argued that product based approaches are more actionable because they are more easily altered to meet the consumer's needs. This, of course, is the very basis of marketing outlined at the start of this chapter.

Hofstede et al. (1999) have attempted to take the product and consumer approaches to micro segmentation and link them together within a segmentation strategy. Such an approach, they argue, links product development to communication strategies that attempt to position products by associating the product aspects to the achievement of desired ends. This is an extension of the means-end chain theory originally developed by Newell and Simon (1972). Attributes lead to benefits, which contribute to value satisfaction, and thus products derive their relevance and meaning.

Hofstede et al. (1999) conducted a study to test the means-end chain theory study across 11 EU countries and involving 2961 respondents. A single product category was chosen, namely, yoghurt. Four international segments were found, based on consumer sociodemographics, consumption patterns, media consumption, personality and attitudes. The authors show that the model has a high predictive validity, and outperforms traditional clustering approaches to international market segmentation.

In terms of practical implications for international marketing strategies, the model lends itself to different types of target market selection and differentiation strategies. Thus companies could:

- Develop specific products for specific segments
- Target a single segment with a number of products (market specialization)
- Target the same product at a number of segments (product specialization) but position it differently depending on the segment-specific benefits

- Develop a mass market product based on commonalties among the segments.

There are obvious parallels between the development of a segmentation strategy, the new product development process, and the communication strategies adopted by companies. There are clear implications as to the importance of the integration of marketing activities.

Whilst the use of the means-end chain theory model involves a quantitative methodology, researchers have used qualitative approaches to segment international markets. In addition, while the model outlined above worked well in a European context, it has not been tested across more diverse cultures. Ueltzhoffer and Ascheberg (1999) set themselves a substantial task by stating that they wished to develop a segmentation system which would:

- Align itself to the subjective reality of the consumer
- Constantly adapt its target group structure to the changes occurring in the market and in society
- Register, understand and integrate the latest social trends
- Not be restricted to regional or national markets, but which will be a transnational, globally deployable socio-cultural market segmentation system.

The model which was developed is based on the Everyday-Life approach, which integrates way of life, basic values and structures in consumer society. It is argued that this model allows the closer monitoring of the connection between changing

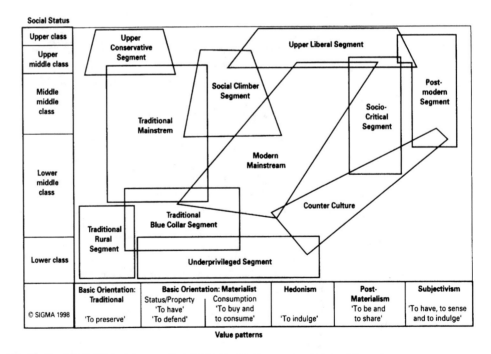

Figure 6.3 **Transnational consumer cultures. Source: Ueltzhoffer and Ascheberg (1999).**

values, postmodernization and consumer behaviour. Thus by understanding consumer culture (social milieus) it is possible to draw up socio-cultural groups with which to target products and services. Figure 6.3 illustrates the implementation of this thesis.

Overall Ueltzhoffer and Ascheberg argue that the Everyday-Life approach creates more stable socio-cultural maps, which reflect the realities of consumers and their basic values. By combining product acceptance and brand perception with the subjective socio-cultural identity of consumers, marketing strategies can be more precisely targeted within and across national boundaries.

Conclusions

Marketing is dynamic because customers are dynamic. Few markets stand still, and companies which stand still tend to find their position over time being eroded by new ideas, fresh ways of doing things or simply fashion cycles. By truly trying to understand the customer, the better companies can keep in touch with their markets. However, although technology alters the way in which market research is conducted, the vital role performed by people in assessing the nuances and cultural influences will still be vital, even if the skills have changed. Market research can be costly and expensive, but it does not have to be that for the smaller company. Informal methods of data collection, simply by keeping close to the key players in any channel, can pay dividends for the smaller company. The best market research is ongoing, continuous and open ended.

Selecting international markets in which to operate is a crucial element of international activity. In this chapter a number of systematic approaches have been outlined. These, however, have been offered for consideration with the warning that a pragmatic and more intuitive approach to market selection may take place. This will be especially true in the micro or smaller firm, where the personal networks and cultural background of the entrepreneur or owner manager will be highly influential. Micro-segmentation, as we have seen, can play an important role in narrowing the range of customers a company can chose to serve, and as a result make it more efficient.

The activities associated with understanding the customer's values interact and feed through into the next stage of the marketing cycle, particularly in relation to the development of the brand. Market research helps to identify and show ways in which the best use of brand equity can be made within different cultural contexts, whilst informing management of buyers' current and future needs. As the marketing cycle in Figure 6.1 implied, these activities are linked, and marketers must ensure in any organization that a dialogue takes place between those responsible for understanding and creating customer related values. The next chapter will continue the discussion of the marketing cycle, by considering the marketing activities associated with creating and communicating customer related values.

Questions for discussion

1. Apply the conceptualization of the marketing cycle discussed in this chapter to the work undertaken by your educational institution with undergraduate or postgraduate students. What happens at each stage of the cycle? How could it be improved?
2. You are to develop a new consumer product for the food sector. Decide the new product's characteristics and then outline what market research you would undertake and why?
3. Why should companies undertake to screen international markets? Why, in some cases, will systematic screening not take place?
4. Compile a list of the key secondary sources of business information available in your country.
5. For the sources identified in question 4, define a number of criteria to judge their usefulness to the smaller business, for example, cost, how recent is the information, breakdowns available, etc. Use a five-point scale (1 very poor; 2 poor, 3 average, 4 good and 5 very good) to produce a ranking of these sources.
6. Select a country and product or service. Using only the Internet, see what information you can find out to assist with a proposed market entry to that market.
7. Discuss the potential problems of using international statistics in a market screening process.
8. Research and discuss how technology is changing the conduct of market research.
9. Quantitative market research and qualitative market research are distinct approaches and should never be mixed. Discuss and justify your views.
10. Understanding what customers are looking for in products and services is a one-off activity. Discuss.

References

Bathie, D. (1998), *Principles of Marketing, Retail Marketing MBA Module 1*, Institute for Retail Studies, University of Stirling.

Green, R.T. and Allaway, A.W. (1985), Identification of export opportunities: a shift-share approach, *Journal of Marketing*, 49 (1), pp. 83–88.

Hollensen, S. (1998), *Global Marketing: a Market-Responsive Approach*, Prentice-Hall, London.

Hofstede, F., Jan-Benedict E.M. Steenkanmp and Wedel, M. (1999), International market segmentation based on consumer-product relations, *Journal of Marketing Research*, 36 (1), pp. 1–17.

James, D. (1999), Precision decision, Marketing News, Sep. 27, pp. 23–24.

Laflin, D. (1999), Planning a successful research project, *Marketing News*, Jan. 4, p. 21.

MacFarlane, I. (1991), Do-it-yourself marketing research, *Management Review*, 80 (5), pp. 34–37.

McKie, A. (1996), International research in a relative world, *Journal of the Market Research Society*, 38 (1), pp. 7–12.

Moseley, D. (1996), Information needs for market entry, *Journal of the Market Research Society*, 38 (1), pp. 13–18.

Newell, A. and Simon, H.A. (1972), *Human Problem Solving*, Prentice Hall, Englewood Cliffs, NJ.

Pawle, J. (1999), Mining the international consumer, *Journal of the Market Research Society*, 41 (1), pp. 19–32.

Papadopoulos, N. and Denis, J.E. (1988), Inventory, taxonomy and assessment of methods for international market selection, *International Marketing Review*, 5 (3), pp. 38–51.

Stewart-Allen, A.L. (1999), Do your international homework first, *Marketing News*, 33 (1), p. 25.

Ueltzhoffer, J. and Ascheberg, C. (1999), Transnational consumer cultures and social milieus, *Journal of the Market Research Society*, 41 (1), pp. 47–59.

Further Reading

Dibb, S. and Simkin, L. (1997), A program for implementing market segmentation, *Journal of Business & Industrial Marketing*, 12 (1), p. 51; (15) InfoTrac http://www.galegroup.com/

Hassan, S.S. and Katsanis, L.P. (1994), Global market segmentation strategies and trends, in: Kaynak, E. and Hassan, S.S. (eds.), *Globalization of Consumer Markets: Structures and Strategies*, International Business Press, New York, pp. 47–63.

Hassan, S.S. and Kaynak, E. (1994), The globalizing consumer market: issues and concepts, in: Kaynak, E. and Hassan, S.S. (eds.), *Globalization of Consumer Markets: Structures and Strategies*, International Business Press, New York, pp. 19–25.

Kale, S.H. (1995), Grouping Euroconsumers: a culture-based clustering approach, *Journal of International Marketing*, 3 (3), pp. 35–48.

Keillor, B.D. and Hult, G.T.M. (1999), A five-country study of national idenity: implications for international marketing research and practice, *International Marketing Review*, 16 (1), pp. 65–82.

Kristiaan, H., Jedidi, K. and DeSarbo, W.S. (1993), A new approach to country segmentation utilizing multinational diffusion patterns, *Journal of Marketing*, 57 (4), pp. 60–71.

Li, T., Nicholls, J.A.F. and Roslow, S. (1999), The relationships between market-driven learning and new product success in export markets, *International Marketing Review*, 16 (6), pp. 476–503.

Walters, P.G.P. (1997), Global market segmentation: methodologies and challenges, *Journal of Marketing Management*, 13 (1–3), pp. 165–177.

White, D. S. and Griffith, D.A. (1997), Combining corporate and marketing strategy for global competitiveness, *Marketing Intelligence & Planning*, 15 (4/5), pp.173–178.

Wood, V.R., Darling, J.R. and Siders, M. (1999), Consumer desire to buy and use products in international markets: how to capture it, how to sustain it, *International Marketing Review*, 16 (3),pp. 231–256.

In addition the following journal has published a relevant special issue:

Journal of the Market Research Society (1999), Special Issue: Research on the Internet, 41 (4).

CHAPTER 7

Creating and communicating customer values

Chapter objectives

After studying this chapter you should be able to:

- Appreciate what is meant by creating and communicating customer values
- Explain the marketing activities associated with creating customer values
- Explain the marketing activities associated with communicating values, including the role of communication, the standardization – adaptation debate, and how to construct a basic communications plan

Introduction

This chapter continues to use the framework outlined in the previous chapter, by devoting its attention to the creation and communication activities within the marketing cycle. For many people the communications aspects of marketing are the most familiar. After all, if you turn on the television, open a newspaper, drive or walk around our cities, a company is trying to grab your attention – be it from a hoarding/billboard, a leaflet in the street or a message emblazoned on the side of a taxi or bus. We ourselves can even be considered as part of the marketing message, as we visibly display various brand names on our clothing.

As a student of marketing, you know that marketing is more than simply the very obvious activities of communication or promotion. We have already seen in Chapter 6 how understanding the customer is a vital part of the marketing process. It is the precursor to creating products and services which customers actually want. Their needs and wants have to be incorporated into the products or services before going on to tell the same customers that you can offer these to them. Communication is perhaps the most visible marketing activity, but to fully work it must be integrated with all other parts of the cycle. Clearly, simply understanding customers and producing good products or services is crucial to the success of a business, but unless potential customers are told about the product then who is going to buy it? Communication entails many marketing decisions; who to 'speak' to; how to reach them; what to tell them? Within this chapter we will look at the issues surrounding the creation of products or services including the development of global brands and issues to do with pricing and packaging. In the next section the basics of communicating value will be discussed, before going on to consider the role of advertising. Finally, the standardiz-ation versus adaptation debate will be discussed before concluding the chapter.

Creating customer values

In an average week of reading papers or watching television it would be hard to avoid the topic of globalization. Surf the Web and you have an even more direct link to a global network of possibilities. Holbert (2000) views globalization 'as the process in which the world is shrinking virtually while growing with real oppor-tunities; where the mighty dominate, but anyone with Web savvy can become an instant international marketer; and capital...now crosses increasingly porous borders.' Is globalization the new imperialism, with McDonalds, Coca-Cola, Bene-tton, Sony and Microsoft the new colonizers?

It is good that in the 'global village' we can share in its riches. The millennium celebrations at the start of this new century were the first global party, but not everyone was there. Different cultures and poverty kept some away. Marketing does not want to make the world entirely uniform. Local variations enrich all our lives, but they have to be good to compete and marketing can help. Those who cannot afford to buy from the colonizers, or who sacrifice more fundamental purchases in order to buy them, must be a part of globalization. There is a danger of exclusion for some despite all the talk of a shrinking world. e-Commerce is of no interest if you have no online access or little prospect of it. Globalization has a dark side, and marketing can be seen as its partner, when instead marketing should be helping to offer a choice of purchasing options, the international brands and the local. This is a better future than the imperialistic marketing envisaged by Levitt as we saw in Chapter 4.

In this section we will consider the development of global brands, the role of country of origin as an extrinsic product cue, pricing and packaging as they relate to the creation of value.

Global brands

There is a famous scene in Tarantino's movie, Pulp Fiction, where John Travolta and Samuel L. Jackson discuss the different names for a Big Mac around the world. Whether Le Big Mac or Royale with Cheese, there was never any dispute that the overall brand was McDonalds. This brand, along with Marlboro, Nike and Coca-

Cola, belongs to a small but distinguished group of truly global super-brands. This kind of recognition is the dream of many less well known brands who have to find their way around the problems of global design. Problems, as we saw in Chapter 3, arise with names causing an embarrassing faux-pas, colours, symbols or the logistical challenge of harmonizing a myriad of names and designs under a new brand identity.

Few brands can reach the level of standardization normally associated with McDonalds, Marlboro, Nike and Coca-Cola, whose positioning, advertising strategy, personality, look and feel are in most respects the same from country to country. Therefore it is not unusual to find a strategy based on regional flexibility. The key is to establish core brand values and come up with a design solution appropriate to disparate regional markets. Even strong brands like McDonalds have to change sometimes – for example, in Sweden the packaging was altered to use woodcut illustrations and an overall softer design, to appeal to the Swede's perceived interest in food value and the natural world.

The dominance of globalization was reflected more in the textbooks of the 1980s and early 1990s, whereas by the late 1990s there was more often an appreciation of the environmental maxim 'think global, act local'. Marketers are attracted to globalization through demand motives such as internationally shared tastes, preferences and the expectation that products everywhere should be sold at the same price. However, any attempt to devise a 'world consumer' would seem only to result in the lowest common denominators being used, and would be a useful as any 'average'. Even within Europe the pan-European consumer can be difficult to identify as, for example, in the washing machine market where there are contrasts between consumers who prefer a top or front loading machine. However, companies like Gillette have attempted to capitalize on pan-European brands (see Box 7.1).

BOX 7.1: THE GILLETTE SENSOR STORY

In the 1980s Gillette discovered that price competition from truly disposable razors, e.g. Bic was eroding their profit margins and brand loyalty. To compete on price would be futile in the long term. Instead the company focused on its concept of a shaving system where only the blades were replaced but the shaver was durable.

The intention was to create a product which would serve US, Canadian and European customers, thus covering the North Atlantic marketplace. Thus Sensor was launched in 1989. The name was selected for its ease of pronunciation in many languages as well as for its technological imagery. As part of its intention to build a North Atlantic and then a global brand, the company used the Gillette name as a super-brand to capitalize on the company's dominance in the industry.

The gamble paid off and Gillette Sensor succeeded. On the back of this success the company has brought greater consistency to its other products across diverse markets. Thus names and graphics have been given greater unity and fragmentation reduced. This strategy has successfully boosted sales, and increased customer loyalty in what was becoming an undifferentiated, purely price-driven business.

(adapted from Ackerman, 1991)

Table 7.1 Mandatory and cultural reasons for adaptation

Mandatory	Cultural
Legal reasons	Consumer tastes – beer can be preferred bitter, foamy, bubbly, sugary and have different strengths
Taxes and tariffs	Disposable income
Technical requirements	Labour costs
Nationalism	Physical differences
Climate	Language
	Illiteracy

Culture acts as a natural entry barrier to pure globalization, and there is probably a greater recognition of this now amongst marketers than there was in the 1980s. If consumers share global values, then a globalization approach becomes easier and the economies associated with standardization will come into play. However, global strategies can also be pursued with the input of good local market research, and by making use of cultural 'insiders' to advise the company. Acquisition of local companies can also accelerate organizational learning in the local market and thus assist the globalization process. Compromises can be forced on a company either because of cultural differences or as a result of mandatory regulations (Table 7.1).

However, a global brand may not be an appropriate solution for every country. Aaker and Joachimsthaler (1999) suggest three difficulties with this concept. First, economies of scale may not be achieved. Cultural differences make the development, for example, of a global advertising campaign more difficult, and even a large agency may have trouble executing it well in all countries. Cost savings from 'media spillover' where people in France view German television advertisements are, they argue, exaggerated due to language and cultural differences. Second, putting a global brand team together and developing a superior brand strategy for one country is difficult enough without trying to devise one for a world-wide launch. Teams would have to assimilate too much information, be extremely creative and anticipate all the difficulties of a global execution. Finally, global brands cannot be imposed. Sometimes brands mean different things in different markets, for example, Honda means quality and reliability in the US and Europe but in Japan the quality of cars is taken as given and Honda represents speed, youth and energy. The name itself can be a crucial part of success in branding and a company in the US specializes in developing brand names (see Box 7.2).

BOX 7.2: WHAT'S IN A NAME?

There is a company based in California, US which specializes in coming up with brand names for products. This company is Lexicon Branding. What the world knows as the Pentium chip could also have been called Razor, ProChip or Intellect had executives at Intel thought differently.

Coming up with a number of options is not an easy task. David Placek, founder of Lexicon, must first gain an understanding of the product, the demographics of the consumer and an idea of what the name should evoke. Three teams took eight months to come up with Slates for Levi Strauss's new dress trousers. The also-rans were Darts, Batten, Dress Gear and Flints.

One of the biggest turnarounds the company has been involved with was when Apple had a new laptop known simply as a Macintosh portable. Lexicon provided the verbal lift and sales of the PowerBook soared.

(adapted from Malik, 1999)

Aaker and Joachimsthaler go on to argue that rather than developing global brands, firms should concentrate on creating strong brands in all markets through global brand leadership. This they define as 'using organizational structures, processes and cultures to allocate brand-building resources globally, to create global synergies, and to develop a global brand strategy that co-ordinates and leverages country brand strategies.' In a study of 35 companies across Europe, the US and Japan, they found that four common ideas about effective brand leadership emerged from the interviews. These were:

- Stimulate the sharing of insights and best practices across countries
- Support a common global brand-planning process
- Assign managerial responsibility for brands in order to create cross-country synergies and to reduce local bias
- Execute brilliant brand-building strategies

However, global brands have not had it all their own way. Studies of the sources of our favourite brands have linked Nike sneakers to abusive sweatshops of Vietnam, Barbie's outfits to child workers in Sumatra and Shell's oil to the polluted and impoverished villages in the Niger Delta. These stories seem to be providing a focus for protest by activists against the 'brand bullies' as discussed by Naomi Klein (2000) in her book 'No Logo'. This will be discussed further in Chapter 10.

Controlling global brands can be a problem for companies. Pepsi spent £200 million (pounds sterling) on introducing its new blue cans all over the world in 1996 at the start of a 3 year programme. However, the company experienced problems because gray marketeers were selling the old style cans more cheaply in the markets where the new design had already been introduced. This resulted in brand dilution and customer confusion. The gray traffickers are attracted by currency fluctuations and differences in taxes. Thus the goods flow from continental Europe into the UK, from Switzerland into France, from France to Belgium and from Norway into Sweden (The European, 1998). See Box 7.3 for further details.

BOX 7.3: SHADES OF GRAY

Gray markets occur when branded items are distributed through unauthorized channels. Often this flow takes place across national boundaries where price differentials can be capitalized upon. Thus gray marketers will purchase goods either from an authorized dealer or directly from the manufacturer, and then re-sell the product in a higher-priced market at a profit. Technically they are not contravening any law, but they may be in breach of license agreements or government trade regulations.

Some consumer groups argue that such trade promotes competition, but the manufacturer tends to view it as an impairment on the trademark owner's ability to get a full return on their investment or protect the brand image.

In 1998 after some high-profile examples of gray market activity, the EU imposed a ban on it resulting in an increase in legal actions taken against retailers and importers handling unauthorized goods. Some UK based supermarkets were using the gray market sources to obtain fashionable brands of clothing. However, the Advocate General of the European Court of Justice ruled in January 1998 that trademark owners could prevent the selling of their branded goods if the goods had been imported, without their authorization, from outside the EU. Tommy Hilfiger Corp. also entered into legal proceedings against Tesco Stores Ltd., claiming that they found counterfeit items amongst Tesco's Tommy Hilfiger goods.

In another case before the European Court, Silhouette, a manufacturer of fashionable spectacle frames, sold a shipment of an outdated model to a trading company in Bulgaria with the stipulation that the frames could be sold only there or in the states of the former Soviet Union. However, Hartlauer, a retailer of lower-priced spectacles (which Silhouette had refused to supply in Austria), subsequently acquired the frames, re-imported them and offered them for sale in its shops. Silhouette, fearing damage to its upmarket brand, sued to stop the sale.

A study by Myers and Griffith (1999) revealed that gray market activity occurs in almost every manufacturing industry, and not just in less developed or volatile markets. They advise that in order to combat gray market activity managers must:

- Co-ordinate distribution channels horizontally
- Keep apprised of changing regulations
- Pay attention to differentiated products across markets
- Restrict the autonomy to set prices
- Stay in touch with distributors

(adapted from Robinson, 1998; Myers and Griffith, 1999; and The Economist, 1998)

Country of origin

The country of origin of a product, which is normally communicated through the phrase 'made in...', is an extrinsic product cue, an intangible product attribute, that is distinct from physical product characteristics or intrinsic attributes, for example, taste, design, performance. As such, a county of origin cue is similar to price, brand name, or warranty, in that none of these bear directly on product performance (Peterson and Jolibert, 1995). This construct is not just important in consumer markets where it may be more visible, but it also applies in business to business marketing as well. This is a well researched area within international marketing, however, those involved are unsure of how far country of origin effects can be generalized. In a sense, this area of research has suffered in a similar way to the study of internationalization processes (Chapter 4), as the construct is relatively ambiguous and has been interpreted and operationalized in widely divergent ways in the literature. In addition, methodologies and research designs have differed, with little systematic exploration across cultures.

Taking what has been broadly established by the research, most would agree that country of origin has an impact on how consumers evaluate products, but its effect is mixed. Some research suggests that it signals product quality, but other work suggests it is only a weak attribute. Any categorization of a product based on country of origin – for example, Japanese cars are very reliable – is based on a stereotype. Such a view is potentially less accurate, context dependent and likely to vary across situations.

Inevitably, often the consumer is basing his/her perceptions on a stereotype which can be highly inaccurate, but in general, products from developed nations are seen as better quality and have a more positive image than those from developing nations. Consumers will also use country of origin in effect to compensate for their lack of knowledge or familiarity with a product. Thus high familiarity reduces the impact which country of origin information may have on a product evaluation. When consumers are not familiar with a product they will use the country's image as a 'halo' in evaluating the product.

This is borne out in a study by Maheswaran (1994) in which the influence of consumer expertise and attribute information on product evaluations was explored. It was found that when attribute information was unambiguous, experts based their evaluations on attribute strength, whereas inexperienced consumers relied on country of origin. When attribute information was ambiguous, both experienced and inexperienced consumers used country of origin in their evaluations. The research went further and found that experienced consumers used country of origin to selectively recall product attributes, whereas inexperienced consumers used it to differentially interpret attribute information.

Another aspect of country of origin is the aura of sophistication which international brands can convey. Thus in developing countries even the poorest people will aspire to own something western. In addition, if the item is expensive and may have a risk of malfunctioning, then county of origin is used to evaluated this risk. Kaynak et al. (1995) found in a study in Azerbaijan that Japanese and US products were perceived to be better in design and technological level than products from Russia, China and Hong Kong. Similar evidence was found by Zain and Yasin (1997) who found that Uzbekistan consumers rated the quality of products from Japan and the US higher than those from India and China. This is potentially an important factor for international marketers, as the opportunities for trade open up in the former Soviet republics. Conversely, for exporters from developing countries, they can have difficulty persuading consumers in developed countries to purchase their products, as domestically produced products are more highly rated. This influence is reduced with higher education levels, amount of disposable income and experience of international travel.

Thus the use of the country of origin attribute can be managed as part of the marketing activities of the business. If the country of origin has a favourable reputation in the appropriate product category in the national market, then the country of origin has value to add to the communications strategy. On the other hand, if this is not the case, then it may be better to revert to a local name for particular markets in order to 'conceal' the country of origin. In instances where nationalistic feelings are prevalent, perhaps in a newly independent nation, this is also a possible strategy. It is not impossible to overcome negative images through improved advertising or national export promotion campaigns, which seek to enhance the general image of the country and the image of products sourced from it. Box 7.4 illustrates the selective use of country of origin by L'Oreal to appeal to different mind-sets.

BOX 7.4: GLOBAL BEAUTY

In Shanghai there is a launch of a new product – Maybelline. With the backdrop of a New York skyline and a pulsing rhythm a make-up artist transforms a model's face while a Chinese saleswoman delivers the punch line. 'This brand comes from America, it's very trendy. If you want to be fashionable, just choose Maybelline.' Few will realize that this 'American' brand belongs to the very French company L'Oreal.

The French company L'Oreal has taken a different approach to global branding. Whereas Coca Cola attempts to focus on selling one brand globally, L'Oreal's strategy is to convey the allure of different cultures through its many products. This can include Italian elegance, New York street wise mentality or French beauty. By embodying country of origin into their products, L'Oreal has made a marketing virtue out of what others regard as a narrowing factor.

The company attempts to capitalize on the two dominant beauty cultures, namely French and American, by having two creative bases, one in Paris and one in New York. This provides contrasting approaches based on two totally different mind-sets, backgrounds and creative directions.

L'Oreal acquired Maybelline in 1996 and gave it an 'urban American chic' makeover. From 1996 to 1999 sales have doubled from $320 to $600 million and the brand is available in more than 70 countries. Sales outside the US account for 50% of the total.

(adapted from Business Week, 1999)

Pricing

Pricing has been relatively neglected in terms of academic marketing research. This has been noted by Rao (1984) while Cavusgil (1988) stated that the neglect of international pricing was even more acute. Clark et al. (1999) comment on its continued neglect over the previous 25 years. Pricing is not simply an economic decision, it can also be seen as a marketing tactic, through the use of discounts, special offers and various incentives. It is an important decision for any business because, quite simply, it generates revenue for the business.

In the domestic market, basic pricing strategies may include cost orientated pricing, where a fixed amount or percentage is added on to the cost of the product, for example, cost-plus pricing or mark-up pricing. Demand may also be used to set prices; thus the price is high when demand is strong and lower when demand is weak. Alternatively pricing could be based on the strategies adopted by competitors, and the company will price above, below or at the same level as a competitor. From a marketing perspective, the pricing strategy could be marketing-led. Thus, market-orientated pricing takes into account a wide range of factors, which makes it more complicated than cost-orientated or competition orientated pricing. These factors include the marketing strategy; competition; value to the customer; price-quality relationships; costs; product line pricing; negotiated margins; and the effect of intermediaries and political factors.

In setting a price for international markets companies have to take into account a variety of company and market factors (Figure 7.1). The company is exposed to additional cost, for example, in additional packaging costs which may not be required in the domestic market, and difficulties can arise in the international market as a result of inflation, volatile exchange rates, the activities of gray marketers and difficulties in transfer pricing (see Box 7.5). Additional costs can be generated via transportation costs, warehousing, insurance, tariffs and taxes, legal costs and the cost of employing staff dedicated to the exporting activity. Political factors too can affect the pricing strategies of companies, due to governmental influence on the wider marketing environment via antidumping legislation, tariffs, lack of 'hard currency' and government intervention in currency markets.

BOX 7.5: TRANSFER PRICING EXPLAINED

Transfer pricing is associated with multinational companies with subsidiary companies in many countries. The multinational can sell products or services to its own subsidiary companies through an internal account. A subsidiary can show a higher or lower profit or obtain goods at a higher or lower price. The prices will be set by the head office and may have little relationship to the real value of the goods. Thus, transfer pricing allows the subsidiary to adjust the amount of tax it pays on profits; or to import goods at lower costs and pay less customs duties or it could be used to repatriate funds from the subsidiary to the head office.

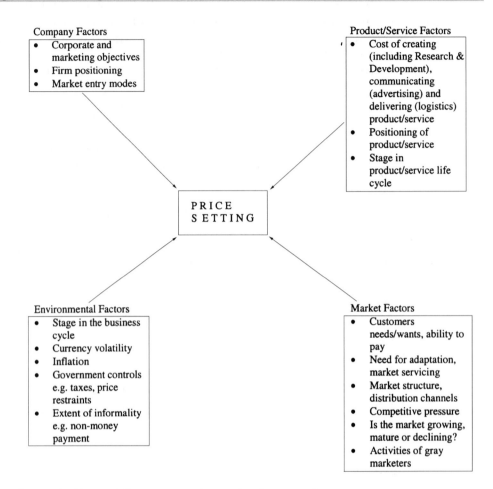

Company Factors
- Corporate and marketing objectives
- Firm positioning
- Market entry modes

Product/Service Factors
- Cost of creating (including Research & Development), communicating (advertising) and delivering (logistics) product/service
- Positioning of product/service
- Stage in product/service life cycle

PRICE SETTING

Environmental Factors
- Stage in the business cycle
- Currency volatility
- Inflation
- Government controls e.g. taxes, price restraints
- Extent of informality e.g. non-money payment

Market Factors
- Customers needs/wants, ability to pay
- Need for adaptation, market servicing
- Market structure, distribution channels
- Competitive pressure
- Is the market growing, mature or declining?
- Activities of gray marketers

Figure 7.1   The key influences on setting a price. Source: author.

Market-orientated pricing

Of course the consumer sees price from an entirely different perspective. The consumer will view the price of a product as a signifier of its quality. High price indicates high quality and similarly for low priced goods. The greater the perceived quality of a product, the more tolerant the consumer will be to price changes, and therefore other signifiers of quality, for example, performance, style, prestige and design, become important marketing tools. Four central pricing techniques are associated with marketing-orientated pricing (Winkler, 1989).

1. Higher price strategies. These include skimming, which concentrates on the top layer of the market; and prestige pricing, which prices products at an artificially high level in order to maintain an image of extreme quality, which distinguishes the product from the rest of the market. A third high price strategy is umbrella

pricing, which encourages competitors to shelter under the higher prices of the quality or volume leader in the market.

2. Competitive pricing strategies include price matching, copying the competition closely; flexible pricing, changing prices to suit current competitive or market situations; trading down prices, to open up demand in new segments of the market; pricing points, using for example $89.95 to make it 'seem' cheaper than $90.00; market pricing, using different prices in different markets; diversionary pricing, supplying a product free at installation against a contract to supply and service the product over its lifetime; phase out pricing, maintaining or raising prices to maximize profits when a product is at the end of its life cycle; discount pricing, special prices for particular orders; promotional pricing, the use of time-limited special prices to increase sales, perhaps including free goods or credit.

3. Low price strategies include pre-emptive pricing, to discourage others from entering the market; penetration pricing, to gain a large share of the market, perhaps when entering the market for the first time; predatory pricing, to use very low prices to prevent competition from entering the market, or to force existing competition out of the market; loss leader pricing, to use low prices for a limited period to attract customers to other goods sold at full price.

4. Negotiated pricing strategies include bundling prices, putting a complete deal together involving a number of products or services sold under a single price; unbundling prices, the reverse, where a package is split up and negotiated piece by piece; packaging and add on pricing, where parts of the deal vary in price depending upon the prices for the rest of the deal; buy it and cook it pricing, where a very low initial price is agreed, perhaps at a loss, because it is known that later variations to contract, or agreed later price increases or inflationary factors will make the deal highly profitable in the end.

The above discussion provides some insight to the links between different pricing approaches and marketing strategy. Price is not just a number, it is a marketing tool to be used and manipulated like any other marketing tactic. In contrast to the large number of options outlined above, Clark et al. (1999) identified three basic pricing strategies for export markets which are identified in the literature, namely, cost-plus, profit contribution and incremental cost. Cost plus indicates that firms are adding a fixed amount, in effect a predetermined profit margin, to their total cost of producing a product. The profit margin is then a potential casualty of currency fluctuations due to exchange rate variations. In addition this is a form of pricing in which no account is taken of the market conditions, thus, if the market is very competitive, sales may drop. Usually firms will be forced to respond to external competition and abandon strict cost-plus pricing in these circumstances.

Profit-contribution pricing recognizes that demand conditions can often differ from market to market. Prices are set to obtain the maximum profit margin within each geographic market. If this method is to work, then the activities of gray marketers must be minimized. Gray markets exist when traders can import goods from another market where the selling price is cheaper than the price they normally pay (previously discussed in Box 7.3).

Incremental cost pricing plays down the role of fixed costs in setting export prices, and focuses on the incremental cost of exporting. Thus, exporters regard fixed costs as covered by domestic sales, and so price exports at anything above their domestic variable costs. This policy is based on the assumption that exporters have excess capacity and that arbitrage between domestic and international markets is not possible. In effect this method represents a middle ground between cost-plus and profit-contribution as it neither adheres to full costs or market conditions. The company has flexibility to maximize excess capacity sales, which frees it from exchange rate fluctuations. However, it is possible that prices in the export markets fall below domestic levels, which may result in the company being accused of dumping (see Box 7.6).

BOX 7.6: DUMPING EXPLAINED

Products will be classified as having been dumped if they are sold below the cost of production or if they are sold in the international market below the price they are sold for in the domestic market. The legal definitions are more precise, and the World Trade Agreement allows governments to act against dumping where there is genuine injury to the competing domestic industry. In order to do that, the government has to be able to show that dumping is taking place, calculate the extent of dumping (how much lower the export price is compared to the exporter's home market price), and show that the dumping is causing injury. Anti-dumping action involves charging extra import duty (a countervailing duty) on the particular product from the particular exporting country, in order to bring its price closer to the 'normal value' or to remove the injury to domestic industry in the importing country.

Recent examples of dumping disputes include the EU imposing anti-dumping duties on imports of unbleached cotton fabric from China, Egypt, Indonesia, Pakistan and Turkey. The American steel industry has accused Japan, Brazil and Russia of dumping, and South Korean memory-chip manufacturers have been hit with heavy duties. In addition, countries such as Mexico, Argentina and Brazil have accused the US of dumping.

How to avoid mistakes in pricing

There tends to be two common errors in pricing decisions. Either price is set without having a specified long-term objective in mind, or it is calculated without using other information from the market. In order to avoid these mistakes the following principles should be followed:

- Allocate responsibility for the collection of data on pricing; for studying alternatives; for making the pricing decisions and implementing them.
- Set pricing objectives. There should be company guidelines on the overall strategic approach to pricing, including how it relates to the management process and especially the financial objectives.

- Construct a plan and a timetable for the pricing process.
- Identify the influencing factors, for example, major customers, reaction of competition, likely demand levels, cost factors, supply problems, implications for intermediaries and for the longer term.
- Review market information. Gather market information and assess demand in different market segments. Examine possibilities for low and high price products.
- Review the competition. Look at their strengths and weaknesses; identify those which have to be covered to enter the market; what unique edge can be built into the offering; how can pricing be used be used competitively and how will the competition react to the pricing strategy.
- Review the cost data. A plan for the long-term return on investment should be put in place, as well as the possibility for cost reductions and efficiencies when prices are lowered as the market matures.
- Establish the strategy. Broadly; top of the market; competitive; penetration or specialist niche markets.
- Set price. Finalize the terms of sale and any discount structure as appropriate.
- Set cost and volume objectives, which in turn become the production targets.
- Review price performance in the market.

Packaging

As we have seen, the fewer changes an exporter has to make to a particular product, then the less costly export activities will be. However, cultural influences can militate against the cost conscious package designer. From a marketing perspective, an investment in researching and designing appropriate packaging and choosing the right name can bring huge rewards. There is another side of packaging, namely that concerned with protective packaging and the safe transportation of goods, and this will be dealt in Chapter 8.

This section will concentrate on the role of packaging in attracting the consumer to the product. The keys to effective packaging that works for you while it sits on supermarket shelves are graphic design, structural shapes and materials that capture the essence of a product brand and are easily recognizable. Knowles (1996) states that 'In our over-communicated, hyperactive, commercially obsessed world, ideas travel faster, innovation is imitated quicker and much marketing is rapidly decoded and disregarded.' As consumers in many international markets feel their lives getting busier, they shop more impulsively for many relatively routine items. Thus, packaging on supermarket and hypermarket shelves must work in a split second, communicating recognizable brand values. This is true of other sectors as well where, for example, the BMW and VW logos work very efficiently to convey a whole host of meaning. Of course this will work best if the packaging fits into a well developed coherent marketing identity. The importance of a holistic marketing approach cannot be over stressed. Packaging is not just for the 'techies' it should be a marketing concern.

Good packaging can, to some extent, replace traditional advertising strategies if interest and loyal customers can be built through eye catching design. Think of the Guinness poster campaigns, which since the early 20th Century have become an advertising icon, and to some extent an art form. All the big global brands have a very distinctive look, from the Nike swoosh to the Coca-Cola wave. J&B whisky's success in the hypermarket may owe as much to its bright yellow label as to its taste. Glenfiddich's green triangular bottle certainly gives a robust feel when handled. Different cultures can have their varying preferences, as Box 7.7 illustrates.

BOX 7.7: SOME PACKAGING QUIRKS

Cans are more popular in France and Spain than card or foil. Soups are traditionally supplied in packets. The French suspicion of canned drink is not a problem for Coca-Cola but does affect sales of fresh orange.

Germans prefer to see their cakes wrapped in foil whereas the French prefer a cellophane window in order to be able to see the cake.

French consumers have strong colour associations – blue is seen as the colour of the Nordic lands, whereas green is seen as being associated with Scotland and Ireland. A rampant lion is associated with Peugeot or with Normandy rather than being seen as a Scottish symbol.

In France and Germany where knowledge of Asian and Latin American food is low the ingredients for a curry sell better if they are put together in a kit rather than being sold separately in different supermarket aisles.

(adapted from Ensor, 1997)

Clearly packaging has an important role to play in attracting the consumer. However, it is worth noting that as e-commerce takes off, certain products, for example, music, software, news, and movies, can be delivered electronically with no discs, tapes, papers or boxes required.

Communicating customer values – the basics

Communication is essentially about transmitting a message in order to elicit a discriminating response. The responsibility for the sending of the message rests with the sender. If the message is misunderstood, then it is the fault of the sender, not the receiver. Marketing communications are designed to achieve a particular objective or set of objectives. These must be defined before a communication strategy is put in place and implemented. At a very basic level we can think of communications involving the elements (Figure 7.2).

The methods of communication available to the marketer include advertising, personal selling, publicity and sales promotion. Advertising is any paid form of non-personal communication that is transmitted to targeted customers via mass media, for example, television, newspapers, magazines, direct mail, billboards. It is

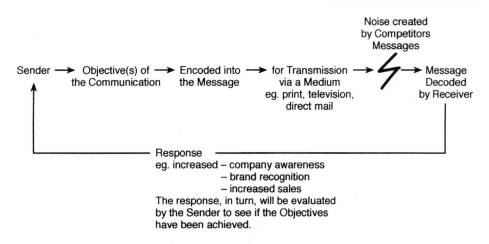

Figure 7.2 A basic communications model. Source: author.

largely impersonal and one-way communication. The objectives of advertising can be to:

- Shift customer attitudes
- Build brand awareness
- Promote products/services
- Promote an organization
- Support the sales force
- Reinforce current customer purchasing
- Even out sales fluctuations.

Personal selling, as the name implies, is all about having a face-to-face exchange with the customer. The marketer can tailor the message to the customer's needs and deal very specifically with any issue or questions which the customer may have. Personal selling aims to:

- Find prospective customers
- Convince prospects to purchase
- Maintain customer relations
- Generate customer and market intelligence.

Publicity is communication about a business or its products through a news story format, which is transmitted through a mass medium without media costs being incurred. The news story format gives the message greater credibility for some people than pure advertising. Publicity can:

- Provide information but is not persuasive
- Build product and brand awareness
- Build awareness of the company.

Sales promotion is any activity, or material, that acts as a direct inducement to distributors, salespeople and/or end users, to buy the product or service. Sales promotions are essentially short-term, tactical communications tools used to achieve specific objectives including:

■ To identify and attract new customers
■ To introduce a new product
■ To educate customers as to product improvements
■ To bring customers into a retail outlet
■ To obtain more shelf space in retail outlets.

The application of these methods will vary with the context, and the objectives which the communication is trying to achieve. There will also be variations in the suitability of methods for small and large firms, and whether the company is operating in the consumer or business markets.

Before moving on, it is worth commenting on the role of public relations in the international communications toolkit. Clearly as a business function public relations is often dealt with separately from marketing communications, but there is an overlap, especially when something goes wrong with a product or service.

The rapid and planned response to a crisis can benefit a company, in terms of being perceived as being a good corporate citizen, even when something has gone wrong. Conversely, a confused and unfocused response can cause damage to a company and its brands which will take time to recover from. In June 1999 Coca-Cola took a battering after it was forced to withdraw product from the retailers' shelves in Belgium and France (Schmidt, 1999). It only took 7 days to undermine a 113 year history, which left the market leader scrambling to give the product away in order to build up consumer confidence. It was 7 days before the company responded to reports of people becoming ill after drinking Coca-Cola products in Belgium and Northern France. When it did respond, it claimed that its products could not have been responsible. It may well be that the media blew the event out of all proportion, but from a marketing and public relations perspective, the company lost control of the plot and left the media to run riot: '200 Poisoned by Coca-Cola' in Svenska Dagbladet, a Swedish newspaper; 'Alarm Across Europe for Coca-Cola Products' in an Italian newspaper.

There are three marketing lessons for the company; first stay close to the customer. Belgium at that time was just emerging from a scandal in which dioxins had entered the food chain. The result was that poultry, pork, egg and other meat products were banned from markets across Europe and Asia. The Coca-Cola problem came at a time when consumers and government officials were highly sensitive to such health issues. Second, take charge of the situation immediately. In the absence of a strong response the media will run with unofficial sources and no comment will look like guilt. Thirdly, basic product control is vital, even when you do have over half the soft drinks market in the world. Since Coke does not own all its bottlers throughout the world, they need to work to enforce quality control standards. The problem was caused by lapses in quality control at two bottling plants.

As for the correct response, Coke should have made a statement to say we have a problem which has occurred because we do not control our bottling standards throughout the world, but we are making every effort to correct the situation. Still, for a smaller business there is some comfort in watching big brother get it wrong.

The role of advertising

Probably the earliest advertising model was based on a hierarchical approach and is attributed to E. St. Elmo Lewis in 1898 (Strong, 1925), namely, Attention > Interest > Desire > Action, otherwise known as the AIDA model. Initially this was a model for personal selling, but later became associated with advertising. In a study by Vakratsas and Ambler (1999) in which they attempt to establish the current state of knowledge about how advertising works, they state that advertising is an input for the consumer; scheduling of the media, message content, and repetition are components of this input, and are part of the strategy to trigger a response in the consumer. They also identify a range of intermediate responses which suggest that advertising has a mental effect, consciously or unconsciously, before behaviour is influenced. This mental effect includes awareness, memory or attitude towards the brand. Thus the authors identify a cognition, or thinking, element and a feeling component as two major intermediaries.

A third crucial element is experience. Consumers normally carry a memory of product usage or experience, especially for frequently purchased goods. This influences attitudes and is identified as a third intermediary. All three intermediaries filter the effect of the advertising input.

A taxonomy of models is presented which classifies advertising models into:

- Market response models (those which relate advertising, price, and promotional measures to purchasing behaviour measures such as sales, market share and brand choice).
- Cognitive information models (consumer preferences are not changed by advertising, their decisions are rational. Advertising provides information and helps reduce search costs by, for example, reducing shopping time).
- Pure affect models (consumers form their preferences on the basis of liking, feelings, and the emotions triggered by the advertisement rather than the product/brand attribute information).
- Persuasive hierarchy models (to generate sales, advertising must inform and then persuade, this suggests an order in which things happen. The elaboration likelihood model is an example of such an model. This model distinguishes between elaborate (attribute evaluation) and non elaborate (paying attention to execution elements, for example, celebrity endorsement) information evaluation.
- Low-involvement hierarchy models (product experience is the main factor and advertising reinforces existing habits, frames experience in relatively routine purchasing situations).
- Integrative models (different hierarchies of cognition, affect and experience are

assumed based on product category and level of involvement, context may also influence the strength of each effect.

- Hierarchy-free models (this group discounts the persuasive school of advertising and rational decision making. Instead advertising is seen as part of the totality of the brand including seeing brands as myths and advertising as myth-making). The authors conclude that the concept of hierarchy cannot be empirically supported – despite these models being around for over 100 years – and they are also deficient by excluding experience effects.

Advertising has a specific role which takes place within the context of an advertising goal, product/service category, competitive environment, stage of the product life cycle, and target market. The goal of advertising can vary. It is not just to increase sales or market share. It may also be used to support a premium price, or to respond to competitive activity or to maintain the current market share. The launch of new products requires a lot more advertising support than existing ones if they are to break through, raise awareness and establish an image. Experience and service goods need more creative advertising than industrial or search goods, which rely more on rational/informational approaches.

Standardization versus adaptation

A perennial debate since the 1960s within international marketing is the extent to which the same advert can be used around the world without adaptation. In much the same way as the debate has raged in connection with product standardization, so to in relation to communication strategies the lure of a global mix has been courted. The basic argument of supporters of this approach is that a single message with only minor modifications can be used to reach all targeted consumers because they share identical, or very similar, needs and wants. The attractiveness of this approach is based on a number of perceived advantages:

- It allows the multinational company to maintain a consistent, uniform approach world-wide
- It reduces confusion in areas of media overlap and amongst buyers who travel frequently
- It allows the development of a single campaign across numerous markets
- It allows cost savings in terms of media costs, advertising production costs including graphics
- Good ideas are rare and should be exploited wherever possible
- Many national subsidiaries lack the financial and managerial resources to construct effective campaigns
- It allows companies to respond to the increasing convergence of consumer tastes, partly as a result of developments within communications.

The alternative viewpoint argues that separate messages should be used to reach different buyers in different countries. A single message cannot be used because of cultural, economic, legal, media and product variations. For a practical approach to standardization see Box 7.8.

BOX 7.8: PRACTICAL STANDARDIZATION

Brand owners are strongly attracted to the idea of delivering the same message with the same execution and promotional methods across several European countries. How feasible is this, given the language and cultural differences, as well as the legislative anomalies which exist?

Andrew Kingham from The Marketing Store World-wide (TMSW) believes that while it is not entirely possible, brand owners can come close to achieving their ideal by standardizing the way you develop campaigns across Europe. 'Lots of companies are using global campaigns with local market adaptations. You have to dial down into the detail to what does and does not work'.

TMSW did this with an integrated on-pack Pepsi promotion which ran across nine countries offering exclusive Spice Girl prizes. A menu of different operations was offered to each country to ensure that the promotion was tailored to the market needs and legal situation of each.

(source: Murphy, 1999)

Even in countries who, on first sight, appear to be very similar, there can be distinct cultural differences in purchasing behaviour that make a standardized approach unworkable. Ferley et al. (1999) in a study of US and Canadian consumers illustrate that while there are many similarities in product usage patterns between the two countries, there are also many differences which national and international marketers should recognize in order to optimize the chances for product success. The data in the study shows similar product usage for household ownership of burglar alarms, cat (but not dog) ownership, usage of fresh vegetables, ketchup, vinegar and ownership of swimming pools. Some social behavioural data also show similarities in uptake of hunting, golf, attendance at baseball games and car racing. As for significant differences these are detailed in Table 7.2.

Table 7.2   Household usage of selected products (source: Ferley et al., 1999)

Product	US market (%)	Canadian market (%)
Bottled water	40	25
Iced tea	51	35
Sparkling water	24	16
Headache medicines	89	70
Computer usage for communications	25	15
Root beer	38	17
Sports drinks	36	11
Table syrup	81	58
Toaster products	45	23
Hot sauces	21	3

There are, of course, incidences where Canadian usage outstrips the US for example, in wine (Canada 50%; US 30%) and even where consumption patterns are geographically skewed, as in sparkling water consumption, which is skewed towards the larger cities. Within Canada consumption is highest in Montreal while in the US it is Los Angeles.

The authors argue that geographic variation characterizes most consumption. By understanding it much valuable information can be gained about neighbourhoods and the types of product and services which they use. This can provide useful input to marketing activities, including communication strategies, even within two countries which, on the surface, appear more similar than they actually are.

One of the most recent and comprehensive studies into standardization comes from Papavassiliou and Stathakopoulos (1997), who have identified the factors which determine the degree of standardization as those associated with the firm, intrinsic factors and local factors.

Local environmental factors

Cultural variables

The cultural environment has already been explored in Chapter 3, but clearly the set of beliefs, values, norms and attitudes held by consumers is of crucial importance when attempting to find ways of communicating with them (Box 7.9). This will affect the level of humour, sexual innuendo, degree of exposure of the human body, individual gratification versus benefits to the group, and the hard-sell versus a soft-sell approach.

BOX 7.9: OOPS, I DON'T THINK YOU MEANT THAT

Lost in translation:

In Taiwan, the translation of the Pepsi slogan 'Come alive with the Pepsi Generation' came across in translation as 'Pepsi will bring your ancestors back from the dead'.

Ford had to rename the Pinto in Brazil when it discovered the name was Brazilian slang for 'tiny male genitals'. The replacement nameplates substituted 'Corcel' meaning horse!

Parker Pen marketed a ballpoint pen in Mexico with the line 'It won't leak in your pocket and embarrass you'. Unfortunately this translated as 'It won't leak in your pocket and make you pregnant'.

(source: Rogers and Marsh, 1997)

Economic variables

Amongst the many relevant economic variables are the rate of economic growth, per capita income and distribution of income, attitudes towards wealth and monetary gain and the development and acceptance of international trademarks. Some studies have suggested that advertising standardization is more likely in less affluent countries than in the better off nations, because of under supply, less competition and less sophisticated consumers.

Legal framework

Legal frameworks vary from nation to nation and this can prevent companies adopting a standardized approach. Comparative advertising is not allowed in some countries, for example, Hong Kong, Korea and Belgium. Even where its use is permitted, the usage can be quite low. Donthu (1998) reports that although the recall of comparative adverts was high, they were not particularly popular with consumers, especially in countries where they are not widely used, for example, Australia, Brazil, France and Japan.

Table 7.3 illustrates the variation in what is and is not allowed in sales promotions across some EU members. This is under review and it is likely that a new system, perhaps based on mutual recognition, will be introduced in 2000. This would allow sales promotions to take place in any country provided the method used was legal in the company's home country.

Murphy (1999) reports that some advertising executives suggest that there is a difference between the legal framework as written, and that which is actually implemented. Bending the local rules is one strategy which some agencies appear to be adopting. This, of course, could be a high risk strategy if the authorities chose to implement the letter of the law when it is your campaign which is running!

Degree of competition

In more competitive environments, it is argued that such factors as industry structure (oligopoly versus monopoly), the influence of suppliers, the company's market

Table 7.3 Legal constraints on sales promotions (source: UK Institute of Sales Promotion)

Tactic	Germany	France	UK	Netherlands	Belgium
On-pack price reduction	Yes[a]	Yes	Yes	Yes	Yes
In-pack gift	??[b]	??	Yes	??	??
Extra product	??	Yes	Yes	??	??
Money-off vouchers	No[c]	Yes	Yes	Yes	Yes
Free prize contest	No	Yes	Yes	No	No

[a] Yes, legally allowed.
[b] ??, under review.
[c] No, not legally allowed.

position (leader or follower) and the consumers' bargaining power (ability to find a substitute product) all influence the degree of standardization. If local market conditions are subject to local and other international competitors, then advertising may have to adapt to the local conditions and not follow a standardized approach.

Support infrastructure

Clearly the availability of media options, and staff experienced in the design and execution of programmes can affect a standardization policy. Standardization is more likely when there are similarities between countries in their media structure. However, a television campaign may have to shift to print if the penetration of television ownership is so low as to make it unfeasible.

Consumer profile

A consumer profile encompasses the demographic, psychographic and behavioural characteristics of the consumers in the target market. It may be that consumers decode a different meaning from the same advertisement, or they have different consumption patterns across markets. Studies have looked at the use of different media by consumers – for example, French consumers tend to watch less television and subscribe to fewer magazines than US consumers; while Latin American consumers are exposed to more radio and less print; and Asians spend more time watching television than on radio and newspapers.

Country of origin effect

In the context of advertising this normally has three facets: general country attributes associated with economic, political and cultural perceptions; general product attributes associated with the capacity of the country in question to produce good quality products; and specific product attributes including product marketing, and firm goodwill-related characteristics of the specific products. The question for advertisers is how stable a positive country of origin image is across markets. The greater the stability, then the greater the potential for standardization.

Factors related to the firm

Managerial and financial issues

A company's broader business strategy will largely determine its communication strategy. If the former is orientated towards standardization, then it is likely that this will be reflected in the communication strategy. Thus, a centralized organization will make all decisions about campaign preparation, media selection and budgets in the 'home' head office, while a decentralized organization will hand over such responsibilities to its subsidiaries. In reality a compromise between these two extremes is probably the best option. Papavassiliou and Stathakopoulos (1997) also suggest that a shift towards standardization is also likely if the firm is experiencing financial difficulties. Such a move allows the firm to economize on media costs, advertising production costs and illustrative advertising material.

In addition to formal organization structure, the attitudes of the managers also have an impact. Those culturally orientated managers (i.e. host-country orientated) are more likely to favour adaptation than non-culturally orientated managers (i.e. home-country orientated). There are advantages to the organization in allowing local input, in that it will attract more talented people if the jobs available have greater responsibilities. Empowered local mangers can also play a vital role in creating new communication ideas and in establishing links with local firms through formal and informal networks.

Product characteristics

The product aspects which most affect the standardization decision are product type, product involvement, product life cycle and culture-bound appeal. There is a generally held belief that standardization is easier in business to business markets than in consumer markets. Within business markets, some adaptation is necessary / possible within the selection of creative tactics, while in the consumer market a greater degree of standardization is possible for durable rather than non-durable goods. The reason for this is that the latter are more influenced by tastes, habits and customs which will vary between societies.

Product involvement tends to be categorized as high or low-involvement. High-involvement purchasing decisions tend to be viewed as more important, more expensive and have a higher degree of risk than low-involvement decisions. Rational appeals tend to be used in high-involvement decisions, which require more information, than low-involvement appeals which tend to target emotions. This characteristic means that standardization is less likely, as the information may need to be tailored across different markets. This issue requires more research in order to fully substantiate the distinction outlined.

The life cycle of an individual product can also affect the possibility for standardization. If the product is in the same stage of the life cycle across different markets, then a degree of standardization is possible which, of course, would not be the case if the product were at different stages. Clearly, different communication tactics, for example, are needed at the product introduction stage compared with maturity.

The final product related influence on standardization is the product's appeal in each international market. The general belief is that when a product is 'culture-bound', namely when different product attributes appeal to different cultures, standardization is inappropriate. There may also be variation in the level of appeal of those attributes which do permeate international markets, thus also making standardization difficult.

Intrinsic factors

Advertising objectives

Where the objective of advertising is to provide information (basic product/service information, benefits to the consumer, where they are available) and to achieve memorability, then a single advertising message with only minor modifications, perhaps including translation, can be used to reach consumers in different countries. By following this strategy, the planning and development costs are reduced, and improved co-ordination and control of the campaign is possible. In addition, comparisons can easily be made of the effectiveness of the campaign across different regions.

While a degree of standardization is possible when information provision and memorability are the key objectives, the situation is different when the task is to persuade the consumer to purchase. As a result of differences in the culture, economic, legal and media scene and in the product – for example, usage, positioning, life cycle – dissimilarities must be taken into account, and the message adapted to each country.

However, even when persuasiveness is the objective, it may be that a standardized message can be used if there are similarities between target groups, or in product positioning, increased mobility of consumers, limited knowledge of regional markets, or a centralized approach by management to managing the business.

Company-agency dynamics

The environment within which the advertiser and the agency have to operate determines the criteria for the selection of an advertising agency. Previous experience of both the advertiser and the agency in dealing with standardization issues will influence the selection. Research has shown that the nature, for example of television advertising messages, was influenced by the advertising environment in terms of the types of products and services available, advertising expenditure per capita, government control of advertising, availability of commercial breaks during broadcasting and the availability of advertising personnel.

Creative strategy

The creative strategy is the overarching policy or principle which determines the character of the advertising message. Most strategies can be divided into those which elicit either rational or emotive responses. Rational appeals contain information for the customer based on the customer's language, and because language and the perception of its meaning can vary, adaptation is necessary. On the other hand, emotional advertising is focused on moods and atmosphere, which can be shared to a greater degree across national boundaries.

Simon (1971) developed a list of ten creative strategies namely: information, argument, motivation with psychological appeals, repeated assertion, command, brand familiarization, symbolic association, imitation, obligation and habit-stating. Research based on these categories has found differences across countries in the application of similar creative strategies. In addition, the shift from mass-market appeals to niche marketing tends to require more customized communication strategies.

Media strategy

This is perhaps the most obvious area where a standardized approach is almost impossible. There is an enormous heterogeneity in the make up of the media structure amongst countries, which gives rise to media having different significance, different target groups, different reach and frequency in each country. This difference is due to variations in culture, and economic and sociological differences amongst countries.

It is difficult to generalize in a meaningful way, but consumers in developed countries tend to read more newspapers than those in developing countries or in countries where literacy is a problem. Europe has a greater number of local magazines with small circulation's compared to the US where a few national titles dominate. Television is important in developed markets but can be heavily regulated by governments, for example in Sweden and Italy, and as cable and satellite provision grows there is a dilution of its reach.

The use of international media which reach more than one nation can be an important feature of media strategy, for example, Business Week, Radio Luxembourg, CNN.

Other elements of the communication mix

Some international firms attempt to standardize their communication mix (advertising, sales promotion, packaging) in all of the countries where they operate. These firms aim at an international product and company image, based on the standardization of their communication mix, or at transferring their profitable national communication mix to international markets. A standardized mix can increase the contacts with the brand name and the trademark.

Support activities and barriers

Advertising standardization has qualities similar to other good decision making: clear strategic vision, access to reliable information, flexibility in implementation, and a willingness to alter direction when the market and competitive conditions change. Without these qualities, advertising standardization is no longer a viable competitive tool.

The opportunity to improve on advertising effectiveness depends on the degree of similarity of different national markets. Basic institutional and cultural conditions will provide the framework on which the judgement can be based. On the other hand, the heterogeneity of customer groupings will act as a barrier to standardization, and there will be many reasons why a wholly standardized campaign cannot be conducted.

Thus, Papavassiliou and Stathakopoulos (1997) list the requirement for complete standardization of creative strategy and tactics as when mainly:

- There is a great similarity in the cultural environment across different countries
- There is a great similarity in the economic conditions across different countries
- There is no great uniqueness in the consumer profile across different countries
- The strategic orientation of the corporation is not very culturally oriented
- The decision-making process of the organization is very centrally controlled
- It is more about industrial products than about consumer products and consumer durable products
- The products are at the same stage of the product life cycle across different countries
- It is about non-culture bound products rather than culture-bound products
- There is a great similarity of legal condition cross different countries
- The presence of local and international competition is not high in the host countries
- A well developed advertising infrastructure exists in the host countries
- The organization experiences great difficulties with respect to its financial position
- The objectives of advertising are centred on information and memorability rather than on persuasiveness
- The previous experience of advertiser and of advertising agency on how to handle the barriers hindering the international advertising standardization is high
- Little power is in the hands of the regional country managers
- There is a great similarity in the media scene across different countries
- There is a high degree of overlapping regarding the number of national media across different countries
- There is a high degree of orientation with respect to the development of a standardized communication mix across different countries; and
- There is, to a great extent, a presence of support activities and an absence of barriers.

At the opposite end of the continuum is the requirement for complete adaptation of creative strategy and tactics. The specific conditions of this state are that:

- It is, first, about consumer non-durable products and, second, about consumer durable products rather than industrial products
- Advertising objectives centre on persuasiveness rather than on information and memorability: and
- All the other determinants, listed in the standardized state, exist in a high degree but in the opposite direction.

In essence this listing provides all international marketers with a practical checklist of how to judge the potential for a standardized advertising campaign. As with any continuum, there are many points along the scale where there is significant variation to demand a different approach by management. However, this attempt by the authors does provide a comprehensive approach to the academic understanding of the standardization versus adaptation debate, while at the same time providing a checklist which could be both a research tool and practitioner guideline.

While the standardization debate has been ongoing for some considerable time, as was acknowledged at the start of this section, the marketer should not be deflected from the primary motivation of devising relevant and timely communication campaigns with clear objectives which are focused on the target customers. To some extent, everything else is a distraction. In a study of the attitude of multinationals to standardization Harris (1996) studied the attitudes of 38 US and European multinationals, 27 of whom practised standardization of some form. Table 7.4 summarizes their rationale for such an approach.

Following the survey of the companies a series of personal interviews were conducted with eight executives. It emerges that a simple categorization of why multinationals standardize is not possible. Many different degrees and types of standardization are practised, from the corporate logo to complete executional standardization involving copy and media. Length of experience also seems to influence behaviour, in that those companies who have only just begun to standardize are partly doing so because their perceive that more companies are going down this route, so they feel pressured to conform. The strategy is also given credence by the perceived success of standardizes such as Levi-Strauss, Philip Morris, Pepsi-Co and Coca-Cola. Broader managerial reasons in support of standardization are seen as being just as important as economic reasons. Thus, national subsidiaries often do not possess the skills and financial resources to develop

Table 7.4 Why standardize? (adapted from Harris, 1996)

Attitude statement	Mean score*
Standardization can significantly reduce production costs	3.6
Standardization is good because the top talent works on one good idea	3.5
Given the increasing degree of international communication, it makes sense to standardize	3.5
Having an international image is suitable for our brand	3.5
The media and communications revolution has done much to reduce or harmonise cultural differences	3.3
Standardization is the best way to control subsidiary activities and achieve effective co-ordination	2.5
Via standardization we can achieve economies of scale in human resources	2.4
We sometimes doubt the ability of our subsidiaries to produce effective advertising	2.3

*1 = not very important and 5 = very important.

coherent advertising strategies, and ironically standardization comes about as a result of attempting to transfer skills to the subsidiaries.

This study helps to show that the often dichotomous debate between standardization and adaptation is one which has gone on for too long. It is a distraction from the main objective of communicating effectively with potential customers. It should be obvious that, in a complex world with many products/services competing for attention, the best companies will adhere to a flexible market-responsive policy. It matters little how the advertising is undertaken, but rather whether it is effective. A practical guide to preparing a marketing communications plan is given in Box 7.10.

BOX 7.10: DEVELOPING A MARKETING COMMUNICATIONS PLAN

Preparing a marketing communications plan

These do not have to be complicated – in fact the more concise they are, the better the plan. Keep it simple, uncluttered by technical terms and keep it focused on what you are trying to achieve. Lamons (1999) states that if you cannot articulate *what* you intend to do, *who* you'd like to do it to and *how* you intend to go about it in just a few double-spaced pages, then you probably need to do more thinking and editing. His ten point plan includes:

1. Situation analysis – this should cover the firm's environment, industry trends, competitive situations, legal or legislative issues, and historical performance for the plan subject.
2. Marketing objectives – this should focus on what you plan to achieve, perhaps stated in terms of market share or sales revenues.
3. Marketing strategies – this is how to achieve the marketing objective, for example, by introducing new products/services, altering pricing strategies, target markets or channels.
4. Target audiences – this is who you need to reach. This may involved targeting a segment and explaining what benefits are in it for them.
5. Communication objectives – these should be measurable, so that the impact of plan can be evaluated numerically were possible. Likely to include increasing awareness, changing attitudes, generating sales leads, encouraging product trial, distributing promotional material and making technical presentations.
6. Communications strategies – these are the activities which will be undertaken to achieve the communication objectives, including advertisements, brochures, direct mail, trade shows/exhibitions, website development and promotions.
7. Budget – what is it going to cost?
8. Timetables – this is important to ensure integration of different activities, for example, a new brochure to launch a product at a trade show.
9. Media flowchart – this can show which issues of which publications are planned along with cost. Separate charts can be prepared, for example, for radio, Internet, television.
10. Appendices – other material can be included here, such as trade show schedules, media information and anything which interrupts the flow of the plan and would distract from the 'who, what and how' focus.

Conclusions

In discussing the creation of product value from a marketing perspective, we have looked at the development of global brands. This gives rise to the standardization/adaptation debate and both can have a role to play in response to market needs. A picture of 'standardize when possible, adapt when necessary' becomes a pragmatic approach to international marketing in the consumer market. The story is different in the business to business market, where products are less influenced by culture, particularly where they are consumed in the manufacture of products or included within them, for example, computer hardware, heavy equipment and machine tools. In these instances standardization is more likely.

The consumer is also influenced by the 'made in...' label on products, as well as pricing and packaging cues. The perception of these signifiers can be crucial to their purchasing behaviour and so becomes another element to understanding the customer. This is always more complex in the consumer market than in the business to business market. However, regardless of the market being operated in, and regardless of the size of the firm, the basic underlying marketing principles reviewed in this chapter and the previous one, to do with understanding and creating customer values, remain the same. It is only in their application, whether by market, or over time, that they will vary. The activities associated with understanding, creating and communicating customer values remain intact through the development of the brand. Market research helps to identify and show ways in which the best use of brand equity can be made within different cultural contexts, whilst informing management of buyer's current and future needs. As the marketing cycle in Figure 6.1 implied, these activities are linked, and marketers must ensure in any organization that a dialogue takes place between those responsible for understanding, creating and communicating customer related values.

Any business which wishes to develop international advertising must consider factors beyond simple translations if they are to succeed. Market conditions vary, especially where the product is culturally sensitive, for example, food and drink products. Advertising is so intimately linked with popular culture, the social fabric, laws, marketing conditions, buying habits, aspirations, sense of style, and humour of a people, that messages can not be communicated in precisely the same way in different countries. Experience shows that if you treat international market adaptation of an advertising or direct marketing campaign as a production detail, rather than as a full-scale planning and creative issue, then there is a good chance of failure. Consumers have an ability to spot advertisements which were originally aimed at other people. The art of multi-local advertising is to harness the skill and sensitivity of local copywriters, working closely with the lead agency, to eliminate any trace of a foreign accent from the material. If this can be achieved without the diluting the family resemblance between the different market versions, then the elusive balance between thinking globally and acting locally has really been achieved (Anholt, 1995).

In a survey of 63 Finnish managing and marketing directors (Schultz, 2000) representing more than 40 leading firms including Nokia, Finnair and Sonera they were asked 'What is your greatest concern in the context of marketing communications?' The responses were collapsed into the following seven areas:

- Firm efficiency and profitability as a result of marketing communications programmes
- Organizing the firm's communications activities (in the unit, area, brand or customer group)
- Integrating marketing communications
- Obtaining information from customers and potential customers
- Reaching customers in a cluttered communications landscape
- Message and content issues; and
- Using communication tools, particularly databases.

The concerns of the managers in this sample seem to be with content and strategy, which Schultz argues is no different to what communications managers have struggled with for the last 50 years. He sees a need for basic research to understand the market and communications basics before rushing ahead with campaigns. After all, what is a few thousand dollars on research, when you spend $2 million on a 30 s commercial in the Super Bowl?

The next chapter will complete the discussion of the marketing cycle by considering the marketing activities associated with delivering customer values.

Questions for discussion

1. Do global products exist, or is it global brands which exist? Make a list of global products, services or brands. How can they be categorized? Does this categorization help you to decide what it is about them which makes them global?
2. Using Germany, France, the US, Taiwan and Mexico, list your perceptions of a product produced in each of these countries across the following sectors: consumer electronics, female clothing, cars. What does the list tell you about your perceptions? How accurate do you think you are?
3. Does the 'Made in' label affect your purchasing patterns? How? In which instances?
4. For the countries listed in Question 2, or for others of your own choosing, what economic, social, cultural and political assumptions are you making about each country?
5. Select a product or service which is high-price and which you purchase infrequently. How do you evaluate the product? What role does price and packaging have on your conclusions? How important is product design?
6. List five current advertising campaigns that have attracted your attention. Analyze what it is about the creative strategy or creative tactics that appeals to you.
7. Discuss the problems which can be caused by culture in terms of an international advertising campaign.
8. How does the media structure of your country compare to any neighbouring

country? What similarities or differences exist? How would this affect an international marketer?

9. Can you identity a recent example of where a company has failed to deal adequately, in terms of public relations, with a crisis in relation to its product or service? What went wrong and why? Is there an example of where a company has handled a crisis in a professional manner?

References

Aaker, D.A. and Joachimsthaler, E. (1999), The lure of global branding, *Harvard Business Review*, 77 (6), pp. 137–144.

Ackerman, L.D. (1991), Gillette: rewriting the rules, *Management Review*, 80 (9), p. 30.

Anholt, S. (1995), Global message, Grocer, 217 (7199),pp. 38–39.

Business Week (1999), The beauty of global branding, *Business Week*, June 28, 3635, p. 70.

Cavusgil, S.T. (1988), Unraveling the mystique of export pricing, *Business Horizons*, May/June, pp. 54–63.

Clark, T., Kotabe, M. and Rajaratnam, D. (1999), Exchange rate pass-through and international pricing strategy: a conceptual framework and research propositions, *Journal of International Business Studies*, 30 (2), pp. 249–268.

Donthu, N. (1998), A cross-country investigation of recall of and attitude toward comparative advertising, *Journal of Advertising*, 27 (2), p. 111; (12) InfoTrac http://www.galegroup.com/.

Ensor, J. (1997), Interpreting the European market, *Grocer*, March 15, p. 67.

Ferley, S., Lea, T. and Watson, B. (1999), A comparison of US and Canadian consumers, *Journal of Advertising Research*, 39 (5), pp. 55–65.

Harris, G. (1996), Factors influencing the international advertising practices of multinational companies, *Management Decision*, 34 (6), p. 5; (7) InfoTrac http://www.galegroup.com/

Holbert, N.B. (2000), Worldwide marketing must not assume imperialistic air, *Marketing News*, Feb. 14, p. 20.

Kaynak, E., Kara, A. and Nakip, M. (1995), Life-styles, household decision-making, ethnocentrism and country-of-origin perceptions of Azerbaijani consumers, in: Kaynak, E. and Eren, T. (eds.), *Innovation, Technology and Information Management for Global Development and Competitiveness Proceedings*, Istanbul, pp. 356–368.

Klein, N. (2000), *No Logo*, Flamingo, London.

Knowles, A. (1996), Packaging says it all, *Marketing*, Nov. 14, p. 31.

Lamons, B. (1999), Simple marcom plans are your best bet, *Marketing News*, Feb. 1, p. 8.

Maheswaran, D. (1994), Country of origin as a stereotype: effects of consumer expertise and attribute strength on product evaluation, *Journal of Consumer Research*, 21 (2), pp. 354–367.

Malik, O. (1999), A good name should last forever, *Forbes*, Nov. 16, p. 88.

Murphy, D. (1999), Cross-border conflicts, *Marketing*, Feb. 11, p. 30; (2) InfoTrac http://www.galegroup.com/.

Myers, M.B. and Griffith, D.A. (1999), Strategies for combating gray market activities, *Business Horizons*, 42 (6), p. 2; (8) InfoTrac http://www.galegroup.com/

Papavassiliou, N. and Stathakopoulos, V. (1997), Standardisation versus adaptation of international advertising strategies, *European Journal of Marketing*, 31 (7-8), pp. 504–527.

Peterson, R.A. and Jolibert, A.J.P. (1995), A meta-analysis of the country-of-origin effects, *Journal of International Business Studies*, 26 (4), pp. 883–901.

Rao, V.R. (1984), Pricing research in marketing: the state of the art, *Journal of Business*, January, pp. 539–559.

Robinson, P. (1998), Shades of grey, *Grocer*, 221 (7360), pp. 36–38.

Rogers, D. and Marsh, H. (1997), Why brave the new worlds? *Marketing*, Oct. 30, p. 19.

Schmidt, K.V. (1999), Coke's crisis: what marketers can learn from continental crack-up, *Marketing News*, Sep. 27, p. 1/11–12.

Schultz, D.E. (2000), Marketers still in need of basic training, *Marketing News*, Feb. 14, p. 12.

Simon, J.L. (1971), *The Management of Advertising*, Prentice-Hall, Englewood Cliffs, NJ.

Strong, E.K. (1925), Theories of selling, *Journal of Applied Psychology*, Feb. 9, pp. 75–86.

The Economist (US) (1998), *Shopping: a grey market*, 349 (8097), p. 2.

The European (1998), Pepsi discovers branding blues, *The European*, Aug. 17, p. 22.

Vakratsas, D. and Ambler, T. (1999), How advertising works: what do we really know? *Journal of Marketing*, 63 (1), pp. 26–41.

Winkler, J. (1989), *Pricing for Results*, Heinemann, London.

Zain, O.M. and Yasin, N.M. (1997), The importance of country-of-origin information and perceived product quality in Uzbekistan, *International Journal of Retail and Distribution Management*, 25 (4/5), pp. 138–146.

Further Reading

Crick, D. and Bradshaw, R. (1999), The standardisation versus adaptation decision of 'successful' SMEs: findings from a survey of winners of the Queen's Award for Export, *Journal of Small Business and Enterprise Development*, 6 (2), pp. 191–200.

D'Astous, A. and Ahmed. S.A. (1999), The importance of country images in the formation of consumer product perceptions, *International Marketing Review*, 16 (2), pp. 108–125.

Delene, L.M., Meloche, M.S. and Hodskins, J.S. (1997), International product strategy: building the standardisation-modification decision, *Irish Marketing Review*, 10 (1), pp. 47–54.

De Mooij, M. (1998), *Global Marketing and Advertising: Understanding Cultural Paradoxes*, Sage, London.

Elliott, J. and Emmanuel, C. (2000), International transfer pricing: searching for patterns, *European Management Journal*, 18 (2), pp. 216–222.

Geuens, M. and De Pelsmacker, P. (1998), Reactions to different types of ads in Belgium and Poland, *International Marketing Review*, 15 (4), pp. 277–290.

Grier, S.A. and Brumbaugh, A.M. (1999), Noticing cultural differences: ad meanings created by target and non-target markets, *Journal of Advertising*, 28 (1), p. 79; (14) InfoTrac http://www.galegroup.com/.

Grimes, A. and Doole, I. (1998), Exploring the relationships between colour and international branding: a cross cultural comparison on the UK and Taiwan, *Journal of Marketing Management*, 14 (7), pp. 799–817.

Harker, D. (1998), Achieving acceptable advertising: an analysis of advertising regulation in five countries, *International Marketing Review*, 15 (2/3), pp. 101–118.

Leonidou, L.C., Hadjimarcou, J., Kaleka, A. and Stamenova, G.T. (1999), Bulgarian consumer's perceptions of products made in Asia Pacific, *International Marketing Review*, 16 (2), pp. 126–142.

Li, T., Nicholls, J.A.F. and Roslow, S. (1999), The relationships between market-driven learning and new product success in export markets, *International Marketing Review*, 16 (6), pp 476–503.

Myers, M.B. (1999), Incidents of gray market activity among U.S. exporters: occurrences, characteristics, and consequences, *Journal of International Business Studies*, 30 (1), pp. 105–126.

Tai, S.H.C. (1997), Advertising in Asia: localise or regionalise? *International Journal of Advertising*, 16 (1), pp.48–62.

Tersine, R. and Harvey, M. (1998), Global customerization of markets has arrived, *European Management Journal*, 16 (1), pp. 79–90.

Tzokas, N., Hart, S., Argouslidis, P. and Saren, M. (2000), Strategic pricing in export markets: empirical evidence for the UK, *International Business Review*, 9 (1), pp. 95–117.

Whitelock, J. and Rey, J.-C. (1998), Cross-cultural advertising in Europe: an empirical study of television in France and the UK, *International Marketing Review*, 15 (4), pp. 257–276.

CHAPTER 8

Delivering customer values

Chapter objectives

After studying this chapter you should be able to:

- Appreciate what is meant by delivering customer values
- Explain the marketing activities associated with delivering customer values, in particular, customer value management and customer satisfaction
- See the potential of the Internet for augmenting the delivery of customer values in the future dotcom world

Introduction

This chapter continues to use the framework outlined in Chapter 6 by devoting its attention to the delivery activities within the marketing cycle. Delivering customer related values is the final marketing activity before an exchange can take place.

Over the past 30 years there has been a gradual evolution in the way logistics decisions have been conducted. From the end of the 1960s to the mid-1970s the emphasis was on cost reduction. Computers were used mainly to increase efficiency. The elements of the distribution system, namely, purchasing, transportation, warehousing, materials handling and physical distribution costs, were traded off under the principle of least cost.

From the mid-1970s to the mid-1980s revenue generation became the paramount concern during an era of zero-growth, following the oil crises in 1973/1974. There was an attempt to integrate logistics with marketing and product development as a means of competing.

The next phase of change up until the early 1990s was focused on capital rationalization. The activities of suppliers and customers were integrated to facilitate the flow of materials. Multiple sourcing was gradually replaced by dependent and single sourcing. In most cases attention was devoted to the individual company and not the whole marketing channel. This gradually changed from the early 1990s until the late 1990s when the concept of time based competition caught on and companies began to think about the interplay throughout the entire channel. This was the beginning of companies thinking about more holistic supply chain management.

The latest change in the gradual evolution of companies and their logistic management is the design and development of highly efficient networks based on virtual integration. Environmental concern is a major factor, and e-commerce requires the development of e-logistics, with potentially gigantic improvements in effectiveness and efficiency.

For most consumers the process of delivering values takes place in the retail environment. This is supplemented by other channels including direct marketing and, increasingly, by the Internet. For business customers, delivery may be directly from the manufacturer or from an intermediary of some sort. In this chapter we will consider, in the Section 'Delivering customer values', customer value management; customer satisfaction and, briefly, delivering value in the dotcom future. In the Section 'Delivering value: examples from Sweden and Japan' Sweden will be used as an example, to illustrate how logistical advantages can be used to promote inward investment, while satisfying companies' needs for regional bases. The case of Japan will be used to show how deregulation of the distribution network has allowed more international companies to enter the market and in turn have an impact on the operating methods of domestic companies. Finally in the Section 'Role and importance of packaging' the role and importance of packaging will be discussed.

Delivering customer values

In this chapter we shall look at the delivery of values from a marketing perspective. The focus here will be on those activities and systems which the marketer can activate to add value to the basic product or service being offered.

Thus, in Chapter 7 we talked about the creation of values which are inherent in the physical product or service, as well as the service features which are part of the offering, for example, delivery, installation, financing. In addition to this are the expected psychological benefits to be gained from possession and use of the product. Delivering values is really about the system and people elements of the business, which are essential to the delivery of these customer values. By focusing on such elements it is believed, from a marketing perspective, that value to the customer will be greatly increased.

Under the framework of understand, create, communicate and deliver which we have been using, each stage of the marketing cycle builds on and extends the previous one. So, delivering customer related values is the accumulation of all previous activities. In some of the literature this has been referred to as customer value management (CVM) namely, competing and differentiating a business by delivering ideal, customer-defined value at each interaction with its targeted customers (Thomson, 1998).

This sounds great but how is it actually achieved? In this chapter and the previous one we explore the framework of understand, create, communicate and deliver, but what are the practicalities which lie behind delivering value and how can it be managed? In this section we shall look at the implementation of such a framework, with examples of how companies have adopted such an approach as their business strategy.

Customer value management

CVM requires that a company aligns its infrastructure and capabilities to the ideal outcomes which a target set of customers would wish to see. Thus, the customer becomes the firm's design point; the company examines every interaction with a customer for its potential to deliver ideal, customer-defined value. It is worth pointing out at this stage that while some proponents of CVM coming from a strategic background may not recognize it this, of course, is the basic essence of running a business based on a marketing philosophy. As for implementation, there are three key steps.

First, the company's customers and marketplace must be segmented. Technology is essential to the successful mining of databases. Companies such as Comercia Bank have identified their high (current and future) value customers as well as groupings of customers with shared needs and wants, based upon their previous buying patterns. By exploring the underlying structure of the values which are driving their purchasing patterns, the company can develop targeted marketing campaigns that appeal to these values. It is also possible to design customer-facing processes and services to align with and deliver specific values appropriate to the targeted segment.

In addition to using its own databases, a company can purchase databases of non-customers. Through analyzing these and identifying mirror-image customers, a company can identify potential customers who display the same behaviour as existing customers and who share the same underlying values. By understanding what appealed to its existing customers, the company has a platform from which to appeal to the potential customers.

The second step is to develop an outside-in vision of the firm, that is, to get a sense of what each customer segment actually wants from it (see Box 8.1). This essentially takes us back to the basic marketing principle of understanding customer buying habits. In many ways this is more crucial than customer satisfaction in terms of business and marketing strategy. Customer satisfaction does have a role to play in the aftercare of customers and clients, but you only get to play in this field if you have a customer willing to purchase from you in the first place. All customers are not equal, they will look for different things. A company should stratify customer needs and values into a buyer behaviour driver hierarchy, for example, basic, attractor and satisfier.

BOX 8.1: MASTERCARD'S OUTSIDE-IN VIEW

When MasterCard wanted to gain an outside-in view of what its customers valued when using its call-centres, it found that customers rated responsive service higher than interest rate charges. Thus the company developed a call centre strategy which has been defined by its customers, and includes the business capabilities and infrastructure needed to align its business with what customers value.

Basic needs are must-have needs which will result in the loss of customers if they are not met, for example, a bank statement must be accurate, coffee at a restaurant must be hot, self-assembly furniture must have all the pieces in the pack.

Attractor, ideal-value needs set a company apart from the competition and attract customers if fulfilled. Easy to reconcile invoices may attract a corporate customer who deals with large volumes of invoices.

Satisfier needs are those which create customer delight and get good scores on customer satisfaction surveys, but do not affect buying behaviour or attract new customers. Thus knowing every customer by name will be appreciated, but will not cause customers to leave if not provided, or attract new customers if done well.

The third and final stage is to develop a strategic vision of the specific processes, capabilities, and infrastructure that the business needs to ensure the delivery of ideal customer-defined, high-value outcomes. This should align the company's ability to perform with the promises it is making. The targeted marketing strategy, in turn, aligns the promises with each of the desired customers' or segments' values.

Clearly in implementing CVM the company has to be consistent with the business it is in. Thus a low-cost product or service provider will meet basic must-have needs. CVM should be used to increase profitability by implementing low-cost processes that do not deliver expensive, non-essential customer services. On the other hand, a company which wishes to add value to customers must satisfy the basic must-have needs and selectively provide higher value to the segment. The company can put in place processes which satisfy both low value and high value customer segments, and thus balance the 'value received from' and 'value provided to' a particular customer (see Box 8.2 for an example).

BOX 8.2: KNOWING YOU, KNOWING ME

NationsBank is using CVM to implement a customer-defined vision of ideal interactions with the bank via telephone banking. Customers have identified the types of information which they prefer to access directly rather than via a customer service representative (CSR). They have also defined what features an automated voice system should have in order to provide added value, and make what is for the bank a low cost channel attractive to them. For those pieces of information where the customers prefer to deal with a CSR, the customers have defined what capabilities the CSR must have to satisfy their basic needs, for example, immediate access to their account, characteristics of a trusted advisor.

   As a result of this NationsBank can implement processes, organization and technology which align exactly with what their customers want from an ideal telephone banking channel.

Adapted from Thomson (1998)

Becoming truly focused on customer values is not just a game for the MNE or larger domestic players. SMEs can and must be concerned with such development too. They must not be put off by fears of expense and the time involved, rather it should be seen as an investment in business for its long-term survival. For the micro-business the implementation of CVM may not require the purchase of huge data sets, since much of the data will be carried in the owner's head, but the principles behind CVM can be implemented. As with all business techniques it requires tailoring to specific individual situations. This is not the failure of the technique to meet needs, but rather the acclimatization of first principles to a particular situation and that is where it begins to get interesting from an entrepreneur's point of view.

Customer satisfaction

One of the crucial elements of delivering value is customer service, which basically comes down to making sure that each customer has a satisfactory experience with the product or service bought, how it was bought, and with how the product performed after purchase or how the service was delivered.

   Customer satisfaction is seen as leading to loyal customers, but Dahlhoff (1999) points out that there are a number of misconceptions about what it takes to create a satisfied customer. Firstly, it is not just enough to deliver the essentials to the customer, there must be extras if superior customer service is to be achieved. Thus, most people expect the automated teller machine to be available 24 h a day, itemized telephone bills, well-staffed call centres. Most suppliers can achieve this level of service, and therefore any business providing the same will not distinguish itself from the crowd. Supplying extra gratification to the customer, for example, a no quibble returns policy, dealing adequately with complaints, using upgrades on flights and car rentals selectively, can create that extra gratification.

Second, customer satisfaction does not automatically lead to loyal customers. Many customers will have a set of products which they regularly buy from in any category. Product A may have been purchased for the past 4 months and given satisfaction. However, Product B, also in the customers relevant set, may have a price promotion which causes a customer to switch. Temporary unavailability of the product or the wish for variety can also cause switching.

Third, many believe customer loyalty schemes can compensate for customer dissatisfaction. This is a myth. Few customers will swap quality and good service for a few bonus points.

Finally, it is thought that companies should conduct regular identical surveys to gauge customer satisfaction. This is true, but only where markets are very stable in terms of how customers evaluate the product. In the mobile phone market, for example, customer satisfaction has shifted from quality of outdoor reception, to indoor reception and tone as well as design features. Surveys must be designed to contain the most current evaluation criteria for measuring customer satisfaction.

When these issues are translated to the international market, other factors can also come into play, not least the role of culture. Regardless, it is vital to communicate with international customers. Indeed often, at least in the short term, just communicating that the company is aware of areas which need addressing or changing is enough to alleviate dissatisfaction in the short term. Mitchell (1999) identifies three key issues in addressing customer satisfaction globally. First, regional market characteristics. Thus, if levels of customer service offered locally are generally deficient, then it will be easier to excel in the eyes of the consumers. Satisfaction will be higher than in markets where customer service is high in all sectors. The extent of local presence which is related back to the market entry decision can also be a factor. If there is no local presence then customers may experience delays in obtaining equipment, parts, or customs delays or problems of compatibility. Where distributors or agents are used, then technical support, warranty, and service can be the key to finding and retaining customers. Clearly it is crucial to the company that a credible vendor is employed as the intermediary, as the vendor will be seen as an extension of the product and brand. Customer satisfaction, loyalty and retention approaches should include evaluations of all intermediaries in order to ensure that all aspects of the product and brand name are evaluated by the consumer.

Second, it is important to understand how customers' opinions might vary with culture across regions and markets. It may not be enough to follow careful translations and market adaptations. For instance, culture can affect an individual's use of a 1–10 ranking scale. A less than pleased Latin American customer may still rank your company as a 7 or 8 while in the UK a customer wanting to rank your company in the same way may use 5 or 6, whilst Asian respondents will use the centre of the scale. Analysis by country, region or even client types may be safest so as not to bias the results.

Finally, relationships and etiquette. Overall satisfaction will be partly based on the form and development of relationships with vendors. However, the concept of relationship can vary between countries. In the US, for example, executives feel they are developing a relationship by responding by mail or via an interactive voice response system. In Latin American countries relationships can only be forged by personal communication by phone or in person. It is also important to show a concern for a client's issues and plans for the future. In Asia there is a strict hierarchical etiquette, so a request for a busy senior executive's time to participate in a market research survey should come from an equal and be personalized. Those conducting the data collection should be native in the appropriate language and experienced in the protocol of the business.

By addressing such potential culture clash issues, and by measuring variables which are important to the customer, a company can hope to make some progress in global customer satisfaction (see Box 8.3).

BOX 8.3: ARE YOU BEING SERVED?

A survey by the Marketing Society revealed that only 20–40% of company boards regularly discuss marketing measures related to customers, while profits are discussed at almost every meeting. There would appear to be an over-emphasis on financial measurement, while at the same time forgetting that customer attitudes, beliefs and actions are the ultimate driving force behind profits.

The poll of nearly 100 chief executives, managing directors and senior marketers also revealed that 43% of the companies questioned admitted that, apart from their sales and marketing directors, no other directors were required to meet customers regularly. Some 60% agreed that service levels were higher in US companies than in the UK.

Source: Tylee (1998)

Customers will pay higher amounts for equally high levels of service. In markets where a number of competitors are able to offer products with similarly high standards, then it is necessary to build the brand public relations in order to come out on top. This is all about advances made at the margins, often in the simplest of ways. Bell (1998), in four basic ways, (see Box 8.4) illustrates how this can be achieved.

> ### BOX 8.4 TOP TIPS ON SERVICE AND ATTITUDE
>
> 1. Does the salesperson that gives you, the boss, a charming smile lapse into offhand sullenness with your customers behind your back?
> 2. Is your switchboard answered immediately? Ring in regularly and check. Anything over three rings is a disgrace; anything over ten is a sacking offence (if it is busy get them to at least acknowledge a call before returning).
> 3. Do their switchboard voices smile over the phone, or do they rudely click off without a comment?
> 4. Does a system exist to ensure customer calls are promptly returned, remembering that to snub a customer is a sin never to be redeemed?
>
> Obvious stuff? Yes. Repeatedly overlooked? Yes. Ignore them and your reputation will suffer.
>
> *(Source: adapted from Bell, 1998)*

American Express's brand strategy is based on improving customer service with the help of its highly trained staff and through partnership with other firms to develop better products and services. Its core strategy can be summarized in five key points (Lafferty, 1999).

First, to capitalize on the American brand name. Thus the name is applied to products and services when those products and services are critical to the brand positioning. It is not used when the products are not critical to the brand.

Second, the company focuses on serving individuals whether directly or through intermediaries.

Third, the company works with and through partnerships. This is a change in the company's direction, as in the past the company was very vertically integrated. The company manufactured everything it sold and serviced everything it manufactured. Today the company also partners, for example, with Microsoft in constructing technology-based travel solutions for corporations; with external sales agents to find outlets to accept the AMEX card; through outsourcing some customer service or processing activities. Perhaps crucially, AMEX works with other organizations to reach their customer base. These partnerships involve a package of services: marketing, direct mail, credit management, modelling, customer service and operations. These services help the partner companies better achieve their objectives locally, while giving AMEX global scale and knowledge without necessarily having local resources in place.

Fourth, AMEX focus on creating a customer service advantage through people, highly trained and dedicated, and through world class technology.

Fifth, products and services are provided to customers through whichever distribution channels they wish to use, namely, direct sales, telephone and the Internet.

Delivering values in the dotcom future

In some ways the future will be more like the past. Customers will be better known to companies and they will receive, or at least will perceive that they receive, a more personal service. Delivering values will be strongly influenced by developments in information technology and e-commerce. IBM defines e-commerce in terms of business benefits that go beyond improving processes to leveraging the Web to bring together vendors, suppliers, and employees in ways it was never thought possible, and Web-enabling your business to sell products, improve customer service, and get maximum results from limited resources.

Companies are developing global information systems with database software and e-commerce solutions which allow them to see the status and current location of their orders wherever they are in the supply chain. 'Value' in a sense is not only being delivered to the customer but also to the international merchandiser, retailers and manufacturers along the way. Even here at this leading edge of technology we cannot shake off culture. Many of the advantages of these solutions could be lost if cultural and language issues are not addressed in the technical implementations. Thus companies which provide multilingual and multicultural service and support including translation, localization and guidelines on cultural practices, are thriving as part of global e-commerce solutions (Baker, 1999).

The Internet has gone through a number of stages. First, it was used as a marketing tool to stake a claim in cyberspace. Initially many companies simply put their brochures on the Web and, as a consequence, often put files on the Web which took forever to download. Over time this approach became more sophisticated, and companies better presented their image/identity. At the next level, the Internet became a one-way transactional vehicle for clients to supply information to an organization or for the organization to distribute information to its clients. This, for some companies, leads to electronic commerce (e-commerce). Since 1998 UPS has been moving into e-commerce and as their vice president of marketing stated (McGovern, 1998) 'UPS is moving beyond the shipping room, beyond facilitating the physical flow of goods. Through alliances with leading e-commerce providers, we are positioned to facilitate the flow of information and funds, the other two elements critical to commerce'. UPS will 'ship' digital files for customers which, for example, may contain documents, images, video, or software.

In terms of delivering value, these services are currently adding value to the service offered by UPS and similar providers who are facilitating the logistics process electronically. Of course, at some point in the future, such a service will simply be a prerequisite for conducting business, but until then there are advantages to be exploited by the first movers who are able to deliver information more effectively than others, which can lead to lower costs and better decisions. There is further discussion of the Internet in Chapter 10.

Delivering value: examples from Sweden and Japan

Sweden

Perceived advantages in logistics can be used as a marketing tool to promote a

Figure 8.1   Logistical reach from Sweden in 12 and 24 h. Source: Invest in Sweden Agency (http://www.isa.se/)

particular location, thus attracting foreign investment and diversifying a regional economy. Sweden is one country which, within its regional setting of northern Europe, is promoting itself as a distribution base for Scandinavia, western Russia and the Baltic states. It claims to be the only country in the Baltic Sea region which can guarantee 24 h distribution to all major destinations in the area, covering some 100 million people (Figure 8.1). The attractions of such a location to the international marketer are obvious.

This position is further enhanced by state-of-the-art technology and widespread use of IT and electronic data interchange to offer solutions for just-in-time delivery and a seamless flow of materials and information. Value-added logistics (VAL) centres are available for integration of pre-sale or after-sale activities. All of the main providers have well-established international networks, and there is a significant and growing presence of foreign third-party logistics providers (Table 8.1). Significant multi-modal mainports exist with inter-continental air gateways and container shipping ports. The new fixed Oresund link between Malmo in Sweden

Table 8.1 International companies with distribution activities for Scandinavia located in Sweden. Source: Invest in Sweden Agency http://www.isa.se/

Company	Distribution point
Avex (US)	Stockholm
Bayer (Germany)	Göteborg
Bosch-Siemens (Germany)	Jönköping
Bridgestone (Japan)	Jönköping
Elkjöp (Norway)	Jönköping
Flextronics (US)	Stockholm
Ford (US)	Örebro
Fujitsu (Japan)	Stockholm
Hitachi (Japan)	Örebro
Johnson & Johnson (US)	Göteborg
Johnson Wax (US)	Jönköping
Linde truck (Germany)	Örebro
Procter & Gamble (US)	Norrköping
Van den Bergh Foods (NL)	Helsingborg
Whirlpool (US)	Norrköping

and Copenhagen in Denmark makes Sweden even more attractive. Further specific advantages include:

Infrastructure for efficient flow of goods, information and funds

Sweden has the advantage of sophisticated and extensive logistics infrastructure, covering all modes of transport as well as information and flow-of-funds. Massive long-term investments in roads, railways, harbours and airports have created rapid and reliable links to all countries in the Baltic Sea region. As one of the world's most advanced IT countries, and with its highly developed banking sector, Sweden meets the demands of the logistics industry and facilitates development of services and products. The Swedish telecom and banking infrastructures have been extending their involvement throughout the Baltic countries since the 1990s.

High environmental standards

Swedish logistics providers have advanced significantly in developing environmentally friendly logistics solutions. Sweden was one of the first nations in Europe to seriously discuss environment issues. By training drivers, by using the most appropriate means of transport and through collective consignments, Swedish logistics providers strive to reduce their impact on the environment. A number of them have been, or soon will be, certified in accordance with the international environmental management standard ISO 14001.

Economic, political and sociological stability

Sweden is an advanced, stable nation which offers an attractive business climate including low levels of corporate taxation and inflation. It is a good base from which to access the emerging Baltic/Russian markets at minimal risk.

It is clear from this review that Sweden has positioned itself as a regional centre for distribution operations in northern Europe. Examples of companies which recently have invested in Sweden include Cat Logistics (US); Dan Transport (Denmark); Danzas (Switzerland); Deutsche Post (Germany); Katoen Natie (Belgium); Rutges Cargo (Netherlands); Schenker (Germany) and Tecnologistica (Italy).

Two examples of how companies have utilized the opportunities offered by a location in Sweden are given below. The first is a partnership between clothing retailer Lindex and logistics providers Schenker-BTL and Wilson, which illustrates how to efficiently serve a fragmented northern European distributions network. This partnership allows Lindex to serve some 300 retail shops in four countries from a base in Göteborg.

Lindex is a Swedish-based chain of ladies' and children's wear outlets which also operates in Norway, Finland and Germany. The company sources most of its products from the Far East. Logistics providers Schenker-BTL and Wilson are responsible for handling the flow of almost all Lindex goods, and have set up a sophisticated system to cover all aspects of the task: from delivery control, inbound traffic and customs clearance, to outbound distribution and IT systems. From a marketing perspective, by allowing the logistics company to concentrate on the physical handling of the goods, Lindex can devote more attention to planning and control activities which enable it to allocate goods to the stores more effectively. The traffic from the Far East includes several sea-borne departures a week from Hong Kong and air cargo flown by SAS into Göteborg. The Schenker-BTL logistics centre in Göteborg receives, checks, and registers all the goods, which are then sorted shop by shop. Lindex personnel are on-hand to perform quality control. The logistics centre is also responsible for the recycling of packing material, quality and quantity control, re-allocations, storage for new shops, and handling of returned goods. There are daily departures to all Lindex markets, unless store demand dictates otherwise. Key people from all levels within the partner companies meet regularly to discuss and improve the co-operation. This relationship is a good example of an advanced supply chain partnership which depends on a high level of commitment from the partner companies.

The second example is Bayer who have reduced their inventory points in the Nordic and Baltic countries from 40 to two in 18 months while still maintaining the same customer service levels. Göteborg is the centre of their distribution network covering eight countries.

Prior to this reorganization, the company had operated on a country-by-country basis, and offered products in areas as diverse as health care, agriculture, plastics and special chemicals, with little logistics co-ordination between the different product divisions and countries. At the beginning of 1998 Bayer chose to centralize distribution activities for eight countries (Sweden, Denmark, Finland, Norway,

Estonia, Lithuania, Latvia and Iceland) to Göteborg. The city was attractive for a number of reasons, such as the availability of logistics providers, the existence of a large Bayer warehouse, and the need for multi-modal transport alternatives. Bayer now delivers overnight to customers in Denmark, Sweden, southern Norway and to Helsinki in Finland. Within 48 h other areas in the Nordic countries are reached.

Japan

The example of Japan illustrates how changes in the regulatory environment can alter a traditional system of distribution, and thus open up new opportunities for companies and customers alike.

Traditionally, and despite recent changes, Japanese wholesalers still play a more important role than their counterparts in other countries, primarily because of the high degree of fragmentation in the retailing of consumer products. This system has caused confusion for international investors in Japan, more used to direct distribution in systems where there is little need for wholesaler intermediaries.

Because of the importance of the wholesaler in Japan, international investors need to examine how competing companies compensate their wholesalers when formulating a sales promotion programme. Providing incentives for wholesalers is crucial within the Japanese business environment. Thus, Japanese firms have designed intricate and far-reaching systems of rebates and other incentives targeted at the wholesaler. The amount often depends on the type of product, and some producers rely on progressive rebates to motivate wholesalers. Thus, for example, wholesalers who record a higher level of sales might receive a 5% rebate instead of a 3% rebate. The use of a wholesaler is particularly important if the product can be sold in a wide range of retail outlets, such as supermarkets, department stores, and small neighbourhood stores. On the other hand, if the product is to be sold at a single location, such as a department or speciality store then it may be possible to deal directly with that store.

The manufacturer's representative is another intermediary with an important role to play in Japan's distribution system. The main function of the manufacturer's representative is to establish personal relationships between the producer and its wholesalers and retailers, and, toward this end, the representative usually meets with wholesalers once or twice a month and with retailers even more frequently. This allows for an honest exchange of opinions with the wholesaler and retailer about the product and its performance. The manufacturer's representative frequently accompanies the wholesaler's representative on visits to retailers.

With consumer products, the duties of the manufacturer's representative go beyond those of an ordinary salesperson. The chief activities of a manufacturer's representative in this field are collecting information, assuring retailers and wholesalers of continued interest on the part of the producer, and providing support services, including assistance in accounting and merchandising, to smaller wholesalers and retailers. In terms of merchandising, for example, the manufacturer's representatives may offer advice on optimizing the store layout and presenting products in the most advantageous way.

During the 1970s the role of intermediaries such as wholesalers and manufacturer's representatives was protected by stringent regulation which made it difficult for large retailers to enter the market. In 1973 the Large-Scale Retail Store Law was enacted in Japan. The purpose of this law was to control the number of supermarkets and other large retail stores, which was rapidly growing. It was perceived that large retail stores posed a threat to the interests of the wholesaler distribution system, as well as to traditional shopping districts that were mainly served by small stores. Under this law, stores of 1500 m^2 or more were subject to advance review of, for example, the floor area, date of opening, number of closing days, and store operating hours. The overall impact of these regulations and others was to hinder large retail stores from opening. For example in 1989, a total of 134 store opening negotiations were concluded but had, on average, taken 35 months to complete, with 15% of them taking 5 years or more.

During the Japan–US Structural Impediments Initiative talks that began in 1989, the American government demanded that Japan amend the Large-Scale Retail Store Law, asserting that the Law represented a barrier to market entry by foreign distributors. Since then a number of amendments have been made to the law, for example, reducing the co-ordination period for new store openings to 1 year from a year and a half, and stores that formerly were required to close at 7 PM were allowed to stay open until 8 PM. These changes made it easier to open and operate large retail stores. These deregulation measures have led to a significant increase in the number of large-scale retail stores over the past 10 years.

Partly the mood for change has come about from the recession in the Japanese economy, which depressed retail sales in the late 1990s. November 1999 represented the 32nd consecutive month in which retail sales were down compared to the same month the year before. In addition, cultural changes have also had an influence. The changing lifestyles of the Japanese people are bringing about a revolution in the distribution industry as a whole. This has provided the opportunity for foreign-owned distributors to stake out a significant presence in the Japanese market. Table 8.2 provides examples of international companies which have entered the Japanese market in the 1990s. This in turn has influenced the practices of the domestic distribution industry, who are increasingly adopting the formats of their international counterparts. In addition:

- Retailers are now increasingly doing business directly with manufacturers
- The number of large scale retail facilities in suburban locations has increased
- Stores have been able to obtain more favourable rental agreements and fees
- More stores are opening in malls and drawing customers away from big-name department stores.

The example of Toys 'R' Us below illustrates the impact a new distribution format can have. December 1991 marked the opening of the very first Toys 'R' Us store in Japan, a gigantic 3000 m^2 store in Ibaraki Prefecture near Tokyo. Toys 'R' Us is the leading toy retailers in the US, and its arrival in Japan had a significant impact on the distribution system. The toy industry in Japan traditionally employed a multi-layered distribution structure in which manufacturers distributed through whole-

Table 8.2 Foreign distributors entering the Japanese market during the 1990s. Source: http://www.jetro.go.jp/top/index.html

Year	Company name	Country	Genre
1990	HMV	UK	Music and video
	Virgin Megastores	UK	Music and video
1991	Toys R Us	US	Toy
	Blockbuster	US	Video rental
1992	Kinto	US	24 h office service
	The Disney Store	US	General merchandise
1993	Nike	US	Sporting goods
	Burger King	US	Fast food
	Eddie Bauer	US	Outdoor apparel
1994	Esprit	Hong Kong	Ladies apparel
	Lands End	US	Casual apparel by mail order
1995	GAP	US	Casual apparel
1996	The Sport Authority	US	Sporting goods
	Starbucks Coffee	US	Coffee
1997	Foot Locker	US	Sports shoes
1998	Office Depot	US	Stationery
1999	Boots	UK	Cosmetics
	Sephora	France	Cosmetics

salers to retailers. In contrast, Toys 'R' Us Japan Ltd. used a central buying system and integrated inventory management to make large-lot purchases, resulting in lower retail prices. Toys 'R' Us changed the way business was done in its sector and has been a great success.

The Toys 'R' Us success story enticed a number of other foreign-affiliated speciality stores into the Japanese market. Many of the foreign distributors lured into Japan by deregulation have sought to differentiate themselves from Japanese competitors through their unique management techniques and the strength of their brand names. The arrival of these foreign distributors has had a major transformative impact on the Japanese distribution industry.

Role and importance of packaging

Packaging is a marketing issue because a product must arrive in good condition and because in the consumer market, in particular, the design of packaging can influence buying behaviour. Thus, packaging can have an important role to play in the successful entry into a market. Companies can suffer from the two extremes of either overpackaging or underpackaging their goods. In either case money is wasted. Generally speaking when shipping by sea or air, successful domestic packaging does not automatically mean that it will be suitable for the rigours of exporting. However, if the transportation is to be made by land to a contiguous country then it may well work, for example, on continental Europe, or between North America and Latin America. According to Green (1989) 30% of damage to sea going freight is caused by fire, collision, bad weather and in extreme cases by sinking. Approximately 70% of loses may be preventable if packaging has been properly researched and engineered.

The key points to understand in relation to the performance of packaging are:

- The behaviour of each product must be evaluated and understood under the conditions it will be exposed to
- The facilities at the destination must be researched: ports of embarkation and debarkation, points of final delivery, handling equipment and methods used, customs of the trade, weather, politics, storage facilities
- The methods of stowage and the location on the carrier (lower hold, deck, centre or wings); the exposure to moisture (rain, fog, salt water, and condensation); the motions of the ship at sea (a ship can roll as much as 40% each side of centre, six or eight times per minute, and as far as 70 feet for top-loaded cargo), surge, pitch, sway, heave, and yaw
- Whether the goods are travelling by land, sea or air each shipment is subject to the local road conditions, trucking, handling, and potentially unknown delays.

According to Green (1989) the five packaging essentials are:

- The export packaging must meet all of the well thought through and established criteria
- The markings (shipper, receiver, port, weights, handling, cautionary, size, count and country of origin) are of utmost importance. They should clearly identify the contents. Poor marking can mean misdelivery or non-delivery or it may invite pilferage or unnecessary damage.
- Closures or seals can make all the difference between success and failure
- If there is a weakness, export exposure may find it at the end, and the entire effort will have failed
- Export packaging may be more expensive than domestic, but the cost need not be excessive if researched and planned.

In the 'new economy', electronic technology will allow some companies to use electronic commerce to replace the cost of shipping a physical product and will eliminate packaging costs (Richardson, 1999). Thus, music, movies, software, news and books can now be delivered by technology. Even for those products which will continue to be shipped by traditional means, there are changes in how they are packaged because of changing attitudes, brought about partly by the pressure of environmental groups. The message of reduce, reuse and recycle is getting across, either voluntarily or by government backed regulations.

The newer technologies are not just changing the way some products can be delivered, but are also being adopted by shippers of conventional goods as a cheaper means of communication than phones and faxes, and as a means to track the progress of the goods both for the shipper and the customer (McGovern, 1998).

The internet has created another mode for the transportation of one of the logistics key components, namely, information. With the internet, nothing has to be assumed, as real-time tracking can pinpoint the location of a particular delivery.

Studies of packaging suggest that instead of seeing it as a unique and separate activity, it should be managed as part of the overall approach to logistics. This point emerges time and time again; that the business must be seen as a whole with integrated operations and activities designed to serve the needs of the customer. A marketing oriented firm keeps the customer in mind even when apparently mundane elements of, for example, the benefits of corrugated packaging are being discussed. Richardson (1999) quotes an example of a joint venture between General Motors and Suzuki in Canada. The company engaged packaging experts to look at its systems. The company identified significant cost-saving opportunities such as:

- Reduce expendable packaging by 92%
- Decrease or eliminate the recurring costs of expendable packaging and related waste disposal costs
- Improve cube utilization by 5% per quarter with standardized packaging.

Indirect benefits of these changes were also identified as:

- Improvements in inventory accuracy
- Decrease in lifting and repetitive-motion injuries
- Reduction in quality control costs
- Reduction in manufacturing time by putting parts at lineside
- Improvements in floorspace use and the maintenance of a cleaner work environment.

By adopting these changes the company recovered its initial investment in the project within 10 months.

Other examples of cost savings as a result of designing more effective packaging include Kimberly Clark shipped cases with excess headspace. Removing the excess meant the cases could be packed without crushing, and thus the core of the paper roll acted as support, meant the overall strength of the corrugated carton could also be reduced. Reconfiguration of the product within the case can be another simple solution. In shipping 12 items in two rows of six an opportunity is lost to configure three rows of four and take advantage of the fact that this shape of a rectangular box is stronger.

Categories of export packing

The exporter will balance the cost of packaging against protection and the requirements of the customer. Some of the more usual categories of export packing are listed below (Walker, 1995):

- Retail unit packs: cardboard cartons, cellophane bags, plastic containers, polystyrene mouldings, tin cans, bottles

- Internal packing materials: wood wool, wood shavings, straw, chaff, waxed paper, sheets of cellophane film, multi-wall paper bags, plastics or paper linings
- Outer transit packs: hessian sacks, special multi-wall paper bags, steel drums and cans, wooden crates, trusses, wooden cases, sometimes battened, or wire-bound. Plywood cases – occasionally metal edged. Barrels, fibreboard packing cases and plastic or polystyrene containers which can be very strong but light and easily manoeuvred.

Below is a brief classification of some of the relevant types of packing for export goods:

- Bulky raw materials (carbon black, cement, fertilizers, etc.): plywood drums, multi-wall bags/sacks
- Machinery and capital goods: wooden cases sometimes crated, sometimes on flats covered with polythene sheeting as when dispatched by air. Shrink wrapping often used and the goods must not move about within the cases
- Furniture: wooden cases, fibreboard cartons, crates, protective polythene and paper wrapping; often shipping on a knocked down (KD) basis, i.e. partially disassembled or completely knocked down (CKD) i.e. completely disassembled to save freight space and sometimes assembly costs on arrival
- Kitchen and sanitary equipment: can be nested using straw extensively, and then packed in wire-bound crates
- Liquids: casks, metal drums, carboys (especially for acids) suitably encased in straw wrapping
- Instruments (electrical apparatus, radios, etc.): cases or cartons, great care being taken with the internal packing.

Conclusions

As with all the elements of the marketing cycle – understand, create, communicate and deliver – each stage is nested in the other. The final stage involves making sure the promises you have communicated to customers are delivered. As we have seen in this chapter in the examples from Sweden and Japan the development of logistic solutions allows companies to enhance their delivery of customer related values. New information technologies are changing the delivery modes is some sectors. For example Eastman Kodak (Zimmerman, 1999) has retooled its Global Customer Service and Support business to become a revenue-generating unit that offers customers digital imaging and networking consulting, implementation and support services. It has also set up web-related products and services to extend digital technologies to traditional film customers while at the same time advancing its digital camera technology. Kodak's CEO was quoted as saying 'For a lot of customers, we bring value in helping them engineer their image workflow, from capture to output, and that's their business, so we're dealing with their business processes'.

Kodak is also rolling out Picture Maker kiosks across the US and Europe, enabling customers to scan photos and images for enlarging, cropping and other manipulations. A print at home service is also under development, linked to the Web, for archiving and printing.

There will at some future date be no more film in the family camera, and unlike now it will not matter! This example of Kodak and where they are heading illustrates the essence of delivering value in the future – the integration of IT with e-commerce while being firmly focused on the customer whether in business to business, or at home with the consumer. Companies who can keep these principles in mind will be survivors not only in the 'new economy' but also in the old economy.

Questions for discussion

1. Identify two purchasing decisions for high-value products or services. One should be one where you as a consumer where satisfied, and one where you were dissatisfied. Analyze what went right and what went wrong in each of these cases. In the case where it all went wrong, what advice would you give to the organization?
2. Customer satisfaction creates customer loyalty. Discuss.
3. What do you understand by customer value management?
4. Customer care has been thought about as involving three interfaces, namely, the staff–customer interface; the management–customer and the management–staff interface. Use these three dimensions to explore customer care in relation to an organization you are familiar with, for example, your university or college, or somewhere you have been employed. What examples of good and bad practice can you identify?
5. Identify and visit up to six websites belonging to different companies. Categorize how the websites are being used (for example awareness, information provision, e-commerce). Under the following headings rate the sites on a scale of 1 = very poor to 5 = very good: easy to find; ability to navigate online; detailed information on product/services; advice provided online; ability to request further information. After ranking the overall results discuss the positive and negative features of the sites you visited.
6. How has the Internet been used by companies to deliver customer values?
7. How has the Internet been utilized by companies in your own country or region? What has happened to the growth of e-commerce for both consumer purchases and business to business purchases? What evidence can you find? Discuss
8. If a customer complains we know they are dissatisfied. If a customer does not complain we know they are satisfied? Discuss.
9. Produce a list of what you regard as 'good practice' in customer service. Can you divide the list into 'must be present' and 'good idea but not essential'?
10. Why is a concern for packaging an essential part of the marketing cycle? Discuss.

References

Baker, S. (1999), Global e-commerce, local problems, *Journal of Business Strategy*, 20 (4), pp. 32–38.

Bell, Q. (1998), When service is crap brands can go down the pan, *Marketing*, April 30, p. 5.

Dahlhoff, D. (1999), Beaten paths not always right roads, *Marketing News*, May 10, p. 16.

Green, F.W. (1989), Stand the test of export packaging, *Transportation and Distribution*, 30 (8), p. 52.

Lafferty, M. (1999), Inside American Express, *Bank Marketing*, Jan/Feb (101), p. 2.

McGovern, J.M. (1998), Logistics on the internet, *Transportation and Distribution*, 39 (7), p. 68; (4) InfoTrac http://www.galegroup.com/

Mitchell, J. (1999), Reaching across borders, *Marketing News*, May 10, p. 19.

Richardson, H.L. (1999), Cut packaging costs, *Transportation and Distribution*, 40 (8), pp. 79–84.

Thomson, H. (1998), What do your customers really want? *Journal of Business Strategy*, 19 (4), p. 17; (5) InfoTrac http://www.galegroup.com/.

Tylee, J. (1998), Survey slams customer service, *Campaign*, Nov. 20, p. 5.

Walker, A.G. (1995), *International Trade Procedures and Management*, Butterworth-Heinemann, London.

Zimmerman, M.R. (1999), Kodak bid zooms in on digitisation, *PC Week*, April 26, 16 (17), p. 1.

Further Reading

Ghosh, S. (1998), Making business sense of the internet, *Harvard Business Review*, 76 (2), pp. 126–135.

Katsikeas, C.S., Goode, M.M.H. and Katsikea, E. (2000), Sources of power in international marketing channels, *Journal of Marketing Management*, 16 (1–3), pp. 185–202.

Naumann, E. and Jackson, D.W. (1999), One more time: how do you satisfy customers? *Business Horizons*, 42 (3), pp. 71–76.

Smith, A.K., Bolton, R.N. and Wagner, J. (1999), A model of customer satisfaction with service encounters involving failure and recovery, *Journal of Marketing Research*, 36 (3), pp. 356–362.

Stank, T.P., Daugherty, P. and Ellinger, A.E. (1998), Pulling customers closer through logistics services, *Business Horizons*, 41 (5), p. 74; (7) InfoTrac http://www.galegroup.com/.

Walsh, J. and Godfrey, S. (2000), The internet: a new era in customer service, *European Management Journal*, 18 (1), pp. 85–92.

CHAPTER 9

Export documentation, getting paid, organizing insurance and finding finance

Chapter objectives

After studying this chapter you should be able to:

- Understand the purpose of the commercial and transport related documents used to facilitate the movement of goods
- Understand the alternative methods of payment available to international marketers
- Understand the role and importance of insurance to the payment process
- Understand the alternative sources and methods of obtaining finance to support export activities
- Understand the influence of exchange rate fluctuation to the international marketer

Introduction

A general expectation of exporters is that marketing and selling their goods internationally is more problematic than operating solely in the domestic market. Delivery generally takes longer and payment for the goods can also take more time. Companies need to ensure that prospective customers are of good standing, i.e. reliable payers, and that the payment can be received as quickly as possible. Prompt payment is often more crucial for the smaller firm. A good understanding of the relevant export documents can also facilitate prompt shipment and payment.

The mode of payment is agreed between the buyer and seller, and will be set out in the commercial contract with the international buyer. INCOTERMS, devised by the International Chamber of Commerce, are intended to avoid confusion about the cost of an order.

The final decision on which method of payment depends on a number of factors. These can include:

- The usual contract terms adopted in the buyer's country
- What competitors are offering
- The speed with which funds are required
- The life of the product
- Market and exchange regulations
- The availability of foreign currency to the buyer
- Whether the cost of any credit can be afforded by the buyer or the seller.

In this chapter, the documentation required to move goods around the globe will be discussed in the Section 'Export documentation' and reference will be made to the INCOTERMS. The various options for how to get paid will be outlined before going on to discuss the purpose of credit insurance in protecting the exporter while facilitating international trade. The Section 'Export finance' will deal with ways of financing exporting activities over the short- or medium- to long-term. The influence of foreign currency exchange rates will be dealt with before concluding the chapter.

In terms of the global trading system, there are many providers of financial services. Clearly in this book it is not possible to cover them all. Instead the intention is to offer an overview of the services available, together with some specific examples from around the world. The student reader should be encouraged to seek information on relevant organizations within their own country for comparison.

Much of the material covered in this chapter is necessarily of a technical nature, and while it is perhaps less interesting than other aspects of international marketing discussed in this book, the issues discussed are vital to the successful completion of an international order. Thus from a marketing perspective, establishing good financial practice with customers and your financial service providers is crucial to the smooth running of the relationships. Every business decision has a marketing angle if the customer is directly or indirectly involved. Successful companies, particularly small and medium sized ones, recognize this, and see their business operations as a holistic experience. For this reason, the rounded student of international marketing should be competent in the basic financial structures of trade.

Export documentation

Export documents may seem a rather dry topic for study, but they perform a vital role in the link between the international marketer and the international customer. Some appreciation of what their role and purpose is complements the study of international marketing.

The documents are necessary for the movement of goods, for invoicing the customer, for receiving payment for the goods delivered and to satisfy the regulatory requirement of national governments. In addition to the 'basic' documentation the use of bonds and guarantees has become increasingly common in world trade.

Computerization of many of the documents has made the process less cumbersome and reduced the number of errors. This is important because errors can significantly delay the delivery of the goods to the customers.

Commercial documents

Commercial invoice

When sending goods to a buyer the exporter completes a commercial invoice. This is a claim for payment for the goods under the terms of the commercial contract with the buyer. The invoice should include a detailed description of the goods along with unit prices, total weight and terms of payment, as well as packing details and shipping marks. When several packages are being sent in a single consignment the invoice is usually accompanied by a packing list to identify all the items in the shipment.

As part of the details on the commercial invoice, the exporter can use the Customs Cooperation Council Nomenclature (CCCN). The CCCN is a classification number for all the goods subject to customs tariffs in international trade. When an exporter quotes a tariff number on an invoice, it allows customs officials to quickly identify the goods for statistical, duty or clearance purposes.

Pro forma invoice

This may be needed in advance if the importer has to get an allocation of foreign exchange or an import licence.

Customs invoice

Some countries require a separate customs invoice for imports over a certain value. Its purpose is to allow the authorities to check that no duty liable is being avoided by inaccurate pricing. Use of one may save delays.

Certified invoice

This is simply a commercial invoice which has a detailed statement as to the value and origin of the goods signed by the exporter.

Transport documents

Bill of lading

The maritime bill of lading has three important elements:

- It acts as evidence that there is a contract between either the exporter or importer and a shipping company to transport the goods by sea

- It is a receipt for goods shipped and provides certain details as to their condition when placed on board
- It is a document of title which means that the company named on the document has the right to possess the goods. A transfer of title on the bill acts as a transfer of ownership. This element of a bill is vital to the payment arrangements for the goods.

A clean bill of lading is one which has no superimposed clause or statement declaring some defect in the condition of the exported goods or the packaging, or some other aspect of the consignment. An example of a bill of lading is shown in Appendix III.

A 'received for shipment' bill of lading confirms that the shipping company has the goods in custody for shipment. Due to the dominance of containerized transport, it is common for the goods to be loaded at the factory into a container provided by the shipping company. If the shipment is less than a full container load, it is sent to an inland clearance depot to be packed into a container with other goods for the same destination. The container will be transported by road or rail to the port where the received for shipment bill can be converted into a shipped bill, by an endorsement from the carrier when the goods have been loaded aboard ship.

Railway consignment notes

These are used for international transport by rail to an overseas destination. They are not documents of title and are not negotiable.

Air waybill

Valuable or urgent, for example, perishable goods are often moved by air freight. This document is used but is non-negotiable. An example of an air waybill is shown in Appendix III.

Certificates

A certificate of origin (Appendix III) is sometimes required by the importing country's authorities to prove that the goods originate from a particular country. This may be necessary for the buyer to claim a preferential import duty.

Certificates of health, quality or inspection may also be required by the international buyer or the customs authorities.

Blacklist certificates provide evidence that the goods did not originate in, nor were transported via, blacklisted countries. This applies to situations where normal trading relations between two countries have deteriorated due to the political context. This restriction can also apply to any vessel registered in a blacklisted country, or which itself is blacklisted.

Bonds and guarantees

International buyers often require exporters to supply them with bonds as security for tenders, advance payments or in support of their performance obligations under a contract. As buyers increasingly require this type of security, these bond facilities mean that exporters are able to compete more effectively. There will normally be three parties involved in the provision of a contract guarantee, namely the exporter who performs the work or supplies the goods as covered in the terms of the contract; the buyer in whose favour the guarantee is issued; and the guarantor (for example, a bank or insurance company) responsible for issuing the guarantee.

The mechanics of the process are as follows. The international customer asks the exporter to provide a guarantee in support of the work to be undertaken or goods supplied. The exporter requests a guarantee from a domestic bank or insurance company in favour of the buyer. The bank or insurance company then issues the guarantee to the buyer and takes a counter indemnity from the exporter. These guarantees can be either:

■ Simple demand guarantee: this is usually expressed to be payable on first demand of the buyer despite any objections raised by the exporter. Any recourse the exporter wishes to exercise will have to be made via litigation.
■ Conditional demand guarantee: this is still payable on demand but only if the specifically defined conditions laid down in the guarantee document have been met. Clearly the exporter has more protection under this guarantee.

Bid bond/tender guarantee

This document supports an offer and gives the beneficiary a financial remedy if, for example, the tenderer withdraws the tender during the adjudication period; the tenderer fails to sign a contract if the bid is accepted; or if the tenderer fails to produce a performance guarantee if called upon to do so. Usually a tender guarantee will represent 0.5–5% of the contract value.

Performance guarantee

In the event of a successful bid the tender guarantee may be replaced by a performance guarantee securing the buyer against the exporter's failure to perform the contract in accordance with the terms and conditions prescribed. This may be 10% of the contract price but may well vary from 5 to 100%.

Advance payment guarantee

If the contract contains clauses relating to the advance payment of funds ahead of any performance under the contact, this document secures the repayment to the buyer of those funds should the exporter fail to fulfil the contract.

Retention money guarantee

In contracts where there is a period of warranty, it is usual for the buyer to withhold up to 10% of the contract value for a period after the contract has been completed. However, if the exporter provides a retention guarantee, a buyer may be prepared to forego the right to withhold these monies.

Maintenance, warranty bonds

These provide the buyer with protection should the exporter fail to comply with agreed warranties after the completion of the contract.

Customs guarantee

These are required to allow the importation of goods without payment of customs duty at the port of entry. These can be useful where samples of goods are being temporarily imported for trade fairs or exhibitions, and also to enable the free transit of goods across country borders.

Facility guarantee

These are issued in favour of other banks to secure the repayment of any form of banking facility, granted to a mutual customer or a third party (i.e. subsidiary, associated company, agent) of the issuing bank's customer.

Bail bonds

These are issued in connection with persons or ships which, for some reason, have been arrested.

Terms of the guarantee

Expert advice is required to ensure that the terms of the contract with the buyer are consistent with those in the guarantee document.

Unfair calling

It is in the client's interest to consider seeking protection against the unfair calling of a guarantee.

Expiry dates

While an open ended guarantee may be attractive to the buyer, the exporter should ensure that there is an agreed date by which any claim must be made.

Extend or pay

The international customer may insist that the guarantee be extended or paid. The exporter has little choice since a refusal will result in the guarantor having to pay the buyer. By including appropriate conditions within the original guarantee, it may be possible to avoid such difficulties.

International regulations

Local laws and regulations can vary, therefore it is important to be clear about which jurisdiction is being used. It is becoming increasingly common for exporters and buyers to agree to use a common code; for example, New York law is becoming an unofficial standard for some business deals.

INCOTERMS

Most corporate shipping managers responsible for international shipments do not need to know all the intricacies of regulation and documentation. However, a basic understanding of the process involved in getting shipments through customs and into another country can be useful. For the smaller exporter, it may be more useful especially to be clear about who is responsible for which costs during the exporting process.

International transactions are controlled by a set of rules and definitions. The most comprehensive and up to date terms are the INCOTERMS 1990 devised by the International Chamber of Commerce (1990) which address changing export processes, particularly electronic information exchange, and clarify buyer/seller responsibilities. These terms qualify 13 different trade terms in four groups designated by the letters: E, F, C and D. The terms are ranged on a liability scale with the exporter responsibility at a minimum under E terms and at a maximum under D terms as detailed in Table 9.1.

Table 9.1 INCOTERMS 1990

Minimum seller	EXW	Ex works (named place)
Obligations	FCA	Free carrier (named place)
	FAS	Free alongside ship (named port of shipment)
	FOB	Free on board (named port of shipment)
	CFR	Cost and freight (named port of destination)
	CIF	Cost, insurance and freight (named port of destination)
	CPT	Carriage paid to (named place of destination)
	CIP	Carriage, insurance paid to (named place of destination)
	DAF	Delivered at frontier (named place)
	DES	Delivered ex ship (named port of destination)
	DEQ	Delivered ex quay (named port of destination)
Maximum seller	DDU	Delivered duty unpaid (named place of destination)
Obligations	DDP	Delivered duty paid (named place of destination)

Methods of payment

Advance Payment

From the exporter's point of view the best method of payment is to receive the funds in advance. Cash with order (CWO) avoids any risk on orders with new buyers with whom the exporters has little or no knowledge. Payment may even be requested before production begins. In reality this is a rarely used method, as it means a buyer extending credit to the producer which is a reversal of normal trade practices.

An alternative form of this approach is cash on delivery (COD) whereby the goods are delivered, perhaps by courier or haulier depending on the size of the order, and payment is made before the goods are released.

Open account

While advance payment offers the greatest security to the seller, open account is at the other extreme, providing the least security. In this method, the goods and the appropriate documentation are sent to the buyer, who has agreed to pay within a certain number of days (as specified on the invoice) from the date of the invoice. This is usually a maximum period of 180 days but could be 30, 60 or 90 days. The buyer will remit the money to the exporter by an agreed method. Clearly this method depends on a degree of trust between the buyer and the seller. They will respect each other's business integrity, probably through a lengthy period of trading.

A variation of open account is consignment account, where an exporter supplies an international customer in order that stocks are built up in large enough quantities to cover continual demand. The exporter retains ownership of the goods until they are sold, or for an agreed period, after which the buyer remits the price to the seller.

Bills of exchange

An exporter can send a bill of exchange (Appendix III) for the value of the invoice of goods for export, through the banking system for payment by an overseas buyer on presentation. A bill of exchange is legally defined as 'an unconditional order in writing, addressed by one person to another, signed by the person giving it, requiring the person to which it is addressed to pay on demand or at a fixed or determinable future time a sum certain in money, to, or to the order of, a specified person, or to bearer'. The bill is in effect similar to a cheque/check which is drawn on an international buyer, or even a third party as designated in the export contract, for the sum agreed as settlement.

There are different types of bills of exchange. The sight draft is made out payable on demand when it is first presented to the purchaser. If the bill is to be paid at a fixed date or a determinable future date then it is called a term draft because the buyer is receiving a period of credit. In both cases the buyer indicates an acceptance to pay by writing an acceptance across the face of the bill.

By using a bill of exchange in conjunction with the shipping documents, the exporter is given a greater degree of control over the goods. This is because until the bill is paid or accepted by the buyer, the bank will not normally release the shipping documents, so the buyer is unable to take delivery of the goods.

The detailed use of bills of exchange is as follows. The exporter can pass a bill of exchange to a local (domestic) bank. This bank sends the bill to its international branch or to a corresponding bank in the buyer's country. This bank is known as the collecting bank who then presents the bill to the customer for immediate payment if it is a sight draft or for acceptance if it is a term draft. This procedure is known as clean bill collection because there are no shipping documents required.

An alternative to this method is the documentary collection method of payment. In this case, the shipping documents are sent through the banking system with the bill of exchange including the document of title to the goods (a bill of lading). The international bank then releases the documents on payment or acceptance of the bill of exchange by the international customer.

It is also possible for an exporter to use the banking system for a cash against documents (CAD) collection. In this case the shipping documents are sent to the bank, which only releases them once the exporter has confirmed that payment has been received.

In addition, the exporter can send all the documentation directly to the international buyer's bank which is known as direct collection. However, this is a little less secure than using the services of the domestic bank if something goes wrong with the process, for example, if the goods are delayed resulting in the buyer refusing to pay. The domestic bank will be able to assist the exporter with, for example, warehousing and/or reshipment. For the smaller exporter, having another organization on 'your side' may prove invaluable in difficult circumstances.

In all methods of payment using a bill of exchange outlined above, a promissory note can be used as an alternative. This is issued by a buyer who promises to pay the supplier a certain amount of money within a specified time.

Documentary letter of credit

While the documentary bill collection previously discussed provides some degree of security to the buyer and seller an even more secure method is to conduct the transaction by a documentary letter of credit (Appendix III). This document is sent usually via a domestic bank in the exporter's country, and is the means by which the exporter is paid.

The documents must be correctly completed and presented to a bank by the expiry date of the credit. If the terms of the credit are met, an exporter can receive payment from a domestic bank. The buyer is effectively providing the exporter with immediate payment, in return for a guarantee from a bank that the export docu-

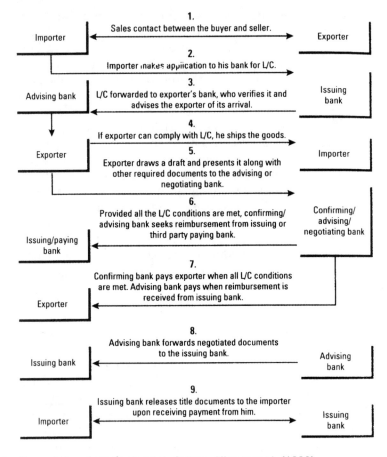

Figure 9.1 How a letter of credit operates. Source: Albaum et al. (1998).

ments required to deliver the goods have been completed to the bank's satisfaction. Figure 9.1 shows how a letter of credit operates.

These documentary letters of credit have two forms; they can be revocable or irrevocable. The former is very rare as its terms means that an international customer can amend or cancel the terms of credit at any time without prior notice to the seller. Most, therefore, are irrevocable, which means that once a buyer's conditions in the letter have been agreed by an exporter, they constitute a definite undertaking by the buyer's bank and cannot be revoked without the exporter's agreement.

Remitting the money

Most banks will offer a range of services to help the exporter receive payment from international customers, whether they are dealing on open account terms or using the security provided by documentary services. Most will offer electronic payments, foreign currency accounts, or electronic banking via a PC in the exporter office. Facilities such as SWIFT (Society for Worldwide Interbank Financial Telecommunications) allows leading banks around the world to process billions of electronic payment messages each year.

Individual banks brand their own particular system but essentially the same basic technical service is being offered, for example, the Bank of Scotland has TAPS (Transcontinental Automated Payment Service) which is relevant for remitters wishing to pay low value, high volume repeat payments such as pensions, salaries, magazine subscriptions and insurance premiums. In the technically complex area of documentary services the bank provides services such as advising, negotiation and confirming letters of credit, and providing discounting and collection services. In payment services the bank has paper systems via international drafts and electronic system via corporate HOBS, a home banking system for business.

Table 9.2 provides an 'at a glance' comparison of the payment options provided by the National Westminster Bank.

Table 9.2   The payment options offered by National Westminster Bank (source: the Internet)

Product	Applications	Time taken to effect instructions	Information we give you	Repeat payment option
Relay	Low cost payments in local currency (certain countries only)	Maximum 6 working days	Will appear on your statement	Yes
Standard transfer	The standard method of making international payments	Varies (usually within 4 working days)	Will appear on your statement plus separate notification	Yes
Urgent transfer	Faster than standard, use when time is critical	Fast (usually 1 or 2 working days)	Will appear on your statement plus separate notification	Yes
Foreign drafts	A banker's draft drawn on an overseas bank	Medium (depends how you deliver it)	Will appear on your statement plus separate notification	Yes
Same day euro	Same day euro payments within the UK	Same day (cut off for submissions 1.30 PM)	Will appear on your statement plus separate notification	Yes

Export credit insurance

The risks

Even when the most trusted customer is involved, sometimes things can go wrong with a contract. A buyer may default through a dispute or insolvency; or a buyer's government may intervene and impose restrictions on the ability of the buyer to pay, or delay payment until after the period for payment has expired. These risks are usually described as 'commercial risks'. Companies who provide credit insurance can tailor protection to the needs of the individual company, and will cover work in progress, binding contracts and goods delivered.

Depending on the market, some may carry more 'political' risks and uncertainties, and without proper export credit insurance the exporter can be left fully exposed to costs. As with other elements of export payments and finance it is often the smaller companies who are most at risk. Political risk arises when payment is not received as a direct result of the occurrence of war or civil war in the buyer's country, a cancellation of the contract by the Government of the buyer's country or when a government implements regulations which either prevent the export or import of the goods, or when measures to prevent or restrict the transfer of hard currency from the buyer's country are introduced by the Government in the buyer's country (see Box 9.1 for an example of the perception of risk from South Africa).

BOX 9.1: PERCEPTION OF RISK FROM SOUTH AFRICA (JUNE, 2000)

Country name: Australia
Short-term credit: Open for cover, no restrictions
Medium- to long-term credit: Generally open for cover
Restrictions: None

Country name: Syria
Short term credit: Applications considered case by case
Medium- to long-term credit: No cover available
Restrictions: Depending on size of contract; weak economy; poor institutional infrastructure (legal, banking, information)

Country name: Suriname
Short-term credit: No cover available
Medium- to long-term credit: No cover available
Restrictions: Shortage of foreign currency; weak economy; poor institutional infrastructure (legal, banking, information)

Country name: Columbia
Short-term credit: Open for cover, no restrictions
Medium- to long-term credit: Applications considered case by case
Restrictions: None

The organizations involved in this business do not just provide insurance. They are also an information resource about companies around the world, as it is in their interests to know the trading records of companies on which cover may be requested. This is an important aspect of risk management, export financing and credit management.

It is worth noting that while the common perception may be of little known customers in distant countries being the most risky, it is often nearer neighbours who are the worst offenders for late or non-payment. The trends are constantly shifting over time as different sectors of economies experience difficulties, but information from the UK office of the Dutch based credit insurer NCM (see Box 9.3) illustrates some of the payment problems for UK based companies. One in five have experienced a loss of payment by an EU company with the figures being one in 11 and one in 18 for France and Spain, respectively.

Trade Indemnity state that on average, companies have 40% of their current assets in the form of trade debtors. Research has shown that companies are not able to predict the majority of failures to which they are exposed, with 25–50% of failures coming from customers considered to be both long-standing and previously prompt paying. In some ways this is a self-fulfilling prophecy in that a customer is always a good payer until he/she is not! Still, with the volume of world trade being what it is the company can use one of those wonderful marketing statistics in its thinly disguised sales pitch: 'one company fails every few minutes of every working day and in some key export markets the situation appears to be worse than ever'.

Given that there are real risks involved in international trade companies generally with £250 000 and more will normally seek to use credit insurance. These will include service companies as well as those trading in goods.

The providers

Trade Indemnity have already been mentioned as one of the key providers of credit insurance. They are a private company, but the origins of the credit insurance industry was as part of national governments' support to exporters. In the UK the Export Credits Guarantee Department (ECGD) was established by the government in 1919 (see Box 9.2 for more details).

BOX 9.2: BACKGROUND TO THE ECGD

ECGD was set up in 1919 to help British exporters re-establish their trading positions following the World War I. This assistance largely took the form of providing insurance against the commercial and political risks of not being paid by international buyers after the goods had been exported.

In 1991 the short-term credit arm of the ECGD which dealt with credit up to 2 years, was sold to the Dutch company NCM Credit Insurance Ltd. (see Box 9.3). This company along with other private providers are the key providers for companies dealing in consumable goods.

ECGD in its current form was established under the 1991 Export and Investments Guarantees Act as a separate arm of the British Government, reporting to the Secretary of State for Trade. It continues to support exporters of British capital goods and services with finance and insurance packages. It can also insure British companies who invest abroad against the political risks of a non-return on their investments.

ECGD issues around £3.5 billion of guarantees a year to cover a variety of projects. Some 55% of the cover is for civil projects, 24% for defence-related equipment and 21% for civil aircraft (mostly the Airbus). In terms of international investments the Department insures £500 million.

The main markets for the ECGD are in the Far East and South Asia, the Middle East, Latin America and South Africa. Examples of recent projects include: double-decker buses for Hong Kong, a library in Egypt, a road in Ghana, a power plant in Turkey, a baby food production line in Russia, a pharmaceutical plant in Croatia, and an offshore oilfield development in Brazil.

(source: http://www.ecgd.gov.uk/)

Internationally, in much the same way as the ECGD operates, many national governments have their official export credit agency, examples of which are listed in Table 9.3.

NCM's mission statement reads 'At NCM we are committed to a dynamic partnership with our customers, fuelled by our people's energy and imagination. Our unique approach to sharing knowledge and information ensures we create the best credit management solutions for our customers.' From a marketing perspective the emphasis is very much on partnership with the business community. By 1999 this company employed 1400 people and had a turnover of 456.5 million euros. A lot of the support offered to customers by NCM depends on economic, political and financial information which it gathers and evaluates. The exporter is not simply purchasing insurance and peace of mind but market intelligence data about markets and customers served. For example, the NCM Data Network is a software package which provides NCM's customers with direct online access to an extensive database of buyer information. This enables customers to establish credit limits, monitor the status of their customers and generally support their credit management process.

More background details on NCM's development are given in Box 9.3.

BOX 9.3: BACKGROUND TO NCM

NCM is one of the four leading credit insurers in the world. Its network of offices covers Belgium, Denmark, France, Germany, Italy, Ireland, Malaysia, Norway, Spain, Sweden, the UK, and the US. The group's headquarters are in Amsterdam.

NCM was founded in 1925 in Amsterdam by a number of Dutch bank and insurance companies, some foreign credit insurance and reinsurance companies, and a German bank. Initially the business focused on reinsurance, but after the late 1950s the business began to focus more on credit insurance activities.

Core activities of the company are insuring payment risks resulting from the delivery of goods and services to companies known as 'commercial risks'. In addition the NCM also insures 'political' risks that go with deliveries to countries in which money transfer is impossible due to a lack of foreign exchange.

In December 1991 NCM began its international expansion by taking over the short-term arm of the UK's Export Credits Guarantee Department. In 1998 Swiss Re, a large reinsurer, became the largest shareholder in NCM. At that time NCM employed 1248 people and had a turnover of 429 million euros.

Table 9.3 Examples of government owned export credit agencies

Country	Agency
Australia	Export Finance and Insurance Corporation http://www.efic.gov.au/
Canada	Export Development Corporation http://www.edc-see.ca/
Denmark	Eksport Kredit Fonden http://www.ekf.dk/engpraes/engprs.htm
Germany	Hermes Kreditversicherungs-AG http://www.hermes-kredit.com/
Hong Kong	Hong Kong Export Credit Insurance Corporation http://www.hkecic.com/
Japan	Export-Import Insurance Department http://eid.miti.go.jp/e/
Malaysia	Malaysia Export Credit Insurance Berhad http://www.mecib.com.my/
Netherlands	Nederlandsche Credietverzekering Maatschappij NV http://www.ncmgroup.com/
New Zealand	EXGO http://www.state.co.nz/
South Africa	Credit Guarantee Insurance Corporation of Africa http://www.creditguarantee.co.za/
US	Export–Import Bank of the United States http://www.opic.gov/

Types of policies

Most insurance organizations offer the same basic policies to their clients. Examples from the Hong Kong Credit Insurance Corporation are given in Box 9.4.

**BOX 9.4: EXAMPLES OF POLICIES FROM
THE HONG KONG CREDIT INSURANCE CORPORATION**

Cover on country risks
Risks covered
- Blockage or delay in foreign exchange remittance
- Cancellation of import licences
- Import bans
- Payment moratorium
- War, civil disturbances and natural disasters

For all events of loss the maximum percentage of indemnity is 90%.

Small and medium enterprises policy
Buyer risks covered
- Insolvency and bankruptcy
- Default in payment
- Failure or refusal to take delivery of goods

Country risks covered
- Blockage or delay in foreign exchange remittance
- Cancellation of import licences
- Import bans
- Payment moratorium
- War, civil disturbance and natural disasters

In general the mechanics of the policy process would operate as outlined below.

1. A company would apply to a credit agency to insure them against non-payment by a foreign organization buying their goods or services.
2. The credit agency will fully investigate the international customer before accepting the risk.
3. The agency will then fix the premium according to the commercial and political perception of the risks in the market concerned.
4. The company completes its transaction with the international customer and gets paid.
5. If payment is not forthcoming then the credit agency can help to collect the overdue account or seek legal assistance.
6. If the debtor defaults, the company is covered by the terms of the agreement, and any salvage collected is shared pro-rata among the parties who have an interest in the debt.

For established relationships, companies can often operate within a discretionary limit without having to approach the credit agency on a case by case basis. For example with Trade Indemnity you can agree a credit limit on each of your customers when you trade above an agreed level. Below this agreed limit (the discretionary limit) the company uses their own sources of information on financial status and trading experience to justify their trading. As long as the company trades within the parameters of the credit limits, and abides by any other conditions of the policy, then it will be covered in the event of one of its customers failing.

Cost

The cost using the services of a credit insurance company will depend on the turnover of the individual client. As an example Trade Indemnity state that in general it will range from 0.1 to 1% of turnover dependent on trading history, the business sector in which the client operates, and the companies on which cover is requested. Trade Indemnity state that most companies' premium is between 0.3 and 0.7%, but could well be higher for some political risks. They also state that most companies have an average bad debt level of 0.7% of turnover, thus making the premium economical.

The Export-Import Bank of the United States also emphasize that costs depend on a number of considerations, such as the terms offered, types of buyers and the countries to which the exports are going. Ex-Im Bank usually insures all of a company's foreign receivables so the premium is 75 cents to $1.25 per $100 of gross value invoice. For small businesses most policies have a minimum advance of $500.

Benefits to smaller companies

Small companies benefit both directly and indirectly from the activities of credit insurance providers. When a company signs a major contract many sub-contractors also benefit. Rolls-Royce, for example, are a major user of ECGD facilities and it is estimated than a major international contract benefits 1500 companies in the supply chain. Approximately 75% of these companies employ between 10 and 250 people. Similarly, Mitsui-Babcock estimate that they place around 500–600 sub-contracts in the UK when they win a contract to construct a power station.

The Export-Import Bank of the United States, for the fiscal year ended in 1999, authorized $3.7 billion in insurance cover, of which 33% was for small businesses. This was made up of 1600 policies of which 83% were to small businesses. The top ten markets where the shipments went are listed in Table 9.4.

An example of a policy targeted at the smaller firm is given in Box 9.5.

BOX 9.5: US EXPORT–IMPORT BANK SMALL BUSINESS INSURANCE POLICY

Ex-Im Bank offers a short-term (up to 180 days) insurance policy geared to meet the particular credit requirements of smaller, less experienced exporters. Products typically supported under short-term policies are spare parts, raw materials, and consumer goods. Under the policy, Ex-Im Bank assumes 95% of the commercial and 100% of the political risk involved in extending credit to the exporter's overseas customers. This policy frees the exporter from 'first loss' commercial risk deductible provisions that are usually found in regular insurance policies. It is a multi-buyer type policy which requires the exporter to insure all export credit sales. It offers a special 'hold-harmless' assignment of proceeds which makes the financing of insured receivables more attractive to banks. This special coverage is available to companies which have an average annual export credit sales volume of less than $3 million for the 2 years prior to application and which meet the Small Business Administration's definition of a small business.

Export finance

It is likely that an exporter will experience some form of delay in payment at some point, whatever the size of the organization. Delays in payment can have a serious implication for the cash flow of the organization unless financing options are used. An exporter may find that they have to allow credit terms to the buyer, not only for the transportation period, but also for the production time. In the case of large scale construction or heavy machinery projects, this could cover a number of years. Further, delays in payment can be caused if there are problems with the project's completion.

As a result a number of financial options are available from a variety of organizations to assist the exporter. There are two types of credit: supplier and buyer credit. Under supplier credit, an exporter allows credit to the customer in the sales contract

Table 9.4   Top ten destinations for shipments supported by the Export–Import Bank of the United States

1	South Korea
2	Mexico
3	Brazil
4	India
5	UK
6	Canada
7	United Arab Emirates
8	Dominican Republic
9	Argentina
10	Hong Kong

and then obtains terms from a domestic bank to cover these terms. With buyer credit a domestic bank provides finance directly to the international customer or an approved borrower, so that the exporter can be paid immediately on shipment of the goods. The finance can be with recourse, in which case the exporter is liable for any outstanding money the buyer does not repay the lender; or without recourse in which case the exporter is not responsible to the lender for any default by the buyer.

Short-term finance

The most straightforward way of financing export sales is for the exporting company to use its existing overdraft facility with its bank. This can cover purchasing materials, manufacturing costs, shipping and credit, as long as it is within agreed limits and the payment from the customer is deposited there when eventually received. This approach may be suitable for a one-off occasion, but will probably be more expensive in bank charges over the longer term than using tailor-made financing packages outlined next.

Advance against bills

One form of short-term finance is for the exporter to obtain an advance of funds from a domestic bank against the face value of a bill of exchange drawn by an exporter on an international customer under the terms of the export contract. The bill is passed to the bank which advances an agreed percentage and will present it to the international customer for collection. If the buyer does not pay the exporter's domestic bank for the bill then the bank has recourse to the exporter for the loss. An advance is only made when the bill is a clean bill collection, i.e. there are no shipping documents involved. The bank will charge interest for the credit period of the advance and a fee for the collection operation.

Negotiation of bills

If more finance is required than just a percentage of the bill of exchange, then one option is to establish a facility to negotiate bills of exchange. The exporter's bank will purchase the bill of exchange along with the shipping documents. The bank then sends the bills for collection to the international buyer and reimburses itself from the money received. If the buyer defaults then the bank has recourse to the exporter, charging interest for the credit period and any collection fees.

Acceptance credits

This is a way of financing which would normally be used only by larger exporters. Under this method a merchant bank, for example, will accept a bill of exchange drawn upon themselves. The bank bill, as it is called, can be discounted, i.e. sold for its face value less a discount charge, in the money market to one of the discount houses that specialize in this business. Once the sale is completed, the proceeds less an acceptance commission are credited to the exporter, and when the bill matures the bank pays it and debits the exporter's account for the face value of the bill. The exporter also has the option to draw another bill on the bank and simply pay the difference between the face value of the maturing bill and the sale proceeds of the new one.

A company can make use of some flexibility within the system by drawing funds when there is the best discount rate in the market. This is more advantageous than being tied to overdraft interest rates.

Documentary acceptance credits

It is possible to use a confirmed irrevocable letter of credit to gain access to funds. This document would be presented to a domestic bank along with a bill of exchange and the documents required under the terms of the credit. The bank can also accept a term bill for extended periods, which the exporter can then discount with any bank for cash. Any cost is charged to the exporter unless arrangements have been made for the buyer to carry such costs.

Factoring

If the exporter has a sufficiently large international turnover, then it may be easier to hand over all the potential problems of payment collection to a specialist organization which deals with debt collection and trade finance. The historical origins of factoring are described in Box 9.6.

BOX 9.6: THE ORIGINS OF FACTORING

The origins of modern factoring are rooted in the old colonial practice of using mercantile agents. Due to the risks involved in trading over great distances with slow communications in the colonial markets from the 16th Century onwards, European producers would appoint such agents or factors to receive, sell, distribute and collect payment for their goods.

This method of doing business ensured that producers could sell their goods abroad without fear of non-payment. It developed strongly on the east coast of North America especially in the textile, clothing and related industries. Factors gradually began not only to hold stock and sell goods on the behalf of principals, but to guarantee payment as del credere agents.

In time it was this role of guaranteeing payment for goods which began to supersede the factor's selling functions. In tandem with this change, the burgeoning domestic cotton and textile trade of the US was increasingly using factors to ensure payment for goods.

(Source Association of British Factors)

Factoring companies provide:

- Sales accounting and collection
- Credit management which can include 100% protection against bad debts
- A financial facility against sales invoices.

The benefits of using the services of a factoring company are:

- Savings in management time
- The elimination of bad debts
- Precise cash flow management
- The availability of funds which would otherwise be financing debtors.

In addition to the basic factoring package of services, many factoring houses offer additional assistance to exporters which might include:

- Advice on trading terms
- Local collections and advice on the resolution of disputes
- Protection against exchange risk when invoicing in foreign currency
- Quicker transfer of funds to the domestic country
- Expert local knowledge of international buyers' credit standing
- Financial facilities in a variety of major currencies.

The mechanics of factoring are as follows. An exporter can sell trade debts to a factoring company, and in return will receive up to 80% of the face value of the debts. The factoring company handles the sales accounting and carries out the task of collecting the debts from the international customer. The factoring company will monitor the sales records of the exporter, and when it receives the final payment it will credit the exporter with the remaining 20%, minus the service charge. If the overseas buyer defaults on a debt there is no recourse to the exporter. From the factoring company's point of view they have to be confident that the internationally based company is of good standing in credit terms.

A factoring company may be prepared to purchase the goods destined for the international customer for cash. The exporter then acts as the factor's agent, delivering the goods and collecting the proceeds.

In certain cases, where the buyer does not know that the exporter has raised finance through a factoring house, it is called undisclosed factoring. The exporter still deals directly with the buyer for payment of the contract.

Factoring companies normally charge for their services in two ways: a fee for the services and a separate charge for the finance made available against sales. The service fee is determined for each client depending on the volume of sales, industry sector, average value of invoices, number of customers and whether credit protection (insurance) is included. Usually the charge will be between 0.5 and 2.5% of gross annual turnover. The charge for finance will be related to the prevailing bank base rate and may be similar to charges for overdrafts.

Confirming house

A confirming house is effectively an agent for an overseas buyer. The confirming house, acting for the buyer, places an order with an exporter and deals directly with the exporter to complete the contract. In this case there is no international credit risk or financial burden for the exporter, because the confirming house gives short-term credit to the international buyer who pays a commission for the services provided. A specialized form of a confirming house is a buying house, which makes purchases, for example, in the UK for international retailers and other international purchasers.

Export finance house

In instances where the exporting company sells only occasional large value capital or semi-capital goods abroad, it may be appropriate to use an export finance house to handle the contract. This type of organization is particularly useful where a buyer is being supplied by a number of companies, none of which wishes to assume responsibility for arranging the financing for the contract. The export finance house provides cash to the exporter on shipment, and credit to a buyer. It deals with the credit assessment of a buyer and takes out insurance as appropriate. If a buyer defaults there is no recourse to the exporter.

Export houses

Export houses do not directly finance export orders, but they indirectly provide a source of credit. The use of this export mode is related to the discussion of market entry modes in Chapter 4. The export house will act either as an export merchant, buying and selling goods internationally, or as an export agent where an exporter receives payment for goods upon shipment and the export agent provides credit to the international customer, promotes the goods abroad, holds stock in the domestic market, and even acts as a complete export sales department.

Countertrade

Countertrade can be regarded as a means of financing exporting activities, especially in new or emerging markets. It involves barter, which is the direct exchange of goods without transfer of funds, and the more frequently used counter-purchase. This is an arrangement whereby an exporter, in part or in total consideration for goods exported, contracts to purchase goods from the end-user.

Medium-term finance

Most of the methods so far discussed for financing export are suitable for periods of up to 2 years. Beyond that timescale there are other methods which a company can consider. These will now be outlined.

Leasing

Where a large item of capital equipment is involved, an exporter may find it more beneficial to sell the product to a leasing company, which then provides it to the international customer on a lease agreement. The advantage of this to the exporter is that immediate payment is received from the leasing company without further recourse.

Instalment finance

An exporting company can also finance the export order by arranging hire purchase for an international customer, either through a finance house in the home market or in the buyer's country. The finance company will purchase the goods from the exporter and receive instalments from the buyer, perhaps via a finance company in the buyer's country.

Merchant banks

These banks specialize in the provision of medium- and longer-term export finance. In addition, for certain projects, it is possible to arrange other types of finance, for example, co-financing loans from international agencies or aid funds and equity participation. Fixed rate finance can be raised on the bond market by way of private placement or public offerings to finance major international projects. Alternatively it is possible to issue floating-rate notes which provide medium-term finance at floating interest rates, but subject to a minimum fixed rate.

Forfaiting

This is a form of fixed rate trade finance which involves the discount, without recourse, of an exporter's trade debts. The debts can be in any form but the most common are bill of exchange or promissory notes held by the exporter as evidence of the buyer's future obligation. This method can be used to provide finance for international customers for up to 7 years. Usually the bill of exchange is supported by a bank guarantee from a bank in the buyer's country, but this is not essential and non-bank supported debt can also be forfaited.

Assuming that a guarantee is required the forfaiting company needs to know from its client:

- The currency and total amount to be settled
- Period to be financed
- Exporting country
- Name of importer and country
- Name and country of guarantor
- Type of security (letter of guarantee)
- Nature of instrument (bill of exchange)
- Nature of goods and delivery date

- Any necessary licences or transfer authorizations required
- Place of payment of paying instrument
- Repayment schedule.

The main benefits of forfaiting for the exporter are:

- Immediate cash after delivery
- No recourse
- Up to 100% of the value of the contract can be forfaited, but this is more usually 80–90%
- Speed and flexibility
- Finance at fixed rate of interest
- Minimal documentation.

Buyer credit

For larger and more complex contracts, it is often the best course for the finance to be provided in the form of a loan direct to an approved borrower in the country concerned, rather than to the exporter. This borrower does not necessarily have to be the buyer. This can include single project finance and lines of credit.

Under single project financing buyer credit financing is provided with support from a guarantee from an export insurance organization, e.g. NCM. A large amount of finance is provided at preferential interest rates. Usually about 80–85% of the contract costs are covered. The balance of the financing will be provided by the buyer, perhaps through a bank loan.

A line of credit can be put in place for a single export contract, but it is also possible to extend credit direct to an international buyer by providing a single loan facility to cover a number of separate supply contracts against a specific project. This would be known as project line of credit, which is often established by the main exporter or contractor.

The finance available under such arrangements is normally 80–85% of the contract value. Ten percent or less of each contract price is usually paid directly by an international customer within 30 days of signature of the contract, and further direct payments made on a pro-rata basis according to the value of each shipment to the buyer. The length of the credit will vary according to the contract but usually range between 2 and 5 years.

Foreign currency for exporters

Many exporters accept payment for their goods and services in the currency of their international customers or in a third currency, for example, US dollars. There are several reasons for this, including the fact that some commodities such as oil are traded in US dollars; a buyer may prefer the price to be in a particular currency because it is more stable than their domestic currency, which basically means they do not expect it to depreciate before the contract is completed. By quoting in this currency an exporter may gain an advantage over competitors unwilling to do likewise.

However there can be problems for the exporter in terms of exchange risk, for example, an exporter may not receive the full domestic value for an order if a buyer's chosen currency has depreciated during the contract period. The exporter also needs to avoid currencies which are not convertible on the foreign exchange market.

In 1999 many members of the EU entered into a new currency called the euro which, it was hoped, would in time become a rival to the US dollar and the Japanese yen as a currency of choice for international trade. Clearly for those countries who are members, instability in the exchange rate between their countries has been removed. Companies in other countries who remain outside the euro zone can still deal in euros and many will have established euro accounts and introduced dual pricing. Box 9.7 provides further details on this new currency.

BOX 9.7: THE EURO EXPLAINED

The euro is a currency which came into being on 1 January 1999 and is currently based on a weighted average of the German mark, the French franc and the other currencies of the nations adopting it. These other nations are Austria, Belgium, Finland, Ireland, Italy, Luxembourg, Portugal, the Netherlands and Spain. The governments involved have worked hard to bring their budget deficits and inflation rates into synchronization with one another, so as to integrate the behaviour of their national economies. Since its introduction it has been used for stock, bond and currency markets. Some larger companies have begun to trade in euros and to conduct their banking in the currency. The euro acts as the common conversion, so if a German wishes to obtain French francs, the marks are converted to the value in euros which is then converted to francs. Euro notes and coins will be introduced on 1 January 2002 and by July 2002 national currencies of the participating countries will no longer be legal tender, and only the euro will remain.

So far the euro has not lived up to expectations as being a currency to rival the US dollar. It remains shaky on the exchange markets and Denmark, Sweden and the UK remain outside the euro zone, whilst Greece is ready to join when it achieves the fiscal requirements. Its future role is in the balance and only time will tell how its importance to exporters will grow.

Forward exchange market

An exporter can protect against the loss caused by fluctuating exchange rates by taking out a forward exchange contract with a bank. The exporter, invoicing a buyer in a foreign currency for payment at an agreed future date, sells those expected receipts to the bank in advance of the due payment date. The bank agrees to buy at a pre-determined forward rate of exchange, which varies according to the time of future delivery be it 1, 3, 6 months or longer. No money is exchanged at the time of the contract, but the exporter is guaranteed a certain amount of domestic currency in place of the foreign currency sales proceeds, no matter what exchange rate fluctuations may take place between invoicing and payment by the buyer.

The forward rate varies form the spot rate, which is the rate a bank is prepared to pay for foreign currency at any moment of time. The forward rate may be at a discount if it exchanges for less than the domestic currency spot rate, or it may be at a premium if it exchanges for more. The difference between the two rates is determined by market forces, including specifically the interest rates being paid on fixed deposits by the bank of the currencies involved.

A fixed forward rate ties in the exporter to delivering the required foreign currency to the bank on the date of maturity of the exchange contract. If the buyer defaults on payment, the exporter must still provide the correct amount, even if this means purchasing it at the spot rate. It may be possible to extend the contract and avoid this situation, but there will still be an additional cost involved. If it is not known to a precise date when the buyer will pay an option-dated contract can be entered into, which allows the exporter to deliver the foreign currency at any time between two agreed dates.

Foreign currency options

A currency option gives the exporter the right, but not the obligation, to buy or sell a specific amount of foreign currency on or before a certain date. This allows some control over the exchange rate fluctuations.

Foreign currency borrowing

An exporter can eliminate exchange rate changes by taking a loan in the same currency as that to be paid by an overseas buyer, so that expected receipts from the buyer are not affected.

Currency accounts

If the exporting company has sufficiently large and regular international transactions, then it may be economical to open accounts in the currencies of the proceeds, instead of converting them into the domestic currency. These can then be used to service international accounts and save fees on foreign exchange dealings. Box 9.8 provides an example of the services offered by one provider.

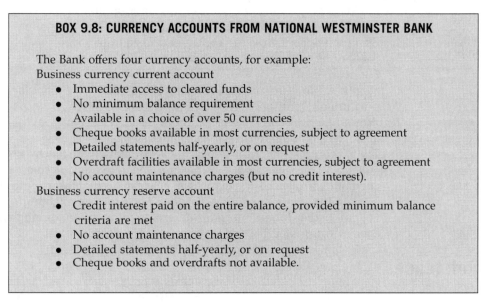

BOX 9.8: CURRENCY ACCOUNTS FROM NATIONAL WESTMINSTER BANK

The Bank offers four currency accounts, for example:
Business currency current account
- Immediate access to cleared funds
- No minimum balance requirement
- Available in a choice of over 50 currencies
- Cheque books available in most currencies, subject to agreement
- Detailed statements half-yearly, or on request
- Overdraft facilities available in most currencies, subject to agreement
- No account maintenance charges (but no credit interest).

Business currency reserve account
- Credit interest paid on the entire balance, provided minimum balance criteria are met
- No account maintenance charges
- Detailed statements half-yearly, or on request
- Cheque books and overdrafts not available.

Conclusions

Although technical in nature, the topics of documentation, payments, insurance, export finance and currency exchange covered in this chapter are by no means static, rather they are an evolving part of the international marketing scene. The evolution of the world economy creates a shifting tide of issues and problems, whether they be the shortage of hard currency in some markets, or high interest rates in others. Political factors leave some markets exposed to higher insurance cost and, in extreme cases, to situations where no cover at all is available to the exporter. Some exporters, foolishly attempt to trade without cover, only to find themselves exposed to losses when the political situation worsens as in Iran, Iraq, Libya, and Yugoslavia in the later years of the last century.

Flexibility is a key word in terms of payments, etc. and the smaller exporter can benefit from a good relationship with banks, credit insurers and financial houses, whilst making good use of the services they provide. Many of the credit insurers are particularly aware that they have to market their own services in an increasingly competitive market, and therefore are keen to add value to what they do. As a result firms can benefit especially from the marketing information and knowledge which is the key to their business.

Questions for discussion

1. What is a bill of exchange and what role does it play in the payment process?
2. What role does a documentary letter of credit play in the payment process?
3. What role do companies like NCM play in international marketing? Using

the Web find other companies who offer similar services to NCM. Select one or two companies and compare the services they offer.
4. Compare and contrast factoring and forfaiting.
5. Select one country as an export market, and evaluate its suitability in financial terms.
6. How has the euro zone developed since 1999? In particular how has the position of Denmark, Sweden and the UK evolved?
7. Why should smaller firms be more concerned with payment problems, and what action can they take to ensure payment?
8. Try to identify any countries in the world which currently it might be difficult to do business with. What are the reasons for this? Can you find current examples of companies who are experiencing payment problems?
9. Explain the ways in which a company can reduce exchange rate risk?
10. Is it important for an international marketer to be concerned with financial considerations? Why?

References

Albaum, G., Strandskov, J. and Duerr, E. (1998), *International Marketing and Export management*, Addison Welsey, Harlow.

International Chamber of Commerce (1990), *Guide to INCOTERMS*, International Chamber of Commerce, New York.

Further Reading

Taggart, J.M. and Taggart, J.H. (1997/98), Exchange rate effects and competitive performance: a comparison of the UK and Irish firms exporting into the EU, *Irish Marketing Review*, 10 (2), pp. 43--52.

See Appendix III for examples of some of the documents discussed in this chapter.
Because of the technical and topical nature of much of the material covered in this chapter, much use has been made of the following websites in writing this chapter.

- Bank of Scotland – http://www.bankofscotland.co.uk/
- Credit Guarantee Insurance Corporation of Africa, South Africa – http://www.creditguarantee.co.za/
- ECGD – http://www.ecgd.gov.uk/
- Export Finance and Insurance Corporation of Australia – http://www.efic.gov.au/
- Export–Import Bank of the United States – http://www.opic.gov/
- Hong Kong Export Credit Insurance Corporation – http://www.hkecic.com/
- HSBC Invoice Finance (UK) Ltd. – http://www.invoicefinance.hsbc.co.uk/home.htm
- National Westminster Bank – http://www.natwest.com/
- NCM – http://www.ncmgroup.com/
- Royal Bank of Scotland – http://www.rbs.co.uk/
- Trade Indemnity – http://www.tradeindemnity.com/

CHAPTER 10

Globalization, the Internet and the marketer

Chapter objectives

- Understand the relevance of international marketing topics within a broader societal context
- Understand the process of globalization as it affects the consumer
- Appreciate the tension between the process of globalization and its human impact
- Understand the opportunities on offer to the marketer which are created by the dotcom world

Introduction

The intention of this chapter and the next one is to select some topics which have a profound relevance to the marketer not only currently, but also in the future. In the space available, it is not the intention to provide an encyclopaedic detail of the topics, but rather to raise the consciousness of the reader, and to stimulate him/her to think about the wider context of international marketing and the kind of society people live in today and how it will change in the future. Inevitably the currency of certain topics can change rapidly. When this book was first under consideration, it seemed that Eastern Europe and the so-called tiger economies of the Far East would be suitable topics for these final chapters. However, while the transition economies and the recovery of the Far Eastern economies are still important, there are other, more generic, topics which the final chapters will focus on. Thus in this chapter globalization and the Internet will be discussed. We have already touched on globalization in Chapter 2, but the discussion now will be more political and radical in its approach. These two topics clearly have a degree of overlap, and as such complement each other.

The Internet is perhaps the ultimate democratizing instrument, but not yet, as there are still the haves and have nots. It does perhaps level the playing field a little more between the MNE and the SME or micro firm. On the Web, size is not important. To a large extent the Web presence is equal, but the customer service back-up must be there to keep the marketing promise. It does perhaps spell the end of geography or at least of distance. In some ways it is turning back the clock, and as supermarkets begin to offer home delivery services, we have a vision of a myriad of small vans scurrying around our towns and cities delivering counter goods from the e-shopping mall. This was the past and may well be the future, but not yet. The Internet offers opportunity for many, and success probably for a few. Internet start-ups will struggle more than the established brand leaders who attempt to transfer their success to the Web.

Earlier in this book we used the terms understand, create, communicate and deliver to describe the marketing process in relation to customers. The Web has the potential to do all of these in certain business sectors. It certainly has the ability to change the traditional interchange with the customer, turning the 'marketplace' into a 'marketspace'. Using the Web, customers will learn about products, buy products and services and assign loyalty differently. Brännback (1997) talks about the Web creating an information space – global billboard for information gathering; a communication space – where information, ideas and experiences can be shared; a distribution space – which is accessible 24 h a day; and a transaction space – where orders will be placed, invoices raised and payments made. Indeed it is not only the marketing function that changes under this new technology, but also the organization's structures, human resources requirement and management of corporate finance.

The future marketing landscape will be strongly affected by the Internet and globalization thus their appropriateness as topics to discuss within this chapter.

Globalization: saint or sinner?

Globalization can be viewed as a relentless transition of the economic and political landscape by self-seeking multinationals, who have scant regard for their employees or the environment, together with the connivance of politicians. Alternatively, it is the rising tide of wealth, good fortune and opportunity which causes all our boats to rise. It would appear to be a phenomenon of the 1990s, but it origins go back much further (see Box 10.1). In the last couple of years there has been an increasing attempt to demonize globalization, which has given rise to sometimes violent protests at World Trade Organization meetings or in centres of the capitalist economy, for example, the May Day 2000 protests throughout Europe.

BOX 10.1: HISTORICAL FOUNDATIONS OF GLOBALIZATION

We can trace the origins of globalization to the expanding early civilizations of the Greeks and the Romans, as they developed their trading routes around the Mediterranean. The Monotheistic religions of Buddhism, Christianity and Islam also played their part. When the countries of Western Europe began their voyages of discovery to the New World and beyond, prompted by improvements in sailing technology, military technology and the spread of the printing press, there was the development of the sense of a wider world community. Then the developments of the industrial revolution established a relationship between the core (manufacturing economies) and the peripheral (raw material supplying economies) which would last until the 20th Century. By the 19th Century the European languages were dominate, and there was widespread technological change which, together with the spread of new beliefs like Marxism and the increasing integration of markets, led to an increased sense of internationalization. The inter-war years were marked by the breakdown of earlier certainties as trade barriers, competitive devaluation's and exchange and emigrant controls emerged. Globalization has not led to a convergence of economic and social experience. Regional incomes are divergent, population growth is uneven across the globe and world trade is dominated by a core group of countries.

(Source: Foreman-Peck, 2000)

In some ways people have been slow to notice globalization, which has crept up on them and, for many, they actually quite like it. Globalization is not a specific target, rather, it is the erosion of the power of national governments which have to share power with transnational corporations. The ability of a national government to control its economy is being reduced either through participation in trading blocs or through the activities of transnationals. Opposition to globalization is difficult, because it is a process and not a specific event like apartheid, nuclear missiles or the Vietnam War. It could be argued that some of these examples at least had nothing to be said in their favour, whereas globalization has aspects which appeal to different people.

As Suter (2000) argues, for the first time in human history many countries have a mass-based consumer economy. More people have more wealth now than ever before, and are faced with a range of global consumer goods on which to spend it. Those opposing globalization will have problems gaining public support, arguing that there should be fewer goods on sale. People like their clothes, Coca-Cola, McDonalds, pop music, television and movies. These they are unlikely to give up to oppose globalization.

A further problem for the opponents of globalization is the diversity of their motives. Some are against the exploitation of workers, others are nationalists who dislike the influence of foreigners in their culture; still more wish to keep cheap, mainly Asian, goods out of western markets, while the developing countries need access to these markets to pay off foreign debts. All this opposition is 50 years too late. Globalization has started and the challenge now is how to make it better for more people. In the take over of Tetley tea, we are seeing the globalization process affecting an outward looking company from the Indian subcontinent for the first time (Box 10.2).

BOX 10.2: TIME FOR TEA

Tetley tea, which is famous in the UK for its Tetley tea folk, has been bought by Tata Tea, the world's largest integrated tea company. The Indian company has paid sterling £271 million. The Indian Tea Association supported the deal, because it puts an Indian firm on the global map for branded tea, which should augur well for local growers. R.S. Jhawar, chairman of the Indian Tea Association said 'For the first time, an Indian tea company has acquired a global brand. It opens a lot of opportunities for us'.

Tata Tea has a 23% market share in India, behind the 44% share of Hindustan Lever, which is a subsidiary of the Anglo-Dutch company Unilever. The combined sales of Tetley and Tata Tea was sterling £418 million (29 billion rupees). Growth is currently reaching 8% per year and this should increase as the company enters new markets.

(Source: The Guardian, 28 February, 2000, p. 22)

The branded multinationals may think they are offering diversity, but in reality there is a powerful view that they are simply creating 'an army of teen clones marching...into the global mall'. Despite the use of polyethnic imagery (setting aside instances where the Ford motor company are found to be airbrushing black faces from their adverts) market-driven globalization does not want diversity. Its enemies are national habits, local brands and distinctive regional tastes. Retail centres around the globe are controlled by fewer and fewer interests. Mergers and acquisitions are realigning commercial interests for the next wave of technology affecting the entertainment, media and retail industries. Take for example the CNN – Time Warner merger, Walt Disney and ABC, America Online and Netscape, Bell Atlantic and Nynes, Vivendi and Seagram. Not all of these have gone smoothly as Box 10.3 illustrates.

BOX 10.3: TRIALS AND TRIBULATIONS OF INTERNATIONAL MERGERS

Vivendi, a French media and utilities group, won acceptance for its bid to acquire Seagram, a Canadian media and drinks company, valued at $34 billion, along with the 51% of Canal Plus, a French pay-TV company, that it does not already own, to create the world's second-largest media group. But investors remained sceptical; Vivendi's shares fell yet again after the deal went through.

Approval of a $230 billion merger between Time Warner and America Online, the deal that Vivendi is striving to emulate in Europe, could face delays. The European Commission announced a further 4 months of antitrust investigations on concerns about domination of digital media distribution.

(Source: Business This Week, 17–23 June 2000, The Economist)

Globally we have all experienced the gradual creeping change, where the downtown is deserted for the big-box discount stores on the periphery. Where the long established café, hardware store, independent bookstore is closed and up pops a Starbucks, Home Depot, the Gap, Borders or Blockbuster. In a twist to the Paul Simon lyric, 'Changes after changes we're more or less the same' the world over. Travel to Hong Kong and you will find Marks and Spencer; in St. Petersburg, Russia there is a British Home Stores. Instead of the open ended and seductive 'Where do you want to go today?' options are really being closed down for the consumer and the real question as Klein (2000) puts it is 'How best can I steer you into the synergized maze of where I want you to go today?'

The types of chains which have come to dominate our shopping centres have changed over time. In the 1960s and 1970s it was fast-food restaurants and car repair outlets, while in the 1980s and 1990s the more common ones such as Ikea, the Gap, Body Shop and the various coffee joints have come with a lifestyle element not unrelated to a healthier, slightly sanitized, New Age hippie.

Franchising too has contributed to this removal of distinctiveness, as every detail of the outlet is designed by the franchiser for the franchisee to run and operate on a day to day basis. We shall discuss this formula more in Chapter 11. The growth of Starbucks for instance helps to illustrate the pace of change. In 1986 the company was based in Seattle with only a handful of stores. By 1992 a total of 165 stores existed in the US and Canada. By 1993 that number reached 275, and in 1996 it reached 1000. By 2000 Starbucks had 2200 outlets in 12 countries, from the UK to Kuwait. Similar patterns can be traced for stores like the Gap and Body Shop, which have averaged between 120 and 150 store openings per year from the mid-eighties.

The growth of these chains depends on: deep cash reserves which allows them to undersell their competitors – the Wal-Mart model; blitz out the competition by setting up chain store clusters – the Starbucks model; or to establish the palatial flagship store which acts a three dimensional advert for the brand – the Nike Town, Disney store model.

Part of the evolution and development of the world's super-brands has been the shifting of production to countries where the costs are lower. Adidas, for example, in 1993 took the decision to close all but one of its factories in Germany, and moved to contracting-out in Asia. By removing the concerns of direct manufacturing from its agenda, the company had more time and money to develop the brand and respond to Nike, which had overtaken it in the style-brand image stakes. There has been some dramatic shifts in the location of manufacturing in certain sectors, for example, Marks and Spencer in 1999 announced that they would be sourcing more clothing from international suppliers rather than from the UK, with an almost inevitable loss of employment at their long standing suppliers. It was of course a stroke of public relations genius to make this announcement in the pre-Christmas period thus damaging further their corporate image. Table 10.1 illustrates the dramatic shift in the pattern of production for the textile, clothing, leather and footwear industries.

In response to declining sales in 1997–1998, Levi Strauss announced job loses of 16 310 at factories in North America and in Europe. Robert Haas, Levis chairman, said the closures not only reflected over capacity but 'our own desire to refocus marketing, to inject more quality and distinctiveness into the brand'. In 1997 this was delivered partly through an advertising campaign costing $90 million, more than had been spent on all brand advertising by the company in 1996.

The jobs, of course, had not disappeared – they had gone to contractors around the world, who in turn may use other contractors to make the goods more cheaply than Levis could. Levis, having pulled out of China in 1993 because of human rights concerns, announced in 1998 their intention to resume production there.

This pattern is common to many of the brand-name multinationals: Nike, Champion, Wal-Mart, Reebok, the Gap, IBM and General Motors. They seek out cheaper

Table 10.1 Percentage changes in employment in the textile, clothing, leather and footwear industries, 1980–1993 (source: International Labour Office)

Country	% Change	Country	% Change
Finland	− 71.7	Mauritius	344.6
Sweden	− 65.4	Indonesia	177.4
Norway	− 64.9	Morocco	166.5
Austria	− 51.5	Jordan	160.8
Poland	− 51.0	Jamaica	101.7
Syria	− 50.0	Malaysia	101.2
France	− 45.4	Mexico	85.5
Hungary	− 43.1	China	57.3
Netherlands	− 41.7	Islamic Republic of Iran	34.0
UK	− 41.5	Turkey	33.7
New Zealand	− 40.9	Philippines	31.8
Germany	− 40.2	Honduras	30.5
Spain	− 35.3	Chile	27.2
Australia	− 34.7	Kenya	16.1
Argentina	− 32.9	Israel	13.4
US	− 30.1	Venezuela	7.9

suppliers in the global mall who will provide them with good quality products made to their specific instructions, using specific material, to their delivery dates, at lowest possible prices. They are not interested in owning and operating factories, buying machinery, dealing with labour or any upstream activity.

This strategy has occasionally come unstuck, as stories of sweatshop labour being used to produce high ticket items sold in developed countries, or as happened with Marks and Spencer goods were labelled Made in Britain when in fact they had been manufactured in Libya.

Klein (2000) in her book 'No Logo' paints a start portrait of export processing zones. These are areas set aside by national governments to attract foreign investment. Normally they will have special financial incentives such as tax breaks, low rents, no import and export duties and primarily, from the investors viewpoint, unlimited access to cheap labour. Thus, in export processing zones (or free trade zones as they can be known) in, for example, Indonesia, China, Mexico, Vietnam and the Philippines, a variety of goods such as clothes, shoes, toys, electronic items are all produced. See Box 10.4 for further details.

BOX 10.4: EXPORT PROCESSING ZONES

The International Labour Organization estimates that there are at least 850 export processing zones in the world, spread through 70 countries and employing approximately 27 million workers. The World Trade Organization estimates that between $200 and 250 billion worth of trade flows through these zones. The largest zone based economy is in China where estimates suggest there are 18 million people working in some 124 zones. The Philippines has 52 zones with some 459 000 people working in them. This is an increase in employment from 23 000 in 1986.

Regardless of location the workers' stories are similar. The working day is long; 14 h in Sri Lanka, 12 h in Indonesia and the Philippines, and 16 h in Southern China. The majority of the workers are young and female, working for sub-contractors from Korea, Taiwan or Hong Kong. These companies are fulfilling orders for companies in the US, UK, Japan, Germany or Canada. The management style can be harsh, the wages below subsistence and the work is low-skill and tedious. The workers are often migrants whose employment can easily evaporate with the end of the last contract.

Klein visited the Cavite export processing zone which is the largest one in the Philippines, covering some 682 acres with 207 factories and employing around 50 000 workers. Having had the 'official' guided visit she managed to gain another insight with the help of a recently laid-off worker. This is what she saw. 'Window-less workshops made of cheap plastic and aluminium siding are crammed in next to each other, only feet apart. Racks of time cards bake in the sun, making sure the maximum amount of work is extracted from each worker, the maximum number of working hours extracted from each day. The streets in the zone are eerily empty, and open doors – the ventilation system for most factories – reveal lines of young women hunched in silence over clamouring machines.'

Since the mid-1980s there has been an increasingly vocal international campaign against these 'sweatshops', as case after case of worker exploitation has come to the attention of the international media. These have included, for example, Guess Jeans in a bitter dispute with the US Department of Labour over the failure of one of its contractors to pay a minimum wage; a Disney contractor in Haiti was found making Pocahontas pyjamas under such poor conditions that the workers had to feed their babies with sugar water; cases in China of children making products for Mattel and Disney; Nike, Adidas, Reebok, Umbro, Mitre and Brine where found to be employing an estimated 10 000 children to make footballs in Pakistan. Such revelations have led to a reassessment of the role of branded goods in relation to their good fortune being based on a system of shantytowns, squalid factory conditions and misery of thousands of workers.

But what has this to do with international marketing? The link should be clear. If nothing else it raises questions, ethical ones, about how we live and how we consume. In the supermarket the meat is cut, cleaned, shrink wrapped, divorced from its origins so consumers do not have to think about the cow, pig or chicken as a living creature. In much the same way our branded goods are packaged, presented in sanitized shopping malls where the link to the Filipino export processing zone is unspoken. The brand is all for many brand-obsessed shoppers, for whom the brand has acquired a fetish-like attraction and talismanic power. In the theme-park inspired stores the conditions of workers in the upstream activities are not thought of; perhaps they should be? Suter (2000) points out that many people in Asia are being exploited in poor working conditions making goods for the western market, but also asks us to remember that life on the farms is not good either; 'Many of the present generation in Asia are doomed to suffering, whether on the farms or in factories'. Their hope is for a better future for their children or grand children, who will have better lives as their countries get richer. In the West previous generations have suffered as economies and societies went through the industrial revolution. No country has yet invented a gentle way to go from a farming-based economy to a modern factory one.

While some of these ideas may be true, is it enough? Where does the next round of manufacturing get done if these countries do manage to improve their standard of living in a generation or two? How far can economic trickle down go? Africa is probably the next stop by the time this Century is half way done. How much would it take for the super-brands to have a responsible manufacturing policy? In low cost countries a small investment in working conditions could go a long way. Sure, some of the profits might be affected, but then consumers in the west may respond to an 'ethical foreign policy'. The issues raised in this brief discussion of globalization are complex. They tend often to be painted in very stark terms. The world is often more complex than it is described, but that does not mean the issues should be ignored. In a globalized world we are all involved in one another. The protests in Seattle, Washington, Prague and elsewhere suggest that we are in a transition. Most of the people in the world today are still peasants. They may not wish to remain so for much longer, and consumers in the US, Europe and Japan may not wish it either. We get the world we create. Does this mean there is a responsibility for marketing within this world? It's your world, you decide.

The Internet

In terms of the wired world, the common perception is that the US holds the lead in the development of e-commerce. It would appear that all countries are equal online but some are more equal than others (Wall, 2000). Table 10.2 illustrates those countries who represent the most and least wired societies in the world. There is delicate mix of economic, political and cultural ingredients which must come together if the Web is to flourish. In terms of culture, North American English is the dominant language, so other English speaking countries have a head start in getting online. Scandinavian countries are adept at speaking English and this also gives them an advantage, whereas the French perceive the dominance of English as cultural imperialism and so it is to be resisted. The diversity of languages in Asia has slowed the progress of the Web there. In societies where management is very much a top down or centralist, then the Web goes against this cultural grain as it is a bottom-up, decentralized, distributed world. Thus, in societies such as Italy, Spain and Latin America, where individualism, entrepreneurship and a healthy disrespect for authority exist, it is argued that this is the right environment for the Web. However, Spain and Italy are among the least wired countries. It is claimed that the weather mitigates against adoption, because in sunnier climates the outdoor life is more important. Conversely in Northern climates adoption has been amongst the highest. However, with the introduction of wireless application protocol (WAP) which provides the ability for mobile phones to read web content, then the Italians, with some 25 million phones, represent a huge potential market.

The importance of the mobile phone and the availability of traditional phone lines will affect the penetration of the Web. For example Scandinavia has the world's highest per capita mobile phone population, and the most telephone lines per 100 people. Compare this with Africa where there are only two lines per 100 inhabitants, and 2.6 million people online in a population of 700 million.

However, by 2003 the virtual map of the wired world is expected to be different. While the US has the lead in e-commerce at present, it is expected that the level of Internet access in Europe will exceed that of the US (Heckman and Schmidt, 2000).

Table 10.2 Our wired world (source: Sunday Times, April 23, 2000)

Most wired	Net population as % of population	Least wired	Net population as % of population
Norway	50	Italy	16
Iceland	45	France	15
US	45	Greece	12
Sweden	44	Spain	9
Canada	43	Poland	7
Finland	38	Brazil	4
Australia	36	Indonesia	4
Denmark	36	Russia	4
Netherlands	29	China	0.7
UK	26	India	0.5

It is also anticipated that by that time Asia's Internet population will have increased four-fold to 80 million, while Web users in Latin America will have grown from 5 million today to 19 million. As a result 46% of global e-commerce will be based outside the US, compared with only 30% today.

Thus, the Web will undergo a transition from an English speaking, US dominated medium to a global marketplace. As a result, even on the Web we cannot get away from one important theme of this book – culture. Research suggests that web users are three times more likely to buy products from websites in their own language, and two-thirds of surfers will click away from a site in another language. By 2005 about 70% of the Internet's one billion users will speak a language besides English.

Just as in traditional commerce, responding to these customers in the future will require more than simple translation of the website. For example, customer service is vital to e-commerce because of the lack of direct contact, so a multilingual customer service operation is important.

In terms of brand management, the Internet and relationship marketing are two emerging trends affecting the global marketplace. Heckman and Schmidt (2000) quote a Cincinnati based company senior vice president who stated that 'e-Commerce, home computers, cell phones and video linkups have bridged the gap of distance and the logistics of time and space, allowing marketers and consumers to know each other on a personal level'. As a result marketers will have to work hard at defining consumer audiences and communicating with them across international borders (see Box 10.5).

BOX 10.5: LANDS' END INC.

This Wisconsin based clothing company allows consumers to identify their body type and then mix and match clothing items thus, creating an intimacy with consumers while providing information to help them make decisions. This information provision is a tangible benefit to the consumer, indicating to them that their needs and wants are understood no matter where they live in the world. This is an e-tailing version of a global brand.

Opportunity

The Internet can provide an opportunity for a firm to:

- Boost profits
- Cut costs
- Improve customer service
- Improve communication with employees
- Enhance a company's corporate image
- Even re-engineer the way it works.

Quelch and Klein (1996) provide a discussion on whether the Internet will revolutionize business, or whether it will become another alternative marketing channel. The answer appears to be dependent on how much added value there is in the Internet communications and transactions; and how this level of added value translates across countries (taking account of the varying pace of technological advancement in emerging markets).

The approach by the company to the Internet may be very different depending on

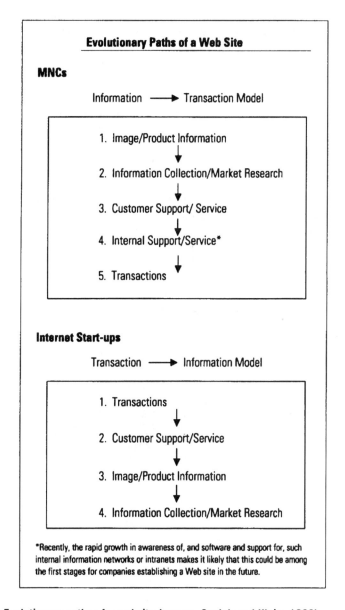

Figure 10.1   Evolutionary paths of a website (source: Quelch and Klein, 1996).

whether it is an established brand or a new start-up. Quelch and Klein identify two models as seen in Figure 10.1.

An established company is more likely to create an information site first and then gradually move towards the ability to conduct transactions, whereas an Internet start up has to be conducting transactions from day one in order to create the market. The development of the brand follows as the company builds a reputation for itself in cyberspace.

In this model it should be easier for the established brand with a financial cushion, to transfer its brand to the Web than for the Internet start-up to succeed. Given a one in three failure rate for traditional start-ups, we should not be throwing our hands up in horror at the failure rate of Internet start-ups. The failure of boo.com in spring 2000 was partly due to its failure to be able to conduct transactions from the outset due to problems with its website. Thus, having raised customer awareness, they could not use the site, and the cost of continuing to finance the venture with no customer revenue left the company continually playing catch-up. This situation was exacerbated by a general downturn in dotcom stocks.

Quelch and Klein (1996) have some concerns about the Web in international marketing. These are:

- Standard pricing – customers will soon become aware of any price discrimination across different markets
- Intermediaries – if a firm is an intermediary, what is its continuing role and value when the customer can deal with the manufacturer directly
- Global operating implications – 24 h order taking and customer response; inventory/shipping expertise; international market expertise; cross-border price/quality issues; language and cultural barriers; import regulations; government influences (tax, data security)
- Website maintenance – the research identified that the annual costs for site maintenance are between two and four times the initial launch cost.

Bowen (1998) suggests that no one has yet come close to realizing the full potential of the Internet; it may be that they never do because the Internet is limited more by people's imagination than by technology. Individuals, whether acting as managers or as entrepreneurs, who have the ability to think laterally will be the major source of competitive advantage. Box 10.6 provides two examples of companies who have used the Internet as a marketing tool.

BOX 10.6: WEAVING THE WEB

The London International Group (LIG) wanted to increase awareness of Durex in the US. The Internet was being used by the kind of young people which the company sought, but a campaign on MTV was launched to drive the traffic to the Internet. Once there, visitors found an offering that followed a delicate line between wit and smut, and the offer of free Durex samples to anyone who filled in and e-mailed back a questionnaire. Within 2 months the company had 45 000 responses which helped build the brand in the US and provided the company with a large amount of useful marketing data.

Transactional sites where products can be purchased have to try and keep ahead of the new entrants where the cost of entry is low. The clever marketing ploy is to play to the Internet's strengths. Amazon, the online bookshop which originated in the US and has 2.5 million books on offer, is often referred to as 'the biggest bookshop in the world'. For Amazon to maintain its competitive edge it has created a community of customers/users who enjoy going into its 'chat areas' to give or read opinions on books, CDs, etc. Amazon is using the Internet's interactivity to provide a service unmatchable by an ordinary bookshop, and at the same time contribute towards building a loyal group of customers.

(Source: adapted from Bowen, 1998)

Establishing a web presence

Companies have three options in establishing their web presence either in-house, outsourced or by acquisition. The examples below offer insights to each of these different routes (Briones, 1999) while a more mechanistic approach to establishing a web presence is offered by December and Randall (1994) in Box 10.7.

Toysmart.com

This company is a retailer of educational toys and had planned to expand from one store and a catalogue operation from 6–10 new stores. However, due to a slow real estate market the company ended up switching its attention to the Internet. At that time it was called Holt Educational Outlet, but the name was changed in 1999 to reflect its new focus. The company wanted to go beyond building a website and actually integrate its entire organization with computer software, including business processes, such as accounting and inventory management.

It was decided to develop an in-house expertise and to hire and train full-time staff to operate the site. While the company recognized it could hire in the help, it felt that this route was not conducive to transferring the knowledge base to the employees. By signing with a software company as a beta site, they got a lot of training as the software was developed and improved. In the end it is estimated the cost of the toysmart.com site, excluding training, was $500 000. A traditional store cost $250 000 to build. In 1998 the company's revenue was $12 million – double what it was in 1996 before the launch of the site. In 18 months after the launch of the site, the sales went from zero to 60% of the company's revenue. The rest comes from its one store.

Fragrance counter

Fragrance counter is an online supplier of fragrances. It is a division of a health and beauty care distributor based in New York. Initially only two people were involved in setting up the site, and as a result they had to outsource the technical capability to launch the site, as neither knew how to build and maintain a site. Using America Online's back-end technology, and the services of a communications company to design the graphics, the site was launched in September 1995. Since all technical set-up and maintenance were outsourced, the biggest problem for the company was inventory. The site was serviced from the same warehouse as the wholesale business, and conflict arose when, for example, there were 12 products on the shelf and a wholesale customer wanted 12 but an online customer wanted a couple. In 1996 Fragrance counter got its own aisle in the warehouse, and expanded to a warehouse within a warehouse in 1997. Also in 1997 the company looked for a web contractor to take it beyond the America Online audience. Again this was outsourced, as the company felt they were merchants first and foremost, and did not want to become top-heavy with technical people. There are disadvantages to outsourcing such as loss of control and additional costs, but outsourcing lets you pick the best available talent and a fresh perspective by selecting an agency with the best technical, creative, media and research capability.

Getty images

The final option is to acquire a business. London based Getty Images is a provider of stock photos and film footage. It has 25 stores world-wide and a revenue of $184 million. In adopting e-commerce the company had a total mind-shift, from a physical business based on sales through representatives, to a digital one where customers control the buying environment. The company had complex pricing and licensing procedures which would not have been compatible with web customers, so long-standing business procedures where radically altered. To make the transition to e-commerce as fast as possible, the company acquired a web based provider of royalty free images. Within 6 months of the acquisition Getty had converted one of its six brands to e-commerce. In order to make the customer experience hassle-free, the company simplified pricing (licensing possibilities were reduced from 92 to 30), the research process, the clearance of credit cards and starting up accounts and provided seven by 24 h help desks and service centres. By 1999 the company offered e-commerce for four of its six brands, and 25% of the Web customers were new to the firm. While acquisition may be an expensive route to e-commerce, especially as more and more user friendly software becomes available, Getty managers believe that it still is a useful option for the larger company. Once acquired, the development of the site is an on-going process; buying or building a site is just the start of the process (Briones, 1999).

BOX 10.7: HINTS FOR ESTABLISHING A WEB PRESENCE

December and Randall outline an approach – web weaving – to creating a presence on the Web. There are six elements and five processes behind this approach.
The elements are:
1. Audience information – knowledge about the target audience as well as the actual ones who use the information
2. Purpose statement – reasons and scope for the Web presence
3. Objective statement – specific goals the Web should accomplish
4. Domain information – knowledge about the subject domain the Web covers, both in terms of information provided to users of the Web and the information the Web weavers need
5. Web specification – describes the elements that go into a web in detail
6. Web presentation – the means by which the information is delivered to the user.
The processes are:
1. Planning – is the process of defining the overall goals for the Web
2. Analysis – is the process of gathering and comparing information about the Web and its operation in order to improve the Web's overall quality
3. Design – is the process whereby the Web designers build on the Web's specification and make decisions about how a web's actual components should be constructed
4. Implementation – is the process of actually building the Web itself via HTML.
Development – is the process of ensuring that the other processes continue and that the Web itself is being presented well to the Internet user. It involves directing the analysis of audience information, usability and use patterns.

(source: December and Randall, 1994)

Usage

Even in 5 years' time the Internet may not be a large player in business to business exchanges in the US. However, it will grow faster than other channels. It is estimated that it will grow at a 49.6% compound annual rate to $53.4 billion by 2004 (Table 10.3). This will be five times faster than its nearest rival, direct mail, which will grow by 10% to $293.3 billion. Other rivals including radio, newspaper, television, telephone and magazines will grow by less than 10%.

As well as general usage, there are examples of companies who are reengineering the supply chain by using the ability of the Internet to remove distance. Womex is, for example, a website which brings together buyers of general goods, mostly in small factories based in Asia. The company has visited numerous companies in Asia, taking photographs of products and putting them on its website. Buyers can then see what is available, along with the information they require on lead time,

Table 10.3   US business to business annual sales – figures in billion of US dollars (source: Marketing News November 22 ,1999, p. 3)

	1999	2004
Telephone	308.3	482.6
Direct mail	181.9	293.3
Newspaper	76.7	120.7
Television	42.6	67.2
Magazine	38.5	58.6
Radio	17.8	28.3
Internet	7.1	53.4

batch quantities and costs, etc. The factories do not even need an Internet connection – Womex can translate the e-mail requests into faxes. The outcome for all involved should be fewer buying trips, greater transparency and more business all round.

There are also examples of companies using the Web to deliver new products online (see Box 10.8).

BOX 10.8: THE INTERNET SEWN UP

A Japanese company has developed the Internet sewing machine. It will be able to log onto a website and download stitching patterns including, in a triumph of marketing, those must-have items of the modern games generation, Pokemon characters. The first of three machines announced yesterday by Jaguar International, Japan's biggest sewing machine company, could be in the shops next month. It will be able to connect to Nintendo's Game Boy terminal, from which it can download the patterns for triangles, squares and more than 80 other letters and patterns to stitch onto T-shirts and other clothing. In September a machine could be launched which automatically stitched Pokemon characters into clothing, but discussions with Nintendo over royalties were continuing. Its launch also depended on whether the Pokemon craze was still going on.

(Source: South China Morning Post, April 23, 2000, p. 5)

As well as direct sales, the Internet will also assist with new product development. The construction of physical prototypes has always been the weak link in the product development chain (Landry, 1999). Ideally marketers would like to create a number of versions of a new product and test them with target customers. However, this can be expensive, and it is more likely that the development team will select a couple of designs for the prototype stage, and then mainly use them to see if a particular design will work, not whether it will impress the target customers.

Landry reports on a study whereby a group of students created nine physical prototypes for a new bicycle pump, and a computer artist created animated pictures of them. Then a different group of students were asked to choose a pump based on the physical prototypes, the animated prototypes on one web page, static images of the pumps on another web page, and purely textual description on a third site. The researchers found a high correlation between the participants' responses to the physical prototypes and the virtual prototypes, both animated and static.

This gives the potential for highly realistic virtual prototypes to be created, and for much easier product testing to take place, especially as the multimedia capabilities of web browsers increase. Customers could look at virtual prototypes, and make selections and changes to the type of product they want, in much the same way as a good salesperson would modify the presentation in view of what the customer wanted. Traditionally managers have focused on one product idea, and designed it as well as possible. In the fast paced Internet economy, managers may need a new approach that gives them more options.

Customer satisfaction and success

A survey (Business Week, 1999) found that only 52% of the uses of e-commerce were satisfied with the service they received (Table 10.4).

This perception is important for the development of the sector. If people are to be encouraged to use e-commerce, then the experience must be good for them if they are to become a repeat customer. If sites do not offer a quick way of getting questions answered, especially at busy festival times, then this could be very damaging.

Krauss (1999) has identified common traits shared by successful companies on the Web. These 'winners':

- Put their customers first
- Stay competitively vital (for example, Netscape giving products away to establish market penetration)
- Are committed to content
- Are community orientated
- Bring childlike creativity to the process
- Are communications savvy (for example, in attacking amazon.com, barnesandnoble.com has a major disadvantage; its name)

Table 10.4   Customer service on the Web

	Percentage of customers who agree (%)
Satisfied with service from e-stores	52
Got no response to e-mail at all	23
Instantaneous support was provided	17
Got response to e-mail within an hour	16

- Remain aggressive, enterprise wide adopters and integrators of technology.

In the future the best web marketers will enable live, interactive online communication between customers and real people internationally. The Web creates a new space for creative entrepreneurs to operate within, and for some this involves linking people's interests to a service via the Web. For instance in April 2000 the Wine-Ark opened in Sydney, Australia (Sydney Morning Herald, 2000). This company brings together the Internet at one end and temperature controlled bricks and mortar at the other end. The company has storage space in the vaults of an old bank building which is now owned by a self-storage company. The cellar is kept at a constant 14°C and 70% relative humidity. Wine-ark provides its customers with an online cellar management service which provides clients with 24 h access to their wine portfolios and a range of related information. Wine storage is charged on a monthly per-case basis and membership also involves invitations to 12 wine tastings per year. It is easy to see how this simple idea could be internationalized, perhaps through franchising, thus creating new opportunities for entrepreneurs globally.

Conclusions

The purpose of the far reaching discussion on globalization was to take some of the academic issues discussed in Chapter 2 and put them in a broader context. Marketing is a social process. It can be a tool for good or bad depending on how it is used. It cannot be divorced from the social context of production and consumption which it facilitates. As yet there has not been enough debate within marketing on the ethical and moral issues which it raises. This must change. In the global context the superbrands bring into focus a number of issues about how we as consumers choose to live and how to spend our money. The later is potentially a key influence over the super-brands.

Globalization sounds like it is involved in the creation of a level playing field, but this is far from the reality. The rich countries generate the foreign direct investment, but they are also the prime recipients of it. Africa has seen little of the available capital for foreign investment in comparison to Asia. The triad countries, as Kenichi Ohmae (1985) once called them, (EU, NAFTA and Japan) dominate the playing field and will do for the foreseeable future.

The Internet too is a force in favour of the level playing field. The crisis in confidence affecting Internet stock in 2000 should not be taken too seriously from a business perspective. New technologies have, throughout history, seen similar heady heights and dizzy falls, be it the Tulipomania crisis in 1637 or the South Sea Bubble in the 1720s. More recently the shares of electricity companies peaked in 1900, car stocks in 1925, radio in 1929 and airlines in 1945. The financial market has a short memory, and indices which dump perfectly profitable stocks for new, untried ones should be regarded as indicative of very little. Many dotcom companies will fail, but many will succeed. There is an enormous change taking place in the world economy, which will profoundly affect the opportunities for companies to reach and serve a truly global market. This change is not taking place evenly as yet but there will come a time when it will be in the interests of the have to include the have not. This may sound like a dream, perhaps one just like all the rest in a historical context, but maybe, just maybe, this time.

Questions for discussion

1. Globalization is a positive process in the world economy. Discuss and justify your position.
2. What role does marketing play in globalization?
3. Multinational companies are getting better at being good global citizens in terms of the environment and employment practices. Discuss and justify your view with examples.
4. What is the current attitude towards globalization of organizations like the World Trade Organization and the IMF?
5. What evidence can you find for the existence of pressure groups who are against globalization? Summarize and discuss their views. Do you agree with them?
6. The Internet is having a democratization effect in the world. Discuss and substantiate your view.
7. How has the use of the Internet evolved since this book was published?
8. Are some societies being left behind in the dotcom world? What evidence can you find? If they are being left behind, does it matter?
9. What is the current level of activity in your country of dotcom companies? How has this evolved over the last 5 years and where is it going?
10. Analyze your own purchasing habits on the Internet. How has the Internet changed your behaviour as a consumer, if at all?

References

Bowen, D. (1998), www+ flair = new business, *Management Today*, May, pp. 84–88.

Brännback, M. (1997), Is the internet changing the dominant logic of marketing? *European Management Journal*, 15 (6), pp. 698–707.

Briones, M.G. (1999), On-ramp - 3 paths to web business success, *Marketing News*, April 26, pp. 13–14.

Business Week (1999), E-tailers had better get service up to speed, *Business Week*, Oct. 4, (3649), p. 226.

December, J. and Randall, N. (1994), *The World Wide Web Unleashed*, Sams Publishing.

Foreman-Peck, J. (2000), *Historical Foundations of Globalisation*, Edward Elgar, Cheltenham.

Heckman, J. and Schmidt, K.V. (2000), International in internet closes US lead, *Marketing News*, Feb. 14, pp. 7–8.

Klein, N. (2000), *No Logo*, Flamingo, London.

Krauss, M. (1999), 7 traits shared by winners on the web, *Marketing News*, Jan. 4, p. 24.

Landry, J.T. (1999),Marketing, *Harvard Business Review*, 77 (1), p. 20.

Ohmae, K. (1985), *Triad Power*, Free Press, New York.

Quelch, J.A. and Klein, L.R. (1996), The internet and international marketing, *Sloan Management Review*, 37 (3), pp. 60–75.

Suter, K. (2000), Globalisation protests have arrived 50 years too late, *New Zealand Herald*, May 4, p. A19.

Sydney Morning Herald (2000), Plenty of room on the ark for ardent imbibers, *Sydney Morning Herald*, April 28.

Wall, M. (2000), The wired divide, *The Sunday Times*, April 23.

Further reading

Baker, S. (1999), Global e-commerce, local problems, *Journal of Business Strategy*, 20 (4), pp. 32–38.

Dussart, C. (2000), Internet: the one-plus-eight 're-volutions', *European Management Journal*, 18 (4), pp. 386–397.

Dutta, S. and Segev, A. (1999), Business transformation on the internet, *European Management Journal*, 15 (5), pp. 466–476.

Govindarajan, V. and Gupta, A. (2000), Analysis of the emerging global arena, *European Management Journal*, 18 (3), pp. 274–284.

Guliz, G. (1999), Localising in the global village: local firms competing in global markets, *California Management Review*, 41 (4), pp. 64–83.

Hamill, J. and Gregory, K. (1997), Internet marketing in the internationalisation of UK SMEs, *Journal of Marketing Management*, 13 (1–3), pp. 9–28.

Martin, J. (1998), Gateways for the global economy, *Management Review*, 87 (11), pp. 22–26.

Poon, S. and Jevons, C. (1997), Internet-enabled international marketing: a small business network perspective, *Journal of Marketing Management*, 13 (1–3), pp. 29–41.

Rugman, A.M. and Verbeke, A. (1998), Corporate strategy and international environmental policy, *Journal of International Business Studies*, 29 (4), pp. 819–834.

Samiee, S. (1998), Exporting and the internet: a conceptual perspective, *International Marketing Review*, 15 (5), pp. 413–426.

Thelwall, M. (2000), Effective websites for small and medium-sized entreprises, *Journal of Small Business and Enterprise Development*, 7 (2), pp. 149–159.

The following websites, may be of interest, as they reflect the increased interest in challenging the processes of globalization and growing consumer power.

Adbusters is a site which philosophical articles as well as activist commentary from around the world addressing issues ranging from genetically modified foods to media concentration. They also promote change through social marketing campaigns, such as, Buy Nothing Day and TV Turnoff Week. http://www.adbusters.org/home/

Corporate Watch is committed to exposing corporate greed by documenting the social, political, economic and environmental impacts of transnational giants. http://www.corpwatch.org

McSpotlight is a site dedicated to tracking the activities of McDonalds http://www.mcspotlight.org/

Boycott Nike is a site dedicated to tracking the activities of Nike, often focusing on labour practices. http://www.saigon.com/~nike/

Primal Seeds exists as a network to actively engage in protecting biodiversity and creating local food security. It is a response to industrial biopiracy, control of the global seed supply and of our food. http://www.primalseeds.org/

The Boycott Board

The purpose of this site is to provide socially-conscious consumers with a means of learning about various boycotts which are in progress. http://boycott.2street.com/

CHAPTER 11

International growth through franchising

Chapter objectives

After studying this chapter you should be able to:

- Understand the concept of franchising as a business format
- Appreciate franchising as an international market entry strategy
- Evaluate critically the growth of franchising in an international context

Introduction

In most developed economies franchising is widely used for operating businesses. It is a system that has enabled business people to develop some of the largest brands around, for example, McDonalds, Dyno-Rod and Holiday Inn. The governments of some developing countries actively encourage business people to use franchising as a way of fostering entrepreneurship. The franchisor gains national and international distribution for the business idea much more quickly than if the expansion had been undertaken through fully-owned outlets. Also, as self-employed individuals, the franchisees, who supply most of the capital for the expansion, are usually more motivated to work hard at building their businesses. Box 11.1 provides a technical definition of franchising from the Russian Franchise Association's Code of Practice.

> ### BOX 11.1: WHAT IS FRANCHISING?
>
> Franchising is a system of marketing goods and/or services and/or technology, which is based upon a close and ongoing collaboration between legally and financially separate and independent undertakings, the franchisor and its individual franchisees, whereby the franchisor grants its individual franchisees the right, and imposes the obligation, to conduct a business in accordance with the franchisor's concept. The right entitles and compels the individual franchisee, in exchange for a direct or indirect financial consideration, to use the franchisor's trade name, and/or trademark and/or service mark, know-how, business and technical methods, procedural system, and other industrial and/or intellectual property rights, supported by continuing provision of commercial and technical assistance, within the framework and for the term of a written franchise agreement, conducted between parties for this purpose.

Historical development

The emergence of the modern concept of franchising occurred in the US just after the Civil War with the activities of the Singer Sewing Machine Company (Goncalves and Duarte, 1994). However, it was not until the beginning of the 20th century that this method of business development gained wider acceptance. The automobile industry and the soft drinks industry were the first to adopt the so-called product and trademark franchising. By the 1930s the petroleum industry was franchising gasoline/petrol service stations. The real expansion of franchising took place in the 1950s, with the appearance of business format franchising. This type of franchising is also known as second generation franchising, and is characterized by an ongoing relationship between the franchisor and the franchisee. This includes the product or service, trademark, as well as the entire business concept – a marketing strategy and plan, operating manuals and standards, quality control and a continuing process of assistance and guidance.

Business format franchising continued to grow and develop throughout the 1950s and 1960s, but it was not until the early 1970s that these successful domestic chains began to apply their franchising concepts internationally. Initially the expansion took place in markets which were most accessible or had good market potential, low cultural distance and the existence of a developed service sector. Thus, Canada became a prime target for international expansion, followed by the UK and Australia. Development of franchising in Japan was facilitated by the use of a master franchise agreement. This reduced the need for direct involvement in the development of operations in what was, especially for Americans, a very unique culture. A master franchise usually has responsibility for more than one outlet and is commonly totally responsible for the development of the franchised business (through other franchisees) in an area. By 1988 Canada, the UK, Australia and Japan accounted for 70% of the total US international franchised outlets.

Franchising business models

'Franchising' is used to describe a number of business models, the most commonly identified of which is business format franchising. However, there are other models which are also dependent on franchise relationships. These include:

1. Manufacturer–retailer – where the retailer as franchisee sells the franchisor's product directly to the public. (for example new motor vehicle dealerships).
2. Manufacturer–wholesaler – where the franchisee under licence manufactures and distributes the franchisor's product (for example soft drink bottling arrangements).
3. Wholesaler–retailer – where the retailer as franchisee purchases products for retail sale from a franchisor wholesaler (frequently a co-operative of the franchisee retailers who have formed a wholesaling company through which they are contractually obliged to purchase, for example hardware and automotive product stores).
4. Retailer–retailer – where the franchisor markets a service or a produce under a common name and standardized system through a network of franchisees, that is, the classic business format franchise.

The first two categories above are often referred to as product and trade name franchises. These include arrangements in which franchisees are granted the right to distribute a manufacturer's product within a specified territory or at a specific location, generally with the use of the manufacturer's identifying name or trademark, in exchange for fees or royalties.

The business format franchise, however, differs from product and trade name franchises through the use of a format, or a comprehensive system for the conduct of the business, including such elements as business planning, management system, location, appearance and image, and quality of goods. Standardization, consistency and uniformity across all aspects are hallmarks of the business format franchise.

Under a business format franchise the franchisees operate the franchise in a standard way under a common trademarked name. The kinds of businesses operating under such a system can include fast food restaurants, courier services, cleaning services, employment or estate agents, kitchen or bathroom installers. The options, in ascending order of initial investment, are:

- Job franchise – usually a one-person self-employed business that the franchisee runs from their own home, such as local deliveries, drain clearance, car repairs.
- Business franchise – generally involves a larger investment in business premises and equipment, employing and training staff, such as fast food restaurants, quick print outlets and card shops
- Investment franchise – here the franchisee is working for a return on their relatively large investment, such as in a hotel or major retail franchise.

With a business format franchise, the franchisees will be operating as satellite enterprises of an already proven larger business under its established trade name. The satellites sell its products or services along specified lines.

The franchisor can expect from the franchisees:

- An initial fee to purchase the business system. The fee should also cover initial training and support
- A continuing management service fee, typically 5–10% of their sales turnover.

The franchisee gains:

- The use of an established trade name
- Prime rights within a particular area
- Support and advice from head office covering central marketing, promotion and administrative back-up
- Continuous market research leading to further development of the product or service concerned.

Why businesses franchise

Companies can expand in a number of ways and full ownership of new outlets is perhaps the most obvious way forward. However, having fully assessed the costs and risks of expansion, some organizations decide to follow the franchising route; why? Combs and Castrogiovanni (1994) suggest three reasons why franchising is used. These are resource scarcity, agency theory and risk spreading.

Resource scarcity means that a company needs access to management talent or other knowledge not available to them, and at the same time may not have a large amount of money to invest in the expansion. Agency theory is about the way in which those people who manage the outlet are motivated and monitored. Since franchisees have considerable financial investments at stake, and since they receive profits from the outlet then they are more motivated than managers of firm-owned units to work hard to make the franchise profitable. Risk spreading, compensating for the decisions surrounding any expansion, is accomplished through franchising. The investment risk is lowered through franchising compared with joint ventures, which can involve large capital investments and legal complications. Franchising creates sales and brand recognition at a much lower cost. In international expansion the political risk and the overall risk of failure are primarily borne by the franchisee.

Dant (1995) identifies seven reasons why successful, growth orientated businesses may well take the franchising route to expansion:

- Access to capital
- Access to management talent
- Access to local market knowledge
- Economies of production
- Economies of promotion
- Economies of co-ordination
- In-built disincentives to agent-shirking (lack of responsibility taken by staff).

The time scale required by franchising is seen as faster than self-owned expansion, which will often require more monitoring. The process of establishing a chain of franchises increases the knowledge of the franchisor, and the time required for each new outlet is reduced as expertise increases. With experience the franchisor develops sensitivity to site selection, store layout, procurement and operating policies appropriate to particular environmental settings.

Box 11.2 provides an introduction to the 'sales pitch' from Allied Domecq for three of its brands, two of which are internationally famous as Dunkin' Donuts and Baskin Robbins.

BOX 11.2: THREE BRANDS UNDER ONE ROOF

The parent company of Dunkin' Donuts, Baskin-Robbins and Togo's is Allied Domecq Quick Service Restaurants (ADQSR) based in Randolph, MA. You can take comfort in knowing that building strong brands is nothing new to us. When it comes to franchising, Allied Domecq QSR brands have more than 130 years of combined experience in operating and franchising quick service restaurants.

We are presently seeking highly qualified and motivated candidates to become part of the Allied Domecq QSR team. Opportunities are now available in many US markets for candidates able to demonstrate significant business management experience and sound financial qualifications. When you become a franchisee with ADQSR you join a network of dedicated franchisees that operate more than 10 000 restaurants worldwide. We understand that franchising is a team effort. As an industry-leading franchisor, we know that our success depends as much on our franchisees as theirs depends on us.

Allied Domecq QSR offers three time-tested restaurant concepts, each with its own highly developed brand identity:

- Dunkin' Donuts: the world's largest coffee and donut shop chain, launched in 1950, has grown to more than 5000 locations throughout the US and 37 foreign countries. Well noted for its fine coffees and breakfast bakery items, this concept fits the demand of consumers by the millions who seek a great tasting breakfast 'on the go.'
- Togo's: founded in 1971, Togo's is California's fastest growing chain of sandwich eateries. Now in eight states, Togo's consumers love their premium quality ingredients, ample portions, and excellent value – a recipe that's hard to beat, whether it's for lunch, a snack, or a light supper.
- Baskin Robbins: a brand synonymous with ice cream, this chain's 31 flavours of sweet, creamy treats are offered in more than 4700 locations from California to Moscow. Ice cream's universal appeal as a snack or dessert makes it a popular draw from midday to closing time.

Combining two or all three of these brand concepts in a single operation is Allied Domecq QSR's unique complimentary 'daypart branding' strategy which allows franchisees to attract customers and achieve sales all day long thus, optimizing return on investment through more efficient use resources.

For more information: visit our website and apply online: www.dunkin-baskin-togos.com or Call 1-800-777-9983.

(Source: http://www.franchise.org/advertise/advertorials/allied_domecq/)

International franchising

When the domestic market becomes mature then a natural progression for the franchising industry is to take the successful package and apply it internationally. If the domestic market is saturated, or if competition limits makes further expansion difficult, then the perceived benefits of international expansion will appear greater. There is little to argue against the idea that a traditional franchise marketing system of locating qualified franchisees, negotiating a relatively standard contract and providing on-going support cannot be implemented in other countries (Storholm and Kavil, 1992).

Markets exhibiting the characteristics of the US market during the expansion of franchising there in the 1950s are particularly attractive. Thus, markets with increasing disposable income, a high level of car ownership, increased leisure time, considerable urbanization and consumer mobility are of interest. Like any market entry decision (see Chapter 4) it is imperative that the international franchising decision is approached with care and thoroughness in researching the territory, the market and the people you will be dealing with.

There are a number of different approaches to international development which the aspiring international franchisor can adopt. These include:

- Company-owned only operations
- Direct franchising
- The establishment of a branch operation
- The establishment of a subsidiary
- The establishment of an area developer
- The granting of master franchise rights
- The entry into a joint venture.

While international franchising involves less risk than some other methods of international expansion, it nevertheless requires extensive resources and effort beyond that required for expansion in the domestic market. See Box 11.3 for some advice on how to be successful internationally.

BOX 11.3: CHECKLIST FOR INTERNATIONAL SUCCESS

- Establish a strong home base which can adequately support the additional burdens of international expansion
- Do not overvalue and thus overprice the franchise opportunity
- Establish a pilot operation and prove the system works in the target territory
- Recognize and come to terms with the differences in social attitudes, culture, taste and lifestyle
- Choose carefully those with whom you will establish a working relationship
- Be patient. Do not underestimate the time it will take to achieve international success
- Do not underestimate the drain on your financial and manpower resources which going international will involve.

Overall the benefits of franchising as an international development strategy include:

- The financial resources required for penetrating international markets are fewer than those needed to expand through foreign direct investment or exporting. International franchisers do not have to expand domestic capacity in order to serve international markets, as would be the case when an exporter tries to penetrate these markets
- International franchising avoids most of the negative factors associated with the exportation of goods to international markets, for example, the logistical problems, payments, insurance and finance
- Internationalization by franchising is less prone to economic and political risks and requires fewer financial resources since the franchisees bear most of these risks
- Small franchise systems can succeed internationally when significant managerial and marketing expertise is contributed by local franchisees
- Expansion of franchising into international markets has fewer negative impacts on both the source country and the recipient country, and therefore meets with a more receptive environment.

However, international franchising is not without its problems, and Mendelsohn (1985) identifies some of the problems that franchisors can face. These are:

- Poor choice of local partner, licensee or staff
- A failure to recognize the need to commit sufficient financial and manpower resources to the venture, whatever method is chosen
- A failure to recognize differences in social and cultural attitudes and in lifestyle
- An underestimation of the time which it takes to become established in the target territory.

The problems associated with failure or setbacks in international franchising are the same as with any other mode of internationalization (Chapter 4) namely that at best retrenchment, or at worst withdrawal to the domestic market, will result. Each situation has to be approached as a unique business situation, but common issues can be used to plan the process. A checklist of critical legal and business issues typical of international franchise transactions is presented in Box 11.4.

BOX 11.4: CRUCIAL LEGAL AND BUSINESS ISSUES IN INTERNATIONAL FRANCHISING

- Franchise structure: direct franchising, area development, area representative, master franchise, management contract, joint venture.
- Use of trademarks and trade names in target foreign country: registration, government restrictions, contract revisions.
- Fees: amount and type of fees, tax on fees, characterization of fees.
- Currency and remittance: restrictions, conversion rates, procedure for remittance (e.g. letters of credit, wire transfer).
- Government review and approval requirements: foreign ownership, trademark licenses, transfers, term, fee amounts, sublicensing, repatriation of fees, competition provisions, development schedules.
- Other statutory requirements: disclosure obligations; consider allocation of cost; and the procedure and timing for preparation.
- Restriction on competition: types of restraints, enforcement.
- Other intellectual property: trade secrets, copyrights, patents.
- Viability of termination and other options: restrictions, assignment of subfranchisees, implications of termination.
- Availability of remedies: litigation, alternative dispute methods, indemnification.
- International department budget: salaries, travel expenses, marketing, trade shows, administration, legal, entertainment.
- Franchisee recruitment strategy: targeted countries, publications, trade shows, organizations, media.
- Franchisee selection criteria: financial, industry, commitment.
- Territorial development requirements: number of outlets, development schedule, subfranchisee support requirements.
- Personnel: assignment of staff for pre-opening training, opening assistance, ongoing support.
- Operations and business manuals: written in a franchisor format.
- Supply and distribution: product availability, import restrictions, selected vendors, distribution network, pricing strategy.
- Site selection and demographic guidelines: space requirements, access, density, incomes, age groups.
- Facility design, adaptability and construction: standardized design and construction plans and specifications, availability of specialized point of sale systems and software compatibility.

(Source: Woolweaver, 2000)

Franchising: some country-specific examples

Australia

In Australia, KFC, Pizza Hut and McDonalds all opened their first outlets around

1970, and while there were a few Australian franchises already operating, new locally based franchises soon began to appear. There followed a decade of steady growth of the franchising sector and an acceleration of this process in the 1980s. At the same time the major banks created sections specializing in financing franchisees, and the state and federal governments began to take an interest in the performance of the franchising sector (McCosker and Frazer, 1999). In 1988 the first comprehensive survey of franchising was conducted by the government. It was found that franchising had been so embraced by local entrepreneurs that the number of business format franchises per capita was greater than in the US. The youthfulness of the franchising sector was characterized by the fact that the number of franchised outlets per system was less than one half of that in the US.

Throughout the 1990s the expansion of the franchising sector continued and subsequent government surveys recorded its growth in 1991 and 1994. The Franchise Council of Australia sponsored a project by McCosker and Frazer (1998) and the findings outline how franchising has become an increasingly important part of Australia's business profile (Table 11.1).

The growth of franchising in Australia can be seen in perspective when compared with the development of the sector in other regions (Table 11.2). When the respective populations are considered, Australia is seen to have considerably higher numbers of franchisors (38 per million) and franchise outlets (2380 per million). The number of franchised outlets per franchisor (17 median) appears a little higher than the 14 recorded for the UK. As part of this growth in outlets, Australian franchisors have been expanding geographically, with 58% of franchisors holding outlets in more than one of the seven states and territories. Of these, 12% held outlets in all states/territories.

Turnover of the franchising sector has increased from A$42.6 billion in 1994 to A$84.1 billion in 1998, indicating a strong contribution to the Australian economy.

Table 11.1   Growth of Australian franchising 1991–1998 (source: DITAC, 1992; ABS, 1994; McCosker and Frazer, 1998) [a]

	1991	1994	Average annual increase (%)	1998	Average annual increase (%)
Total franchisors (including vehicles, fuel)	452	555	7.1	730	7.1
Total outlets	17500	30500	20.3	50100	13.2
Total franchised outlets	NA	24500	14.0	44800	16.3
Total turnover (A$ billion)	32.2	42.6	9.8	84.1	17.6
Total employees	170000	279000	NA	678500	NA

[a] The increasing use of part-time and casual employees makes comparisons of total employee numbers misleading. The 14.0% increase in franchised outlets over 1991–1994 is from ABS (1994, p. 16).

Table 11.2 Franchising growth in Australia, the UK and Japan (source: Purdy et al., 1996; Japan Franchise Association, 1997; McCosker and Frazer, 1998)

	Australia (1998)	UK (1995)	Japan (1996)
Population in millions (1997)	18.4	57.6	125.6
Total franchisors (excluding vehicles, fuel)	693	566	803
Franchisors per million population	38	10	6
Total outlets (excluding vehicles, fuel)	43800	48950	177200
Franchise outlets per million population	2380	850	1411
Franchised outlets per franchisor (median)	17	14	NA
Years franchising per franchisor (median)	7	4	NA
Percentage of franchisors 0–10 outlets (%)	36	43	NA
Percentage of franchisors 101+ outlets (%)	15	11	NA

Employment by franchises has growth from a total of 279 000 in 1994 to 678 500 in 1998. While the majority of this increase has been in casual employees as elsewhere in the economy, the contribution to the national economy is not only significant but increasing.

McCosker and Frazer (1999) have devised a framework for assessing the stage of development of a franchising sector. They propose that franchise size and growth rate, internal support and monitoring structures, expansion into new markets, economic contribution of the franchising sector, internal conflict, and external knowledge and control are factors which may indicate level of maturity.

Their analysis of the Australian economy suggests that under this framework there are signs confirming the stage of early maturity and indicating that the nation has moved into an expanding stage of development. For instance in terms of franchisee selection it appears that an interview, a personal investment requirement and the use of a franchisee profile are the minimum which could be expected from ethical franchisors. Initial support services are also becoming more developed, with 95% providing operating manuals in 1998 compared with 88% in 1991. Ongoing support has also developed strongly with the focus being on regular communication through field visits, newsletters, telephone hotlines, national conferences, the Franchise Advisory Councils and additional training for franchisees and their staff (Figure 11.1).

This framework has the potential, for comparative purposes, to be applied to other economies where franchising is an important player. However, as yet, there has been little on-going comparative study undertaken.

Most recent figures from the Franchising Council of Australia (FCA) state that 24% of Australian franchise systems operate internationally, with a further 27% of systems planning to commence foreign operations within the next 3 years. The FCA puts the number of total systems in Australia at 747 which is broken down in terms of systems and employment as shown in Table 11.3. These systems account for 49 500 outlets.

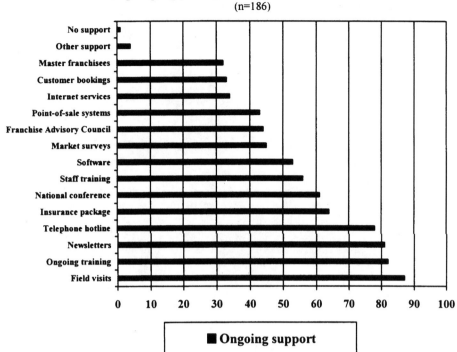

Figure 11.1 Ongoing support by Australian franchisors in 1998 (source: McCosker and Frazer, 1998).

In terms of international expansion one of the most dynamic companies on the Australian franchising scene is Fastway Couriers, a company founded by Bill McGowan, the current Chair of the World Franchising Council. The company began in New Zealand in 1983 but expanded into Australia 10 years later. In October 1999 further expansion took place in the Asia-Pacific region, with offices opening in Singapore, Malaysia and Hong Kong with business to commence in 2000. England is the next target for international expansion, with a master franchisor being sought by the company. Plans are in place to launch the company in China

Table 11.3 Systems and employment in Australia, 1999

	Number of systems	People employed
Business format systems	708	553200
Motor vehicle systems	33	70000
Major auto fuel retail systems	6	28700
Total	747	651900

in 2 years time while Germany, France and Italy are seen as the next markets to target. Further details of the company's activities are given in Box 11.5.

BOX 11.5: THE FASTWAY STORY

Fastway is a 1000 strong franchise organization operating throughout the Asia-Pacific region. In 1999/2000 the system was Franchise System of the Year and in 1998 it was the fastest growing private company in Australia; 3rd largest franchise system in New Zealand and the 5th largest franchise system in Australia. Group turnover is currently A$130 billion.

The business idea was conceived in April 1983 from an idea to operate cost effective hourly pick-up and delivery services between Napier and Hastings (New Zealand).

In April 1984 an evaluation of company drivers showed that no new work was being generated by them. It was then decided that the time was right to introduce franchising, and franchise couriers were sought. A large number of franchises were established which resulted in far greater productivity.

The franchise courier concept not only provided the incentive desired but also freed up working capital which enabled the company to develop further operations and linehaul networks. Never had franchising in the transport industry been attempted (world-wide) before.

The franchising system was then introduced to all branch operations. It was realized that the success of any operation depended on finding the right people to run the company.

The people had to have local knowledge, outgoing personality, knowledge of the industry, the psychological desire to succeed and the ability to run the operation without constant supervision. The introduction of master regional franchisees fulfilled this obligation and the company continued to grow rapidly.

In 1986 the company's founder, Mr Bill McGowan received the award of 'NZ Entrepreneur of the Year'. This award resulted in substantial national news media coverage and led to a rapid growth spurt of the company.

Operations in Australia began in 1993, taking the BRW (Business Review Weekly) Magazine award for No. 1. fastest growing private company in Australia, in 1998. Growth was a staggering 14, 557% for the previous 5 years.

The growth targets which the company has set include:
- Turnover and profitability increases in existing franchises.
- Spread of geographic coverage.
- Further development in transport related services.
- Diversification investment into other activities which directly contribute increased revenue to the courier network.
- The development of the world-wide service.
- Continued growth at the rate of between 18 and 25% per annum and to build on the current turnover base.
- Increased profitability.

France

Franchising first began to show signs of growth in France in the 1970s. At the start of the decade there were fewer than 50 franchisors operating in France but by 1979 that number had grown to 200. The 1980s was a period of rapid expansion with the number of franchisors increasing by 15% per year up to 1988 (Perrier et al., 1999). By the end of the 1980s some 500 networks had been established but only 267 of these still existed in 1996. Common networks in France are, for example, Century 21, Huit a Huit, Jean Louis David, Kookai, Maxi-livres and Climat de France.

In the 1990s there has been a shake out of some of the systems. Partly this has been due to new financial regulations designed to better control the emerging sector and to avoid financial scandals. By 1994, 71% of the networks established before 1982 had disappeared.

Individual sectors have experienced mixed fortunes between 1989 and 1996. Thus:

- The building sector has seen its number of franchisors drop from 26 to 3
- Personal equipment outlets have shrunk by 22%
- Specialist retail food outlets have been cut by 14%
- Hotel and catering sector has increased by 41%
- Non-specialist retail food outlets have increased by 25%.

Most recent figures show that France with 517 franchisors and 28 851 franchisees is the leading European country in terms of franchising (Table 11.4). With an often fierce independence, it is perhaps not surprising that France has developed its own specific networks and has less than 5% international franchisors. Clearly for an international franchisor looking for expansion, there are other countries in Europe which have a more open attitudes and will be better targets for investment. However, of the 35–40 franchisors operating in France they control some 2000

Table 11.4 Franchising activity in Europe

European countries December 31, 1996	Number of franchisors	Number of franchisees	Annual turnover in ECU billions	Employed people
Austria	210	3000	1.6	40000
Belgium	170	3500	2.4	28500
Denmark	98	2000	1	40000
France	517	28851	28.3	320000
Germany	530	22000	14.6	230000
Hungary	220	5000	2.6	45000
Italy	436	21390	12	49658
Netherlands	345	11910	9.2	100000
Portugal	220	2000	1	35000
Spain	288	13161	6.8	69000
Sweden	230	9150	5.7	71000
UK	541	26800	9.7	264100

outlets. International companies are strongly represented in catering and fast-food services. The leading companies are McDonalds, Stefanel, Levis, Hertz in car rental, Midas and Speedy in car repairs.

Perrier et al. (1999) suggest that France has now entered the maturity stage of franchising growth and is experiencing similar trends as those experienced in the US during the surge of franchising there. These trends are:

- A shift from manufacturing to services. Franchising is well suited to exploiting service and people-intensive economic activities, particularly those that require a large number of geographically dispersed outlets serving local markets
- A general increase in the popularity of self-employment which is partly fuelled by large companies outsourcing some of their business activities
- More women in the workforce. The increased participation of females in the workforce leads to dual-career families and to the increasing need and resources to purchase services. As a result home service franchises, for example, cleaning, maid services, child-care, house-minding are on the increase
- An ageing population. New opportunities are being created from the need for special diets and special needs in the fields of leisure and care
- Increased mobility
- Rising disposable incomes.

Russia

Franchising has been promoted as a method of growth for the economies of developing countries because it provides know-how, advanced management and marketing systems and higher levels of employment. The same principle applied in the former communist countries for the transition from planned to market economies. The Russian economy offers a vast opportunity to franchisors but also has many embedded risks (Alon and Toncar, 1999).

There are a number of benefits of franchising for emerging countries. First, franchising does not displace local production. Usually resources, human or capital are under-utilized, and franchising can employ these resources and stimulate the local economic environment by promoting international investment, creating viable small businesses and by restructuring the distribution systems.

Second, foreign investment by franchisors has far-reaching effects in that it often introduces new technology and standards previously unavailable in the host country. Small businesses are typically the source of job growth in developing economies and in transition economies, with the decline of giant state run enterprises. Thus, small international franchisees contribute to this process and can encourage the market-led re-structuring of upstream activities.

Third, because franchising relies on local ownership with its inherent local knowledge, this fits well with the desire for host countries to develop their domestic business skills. These can include marketing, strategic planning and international business skills which are all transferred as part of the business format franchising operation.

The business environment in Russia has been very turbulent for a very long time. In the early years of transition franchisors were faced with very hostile conditions. These included: political disintegration; a conservative backlash that attenuated glasnost and perestroika and an economy struggling with hyperinflation and an increasingly worthless currency. The Russian economy was further hit by the Asian crisis in 1998 which led to further devaluation of the rouble. The Russian economy is subject to a high degree of political risk including government instability, corruption, organized crime, and economic instability. This is coupled with protectionism in the form of limitations on property ownership, and the tax burden on international investor does not help.

In legal terms the civil code in Russia is generally favourable for franchising, as it provides freedom of contracting, trade liberalization reforms and is also supportive of competition, intellectual property and contract law. However, part of the civil code prevents franchisors from setting standards or limits on the prices of franchisee's goods. In addition franchisees are given the right for perpetual renewal of the franchisee agreement on the same terms as the original contract. Clearly this is not a clause which is attractive to the franchisor.

In terms of the social environment, the word franchising does not exist in Russian and so a considerable effort is being made by interested parties to educate the public, businesses and government about franchising. There is, however, an unfulfilled desire for western goods in Russia. This, together with the growth of tourism provides an opportunity for franchisors in the hotel sector. Perhaps the worst aspect of the social environment is the high crime rates, which range from the activities of petty thieves and street gangs to organized Mafia networks. It appears that currently to succeed in business in Russia, you deal both with the official and unofficial channels if you wish to prosper, the unofficial being much more crucial to the success of the venture.

In economic terms the Russian market is attractive because of its huge potential – 150 million consumers. However, poverty remains a serious problem and even in Moscow only about 20% of the population have done well so far during the transition to a market economy. Thus investors have to be prepared for the long-run, as a top executive in McDonalds stated 'we know the pay-off is a long way off. But it's an investment in our future' (Love, 1995). The labour market is strong in the sense that that both skilled and unskilled labour is relatively inexpensive in Russia. High quality and inexpensive labour should facilitate cost reductions and productivity increases. However, monetary instability and poorly developed communications and transportation infrastructure detract from the overall attractiveness of the economic environment.

Finding the finance to invest in a franchise can be a problem, as funding is limited and expensive. Financial sources for franchising in Russia that are available include governmental and international organization, Russian firms and governmental agencies, and wealthy Russian citizens. The US Export–Import Bank, USAID, The British Known How Fund, the US–Russian Investment Fund and the European Bank for Reconstruction and Development will all support franchisees.

Table 11.5   Business environment in Russia

Environment	Description	Unfavourable/ favourable
Political	Very high political risk, government instability, ineffective leadership, increased nationalism, mistrust in government	Unfavourable
Legal	Recently enacted civil code	Favourable
	Laws restricting franchise practices	Unfavourable
Social	Attitude toward franchising	Favourable
	Demand for western products	Favourable
	Crime and corruption	Unfavourable
Economic	Market potential of 150 million consumers	Favourable
	Vast pool of educated, skilled labour	Favourable
	Monetary instability	Unfavourable
	Infrastructure is substantially underdeveloped	Unfavourable
	Substantial number of population concentrations	Favourable
	Relatively untapped market in spite of the presence of major US franchisors and a growing domestic franchise market	Favourable
Financial	Limited amount of capital, especially foreign currency	Unfavourable

A summary of the business environment for franchisors in Russia is given in Table 11.5.

Franchising in St. Petersburg

There has been much recent investment in Russia by US based franchisors including McDonalds, Pizza Hut, Baskin Robbins, and Kentucky Fried Chicken who have developed outlets in Moscow and St. Petersburg. Business services are also represented, for example, Alfagraphics and Xerox. Local systems have also begun to emerge since the 1990s. According to a 1996 study (Sibley International, 1997) there were 14 local businesses developing a franchise system including in food; Togliatte, Russkoye Bistro, Russkaya Trapeza, Zolotoy Tsyplyonok, Alcor (food processing industry) and 1C (computer and software retailing industry).

In 1993 St. Petersburg gave birth to the Fund for Science, Technology and Franchising Development – the first franchise support organization (Seiling, 2000). A year earlier, in 1992, the first book on franchising in Russia was published.

In the early 1990s, several Russian companies started to employ different forms of franchising. In St. Petersburg those companies were Peterburgers, Russian Trapeza, Golden Chicken and others. However, the absence of skilled professionals and detailed information on franchising meant that the majority of companies did not go beyond piloting.

The next phase of franchising development was connected with the arrival of big international franchise companies in Russia (AlphaGraphics, Xerox, McDonalds), introduction of new franchise legislation and projects sponsored by USAID, involving the participation of Sibley International. Sibley conducted a series of seminars on franchising for entrepreneurs and local officials throughout Russia for a year.

Experts assess the current number of franchise companies (franchisors and franchisees) in Russia to be over 200, but its further development is frustrated by the fact that there are currently no more than 20 international franchise companies in Russia. There also appears to be some cultural resistance to successful Russian businesses choosing to franchise (they do not see good coming from good).

Sometimes, Russian companies try to use franchising as a remedy for their problems. But franchising only works if it multiplies a proven successful model. The use of franchising as a cure for an unsuccessful business does not work.

Despite the presence in Russia of big international franchise companies, small Russian businesses cannot afford to become franchisees, because of the high cost of franchises like Carrols, Pizza-Hut, etc.

Those international companies that do offer affordable franchises are not well known in Russia. Russian entrepreneurs are thus faced with the question of whether it is worthwhile to invest in an unknown trademark. The conclusion is that the most attractive way in Russia is when franchisors pilot their own businesses here first, make their trademarks famous and then start to franchise.

Experts assess that the potential number of franchisees (taking account of financial and other capabilities) is some 250 000. These are ready to invest to up to US $100 000. Industries can include both present and well-known ones like fast food, mini laundries, dry cleaners and not yet so popular industries like service franchises (including intellectual services, hotel services).

The Russian market is very attractive for international franchisors. Major obstacles that hindered the development of franchising in Russia have been overcome. These were an absence of legislation, absence of external financing and the absence of trained franchise specialists.

The development of franchising can boom, if a mutual effort is made on the part of Russian and international partners to provide mutual financing and leasing for franchises. Also important is the participation of international specialists in the work of the Franchising Training and Consulting Centre that was created a year ago in St. Petersburg under funding from the Eurasia foundation and USAID. Employees of the centre are mostly Russian specialists. International partners could bring in valuable experience, increase its effectiveness and extend its sphere of involvement.

Development of franchising in the North West of Russia would also be effectively stimulated, if a pilot franchise was based on one of the existing successful businesses in St. Petersburg. This activity is included in the state program for small business development in St. Petersburg in 1998–2000. According to this program, a tender will be announced for potential franchisors who are interested in franchising their business. The program will cover the operational expenses involved in putting the franchise together. If the project is successful, a percentage of future royalties will go to the Fund for Science, Technology and Franchising Development. This money can be used later to fund further franchise activities.

In addition to this, some aid to the development of franchising and finding partners should come from the creation of the Internet web server by the Leasing and Franchising section of the organization for Development of Small and Medium Businesses in St. Petersburg.

Notwithstanding the difficulties outlined in Table 11.5 the potential for franchising is good as local and international agencies work more closely together to foster a more conducive environment for the development of the sector. The most attractive sectors currently continue to be fast-food, retailing, tourist and service industries. In the medium-term the industry will have opportunities to exploit outside Moscow and St. Petersburg by going to more remote areas of the Russian Federation. However, Alon and Toncar (1999) conclude that franchising in Russia is restricted to the largest firms who can make substantial investment with long-term aspirations for growth and profits. Franchisors contemplating entry into the Russia market must proceed carefully, with a long-term planning horizon, and take steps, such as having a local partner, to protect themselves in a market which will remain hostile for another 5–10 years.

Conclusions

Franchising is a system which originated from the US and has since been adopted by other nations around the world, some of which we have discussed in this chapter. It is likely that the franchising concept still has much to offer as a route for international growth. As with any market entry, there are advantages and disadvantages for both the franchisor and the franchisee to be weighed up, but it does seem to be attracting increased attention around the globe. Back in the US, where it all began, there are signs of a further round of international expansion about to start. A survey by the IFA Educational Foundation (Woolweaver, 2000) suggests that domestic sales alone could top the $1 trillion mark by the year 2000. Based on responses of 386 US franchisors, the study noted that if given a choice, 98% of those surveyed would make the decision to establish an international franchise system again. In addition 95% said they were planning to expand the number of their international units.

Another key finding of the study revealed that more franchisors are recognizing the importance of modifying domestic strategies for international operations. Whether it be marketing, training, recruitment or fees, the report said, sophisticated international franchisors understand that the same strategies may not be successful in countries with different cultures, taste, regulations or other distinctions. From a marketing perspective this, of course, is an interesting development, and perhaps indicates a maturity amongst US firms, which have been traditionally regarded as roughshod in their approach to international markets on occasion.

However, the study did find that some of the international expansion activities are still quite reactive. For instance, more than two-thirds of those who made the decision to establish an international franchise system did so as a result of an inquiry from an interested potential franchisee. Similarly, when choosing the location for the first international franchise, US franchisors said that first contact was the method they most frequently relied upon.

However, the companies are expanding their reach beyond the traditional Canadian market which, while remaining the most popular, is today attracting a smaller percentage of franchising activity than it did 6 years ago. Instead the companies are considering expanding their operations into many countries previously not considered, both developed and developing. Asia, South America, Central America and Mexico are the areas of greatest international franchising growth, the study found.

Overall, as a mode of entry franchising is a dynamic and effective way of expanding rapidly around the globe. It is receiving increasing attention from entrepreneurs and from policy makers keen to encourage individuals to become franchisees or to assist successful entrepreneurs to franchise their business. In a sense the development of this business sector encapsulates what has been apparent in much of this book, namely, that consumer tastes and preferences are converging internationally, while acknowledging cultural differences, thus allowing franchising as a business format to succeed.

Questions for discussion

1. What do you understand by franchising?
2. Describe the various franchising business models.
3. Why is franchising a good way for a business to grow in international markets? Are there any disadvantages to franchising?
4. What are the advantages and disadvantages to the franchisee of becoming involved with a franchisor?
5. What evidence can you find in your own country of the growth of franchising? In what sectors? How many people are employed approximately?
6. Using the Internet sites of some of the franchise associations mentioned in this chapter, visit three of the sites and see if you can find out what the recent developments in the industry have been. Do they share any common concerns about the future of the industry?
7. Using the Internet sites of any of the companies mentioned in this chapter, visit their site and see how the business has developed. What are their plans for the future?
8. How crucial is marketing to the success of an individual franchisee or does a successful franchise format market itself? Discuss.
9. Why can franchising fail?
10. Franchising is marketing at its very best, a ready made and successful package of products/services, systems and management process are bundled together for the willing franchisee to operate. Discuss.

References

Alon, I. and Toncar, M.F. (1999), *Franchising opportunities and impediments in Russia*, Paper presented at the 13th Annual Society of Franchising Conference, Miami, FL, March.

Australian Bureau of Statistics (ABS) (1994), *Franchising Sector Survey Results – 1994*, Department of Industry Science and Technology, Canberra.

Combs, J. and Castrogiovanni, G. (1994), Franchisor strategy; a proposed model and empirical test of franchise versus company ownership, *Journal of Small Business Management*, 32 (2), pp. 37–48.

Dant, R.P. (1995), Motivation for franchising: rhetoric versus reality, *International Small Business Journal*, 14 (1/2), pp. 10–32.

Department of Industry Technology and Commerce (DITAC) (1992), *Franchising – Australia and Abroad*, DITAC, Canberra.

Goncalves, V.F.C. and Duarte, M.M.M.C. (1994), Some aspects of franchising in Portugal: an exploratory study, *International Journal of Retail and Distribution Management*, 22 (7), pp. 30–40.

Japan Franchise Association (1997), *Franchise Age*, Japan Franchise Association, Tokyo.

Love, J.F. (1995), *McDonald's Behind the Arches*, Bantam Books, New York.

McCosker, C. and Frazer, L. (1998), *Franchising Australia 1998*, University of Southern Queensland and Franchise Council of Australia, Toowoomba.

McCosker, C. and Frazer, L. (1999), *Signs of maturity in Australian franchising*, Paper presented at the 13th Annual Society of Franchising Conference, Miami, FL, March.

Mendelsohn, M. (1985), *The Guide to Franchising*, Oxford, Pergamon.

Perrier, K., Negre, C., Justis, R.T. and Castrogiovanni, G.J. (1999), Franchising in France, Paper presented at the 13th Annual Society of Franchising Conference, Miami, FL, March.

Purdy, D., Stanworth, J. and Hatcliffe, M. (1996), *Franchising in Figures*, Lloyds Bank and the International Franchise Research Centre, London.

Seiling, S. (2000), *Franchising in St. Petersburg*, www.a-z.ru/raf/.

Sibley International (1997), *Russian Franchise Association: Final Report*, United States Agency of International Development, Washington, DC.

Storholm, G. and Kavil, S. (1992), Impediments to international franchising in the business format sector, *Journal of Marketing Channels*, 1 (4), pp. 81–95.

Woolweaver, C. (2000), International Franchising: Checklist of Short and Long-term Considerations, http://www.franchiseconsulting.net.

Further Reading

Buckley, P.J. and Casson, M.C. (1998), Analyzing foreign market entry strategies: extending the internalization approach, *Journal of International Business Studies*, 29 (2), pp. 539–562.

Fladmoe-Lindquist, K. (1996), International franchise: capabilities and development, *Journal of Business Venturing* 11 (5), pp. 419–438.

Hopkins, D.M. (1996), International franchising: standardisation versus adaptation to cultural differences, *Franchising Research; an International Journal*, 1 (1), pp. 15–24.

Kirby, D. and Watson, A. (2000), Franchising as a small business development strategy: a qualitative study of operational and 'failed' franchisors in the UK, *Journal of Small Business and Enterprise Development*, 6 (4), pp. 341–349.

Martin, J. (1999), Franchising in the Middle East, *Management Review*, June, 38; (4) InfoTrac http://www.galegroup.com/.

McIntyre, F.S. and Huszagh, S.M. (1995), Internationalisation of franchise systems, *Journal of International Marketing*, 3 (4), pp. 39–56.

Stanworth, J., Purdy, D., Price, S. and Zafiris, N. (1998), Franchise versus conventional small business failure rates in the US and UK: more similarities than differences, *International Small Business Journal*, 16 (3), pp. 56–69.

In addition the following journal has published a relevant special issue:
International Business Review (2000), Special Issue: Licensing and franchising across border: theory, management and strategies for the 21st Century, 9 (4).
The following websites will also be of interest:

- British Franchise Association (BFA). Founded in 1977 by eight of the early UK franchising companies with the objective of raising the profile of ethical franchising in the UK. This site includes a listing of numerous national franchising associations around the world. http://www.british-franchise.org.uk/
- European Franchise Federation (EFF). The EFT was formed in 1972 and comprises the national franchise trade associations in different European countries. A secretariat rotates around the membership.
  http://www.british-franchise.org.uk/effintro.html
- The French Franchise Federation (FFF). http://www.franchiseline.com/
- International Franchise Association (IFA). The franchise trade association for the US.
- The Russian Franchise Association. www.a-z.ru/raf/
- The World Franchising Council (WFC) aims to encourage the international understanding and co-operation in the protection and promotion of franchising world-wide. http://www.british-franchise.org.uk/wfcintro.html.

Appendix I - Case studies

The case studies in this section are designed to bring to life some of the topics discussed in this book. Case studies help the student to understand the intricacies of particular business situations. They take you from the pure classroom setting to the point of applying your knowledge and understanding within a practical situation. The cases may involve coming to an agreed decision, setting out a plan of action or resolving conflict. There is not always one correct answer but any recommendations should be consistent with the scenario and be able to be justified. In another way the cases can be used to apply, critique and develop theory in relation to the ambiguity and complexity outlined in the case. In this situation the critical thinking skills of the students are developed and links to broader theoretical issues can be explored. In short this is as close as you can get to the international marketing 'coal face' without leaving the classroom.

It is not possible to cover all the issues raised in the text within the seven cases presented here. Consequently, the cases focus on some of the classic international marketing issues, including, market entry strategies and the internationalisation process (British Medical Group, Moy Park), and the management of the process, for example, via distributors (Tyrone).

It is important to understand some of the subtleties of operating within international markets. Thus, the Conney case goes beyond the basic 'how to do international marketing' and begins to introduce the complexities of interpersonal communication ameliorated through cultural and geographical distance.

Culture is not only relevant in terms of the domestic and international market but also in terms of the internal culture of the company. Thus, how does a company with an established mode of operation adapt itself to the new markets which it enters; or does it have to alter anything? The Wal-Mart case, with its overtly American culture, illustrates this in terms of its market entry into Germany and the UK.

The cases focusing on strategic alliances (Skånemejerier, SIA Glass) also highlight the complexities created by trying to compete internationally in some markets while co-operating in others. This delicate balancing act can be difficult to sustain as the cases illustrate. However, they do take us a step closer to the reality of international markets.

All of the cases presented have questions for discussion and a few have suggestions for further reading. Cases lend themselves to different interpretations with each reader potentially taking a unique perspective and gaining different insights. The discussion created from such multiple readings is the raw energy to drive the classroom debate. By using these cases wisely you will learn much from trying to see the world through someone else's eyes. All this within the safety of the classroom where being unable to justify your position does not affect your financial returns; one day it might.

Ambiguity in a negotiation: the case of Conney – a tool-manufacturing company

Amjad Hadjikhani

Department of Business Studies, Uppsala University, Uppsala, Sweden

Preliminary discussions

One day in spring of 1995, Bernard (manager of the Technical Department at Conney) met Lars and discussed the results of a project for which Lars was responsible and congratulated him on the positive results of the operation. At the end of the discussion, Bernard told Lars that he had received a letter from a manufacturing firm in India called ITR who had asked about the possibility of a joint venture co-operation for a tool-manufacturing plant in India. Bernard said that a man by the name of Feiz (originally from India), who had presented himself as an ITR representative, and a company called Hanfa (a Swedish consulting firm) had also phoned. Conney had no earlier experience with Feiz, ITR, India or other countries in Asia, but Lars became interested and proposed that Bernard arrange a meeting before the summer. In the meeting 2 weeks later, Bernard, Feiz Hanfa's marketing director and Lars met, and from the beginning, it was obvious that Feiz was interested in finalizing the agreement at that meeting. He tried to convince Bernard and Lars that Conney would obtain a good market position in India through this proposed joint venture. However, Bernard and Lars were suspicious in principle about a long-term joint venture since Conney was accustomed to selling tools to Swedish firms in the traditional way – by selling tools and receiving payments. ITR was asking them to enter into a joint venture in a country with a different socio-cultural structure, so from the beginning, Bernard had a rather conservative attitude toward the project.

Feiz showed them a detailed investment calculation in which, after an initial investment of 70 million Swedish Kronor (MSKR), Conney would break even after 2 years, and after 5 years, the sales in India could reach 40% of the total sales for Conney. However, Feiz did not succeed in convincing Lars and Bernard to give an immediate answer; instead, they suggested discussing ITR's request in India and said that they would let ITR and Feiz know when they would schedule a trip to India in the summer of 1995. Lars and Bernard then met with the top managers at Conney and received a very positive response to the idea of the joint venture. According to Lars and Bernard's financial plan, Conney would need to invest about 100 MSKR over 3 years before they would break even, and after 5 years, Conney's sales could reach 85 MSKR, which would be about 15% of total sales. All managers in the meeting declared that since the Asian market was new to them, it would be interesting to go forward and see how negotiations developed. They appropriated 150 000 SKR for the negotiation. During the summer, Lars and Bernard sent a letter to ITR describing Conney's position. At the end of the summer, Feiz was informed that the date of the journey to India would be 26 October. At the end of August, Feiz called Lars and explained that he had been in contact with India's embassy and that they had declared their interest in the project. Feiz also informed them that India's industrial commission would be coming to Sweden in October and that his aim was to make the project one of the topics of discussion in negotiations between India's and Sweden's ministers. Feiz had received this information from Farah, his partner in his consulting firm in India which assisted foreign firms in the Indian market, and mentioned that Farah was acquainted with two of the commission members. It was clear to Lars that such contacts were positive and could assist the project in the future, but it also occurred to him to wonder what would happen if ITR did not go through with the joint venture. By focusing only on ITR, Conney might have to forget the Indian market if they were not successful. It was therefore necessary for Lars to collect more information about ITR in Sweden. In the beginning of September, Lars called a friend in India named Hassy who worked in a Swedish firm in India and asked him if he had any knowledge about ITR. Hassy said that he did not know anything about ITR, but after a few days, he called back and said that according to Indian law, it is easier for companies like ITR to get financial support if they were connected to a reputable foreign company. It became obvious to Lars that there was a risk in concentrating only on ITR. Lars called Feiz the day after and informed him that Conney was interested only in the joint venture contract and not in the accomplishment of a joint venture agreement and that if ITR did not fulfil Conney's demands, there would be no contract. Feiz understood the problem and explained that they would have to put more pressure on the commission.

On 4 October, Feiz called Lars again and said that the Ministry of Industry (involved in the commission) had already bought similar tools from another Swedish firm. Two days later, Lars sent another letter to the embassy declaring Cooney's willingness to enter into a joint venture with the Ministry of Industry. He also mentioned that it would be better to negotiate the matter with the commission members. During this whole process, all the contacts and decisions were made by Lars. Lars only described a summary of the results for Bernard, who formally became the manager of this project. On 12 October, Feiz called Lars and asked if Lars and Bernard could meet with the commission in Stockholm on 13 October. The meeting was arranged specifically for this project. Bernard could not go to the meeting, but both Lars and Feiz went. From the commission, the deputy ministers from two ministries and three department leaders from other authorities were involved. They finally agreed to formulate a letter to the commission so that the project would be discussed at the ministry level of the two countries. In a meeting the next day, the ministers discussed the project and agreed to support it. Up until this time, Hanfa had played a passive role in the negotiations and finally informed Lars and Feiz that they would withdraw themselves from the project.

Project negotiation in India

On 25 October, Lars and two secretaries left Sweden, and the next day, Lars met Hassy and his friend, Paran, in India. Hassy already knew about the ITR project since Lars had phoned him in Sweden. After some general discussion, Lars asked them both if they had any information about ITR, and Paran suggested that ITR would not be the best partner for Conney in India because the firm was not well known. He said that it might be better to enter into a joint venture co-operation with firms having a better reputation. Lars briefly described his meeting with the Indian commission in Sweden, and Paran told Lars that one of the commission members must have been his friend Gova. Paran then called Gova to ask for a meeting. The same day, Lars called ITR and Farah, and they planned to negotiate. Gova also called that day and said that there was another firm called Azadi who was willing to co-operate, but Gova did not disclose the interest of the Ministry of Industry for such a joint venture.

A few hours before the meeting with Gova, Lars met two more of Hassy's friends, Yon and Vaji. They discussed the project, and it became evident that both Yon and Vaji were friends of the Minister of the National Industry, which owned 30% of ITR's stock and thus had a strong influence on ITR. None of them recommended signing an agreement with ITR. Later, Lars met with Gova, Paran and Hassy. After a general discussion, Gova stated that it would be better for Lars to visit other more reputable firms like Azadi as well and that if negotiations with ITR were unsuccessful, Conney could still enter into a joint venture with the Ministry of Industry. The next day, Lars had a meeting with ITR's general manager and other members of the decision board. After discussing ITR's background, Lars stated that a JU was out of the question since the two firms had no knowledge of each other. He added that he would have to make investigations into other potential partners, but it seemed that they did not take Lar's investigation very seriously because they thought ITR was the only alternative. Lars did not discuss the costs of the program with them, but after studying ITR's financial reports, Lars realized that ITR would likely face problems in financing its part of the project. At the end of the discussion, they decided to have another meeting. A few days later, Lars met again with Gova and discussed the problem of the cost of the program. A day before this meeting, Lars also had met another deputy minister who had pointed out the financial problems for even the Ministry of Industry; however, Gova stated that the matter mainly depended on who and which organization or ministry in India undertook the responsibility. They decided to have another meeting.

At a lunch arranged by Homa and Vaji, Lars was introduced to a powerful person in the firm of Azadi, and he and Homa asked Lars if he would meet with one of the leaders in this firm. This company was large and contrary to the other firms, had no contact with foreign firms. He asked Lars to contact him for a meeting, but after a few days, Lars realized that this firm did not have a 'very good' reputation, which made Lars a little uneasy.

In another meeting with ITR, Farah tried to find a solution to the problem, and they discussed several alternatives. One alternative was to have ITR as an agent and sell large quantities to ITR. Another alternative was to make a small investment together with ITR. When they discussed the financial terms, Lars guessed that ITR would have financial problems with both alternatives. ITR already had established contacts with other firms in Germany and the Netherlands that could sell the same tools at lower qualities and prices. Four days after the discussion with Farah, Lars received a phone call from Feiz, and Lars realized that Farah had informed Feiz about the problems in the negotiations and had asked him to come to India. A few days later, ITR's leaders, Feiz, Farah and Lars met again. This time, the leaders provided Lars with complete information about ITR. Lars did not want to bring up the matter of ITR's reputation and Conney's interest in other companies, so he concentrated on the costs of the project. ITR's manager, however, believed that the problem could be solved.

During the time of the meetings with ITR, the Ministry of Industry and Azadi were going on, Lars met with Gova and his colleague several times. Before the last meeting, they formulated a preliminary agreement that contained a request from the Ministry of Industry to present a plan for the joint venture project. If the plan was satisfactory, they could then discuss the proposed joint venture. Lars personally preferred to sign the agreement with the Ministry of Industry and not with ITR since the Ministry was promising a joint venture co-operation with a break-even point after 3 years and sales in the fourth year reaching 20% of total sales for Conney. Moreover, for the sake of cost and reputation, Lars believed that this proposed joint venture was a more appropriate alternative. However, Lars did not realize that the bureaucracy in the Ministry could negatively influence or even jeopardize the whole project because the project was small compared to the total operation of the Ministry. In addition, Lars was not fully aware of the conflicting interested between groups in the two Ministries of Heavy Industry. In the Department of Industry, there was a powerful person who was very interested in signing a contract with Luland, another Swedish company. Later, Lars discovered that there were several other firms from the US and Europe negotiating for similar projects with the two ministries and local firms.

Lars and the two secretaries left India in November after more than a month of hard negotiating with ITR, the Ministry of Industry and Azadi. The negotiations had cost more than 200 000 SKR, and the future of the proposed joint venture was completely unclear. Six weeks after Lars returned to Sweden, Feiz called Lars and told him that the ITR managers were in Sweden and that they had signed a preliminary contract with Conney's competitor in Sweden. In January, Lars began to hear negative comments from his managers. Some accused him of being incompetent and said that he had mistreated the joint venture project in Sweden. Others complained about his lack of ability to negotiate and questioned his decision to negotiate with other companies when he had already begun negotiations with ITR. Some managers stated that Conney should have left the project in the beginning the way Hanfa did since the project had cost Conney more than 200 000 SKR with no concrete outcome to show for it.

Questions

You are representing a consulting company and are invited by Conney to analyze and suggesting solutions for the future. You are going to give a report covering two main areas. The first task is to analyze the current situation and show Conney's managers, particularly Lars and Bernard, that you have understood the situation. You need to show how and why they have gotten into such a condition. The second task concerns the future. You need to provide solutions in the form of strategies by answering the following questions dealing with negotiation strategies and risk in a market with no previous experience and then relating them to personal behaviour in a market when there is no previous market knowledge.

1. How would you describe the penetration strategy undertaken by Conney into the Indian market? What were the other options and the related risks and opportunities?
2. By referring to studies on negotiation and risk in personal interactions between people from different culture, how can you explain the behaviour of Lars and Bernard toward Feiz and organizations from India?
3. What were the mistakes made by Conney's managers, particularly Bernard and Lars, during the whole process of the negotiations?
4. Considering Lars's behaviour, would it have been better for Conney to find and introduce another person more familiar with the cultural situation?
5. Considering Lars's behaviour, was it appropriate to consider several alternatives to ITR, such as Azadi and the Ministry of Industry? Or would it have been better for Lars to focus on one negotiation alternative from the beginning? Why?
6. What is your strategic proposal for the future? Would it be better to forget the market or to replace Lars with someone else? What is your opinion on providing more resources and supporting Lars? If you decide to support Lars, what direction would you propose for him to take?
7. What do you think really happened after Lars left India and returned to Sweden? Give your reasons.

British Medical Group

Angela Carroll[a], Bradley R. Barnes[b]

[a]Huddersfield University Business School, Huddersfield, UK
[b]Leeds University Business School, Leeds, UK

Background

The British Medical Group is a recently established 'umbrella' organization that has been formed from a strategic alliance involving two Sheffield based manufacturers of medical products. Surgimed are manufacturers of general surgical instrumentation from which they produce over 50 types of medical forceps and also manufacture needle holders, bone snips and orthopaedic instruments, retractors and other general surgical instrumentation. The older company is Orthopaedic Innovation who specialize in the manufacture of orthopaedic management systems (bone plates, bone pins, screws) and external fixation systems for fractures that are externally fixed. Surgimed have been operational for 4 years and Orthopaedic Innovation for 5 years. The two manufacturing organizations exist as a result of co-operation between directors Keith Howard of Surgimed and Dave Reed of Orthopaedic Innovation who thought the partnership would achieve long-term export goals. This resulted in Surgimed re-locating within a larger factory and premises at the Orthopaedic Innovation address some 12 months ago. New machinery was recently introduced which enabled production to quadruple without the need for shift work. Surgmied have just five full-time employees, and utilize sub-contraction of labour from their partners. Orthopaedic Innovation who are solely made up of 15 staff employed in the workshop.

Export markets

The organization has been involved with overseas markets for 18 months. During this time markets in the Far East have been established. The value of this business can be seen in terms of orders within:

- Developing markets: China and The Philippines. Value of orders written: £15 000.
- Established markets: Malaysia and Singapore. Value of orders written: £60 000.
- Substantial markets: Korea and Taiwan. Value of orders written: £200 000.

Sales from the above markets currently account for 60% of all sales of British Medical. Export sales are handled by six independent agents (one per country) who work on a commission-only basis.

Establishing international operations

A Chinese–Malaysian student on a MSc in International Marketing at a local university has been based at the organization for the past 18 months as part of a work placement. His salary is subsidized by European funding under the Excellence in Export scheme. He speaks fluent Mandarin, Cantonese, Hokin and English and fully understands the cultural differences that are important when establishing business in the Far East. He was allocated total responsibility for managing overseas activities including researching markets, obtaining export orders and appointing agendas. The student undertook desk research to obtain information on market size, market trends, competition and particular developments in the healthcare and medical sectors. Sources of information used included the Sheffield Chamber of Commerce, Business Link, the Department of Trade and Industry (DTI) and its link with the Commercial Department of overseas embassies, i.e. the Foreign and Commonwealth Office. From the reports generated the organization selected which markets to enter and the student then made local visits in order to appoint the agents and set up order processing and payment arrangements.

Adaptation and market familiarization

Although English is the common business language in Malaysia and the Philippines this is not the case when dealing with mainland China and Taiwan where it is necessary to speak the local dialect. This is a requirement as English is a far remote language and in these markets even the street signs are in Chinese. The students ability to communicate in both Cantonese and Mandarin has been essential for the stages of finding appropriate representation, appointing an agent and negotiating business. Without these linguistic skills both directors have agreed that business would never had developed.

Thus on his own, the student has been responsible for the entire orders that have been written in the Far East. The nature of the business has involved hosting visitors and participating in a recent DTI supported Sheffield Chamber of Commerce Trade Mission visit to Taiwan. More recently the student has been posted to Kuala Lumpur to actually undertake more specific in-market research due to the potential developments associated with an array of 13 hospitals that have been proposed to be built in 1998.

Some local adaptation has been necessary. The products have remained the same as those sold in the domestic market. However payment has been somewhat different and in order to obtain orders it has been necessary to quote and obtain payment in US dollars. Credit terms have also needed to be more flexible to combat competition from Germany. In addition the different regulations associated with trading in each market has implied the need to adapt the fundamentals of the packaging and labelling of goods, much of this depending on whether the shipment is sterile or otherwise or whether the merchandise is bulky or individually packed. Some basic product literature was also translated by the student into Cantonese and Mandarin.

Other potential markets

The Czech Republic and Hungary have emerged as new countries that offer great potential, research has been undertaken, contacts have been established and the company are presently out in the market visiting potential agents.

Research has also been undertaken into other European countries. Germany has been rejected due to the nature of local competition and the fact that the market is self sufficient with an array of high quality producers who are already servicing the market. France and Spain have been identified as potential markets and visits will be made early next year. Portugal and Spain may offer opportunities for export but further investigation is needed.

British Medical have been assisted with the task of researching European markets by the appointment of three French students for 3 months via an initiative supported by the Sheffield Chamber of Commerce.

The future

The organization hope to continue with their international expansion and the directors are optimistic about the future. The Chinese–Malaysian student has now completed his course and British Medical are investigating the possibility of employing him on a permanent basis. Export funding and assistance initiatives are also being considered.

Questions

1. Evaluate the market entry strategy adopted by British Medical Group. Would any other strategy have been feasible?
2. Identify at which stage of the Internationalisation process the organization is currently at, giving reasons for your answer.
3. What barriers to international marketing has the organization overcome and how has this been achieved?
4. What factors may limit further expansion of British Medical?
5. Research the sources of assistance and grants that may be available to UK small firms embarking upon export activities and present your findings.

Further reading

Cavusgil, S.T. (1984), Differences among exporting firms based on their degree of internationalization, *Journal of Business Research*, 12, pp. 195–208.

Cavusgil, S.T., Bilkey, W.J. and Tesar, G. (1979), A note on the export behaviour of firms: export profiles, *Journal of International Business Studies*, 10, Spring/Summer, pp. 91–97.

Johanson, J. and Wiedersheim-Paul, J.F. (1975), The internationalization of the firm, *Journal of Management Studies*, October, pp. 305–322.

Moy Park moves into Europe

Jeryl Whitelock

Department of Business Studies, University of Salford, Salford, UK

In 1988 Moy Park began to seriously considering expanding its sales into markets abroad.

Moy Park was an Irish chicken production company that was part of the portfolio of companies owned by Courtaulds plc, a large company with significant interests in textiles, paints and packaging. Moy Park had come into Courtaulds hands when it acquired Moygashel, a Northern Ireland based producer of high-quality textiles. In 1984, Moy Park was the subject of a management buy-out. At the time, turnover was about £60 million, but the company was not profitable. By the year ended April 1994, total turnover of Moy Park was £130 million, with the company being profitable for some 3 years.

After the buy-out, the company concentrated on making the transition from packing frozen chicken for a commodity market that was in decline, to processing chicken for such enhanced-value products as Chicken Kiev. At that stage they had three plants in Northern Ireland and one in the North West of England, and 80% of sales were in the UK. The main manufacturing base was in Northern Ireland, a fact which caused delivery problems in the UK on occasion – added transport costs and delays as a result of ferry failure, all of which made life difficult where such perishable products were concerned.

The market for processed chicken products was growing fast during the 1980s, initially at 50% per year and slowing to around 20% per year at the end of the decade. The company had built strong relationships with retailers through supplying frozen chickens although they did not have any strong brand identity in this commodity market. Nevertheless, they were able to build on these relationships when they diversified into the new processed range of products, supplying to major UK retailers such as Tesco, Sainsbury and Asda under the retailers' own label. As they were early into the market for further process poultry, Moy Park developed a good reputation for innovation, including employing chefs rather than simply food technologists, and generating new product ideas from other countries through visits to the Far East for example. Consequently they had a strong position within the UK, regarded as the most advanced market for this type of product after the US. However, the power of the retailers in the own brand market meant they were continually under pressure to reduce prices, particularly as competitors, such as Sun Valley, began to enter the market. Part of the Cargill Group, Sun Valley had significant resources to draw on and were able to develop their own brand in the market, whilst also supplying certain retailers with own label products.

Outside the UK, potential for processed products, not only in poultry, was growing in mainland Europe, where plans for an open Single European Market by the end of 1992 were an additional attraction. Despite this, the major chicken suppliers outside the UK were still concentrating on packing chicken, in much the way that Moy Park had done up to the buy-out. Moy Park's UK Sales and Marketing Director had been a driving force in developing the UK further process poultry market for Moy Park, and was now keen to turn his attention to the rest of Europe. The company had undertaken substantial market research on the market for chicken in various European countries, and has good information on consumption patterns, eating trends and sales volume through retailers. Initially, they considered seeking a partner to undertake joint venture manufacture, but, being relatively unknown outside the UK, this did not prove possible. Contract manufacture was a second option that was considered – Moy Park had the skills and experience in the further process poultry market, but making use of processing capacity already in existence outside the UK without additional financial investment seemed to make sense. Processors in France were identified, but they did not share Moy Park's view of the future market for further process poultry in Europe, nor were they willing to invest in the new machinery needed.

The first mainland European market targeted by Moy Park was Belgium. From the research undertaken, many of the trends in Belgium were typical of other European markets, so it presented itself as a self-contained test-market. In particular, the potential convenience foods market was large, with large numbers of working mothers and young singles in the market for buying these products. Also, as a result of the European Institutions, together with a large number of international organizations, being based in Belgium, it was a cosmopolitan market, open to new ideas and products. Finally, Belgium is relatively small geographically and relatively close to the UK. It is often chosen as an export market by UK companies in the early stages of Internationalisation.

Export sales direct to Belgium began in 1988. From the outset, transport was a problem – costs were high for the small quantities initially required in the market for these perishable cook-chill products. Used to orders for 2000 cases, the company was often supplying as little as 15 Chicken Kievs to Delhaize, a major Belgian retailer, so that the market could be tested for these products. Also, although well known in the UK for its reputation as an innovative supplier of quality cook-chill products, Belgian retail buyers were completely unaware of this reputation. Moy Park were competing with Belgian suppliers of poultry products, who were delivering on a daily basis, were on the spot to deal with problems and were well known to the retailers. Nevertheless, the Marketing Director visited the market every 3 weeks to talk to buyers and, of the two major food retailers in Belgium, Delhaize and the UK, Moy Park secured sales with one, Delhaize, and was able to begin to develop its position as a reliable supplier. Minor but necessary product adaptations were made – for example, labelling in grams rather than ounces; reducing the size of portions, which were too large, and too expensive, for the Belgian consumers. Special products were also developed as a result of close collaboration with the Belgian retail buyers, who foresaw a large market for these products that was not being supplied by others, and who were prepared to work with Moy Park to develop the right products – Chicken Cordon Bleu (with cheese and ham) being a particularly successful innovation. Within the company, however, exports were considered an expensive drain on company profits.

The experience gained in Belgium led Moy Park to reconsider France, but it was extremely difficult for an unknown company to get appointments with buyers for such major food super/hypermarkets as Carrefour, consequently they were unable to export direct to retail as they had been doing in Belgium. Instead, a national distributor in the food trade, Voldi, was approached. Voldi was aware of Moy Park's activity in Belgium and felt confident as a result that if goods could be delivered from the UK to Belgium, they could also be delivered successfully to Paris for onward distribution by Voldi. This also offered the advantage to Moy Park of specialist (i.e. chilled) stockholding in France. An agreement was signed in 1989 and Moy Park also established a small office in Paris with one employee, with gave them a presence in the market and allowed the promise of a fast response in the event of any problems.

Moy Park's reputation began to grow and with it sales, to the extent that the original idea of processing products on the mainland, rather than exporting from the UK, was revisited. Sales potential was growing but sales opportunities in more distant European countries such as Italy were being lost because it was difficult to get the product onto the retailers shelves in good time and good condition. Over the 2 years of their exporting Moy Park developed relationships with other poultry producers. In France, for example, the number 2 producer, Bourgoin, had been supplying them with basic standard products (certain chicken parts such as chicken breast, which were needed in larger quantity than the rest of the chicken for further process products). Bourgoin was a very large company and the opportunity of developing a joint venture with them was attractive to Moy Park, not least because Bourgoin was well connected with the relevant ministries in France and could cut through any bureaucratic red tape. From Bourgoin's point of view, the opportunity to make use of Moy Park's experience and expertise in the further process poultry market came at a time they were beginning to consider this market seriously for the first time, but were having problems in developing their own products and making the transition from frozen chicken producer. Moy Park were 5 years ahead of them. A joint venture production company, BMP, was established in Lille in 1990, with both Bourgoin and Moy Park producing their own products independently within the same factory. This location gave the possibility of supplying customers in the UK as well as France and elsewhere on the mainland, while the market in France was developed. Moy Park appointed some 12 sales and marketing staff from and around Europe, often recruiting from other major poultry producers in Germany and Belgium for example. This development gave Moy Park credibility as a European producer, and has allowed them to target other geographic markets such as Germany and Denmark, and also to build up relationships with Pan-

European/global customers in both retail and catering sectors of the food market, as well as major food producers such as Birdseye.

Questions

1. Consider the issues affecting Moy Park's choice of Belgium, rather than for example France, as an initial market for entry.
2. Consider each different market entry method and the factors influencing Moy Park's choice.

Managing a distributor network

Suzanne Horne

Department of Marketing, University of Stirling, Stirling, UK

This company exists but the name has been changed in order to preserve confidentiality. Tyrone is a small biotechnology company employing approximately 50 people and with a turnover of $18 million. It develops, manufactures and distributes its own pharmaceutical products and is known for its 'cutting edge' technology the licensing of which, in itself, contributes to its revenue stream in the form of royalties and contract research. The company is quoted on one of the major stock exchanges and proprietary, intellectual property forms a significant part of its asset base, an important factor in attracting shareholder funding. As one of the new breed of biotechnology companies it is seen by some investors as a high risk/ high potential investment but, unlike so many of this type, it already has a number of products competing in the market place and these, rather than any projected potential, provide a bench mark by which its performance is judged. In an area of the financial markets accustomed to 'hype' this creates a different, sometimes difficult, relationship with financiers focusing attention on actual earnings rather than potential, future revenues. Additionally, the area of licensed pharmaceuticals, is the field of the 'big boys' with long lead times on product development, high investment in research and with intensely competitive markets. Success also attracts attention from financial predators in the form of competitors or speculators.

The survival and success of the company in this difficult climate has derived from the adoption of a niche market approach. The product targets have been of a size which, in each national market are below the level that would be automatically attractive to larger companies with their high overheads and ability to assemble the resources for the highest value sectors of the market. However, a small company, by careful adoption in each market of different strategies which are appropriate to the size and characteristics of that particular sector, is able to control its overhead and can create a global return on a product which, in the context of its more modest standards, is a 'winner'. Within its chosen niche world-wide, Tyrone has secured between 25 and 30% of the market share. Napoleon complained (of Spain) that large armies starve and small armies get beaten. In its pharmaceutical niche Tyrone is a guerrilla army which does neither.

In this success the careful selection and use of distributors has been a major factor. Tyrone has distributors acting for it in more than 20 countries across four continents. The distributors fall into two categories, those that operate independently and those that are sub-companies of the parent. Each distributor, independent or 'own' needs an infrastructure covering general administration, storage, marketing and internal distribution networks. Only in the larger national markets can this degree of overhead be carried as an 'own company'. However, it is in the larger markets that competition is at its strongest and it has been proved many times that the highest success in these situations is achieved by a sub-company which depends for its survival mostly or entirely on the parent company's products.

Where distributors are independent, Tyrone's products are usually fitted into the distributor's range as one of a number of products in the trading scope of that company. The company requires that the distributor has a good knowledge of and is actively working in, the biotech industry and has a trained sales force in this field. There is a distinct probability that they will also be delivering a range of other products to the same client base. The small market size of many of the products which form one of the bases of Tyrone's niche strategy, would make it uneconomical to try to train and maintain an 'own' sales force specifically for this product range as a wholly owned sub-company.

In the case of both independent and sub-company categories, distributors work on a profit margin agreed with Tyrone, however, in the case of a sub-company, a greater share overall remains within the parent holding company. In both cases the distributor agrees with the manufacturer a market price based on the sum of factors in that market. These include competition, market size, distribution costs, etc. and these will differ in each country or territory. Most markets are 'skewed' towards a few major customers and for these, individual contracts may be negotiated. Where a distributor needs to agree a lower than normal price for a high volume or long-term contract, a 'one-off' adjustment in supply price may be agreed with Tyrone in order to preserve the distributors profitability. In return the distributor undertakes sales and marketing within the territory, part of which is to predict volumes for production and maintain intelligence of competitor strategies and products. Since these are 'high tech' products Tyrone expects to input technical assistance where this is required for market development and in the rare instances of a problem arising.

These statements are standard for developed markets where the introduction of one of Tyrone's products may be seen as a 'me-too' unless it can be differentiated in some clear manner that is visible to the market. However, on many occasions a new high-tech/biotech product is faced with developing a new market and this requires educating customers in its uses and benefits. In these cases considerable technical support may be required from Tyrone in support of the distributors and, occasionally this may come from one of the other wholly owned distributors rather than from the parent company. The concern of any distributor handling such a new product is that, once the market has developed successfully, the manufacturer may take over the market with its own sub-company at the expiry of the distribution agreement. There is no defence except for the distributor to prove that he/she can do a better job than the manufacturer.

The manufacturer's relationship with a distributor can often be far from a happy one. Distributors need to feel that the profit return justifies their efforts. If the product yields only modestly in comparison with others in their portfolio then it may receive correspondingly less promotion. This may be good business by the distributor on his own behalf but it does not meet the ambitions of the manufacturer trying to increase market share. Occasionally one type of product may compete indirectly with another, for example a vaccine to prevent disease or an antibiotic to cure it. If both are offered by a distributor this creates an internal conflict of interest for the distributor. Standards of integrity vary in different cultures. A successful product may frequently be copied locally and competes directly with the import. It is not unknown for a distributor to offer both products (usually in contravention of the agreement with the manufacturer) where the margin on the local product is higher. The situation might also arise where there is a desire to maintain a superficially good relationship with the manufacturer, but the distributor owns a sister company, which trades in the locally sourced goods apparently in honest competition.

The role and attitude of a distributor is critical to the success of a product. A long standing, successful relationship with a good distributor allows a manufacturer to introduce new and improved products relatively easily to a market using an experienced team who know the local market well. A manufacturer goes to great lengths to cherish a distributor who does a good job; the distributor values a partnership with a manufacturer that produces a high quality, market leader with a product stream of further developments. The relative concerns, rewards and expectations of each partner need to be established in the earliest days of setting an agreement. This, properly done, should protect both partners against the obvious, potential pitfalls. The old adage that, if it is necessary to take an agreement from the drawer to examine its terms, then already the relationship is in trouble is unfailingly true.

Questions

1. To what extent does the type of product affect the relationship of the distributor with the manufacturer?
2. What factors would you take into consideration before becoming a distributor for such a company?
3. What factors would you take into consideration when choosing a distributor rather than a sub-company?

International relationship building in Skånemejerier – alliances with Klöver Melk and MD Foods 1991–1996

Ulf Johansson

Department of Business Administration, Lund University, Lund, Sweden

Sweden's second largest dairy, Skånemejerier, is based in Scania, the southernmost province in the country. The company produce traditional dairy products that have been protected from foreign competition up until EU entry in 1995. The company is part of the Swedish Farmer's Co-operative, a dominating actor on the Swedish food-industry scene.

Background

By the end of the 1980s Skånemejerier (from hereon SM) began pondering what strategic direction to take in the new competitive situation that the Swedish dairy market would face after deregulation. They could identify several changes in the competition; Arla, both a competitor and partner on the Swedish market, would probably try to expand its interest to the south and large dairy giants like MD Foods, situated close-by in Denmark, and large German dairy companies might also want to have a piece of the cake. Compared to Arla, based further north in Sweden, and MD Foods in Denmark, SM is a relatively small company and these circumstances lead SM to conclude that it was too small to handle future development of the company on its own. In order to continue as an independent company, management felt that it had become essential to seek co-operation with partners in other markets.

The dairy industry in Northern Europe consists of a small number of actors and by tradition, there has been different forums for co-operation, not least in technical areas. Further more, SM and Arla have for some time also been co-operating in producing and selling juice-products, cheese products as well as through trade associations. The first steps towards future alliances with other international actors though, like Klöver Melk and MD Foods, were mainly taken within the technical areas of the industry.

Whilst the initial contacts between SM and MD Foods were established, discussions with Klöver Melk were also taking place. In 1991 Klöver and SM signed an agreement on co-operation which was to be administered by the jointly owned company White Dairies of Scandinavia. This agreement mainly included purchasing and exchange of products but could also be extended to incorporate for instance production development, distribution and marketing. However, it became more a declaration of intent rather than a concrete contract. The main reason for this was that the first few years after the agreement, both companies faced situations on their respective markets that demanded their full attention. In Denmark a price-war on milk started between Klöver Melk and MD Foods, which ended in the two companies closely co-operating and virtually merging. To SM this meant that it not only reached a position of co-operation with one Danish company (Klöver Melk) but with two (MD Foods too). Meanwhile, on its national Swedish market SM had put much effort and energy into the merger with a smaller regional company, Helsingborgs mjölkcentral.

Content of the alliances

The co-operation between SM and MD Foods came to focus on sales of Danish cheese on the Swedish catering market and the sales of Swedish cheese in Germany and the US. MD Foods' Swedish subsidiary also sold SM's dessert cheese to the retailing sector. The co-operation concerning export of SM's products through MD Foods came to an end in 1996 since both companies felt it was difficult to obtain large enough volumes; it became too difficult to sell competing products, to MD Foods' own ones, through the company's channels.

During 1995 Klöver Melk and SM began to revitalize their co-operation. Klöver Melk was invited to become joint owner of SM's dairy (Lindahls) in Poland. During the 1990s SM had started to explore the Polish market, a market that was believed to become very interesting, and on which the company had managed to obtain a market position. At the same time there was a need for a partner with knowledge about the dairy industry and financial assets to make the company develop. This was an important change in SM's relationship with Klöver Melk. The two companies now got a strong common interest, in the form of their Polish dairy.

What has Skånemejerier gained from the alliances?

For SM the assortment for the catering market has grown. The company used to sell MD Foods' Danish cheeses at the same time as MD Foods sold SM's dessert cheeses to the retail market in Sweden. After the national cheese federation (Riksost) was dissolved, it became clear that SM initially had a poorly developed sales organization outside its core market (Scania). This, together with the fact that dessert cheeses demands a different sales approach than hard cheeses, made the change a positive one for SM. There was also an early attempt by SM to include milkshake from

Klöver Melks' Danish assortment on the Swedish market but with little success at the time.

Even though the geographical distance is small, there are significant differences in preferences between Danes and Swedes, a fact that limited the possibilities to enlarge Klöver Melk's range of products with SM's products and vice versa. Both companies had a fairly complete set of assortments and none of them desired to include products from the other that would compete with their own basic products, such as cheese and milk. To achieve this, the companies would have to become more mutually complementary rather than complete full-assortment companies on their own. However, none of them wanted to take that road as co-operative relationships limits the two companies range of action. Also, co-operation on fruit-yoghurts was hindered by existing relations between Klöver Melk and MD Foods and between SM and Arla. To compare, SM's alliance with the Finnish Milko was largely built on a complementarity between the two. Milko is producing Prima Liv (on a licence contract with SM) and until 1998 it also included and sold Pro Viva, a product that SM from then on took over itself.

In terms of distribution and logistics, SM tested a form of distribution of dairy products – to smaller shop units – based on franchising, that was used by Klöver in Denmark. It did not go further than to a test though, and this form of distribution is no longer used.

Neither with MD Foods nor with Klöver Melks has there been any joint product development, although this was originally intended. Due to aspects of the Danish regulations on dairy products, exchange of assortment and product development between the countries have been restricted. For instance, it was not until a few years ago that Denmark accepted the sort of products like mixed dairy and vegetable fat (accepted in Sweden since 1968). At the same time there was an increasing interest from Klöver Melk to take part in more joint product developments with SM – not least after Pro Viva (a functional food) turned out to such a hit.

The flow of information in SM's different alliance with Klöver involved technical development, like allowing access to each others production plants. Also, a benchmarking project was performed by comparing products like juice, cheese and consumer-milk from the two companies' plants in order to find how competitive they were and in which aspects improvements were needed.

SM and Klöver Melk occasionally discussed joint production of various products and in the original agreement of co-operation it was also an important issue. As an illustration of this, in one of SM's plants in Scania, there was under-production of milk with one shift free, meaning that milk from Klöver Melk's less profitable plant outside of Copenhagen could easily have been taken over to Sweden for processing and thus making a shut-down possible on the Danish side. The preconditions for a joint production were nonetheless not ideal as both focused on complete ranges of products, based on the milk delivered from their respective members (the farmers). With increasing excess capacity in the European dairy industry, both companies viewed co-operation in production as important but it never materialized.

Consequences of the alliances on other relationships

The Swedish dairy market for a long time was like a planned economy, where the market was divided between the major participants; SM, Arla and Norrmejerier. All three actors had their base in the same farmer co-operative and were engaged in several forms of business together. When the national borders opened up the three participants had to find new ways and means of improving their competitive position. Old forms of co-operation that had existed between Swedish dairy producers, were no longer possible to maintain. When SM started approaching the Danish companies, the competitors on the Swedish home market did not approve. Some of them felt it was questionable to ally with the potentially most threatening competitor on the Scandinavian dairy market, i.e. the Danes. SM, however, perceived these reactions as plain envy. The fact was that SM was doing what others, not least Arla, had wanted but failed to, i.e. reach an co-operation agreement with a Danish dairy. On top of that came the agreement that SM made with the Finnish dairy company Milko, adding even more to the negative attitude of their Swedish counterparts. From SM's point of view these alliances strengthened their competitive position on the market and thereby gave them the chance to survive as an independent organization within the farmers co-operative. It was especially this latter aspect that, according to SM, stirred up the feelings of Arla and the plans that company had made on the future Scandinavian dairy market.

From the Swedish retailers perspective, SM's alliance with Danish dairy companies could be interpreted as 'hindering' foreign competition to take enter the Swedish market. Thus, it would have been more advantageous for the retailing companies themselves if they had established direct relationships with Danish dairies to import to Sweden. Instead, retailers found the SM's actions positive; firstly it meant that SM and Arla were still separate companies and thus freedom of choice for the consumer was undisturbed and secondly, MD Foods already had its own organization in Sweden that independently negotiated with Swedish retailing.

It is difficult to measure the direct effects of the alliances that SM had made on their position in relation to retailers. Lacking more substantial means of measurement, the most concrete expression of gains was the fact that the company now produced and sold a number of new products – like Pro Viva, Måväl, and Danone yoghurt – on foreign markets such as Finland, Germany, Poland and England.

During 1996 the co-operation between SM and MD Foods selling Swedish cheeses abroad in Germany and the US, under the name Schweden Gold, came to an end. The alliance was by then no longer considered to be a successful means of reaching new consumers in new markets. This was primarily due to the fact that it was directly competing with other products; even if they were sold under another name it was actually cheese that MD Foods also were selling themselves. As a replacement for this alliance with MD Foods, a new one was entered with Norrost GmbH in Germany. SM bought a part of the company, established by the Swedish company with the same name. In respect to their other Danish partner, Klöver

Melk, this new alliance did not cause any problems since Klöver Melk is not allowed to be active on the German market.

Questions

1. What advantages and disadvantages have the alliance with Klöver and MD meant for SM?
2. What would the alternative to the alliances have been and would that have worked better?
3. For the future, do you see alliances as an important part of the company's strategy – or should the strategy change?

SIA Glass's international strategic alliances

Ulf Johansson

Department of Business Administration, Lund University, Lund, Sweden

The Swedish family-company SIA Glass operates in the Swedish ice-cream market. This market has been dominated by Glacebolaget (UK), owned by Unilever, for many years. SIA has expanded rapidly during the last 10–15 years – from 25 million SEK to 150 million today.

Background

At the start of the 1980s, SIA was an unknown producer of ice-cream on the retailing market. The company was better known in the catering industry where SIA had nation-wide distribution. Their concept was built on high quality ice-cream made from dairy cream as well as educating the catering industry on ice-cream, selling their knowledge through 'ice-cream schools'. This competitive advantage was erased when the competitors started to sell cheaper ice-cream (not based on dairy cream) and began to teach the catering industry about ice-cream for free. On the retailing market, SIA's penetration was limited and the company faced a strategic choice; should they compete in the non-dairy segment or strengthen their position in the dairy cream segment? The latter was decided and they went looking for a partner. Mövenpick was eventually chosen.

SIA and Mövenpick - the outset and organization of the collaboration

Mövenpick was eventually chosen as a partner. Their ice cream was higher priced than SIA's but both companies worked in the same segment; premium ice cream made from dairy cream. From Mövenpick's point of view a collaboration with SIA was interesting and promising. The company had evaluated different options for entering the Scandinavian market and this opportunity linked very well to those plans. Compared to the UK, SIA was preferred. In 1986 production of Mövenpick's ice-cream products began in SIA's plant in southern Sweden. The strategy from SIA's point of view was that Mövenpick's products would be added to the existing product-line. SIA's own ice-cream would be priced as before, but it was thought that adding the higher priced Mövenpick products to the product-line, SIA's products would seem less expensive and also more exclusive than before.

Collaboration between SIA and Mövenpick is organized through a written agreement based on sales volumes. The original 5-year contract was extended to a 10-year contract and at present SIA and Mövenpick have entered their second 10-year contract term. SIA can expect Mövenpick to supply product packing, recipes for the different products, access to suppliers of different input products, quality control and standardized promotion material. Concerning the latter, it is up to SIA to adjust the promotion material to suit the demands of the Swedish market. The collaboration is controlled mainly through the budget. However, there are no real sanctions attached to the agreement concerning what happens if sales volumes are not achieved.

Through the co-operation with Mövenpick, SIA also gained access to an international network of contacts with Mövenpick's other partners, mainly Ingman Foods in Finland and Diplom-is in Denmark and Norway. This group of companies have annual meetings when they exchange information and formulate common guidelines for their relationship with Mövenpick. Besides these Scandinavian contacts, all Mövenpick's licensees meet up once a year at a world-wide gathering. Today SIA has several personal contacts with both Mövenpick and a number of their other partners. When the Scandinavian group of partners meet, mainly future product launches are discussed. In order to achieve synergy effects, they try to introduce products simultaneously and can thereby use the same promotional material. Besides the Scandinavian group, SIA meet Mövenpick's other partners at regular intervals, among them the German company Schöller, (producer for most of the European market outside Scandinavia), renowned for its product development and marketing skills.

In the alliance SIA is itself responsible for all marketing investments on its domestic market. SIA, thus invests in the Mövenpick brand name on the Swedish market. Here lies a problem, should Mövenpick prefer to handle the production and distribution themselves. Nevertheless, due to the long-term agreements, this is a potential problem that SIA argues is not likely to occur.

In the case of the other Nordic partners, it is primarily a question of dealing with logistical issues. Through concentrating the production of a certain flavour to a small number of plants, the costs of adjusting the production line set-up, can be reduced. In order to have a fair division of costs between the companies, a system of internally set prices has been made, in which the size of the production costs has been stated. To this cost is then added the cost of raw materials used, which varies depending on the specific product.

What has SIA gained from the alliance with Mövenpick?

SIA has gained access to new products through its co-operation with Mövenpick, both on the retailing and the catering market. Within the retailing sector, SIA has an assortment of nine different sorts of 1-l packages. There are also two variants of ice-lollies, two sorts of ice-cream cups and two multi-packs. To the catering market, not less than 16 different variants is included in their range of products. In total there are roughly 150 different flavours available in the Mövenpick collection of recipes, meaning that the technical restrictions for what product to make are very limited. Not all these flavours suit the Nordic market very well since consumer preferences are rather different from those of, e.g. Germany and Switzerland.

The purchase of the raw materials used in the products included in Mövenpicks assortment, is done jointly by all its partner companies. These purchases only include ingredients that are specific to the different Mövenpick products, such as candied walnuts or crushed coffee nougat. These flavouring materials are not used in SIA's own range of products, simply because Mövenpick would not allow it. Basic raw materials such as milk, cream, sugar, etc. are all purchased individually by each licensee.

There does not exist any joint production development with Mövenpick or any of their other licensees. If SIA has an idea for a new product, this is shown and handed over to Mövenpick in Switzerland and they continue the work to formulate a new product. Should Mövenpick not have the competence itself that is demanded for a complete product, the German licensee Schöller would step in. Concerning discussions with the retailing sector about production of private brands, this has not occurred. Retailers have so far only showed interest in cheaper vegetable based ice-cream, not produced by SIA or Mövenpick.

Information sharing always takes place within the alliance, with both Mövenpick and the Scandinavian partners. As things stand, there is virtually no information that would be withheld from any of the parties, simply because the companies have not been competing on the same markets. An intranet (or the equivalent) does not exist presently but might be developed in the future.

When dealing with marketing, the Scandinavian group of partners have occasionally co-ordinated the promotion material. Mövenpick does supply them with photographs of the products, but no co-ordinated marketing strategy exists. The sales force focusing on retailers and caterers, work with the complete range of products offered on the Swedish market, giving the company substantial large-scale synergies.

SIA produces Mövenpick's products for the Danish market, since the licensee company for Denmark is the Norwegian Diplom-is. The reason for this arrangement is that production in Norway, as a non-EU country, would mean that the cost of export to Denmark would make it unprofitable. SIA also exchange a few products with Ingman Foods in Finland, an arrangement that enables both of them to produce longer series of products and thereby cut down their cost for production line changes.

There are very few things that SIA cannot do due to its co-operation with Mövenpick. However, some things would be less appropriate to do, like launching an ice-cream that would be basically identical to a Mövenpick product but under the name SIA. Furthermore, Mövenpick does not want SIA to introduce products of their own in the same price segment as Mövenpick. These are all issues that lie beyond the stipulations of the written agreement but in practise they become self regulating. Should SIA act in a way that Mövenpick feels is unacceptable for them, they can always resort to the solution of ending the arranged agreement (which SIA does not want).

SIA Glass and Del Monte – background and organization of the co-operation

By the mid 1990s SIA received an proposal from Del Monte about product development of fruit sorbets for the English market. SIA then came up with a recipe for production of several different fruit sorbets. In England the production is made on a licence basis, with SIA licensing their recipes to a producer and Del Monte licensing their brand name. SIA is also producing, selling and distributing the sorbets under the Del Monte brand name on the Swedish market.

Expectations and responsibilities in the agreement were regulated in a 10-year contract between both companies. Each year levels of sales volume are discussed and decided upon, and there is an annual follow-up on the attained versus budgeted volumes. Furthermore, SIA, Arvid Nordqvist and JO-bolaget (the latter jointly owned by the farmer co-operative companies that sell fruit juice under Del Monte's brand name on the Swedish market) undertake co-ordinated marketing analyses. Since it is SIA that developed the recipes and therefore is the registered owner of them, the flow of information is largely going in the opposite direction compared to the one with Mövenpick. Representatives from the companies meet several times per year. In addition, marketing people from Del Monte also travel to Sweden two to three times per year in order to co-ordinate activities with SIA, Arvid Nordqvist and JO-bolaget. Here, the strategies for marketing Del Monte's products on the Swedish market are discussed and the production of the promotion and advertising material is then left to Del Monte's marketing agency. Financially, the co-operation with Del Monte is a substantially smaller commitment than the one SIA has with Mövenpick, since Del Monte itself invests in its brand name on the Swedish market.

What has SIA Glass gained from the alliance with Del Monte?

When looking at the range of products, three sorbets and the ice-cream/sorbets have been added, carrying the Del Monte brand name. The process of developing the recipes have been made together with Del Monte, who have contributed with their knowledge in fruit. No real modifications in SIA's own assortment has been made due to their co-operation with Del Monte and to sell sorbets under the SIA brand name is not in line with SIA's strategy; SIA is supposed to stand for dairy ice-cream products and nothing else.

Shipments to wholesalers and retailers are co-ordinated with SIA's other range of products. Concerning the remaining products, sold on the Swedish market under the name Del Monte, the potential for co-ordinating shipments is limited since the products (juice, canned products and ice-cream) demand different transport solutions. Therefore transportation is an area in which Del Monte has an interest in leaving SIA to make the necessary arrangements.

Between SIA and Del Monte the information on marketing issues has been of main interest. Del Monte needs extensive information in this area in order to enable them to make the best priorities for marketing investments. By sharing information with Del Monte on how the market is developing, SIA can also improve their own skills in marketing and communication, as it gives an insight into how Del Monte uses the information to choose ways of communicating with the consumers. So far, no system of shared computerized information network (e.g. the Intranet) exists.

From the point of view of production, it is SIA that makes the investments and SIA that has the final say in questions that are related to production issues. An exchange of ideas between the companies nonetheless takes place also in this area.

Collaboration in advertising is done together with the wholesaler Arvid Nordqvist and producer of fruit juices, JO-bolaget. Del Monte finances the promotion material as well as advertisements in different media. SIA, together with Arvid Nordqvist and JO-bolaget, pays for the price reductions of the products when there is a price promotion on. As the products under the Del Monte name in Sweden are sold through three sales forces, problems in terms of co-ordination of different promotional activities towards the stores might arise. Accordingly, it may sometimes be difficult to achieve good exposure of the Del Monte products in the stores.

Not surprisingly, the collaboration with Del Monte has meant that SIA has increased its knowledge on marketing considerably. For example, Del Monte uses an advertising agency that is well known as well as expensive, something that SIA would never consider being able to do on their own. SIA has been able to use the knowledge and experience received through Del Monte to better market its own assortment of products.

According to SIA, the alliance with Del Monte has not put any limitations on what the company is able to do on the market. To Mövenpick, SIA's collaboration with Del Monte is quite close to what could be allowed by a partner. Mövenpick also manufactures sorbet but only in 1-l packages. SIA argues that sorbet is an exotic product on the Swedish market and thus package sizes of (maximum) 0.5 l are essential. Through this argument, SIA has this far been able to refrain from selling Mövenpick's sorbet.

Questions

1. What advantages and disadvantages have the alliances with Mövenpick and Del Monte meant for SIA?
2. What would the alternative to the alliances have been and would that have worked better?
3. For the future, do you see alliances as an important part of the company's strategy – or should the strategy change?

Wal-Mart Stores Inc. in Europe [*]

Stephen J. Arnold[a], John Fernie[b]

[a]*School of Business, Queen's University, Kingston, Ontario, Canada*
[b]*School of Management, Heriot-Watt University, Edinburgh, UK*

Wal-Mart Stores Inc. is a US-based retailer. It entered the European market in 1997 by acquiring 21 hypermarkets in Germany from Wertkauf BmbH. In 1999, it bought Asda and thereby acquired 232 stores in the UK market. Whether or not Wal-Mart will succeed in these and other European markets depends upon the applicability of, and ability to transfer, the factors that made it successful in the US domestic market. These factors include a unique organizational culture, low cost operating procedures and customer-focused price, assortment and service practices.

Wal-Mart Stores Inc.

Wal-Mart is the world's largest retailer and it is expected that this US retailer head-quartered in Bentonville, Arkansas will grow even larger. Sales revenues for the fiscal year ending January 31, 2000 were $165 billion. This sales volume is more than twice the size of the next largest retailer in the world, Carrefour/Promodès of France. At current growth rates, Wal-Mart sales will top $300 billion by 2005. In that year, 20% of its sales will come from international sources meaning that Wal-Mart's global sales alone will exceed the entire current annual sales of Carrefour/Promodès. The other 80% of its sales will be sourced at the expense of food chains in the large US market through Wal-Mart's expansion of the Supercenter hypermarket format. An additional doubling of sales and earnings during the next 5 years to 2010 could prove to be a conservative estimate.

International sales accounted for only 9% of Wal-Mart total revenues for the fiscal year ending January 31, 2000. Wal-Mart is a relative newcomer to the international arena having expanded to neighbours Puerto Rico, Mexico and Canada in 1991,

[*] The authors wish to acknowledge the Institute for Retail Studies, University of Stirling, for its role in inspiring this project. The second author was Director of the Institute while the first author was a Visiting Professor. The first author also wishes to thank Professor Harry Timmermans, Director of the European Institute of Retailing and Services Studies, Eindhoven University of Technology, and his colleagues and staff for their wonderful hospitality while he worked on his portion of the paper. Professors Leigh Sparks and Steve Burt, University of Stirling, also provided the opportunity to trial some of the ideas on audiences of practising retail professionals.

1992 and 1994, respectively. It entered South America via Argentina and Brazil in 1994, China in 1996 and South Korea in 1998. It only entered the huge but highly competitive European market via Germany in 1997 and the UK 2 years later. In a relatively short period of time, Wal-Mart evolved from being a national to global competitor – it progressed literally from the Pan-American games to the Olympics of retailing.

The first international markets entered by Wal-Mart quickly felt the impact of the new market entrant. For instance, Wal-Mart became Canada's largest department store 4 years after market entry to exceed leaders Zellers, Sears and The Bay. Eatons went bankrupt and Kmart withdrew from the Canadian market. Wal-Mart is expected to introduce its hypermarket format to Canada and add food to its non-food merchandise as it does in every other world market. Canadian sales in 300 stores that include hypermarkets are projected to reach $24.3 billion when Wal-Mart will dwarf every other national retailer in Canada (food sales of Loblaws, Canada's largest retailer, are currently $11 billion).

Europe was a logical target market for Wal-Mart's most recent move abroad. To Wal-Mart, the highly industrialized and developed European nations have relatively familiar religious, government and economic institutions. An expanding European Union (EU) and common currency will facilitate Pan-European trade. Furthermore, no major retailer dominates Europe as does Wal-Mart in the US and Canada. Finally, there is much room to grow in Europe. One estimate is that Wal-Mart's current global sales equate to only 6% of the total European retail market.

Wal-Mart entered Germany through the acquisition of 21 hypermarkets from Wertkauf BmbH in December 1997 and 74 hypermarkets from Spar Handels AG a year later. Germany is Europe's largest country in terms of population. Wal-Mart's entry into the UK, Europe's second most populous country, involved the acquisition of ASDA, this nation's third largest food retailer, and operator of 232 stores. If size of the population is a determining factor for market selection, France, Italy and Spain are likely targets for further Wal-Mart expansion in Europe. A contributing factor to Wal-Mart's size is that it grew up in the huge US market and other large markets in the world attract similar attention.

An assessment of Wal-Mart's long-term potential in Europe must examine the other factors accounting for its current position and determine whether these factors will also apply in Germany and the UK and any of the other large European markets it might enter. Will Wal-Mart's unique organizational culture succeed with the work forces in each of these countries? Are the operating policies of Wal-Mart superior to the domestic competition? Do consumers in each national market want what Wal-Mart has to offer in its retail proposition?

Wal-Mart organizational culture

The legacy of Wal-Mart founder Sam Walton is a distinct organizational culture (the 'Wal-Mart Way'). In this culture, managers practice a form of servant leadership and every employee is known as an 'associate'. Everyone is on a first name basis.

Associates are empowered to adapt to local circumstances and are encouraged to try out their own ideas. The culture emphasizes experimentation and trial.

Sam Walton's competitive spirit has also been instilled in the associates where there is great motivation to win. Retail at Wal-Mart is about scoring goals, making touchdowns and winning games. The game and team spirit is reflected in the morning cheer: 'Give me a W, Give me an A,…And what does that spell? WAL-MART!…And who is number one? THE CUSTOMER'. Successes are shared in real and pragmatic terms with profit sharing, incentive bonuses, retirement savings plans and equity purchase at a discount.

Employees learn about this culture through on-the-job training as well as through a set of self-administered training videos. Walton's 'Guiding Principles' appear in company flyers and his 'Ten Rules of Business' grace the stairwells and hallways of employee areas and office spaces.

Enculturation into the Wal-Mart Way has various consequences. One outcome is that associates experience more a partnership than a hierarchy. The word 'family' is used again and again by Wal-Mart executives in public presentations. Associate cohesiveness exists that is more than the outcome of everyone wearing the same button-decorated, blue smock.

Being competitive, the associates work hard to succeed. They will investigate the local competition to ensure they have lower prices. Adaptation to the particular circumstances of a local market is rapid because empowered front-line associates instinctively act in the unique circumstances of a new situation by turning to Sam Walton's rules of business. They are not unlike early New World missionaries who relied on religious principles to guide them in unfamiliar circumstances.

The culture is also a powerful force that creates a capacity for constant innovation and reinvention. In terms of technology adoption, Wal-Mart was among the first to adopt elements of the new information technology in terms of electronic data interchange (EDI) and other elements of logistics flow and control. The Supercenters introduced in the 1990s were the result of a long process of experimentation and trial that started a decade earlier.

Wal-Mart operating procedures

Wal-Mart is the exemplar of the low cost strategy and it has fine-tuned low margin, high inventory turnover, volume selling. Volume buying in turn enables lower costs of goods. Furthermore, Wal-Mart demands vendors forgo all other amenities and quote the lowest price. In some circumstances, Wal-Mart buyers go to vendor premises to work on cost reduction.

In addition to becoming a supplier to the world's largest retailer, a successful vendor may also become a category manager. As such, the vendor is given the information and latitude to manage the product category for Wal-Mart. Teams replace one-on-one relationships as best exemplified in the creation of the Procter and Gamble/Wal-Mart vendor-retailer 'win–win relationship'.

A total investment of $4 billion resulted in the Retail Link computer/satellite system. Point-of-purchase information is exchanged with vendor partners in addition to the maintenance of a 104-week rolling history of every item in the Wal-Mart distribution system. The logistics and information systems permit store focused and store-within-a-store (department) operations quite adaptable to local markets. It enables each store and each department manager to know exactly their own sales, margins and profits absolutely and relatively to other stores and departments. Portable scan guns used in the store are reloaded each day to enable an associate to know the status of any product in that store. Each department effectively becomes an individual shop proprietor with all the attendant feelings of ownership.

Wal-Mart executives are not reliant only on computer-generated information. Each week, they fly out to the stores across the nation to gain tacit knowledge about local markets and circumstances. The traditional Saturday morning meeting back at Bentonville enables that knowledge to be shared with others.

Each store is within a day's drive of a distribution centre that replenishes 85% of all inventories (versus 50–65% for competitors). New concepts such as merchandise assembly, cross-docking and accelerated deliveries are continually being introduced into the distribution system. Buyers must respond to any store inquiry within the day (the 'sundown' rule).

Another key to Wal-Mart's success, according to Sam Walton, 'is to identify the items that can explode into big volume and big profits if you are smart enough to identify them and take the trouble to promote them'. Walton dedicated himself to instilling the 'thrill of merchandising' into his 'associate-partners.' Today, merchandising is practised with the prime goal of maximizing inventory turnover and supporting the everyday low price (EDLP) position. Detailed planograms are prepared and featured items are seasonally correct, key items. Furthermore, item promotions are single-priced and are featured on tables, checkouts, end caps, sidekicks and 4-way displayers.

Heavy advertising serves not to highlight specific merchandise items but instead the EDLP and friendly service positioning. The primary media vehicle is television supported by once-a-month, non-sale flyers. The objective is to become the McDonalds of retailing and build a global brand recognizable around the world.

Wal-Mart consumer offer

Wal-Mart premises its retail proposition on four determinants of store choice: low prices, wide assortment, friendly service and community support. Low prices are derivative of a margin schedule that in the US averages 27.5% over various product categories. The margin also varies by international market according to the inherent competitive forces. In Canada, for example, the average competitive margin was 34%. Wal-Mart set its average Canadian margin at 32% and made the Canadian market very profitable for the international division. Other elements in Wal-Mart's pricing policy are to label key items, e.g. toothpaste, soap, and shampoo, at cost or less to have the lowest local prices. Price rollbacks are another important device for communicating a low price image.

As to assortment, the large 16 700 m^2 Wal-Mart Supercenters, 11 100 m^2 department stores and 9000 m^2 SAMS Club warehouse clubs increase the possibility of a one-stop shopping trip. In the Supercenters, there are 80 000 general merchandise SKUs and 10 000 food SKUs. The technologically superior inventory management and logistics system ensures these products are in stock and on the shelf. The EDLP pricing rather than weekly sales and promotions acts to minimize stockouts and ensure high service (in-stock) levels.

The Neighbourhood Market format stores, Wal-Mart's new experimental format, may be an option at this stage of Wal-Mart's international strategy. The 3700 m^2 hybrid food, pharmacy, health/beauty care and convenience store was identified as a 'fill-in' in North American markets and as an alternative to shoppers who were uncomfortable in the larger Wal-Mart stores.

On service, Sam Walton once said 'satisfied, loyal, repeat customers are at the heart of the Wal-Mart's spectacular profit margins, and those customers are loyal to us because our associates treat them better than salespeople at other stores. ... If you want people in the stores to take care of the customers, you have to make sure you're taking care of the people in the stores. That's the most important single ingredient of Wal-Mart's success'. A greeter at the door, often an older associate and always the same person, immediately creates recognition and familiarity when the shopper enters the store. In this way, the impersonal, giant warehouse suddenly becomes a personal, known neighbourhood shop. Associates then practice 'aggressive hospitality' on their 'guests'. The 'Ten Foot/3 Meter Rule' states that if any customer comes with 10 feet/3 m, the associate is to ask if they can help in any way. A liberal return policy, fast checkout and 'satisfaction guaranteed' motto also contribute to a positive customer experience.

Wal-Mart engages in actions that respond to family, community and national norms. Family activities and children of associates are portrayed in flyers, purchases where possible are made from local and national suppliers, and national flags and colours are used in store signs and checkout areas. The origin of these institutional actions traces back to the small town roots of Sam Walton and Wal-Mart. In contrast to other retailers that started in the large metro markets, Wal-Mart began in small towns and cities in the south-eastern US. An important tradition of smaller communities is for the local retailer to be an integral part of the community fabric. Thus, Wal-Mart associates identify a local charity or community activity to support as part of a storewide effort.

Questions

1. Wal-Mart is the world's largest retailer. What lessons, if any, do you learn from Wal-Mart's achievement? If there are lessons to be learned, are they specific to the North American market or do they have applicability in Europe as well?
2. Why do you think Wal-Mart selected Germany and the UK to enter the European market? Do you agree that France, Italy and Spain are likely countries for further expansion in the European market?
3. Why is it that consumers in the US and Canada have responded so favour-

ably to Wal-Mart's retail proposition? Do you think consumers in Germany and the UK will respond in the same way?

4. Will Wal-Mart's unique organization culture succeed with the work forces in Germany and the UK? If you were an employee at Spar Handels or Asda prior to the acquisition, how are you going to respond to your new owners?

5. How will Wal-Mart's various operating practices succeed in Germany and the UK? For instance, Wal-Mart's global branding objective means the replacement of the Wertkauf, Spar Handels and Asda fascias with the Wal-Mart name. In German food retailing, suppliers deliver direct to stores rather than having replenishment controlled centrally by Wal-Mart through distribution centres.

Further reading

Arnold, S. J. and Fernie, J. (2000), Wal-Mart in Europe: prospects for the UK, *International Marketing Review*, 17 (4/5), pp. 416–432.

Arnold, S. J., Handelman, J. and Tigert, D. J. (1998), The impact of a market spoiler on consumer preference structures (or, what happens when Wal-mart comes to town), *Journal of Retailing and Consumer Services*, 5 (1), pp. 1–13.

Ortega, B. (1998), *In Sam We Trust: The Untold Story of Sam Walton and How Wal-Mart is Devouring America*, Random House, Inc., New York.

Simmons, J. and Graff, T. (1998), *Wal-Mart Comes to Canada*, Toronto: Centre for the Study of Commercial Activity, Ryerson Polytechnic University.

Vance, S. S. and Scott, R. (1994), *Wal-Mart: A History of Sam Walton's Retail Phenomenon*, Twayne Publishers, New York.

Walton, S. with Huey, J. (1993), *Sam Walton: Made in America – My Story*, Bantam, New York.

Appendix II - Support for exporters

Support for exporters available in the UK (source: Trade Partners UK – http://www.tradepartners.gov.uk/index.html)

Generous subsidies are available through Trade Partners UK for investigating new market opportunities. They provide:

- Free access to an export development counsellor for initial planning advice and information on sources of help
- Free access to an export promoter for specialist advice on approaching a particular market
- Free use of an extensive self help information centre
- Free information online about markets and sectors, plus signposting to other websites for further research and services
- Tailored market research, at low cost, by commercial staff based in embassies overseas report on conditions, opportunities, buyers, potential partners and other requested information. Interview of candidate partners can be arranged
- Commercial staff based in embassies overseas can help in arranging local visit programmes, including an interpreter if required
- Trade mission sponsorship
- Exhibition and trade fair sponsorship
- Low cost publicity for new product/service including professional copy, translation, targeting of relevant press and media by the embassy in the chosen market(s)
- Free advice on conducting export marketing research
- Grants to cover up to 50% of your export marketing research costs

Support for exporters available in the US (source: The Trade Information Center (TIC) in the US – http://www.ita.doc.gov/td/tic/)

The Trade Information Center (TIC) is a comprehensive resource for information on all US Federal Government export assistance programs. The Center is operated by the International Trade Administration of the US Department of Commerce for the 20 federal agencies comprising the Trade Promotion Coordinating Committee

(TPCC). These agencies are responsible for managing the US Government's export promotion programs and activities.

The TIC provides:

- Referrals and information on all US Federal Government export assistance programs. The publication 'A Business Guide to Federal Export Assistance' describes the resources available from 20 federal agencies to assist US companies develop their export potential.
- General export counselling. New-to-export firms can use a 'Frequently Asked Questions' section to find answers to the most commonly asked exporting questions and links to the most-used resources. Articles of interest to exporters are written by international trade specialists and published in Export America.
- Sources of international market research and trade leads available online.
- Calendar of overseas and domestic trade events and activities sponsored by the US Department of Commerce.
- Sources of export finance. A state-by-state list of service providers nation-wide is available.
- Advice on export licenses and controls. Country-specific export counselling and assistance for Western Europe, Asia, Western Hemisphere, Africa, and the Near East on commercial laws, regulations, business practices distribution channels, business travel, and other market information.
- Lists of opportunities and best prospects for US companies in individual markets. View our list of Top Targets for US exporters world-wide.
- Import tariffs/taxes and customs procedures. Tariff information for particular products is available on the Internet.
- Assistance in overcoming commercial difficulties in doing business abroad.
- US government and foreign contact information related to sources of export assistance. Access the TIC's TRADEBASE –a listing of upcoming trade education events in your area. Use the National Export Directory to locate all US Government trade-related offices around the US, as well as state and local export program offices. Use our Foreign Trade Offices Database to find contact information for foreign embassies, consulates, and trade offices located in the US and customs offices abroad.
- Lists of trade publications and export software. Find a listing of useful export software to expedite your work. See a database of trade related publications.

Support for exporters available in Australia (source: Austrade – http://www.austrade.gov.au/index.asp)

Austrade is the Australian Trade Commission – the federal government's export and investment facilitation agency.

The Austrade Export Hotline is the first point of contact for any business interested in exporting. Austrade's role is to help boost Australia's export earnings, so firms who are ready to export are prioritized and initial advice covering general market information is given to help in deciding how best to proceed. Many of Austrade's services are free or partially subsidized by the government.

Other specific advice available includes:

Entering export markets

Austrade provides advice to companies on which overseas markets hold the highest sales potential for their product, how they can build a presence in these markets, and what sort of practical and financial help is available.

Operating an international network of offices located in 108 cities in 63 countries, Austrade is able to identify potential buyers or agents and to pass on specific business opportunities as they arise. By working with Australian businesses, Austrade can accurately match Australian suppliers with interested local contacts and arrange introductions. It can also engage in long-term partnerships to ensure all possibilities are fully exploited.

Austrade provides information tailored to the specific requirements of each business. Relevant information can include detailed market intelligence such as the competition, the prospects, cultural considerations, distribution systems and government regulations. When the preparatory work is done, Austrade's overseas offices can contribute to a successful market visit.

In-market services

Through our global network of offices, Austrade can provide you with a range of in-market services such as setting up appointments with distributors or other useful contacts, providing on-the-spot briefing on the local business culture and environment, organizing interpreters and office facilities, attending meetings to help overcome language or cultural barriers, organizing product launches and seminars, and preparing publicity material.

Trade fairs

Austrade co-ordinates Australian national stands at more than 100 international trade exhibitions each year. Austrade will assist with stand design and construction, freight forwarding and clearance, and provision of exhibitor facilities. Financial support may be available towards the cost of participating in trade fairs.

Austrade Online

Austrade Online is Austrade's enhanced website, www.austrade.gov.au. It provides a comprehensive, up-to-date export information service, including advice on international trade issues, export programmes and overseas markets.

The 'Australia on Display' section of the site is a searchable database of thousands of Australian companies and their products and services. This can be accessed by potential customers from anywhere in the world. Australian companies can take out a listing free of charge by completing a form available on the site or by calling Austrade.

Financial assistance for exporters

Austrade's Export Market Development Grants (EMDG) scheme encourages Australian exporters to seek out and develop overseas markets. Under the scheme, eligible businesses are reimbursed for part of the export marketing costs they incur.

Appendix III - Examples of export documentation

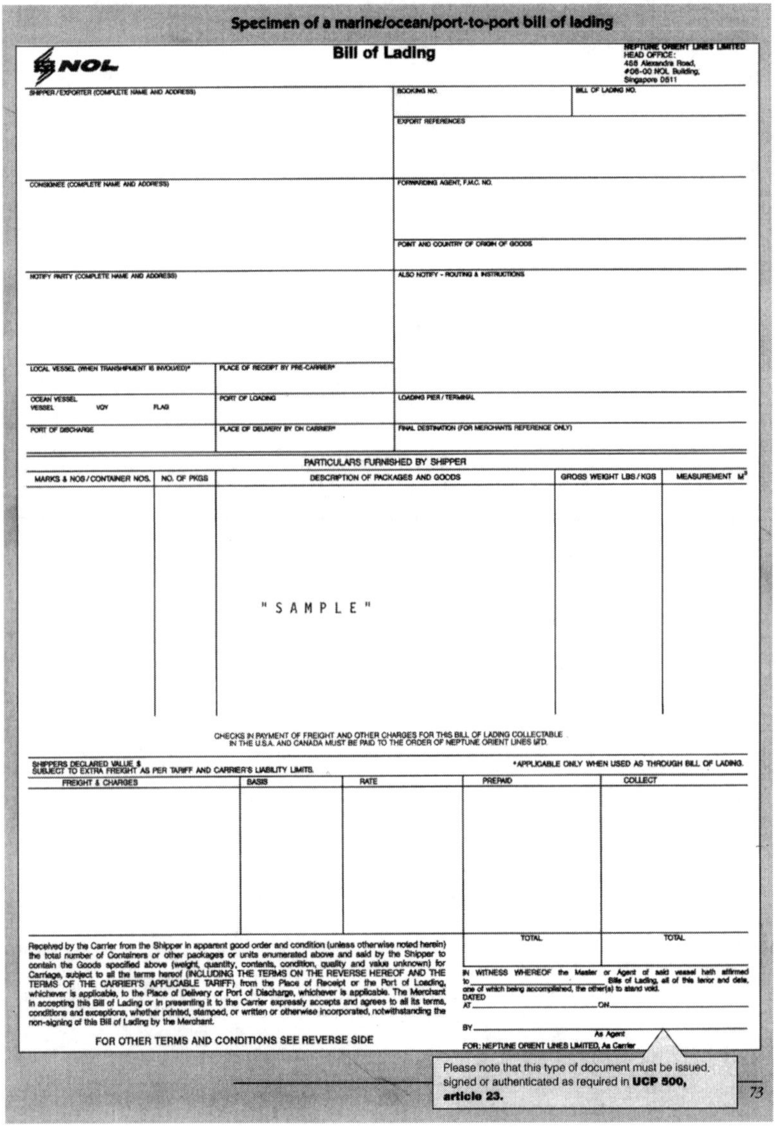

Specimen of a marine/ocean/port-to-port bill of lading

NOL

Bill of Lading

NEPTUNE ORIENT LINES LIMITED
HEAD OFFICE:
456 Alexandra Road,
#06-00 NOL Building,
Singapore 0511

SHIPPER/EXPORTER (COMPLETE NAME AND ADDRESS)

BOOKING NO.

BILL OF LADING NO.

EXPORT REFERENCES

CONSIGNEE (COMPLETE NAME AND ADDRESS)

FORWARDING AGENT, F.M.C. NO.

POINT AND COUNTRY OF ORIGIN OF GOODS

NOTIFY PARTY (COMPLETE NAME AND ADDRESS)

ALSO NOTIFY - ROUTING & INSTRUCTIONS

LOCAL VESSEL (WHEN TRANSHIPMENT IS INVOLVED)*

PLACE OF RECEIPT BY PRE-CARRIER*

OCEAN VESSEL
VESSEL VOY FLAG

PORT OF LOADING

LOADING PIER/TERMINAL

PORT OF DISCHARGE

PLACE OF DELIVERY BY ON CARRIER*

FINAL DESTINATION (FOR MERCHANTS REFERENCE ONLY)

PARTICULARS FURNISHED BY SHIPPER

MARKS & NOS/CONTAINER NOS.	NO. OF PKGS	DESCRIPTION OF PACKAGES AND GOODS	GROSS WEIGHT LBS/KGS	MEASUREMENT M³
		"SAMPLE"		

CHECKS IN PAYMENT OF FREIGHT AND OTHER CHARGES FOR THIS BILL OF LADING COLLECTABLE IN THE U.S.A. AND CANADA MUST BE PAID TO THE ORDER OF NEPTUNE ORIENT LINES LTD.

SHIPPERS DECLARED VALUE $
SUBJECT TO EXTRA FREIGHT AS PER TARIFF AND CARRIER'S LIABILITY LIMITS.

*APPLICABLE ONLY WHEN USED AS THROUGH BILL OF LADING.

FREIGHT & CHARGES	BASIS	RATE	PREPAID	COLLECT
			TOTAL	TOTAL

Received by the Carrier from the Shipper in apparent good order and condition (unless otherwise noted herein) the total number of Containers or other packages or units enumerated above and said by the Shipper to contain the Goods specified above (weight, quantity, contents, condition, quality and value unknown) for Carriage, subject to all the terms hereof (INCLUDING THE TERMS ON THE REVERSE HEREOF AND THE TERMS OF THE CARRIER'S APPLICABLE TARIFF) from the Place of Receipt or the Port of Loading, whichever is applicable, to the Place of Delivery or Port of Discharge, whichever is applicable. The Merchant in accepting this Bill of Lading or in presenting it to the Carrier expressly accepts and agrees to all its terms, conditions and exceptions, whether printed, stamped, or written or otherwise incorporated, notwithstanding the non-signing of this Bill of Lading by the Merchant.

FOR OTHER TERMS AND CONDITIONS SEE REVERSE SIDE

IN WITNESS WHEREOF the Master or Agent of said vessel hath affirmed to _____ Bills of Lading, all of this tenor and date, one of which being accomplished, the other(s) to stand void.
DATED
AT _____ ON _____

BY _____
As Agent
FOR: NEPTUNE ORIENT LINES LIMITED, As Carrier

Please note that this type of document must be issued, signed or authenticated as required in **UCP 500, article 23.**

73

Figure A.1. Bill of lading.

Specimen of an air transport document

Shipper's Name and Address	Shipper's Account Number	Not Negotiable
		Air Waybill
		Issued by

Copies 1, 2 and 3 of this Air Waybill are originals and have the same validity.

Consignee's Name and Address	It is agreed that the goods described herein are accepted in apparent good order and condition (except as noted) for carriage SUBJECT TO THE CONDITIONS OF CONTRACT ON THE REVERSE HEREOF. ALL GOODS MAY BE CARRIED BY ANY OTHER MEANS INCLUDING ROAD OR ANY OTHER CARRIER UNLESS SPECIFIC CONTRARY INSTRUCTIONS ARE GIVEN HEREON BY THE SHIPPER, THE SHIPPER'S ATTENTION IS DRAWN TO THE NOTICE CONCERNING CARRIER'S LIMITATION OF LIABILITY. Shipper may increase such limitation of liability by declaring a higher value for carriage and paying a supplemental charge if required.

Issuing Carrier's Agent Name and City	Accounting Information

Agent's IATA Code	Account No.

Airport of Departure (Addr. of First Carrier) and Requested Routing

To	By First Carrier	Routing and Destination	to	by	to	by	Currency	WT/VAL	Other	Declared Value for Carriage	Declared Value for Customs
								PPD COLL	PPD COLL		

Airport of Destination	Amount of Insurance	INSURANCE — If carrier offers insurance, and such insurance is requested in accordance with the conditions thereof, indicate amount to be insured in figures in box marked "Amount of Insurance".

Handling Information

No. of Pieces RCP	Gross Weight	kg/lb	Rate Class / Commodity Item No.	Chargeable Weight	Rate / Charge	Total	Nature and Quantity of Goods (incl. Dimensions or Volume)

Prepaid	Weight Charge	Collect	Other Charges
	Valuation Charge		
	Tax		
	Total Other Charges Due Agent		
	Total Other Charges Due Carrier		

Shipper certifies that the particulars on the face hereof are correct and that insofar as any part of the consignment contains dangerous goods, such part is properly described by name and is in proper condition for carriage by air according to the applicable Dangerous Goods Regulations.

_____
Signature of Shipper or his Agent

Total Prepaid	Total Collect

Executed on (date)	at (place)	Signature of Issuing Carrier or its Agent

ORIGINAL 3 (FOR SHIPPER)

Please note that this type of document must be issued, signed or authenticated as required in **UCP 500, article 27.**

81

Figure A.2.   Air waybill.

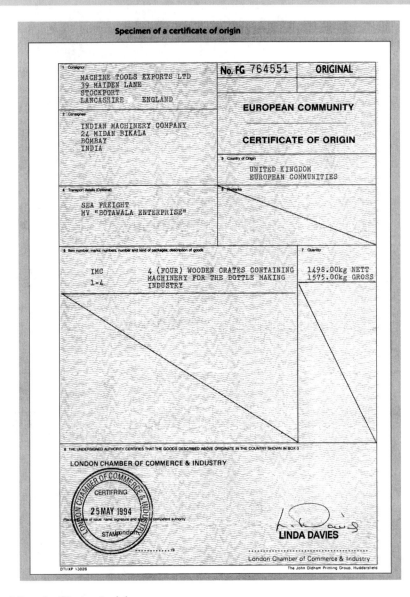

Figure A.3.   Certificate of origin.

Specimen of a draft

Exchange for US$100,000.-   Tampa, May 27, 1994

At sight of the bill of exchange pay to the order of ourselves
One hundred thousand and 00/000 US dollars

Drawn under The French Issuing Bank, Paris, France Documentary Credit No. 12345

Value received and charge same to account of

TO: The French Issuing Bank
           38 rue François 1er
           75008, Paris, France

                                            The American Exporter Co. Inc

---

UNCITRAL **bill of exchange format**

Tampa, May 27 1994
US$100,000

At sixty days after sight for values received,

pay against this bill of exchange to the

order of ourselves

the sum of US dollars one

hundred thousand

effective payment to be made in US dollars

only without deduction for and free of any

tax, import levy or duty

present or future of any nature under the

laws of the United States or any political

subdivision thereof or therein.

This bill of exchange is
payable at
The American Bank in Tampa

Drawn on The American
Advising Bank, Tampa

Accepted ....

For and on behalf of
The American Exporter Co. Inc.
Tampa, Florida

Figure A.4.   Bill of exchange.

Irrevocable Confirmed Documentary Credit

Name of Issuing Bank: The French Issuing Bank 38 rue François ler 75008 Paris, France	Irrevocable Documentary Credit	Number 12345

Place and Date of Issue: Paris, 1 January 1994	Expiry Date and Place for Presentation of Documents
Applicant: The French Importer Co. 89 rue du Commerce Paris, France	Expiry Date: May 29, 1994 Place for Presentation: The American Advising Bank, Tampa

	Beneficiary:
	    The American Exporter Co. Inc.
	    17 Main Street
	    Tampa, Florida

Advising Bank: Reference. No The American Advising Bank 456 Commerce Avenue Tampa, Florida	Amount: US$100,000.- one hundred thousand U.S.Dollars

Partial shipments [X] allowed [ ] not allowed	Credit available with Nominated Bank: The American Advising Bank, Tampa
Transhipment [X] allowed [ ] not allowed	[X] by payment at sight [ ] by deferred payment at: [ ] by acceptance of drafts at: [ ] by negotiation
[ ] Insurance covered by buyers	
Shipment as defined in UCP 500 Article 46 From: Tampa, Florida For transportation to: Paris, France Not later than: May 15, 1994	Against the documents detailed herein: [X] and Beneficiary's draft(s) drawn on: The American Advising Bank

Commercial Invoice, one original and 3 copies

Multimodal Transport Document issued to the order of the French Importer Co.
marked freight prepaid and notify XYZ Custom House Broker Inc

Insurance Certificate covering the Institute Cargo Clauses and the Institute War
and Strike Clauses for 110% of the invoice value endorsed to The French Importer Co.

Certificate of Origin evidence goods to be of U.S.A. Origin

Packing List

Covering: Machinerie and spare parts as per pro-forma invoice number 657
dated December 17, 1993 - CIP INCOTERMS 1990

Documents to be presented within [14] days after the date of shipment but within the validity of the Credit.

We hereby issue the Irrevocable Documentary Credit in your favour. It is subject to the Uniform Customs and Practice for Documentary Credits (1993 Revision, International Chamber of Commerce, Paris, France, Publication No. 500) and engages us in accordance with the terms thereof. The number and the date of the Credit and the name of our bank must be quoted on all drafts required. If the Credit is available by negotiation, each presentation must be noted on the reverse side of this advice by the bank where the Credit is available.

This document consists of [1] signed page(s)   The French Issuing Bank

Figure A.5.   Documentary letter of credit.

Subject index

Company names and products are in bold.

Commercial documents 213
Commercial risk 88, 222, 225, 226, 228
Communication
    cultural factors 61–4, 71
    customer values 3, 11, 139, 157–8, 170–84,
        185–6
    export success 99
    technological advances 77
Comparative advertising 177
Competencies 120–3
Competition
    global rankings 2
    pricing 165, 167, 169
    SMEs 108
    standardization 177–8
    time-based 191–2
    understanding the customer 140
Complementary marketing 93
Conditional demand guarantee 215
Confirming house 232
Conney 283, 284–8
Conoco 69
Consortium exporting 93–4
Consumer profile 178, 182
Contracts
    exporting 211, 213, 215, 216, 232, 234–6
    management 95, 129
Contractual joint ventures 96
Corporate culture 46, 48, 96, 311–12
Costs
    credit insurance 227
    indirect market entry 91
    Internet 250
    packaging 206, 207
    pricing 165, 167
    reducing 191
    subsidiaries 95
Countertrade 232
Country of origin effect 53–5, 59–60, 162–4,
    178
Courtaulds plc 293
Creating customer values 157, 158–70
Creative strategy 180–1, 182

Credit
    export finance 218, 219–20, 228–30, 231,
        232, 234
    insurance 116, 212, 222–7, 237
Croatia 224
Culture 11, 45–76, 123–4, 151, 160
    advertising 176, 181, 182, 185
    customer satisfaction 196–7
    ethnocentrism 39
    Internet 199, 248
    managerial skills 37, 38
    packaging quirks 170
    polycentrism 39
    SMEs 123–5
Currency accounts 236
Customer value management (CVM) 192,
    193–5
Customers 4, 11, 100, 113
    creating/communicating values 3, 61–4,
        139, 157–89
    cultural issues 56–9, 61–4
    delivering values 3, 64, 139, 191–210
    satisfaction 3, 193, 194, 195–8, 255–6
    understanding values 3, 56–9, 137–55
Customs Cooperation Council Nomencla-
    ture (CCCN) 213
Customs guarantee 216
Customs invoice 213
CVM *see* customer value management
Cyprus 32
Czech Republic 7, 28, 32, 131, 291

Dan Transport 202
Danzas 202
Debts 223, 226, 230–1, 233
Decentralization 18, 129, 178–9
Del Monte 308–9
Delays in payment 228
Delhaize 294
Delivery 64, 92, 93, 139, 191–210
Denmark 32, 33, 225, 235
    case studies 295, 301–2, 303, 306, 307
    culture 39
    SMEs 128